F
497
A8
B9
1975

A Bicentennial Publication
Reprinted in 1975 by Ohio University Press

Printed in the United States of America
by the Watkins Printing Co.

ISBN 0-8214-0203-X
LC 75-23393

Designed by Harold M. Stevens

ATHENS COUNTY COURT HOUSE

INDEX

OUTLINE MAP OF
ATHENS COUNTY, OHIO

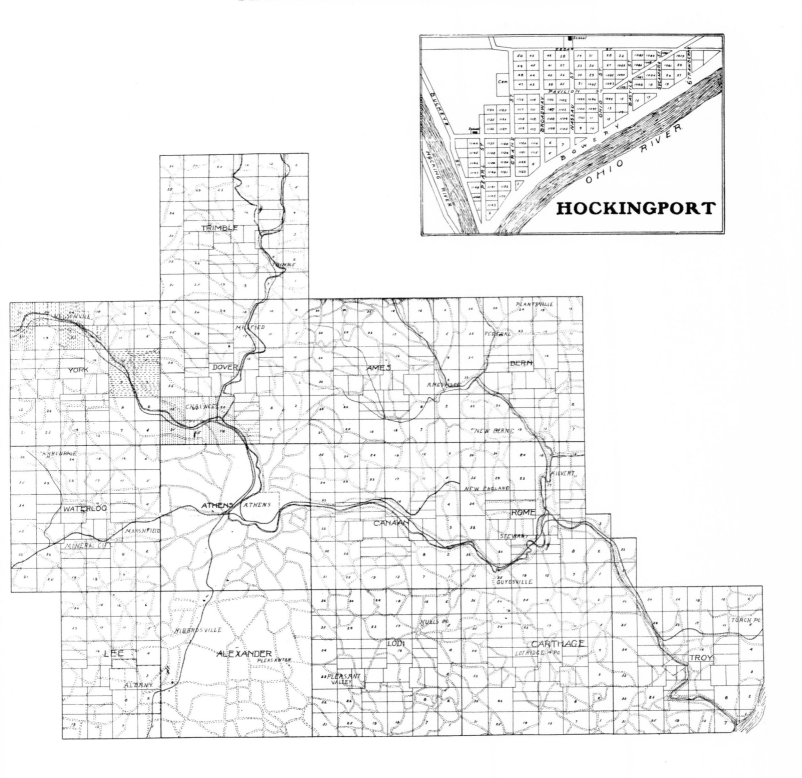

HOCKINGPORT

ATHENS

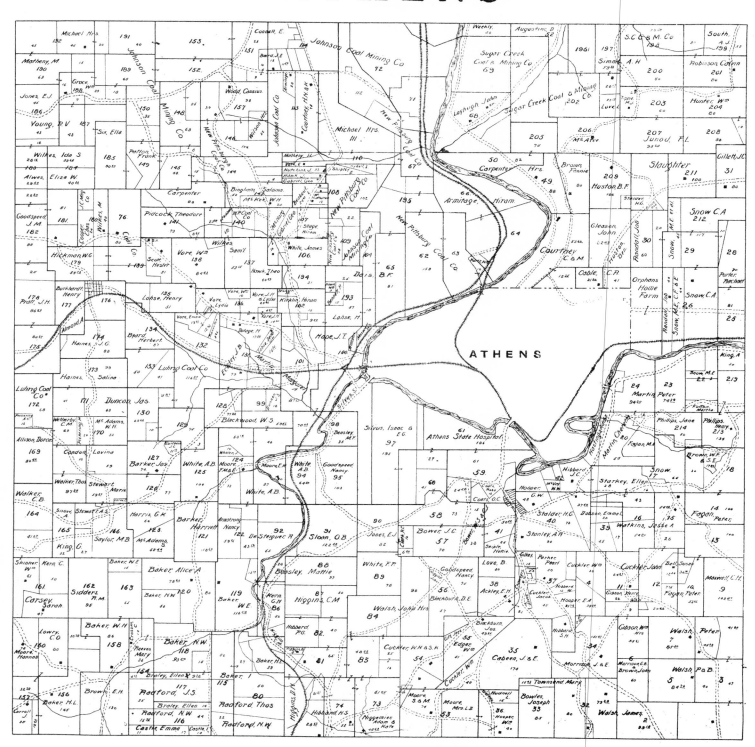

DOVER

ALEXANDER

Carroll, Jesse · Gabriel, Elizabeth · Rawlings, G.H. · Vorhes, Wm · Blakeway E.G. · Radford · Hibbard, H.S. · Walsh, Kate · Tribe, Henry · Moore, Winifred · Chappell, Orin · Miles, Benj. · Parker, Andrew · Rogers, J.C. · Rogers, Wm · Nice, Isaac

Johnson, Issiah · Blackwood A.J. & Martha · Stewart, Jas. · Castle, Isaac · Maxwell, Geo. H. · Hooper, Wm · Chappell, D.C. · Robinson, E.O. · Lillie, Geo. & George · Rogers, J.C.

Johnson, Hannah · Figley, Ella · Drake, Dan'l · Drake, W.H. · Lash, Geo. B · Davis, Mary E · Parker, A.J. · Allen, J.H.

Masters, Henry · Figley, T.J · Parker, W.G. · Parker, Adah · Fisher, John · Alderman, W.J. · Lash, Leander · Lash, J.C. · Gilkey, Sarah · Parker, Andrew · Ballinger, Oliver

Parker, W.J. · Masters · Parker, Adah · Dent, A.S. · Gift, Julian · Matheny, John W · Biddle, John F. · Patterson, R.M. · Lash, Wm · Gilkey Jas. · Curtis, Sam · Hooper, S.F. · McLean, Anno · Cuckler, Emma · Kinney, Alvire · Robinson, Thos.

Vorhes, Clayton · Dent, A.S. · Antle, M.L. · Lash, Wm · Gilkey · McClenahan, P.F. & E.F.

George, Benj · Evans, Martha · Wakefield, Geo. · Fisher, O.A. · Fisher, O.A. etal. · Johnson, Wm · Johnson, O.L. · Patterson R.M. · Herbert, Ford · Wood, J.M. · Walker, Herman · Beal, Sam'l · Leighty, Mary · Crossen, Israel · Johnson, Tabitha · Mathews, H.A. · Tippie, E. · Barnhill · McClenahan · Perry, Isaac C.

Vorhes, Peter · Crossen, R.J. · Tippie, Cassa's · Beal

Mosure, Mary · Vorhes, Sam'l · Masner, J.H. · Border, Wm M. · Moore, A.W. · McGill, Elijah · Border, M. · Hooper, H.D. · Patterson R.M. · Parker, G.B. · Pratt, Jas. E. · Pierce, C.M. · Bennett, Rosalie · Pugh, Willis · Pugh, Mary · Sewell, Henry.

Coe, J.P. · Armstrong, Elmer · Johnson, Ida · Vorhes, Peter · Stanley, A.C. · Andrews, Mason · Haner, J.C. · Harner, P.F. · Oxley, W.C. · Oxley, Ross · Mason, C.A. · McPherson · Kenney, Emma · Eaton, Herman · Pierce, D.C. · Pierce, C.M.

Vorhes, Peter · Howard, L.B. · Harner, P.F.

Wines, S.M. · Coe, John P. · Matheny, Cha's. · Dowler, E.M. · Parker, G.B. & Sarah · Henry, Martha · Gilkins, Wm · Pierce, D.C. · McPherson, F.M. · Parker, E.B.

Fickey, Dan'l · Wines, Loretta · Matheny, H.A. · Patterson, Lizzie, & R.M. · Parker, E.E. · Gilkey, J.W. · Runyon, Sarah A. · Henry, E.C. · Kenny, Weyar · Kinney, David W.

Murphy, O.O · Irwin, Isabelle · Wines, Elvira · Stanley, A.C. · Parker, Mary H. · Gilkey, J.W. · Rusk, N.W. · Dorsey, B.G. · Kinney, F.A. · Henry, Wm · Martin, Geo. & F.S. · Parker, Sheldon · Cuckler, Bettie · King, Henry · Morrison, Nancy

Brooks, Sarah J. · Rathburn, Sarah · Snowden, Henry · Woodruff, Ella · Martin, Edw. · Martin, Geo. · Kennig, M.V.

Lewis, E.E. · Lowther, Frank · Howard, Sam'l · White, W.A.M. · Wines, Elvira · Lowther, Wm · Brooks, Flora Hts · Robinson, Mott · Mitchell, Mary A. · Dickson, J.W. · D.S.F. · Woodruff, Wallace Isaac

Luckett, Sylvester · Adair, Jas. · Cooley, A.A. · Reeves, C.W. · Brooks, Eliza · Haning, M. · Willsee, C.H. · Robinson, Wm · Robinson · Helwig, J.

Blake, S.B. · Daines, Frank · Russ, E.C. · Riley, J.W. · Stotts, Isaiah · Reeves, Rebecca · Reeves, R.J. · Wood, Lucy E. · Runyon, W.G. · Woodyard, S. · Chase, C. · Robinson, Jesse

Townsend, N & Perry · Goodin, Mary & S. · McKnight, Loran · Dickson, C.F. · Brooks, Sam'l · Martin Geo. & Wm · Jeffers, Hattie · Chase, Oscar · Woodyard, A. · Ellis, John · Ellis, Granville

Smith, J. · McHenry, Jones · Woodyard, J.C. · Enlow, Eliza L. · Haning, J.M. · Jeffers, Lewis · Chase, Elwood · Crider, E. · Haning, J.J. · Carbaugh

Zimmerman, Jos. · Coe, S.J. · Reeves, M.C. · Jordan, S.A.D. · Bolin, Grant · Bolin, T. · Robinson, V.E.K. · Jack, L. · Santers, Horton · Carbaugh, Jacob · Masters, Margaret · Price

Tewksbery, Margaret · Bower, Wesley · Woodyard, J.C. · Petit, Mary · Martin, Wm · Bolin, N.D. · Tousley, Tom · Brooks, M. · Atkins, Frank · Santers, Simon · Woodyard, A.

CARTHAGE

ROME

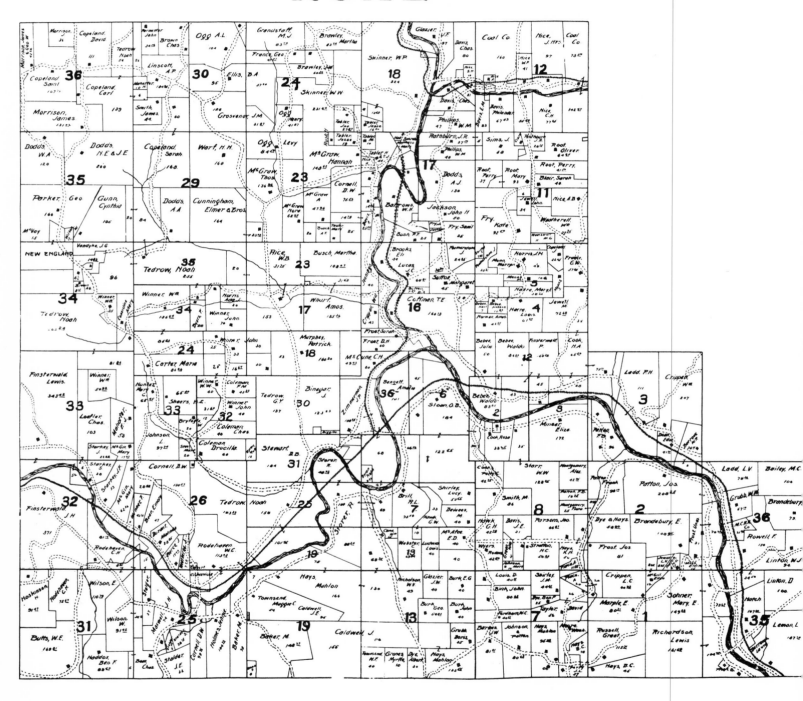

TROY

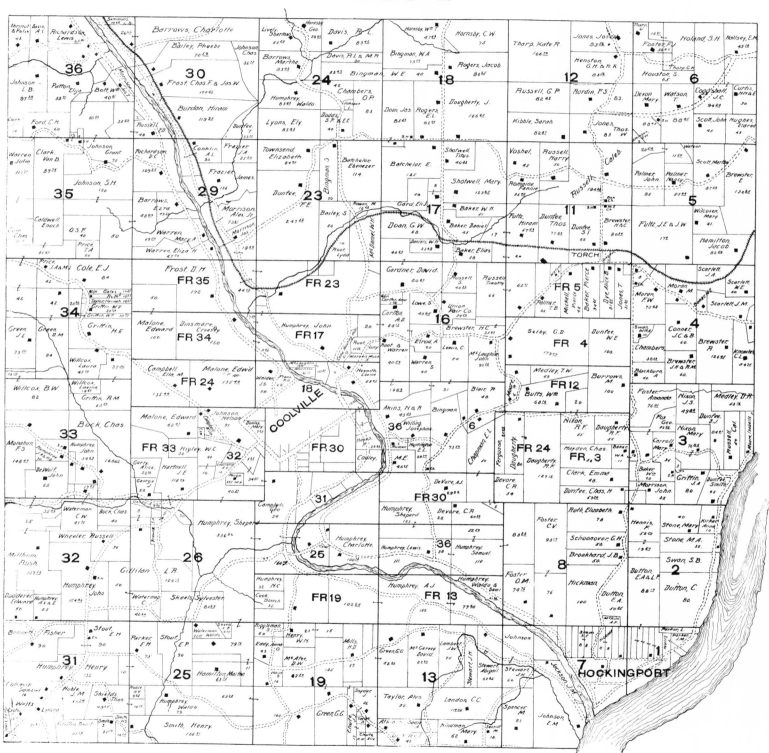

WATERLOO

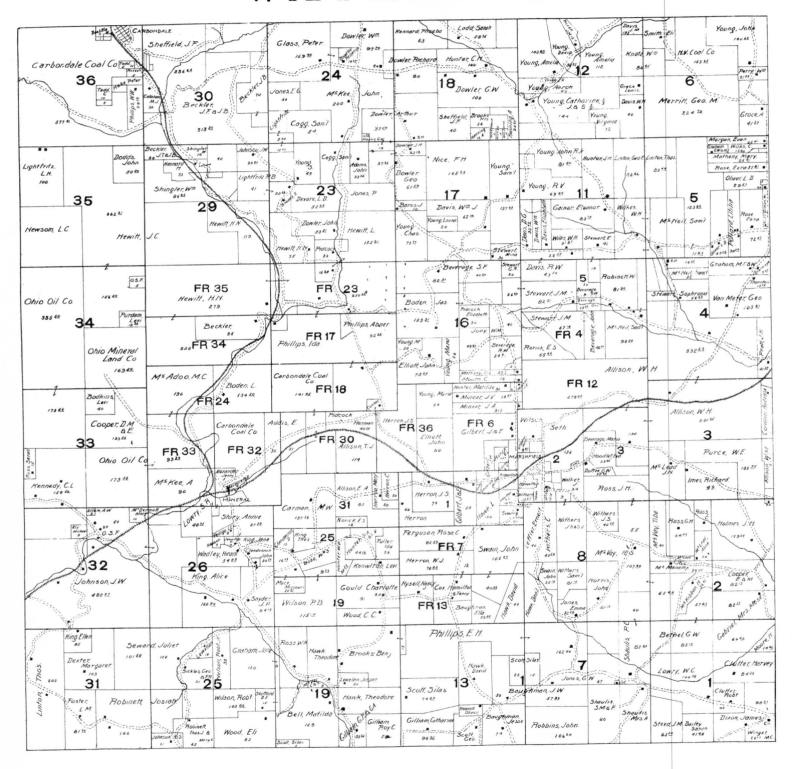

CANAAN

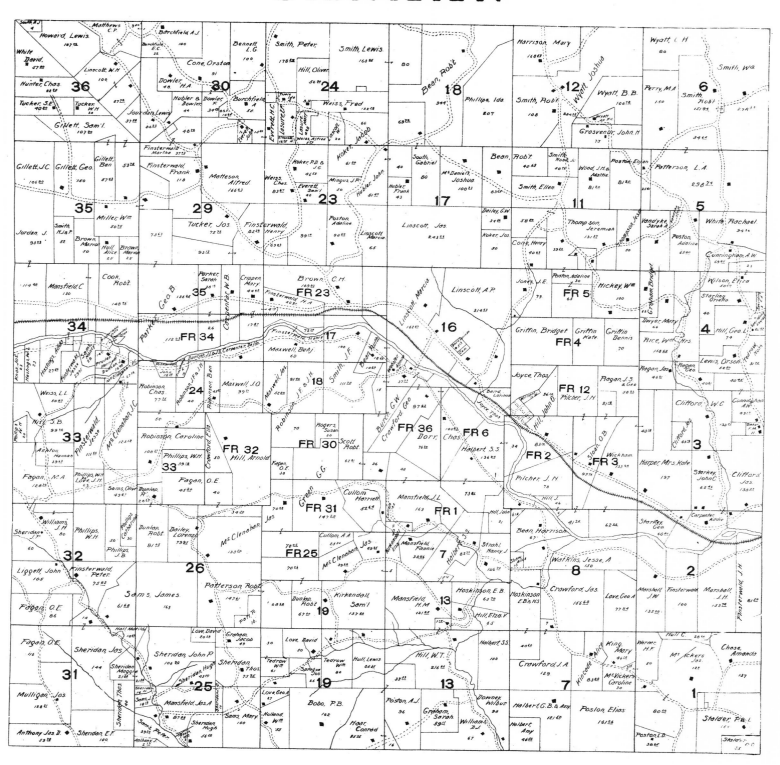

LEE

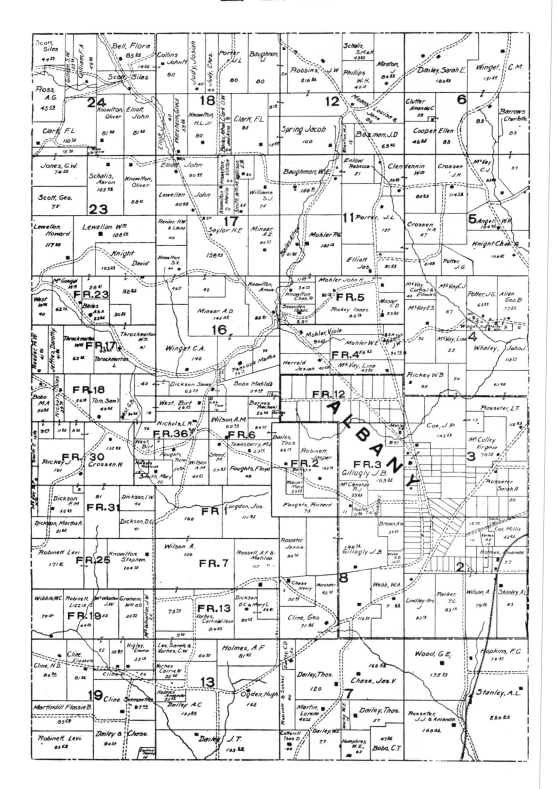

LODI

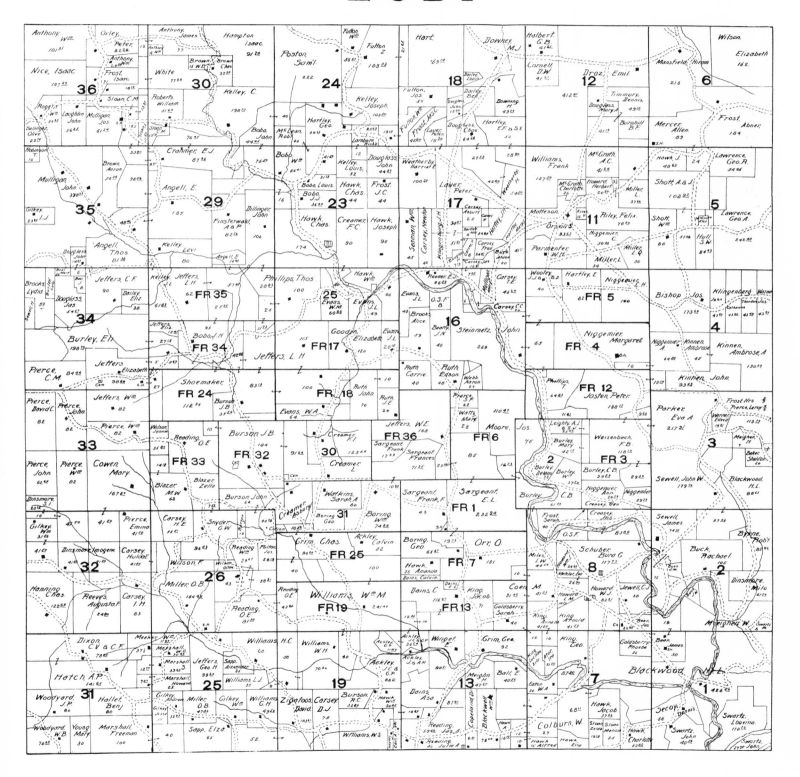

BERN

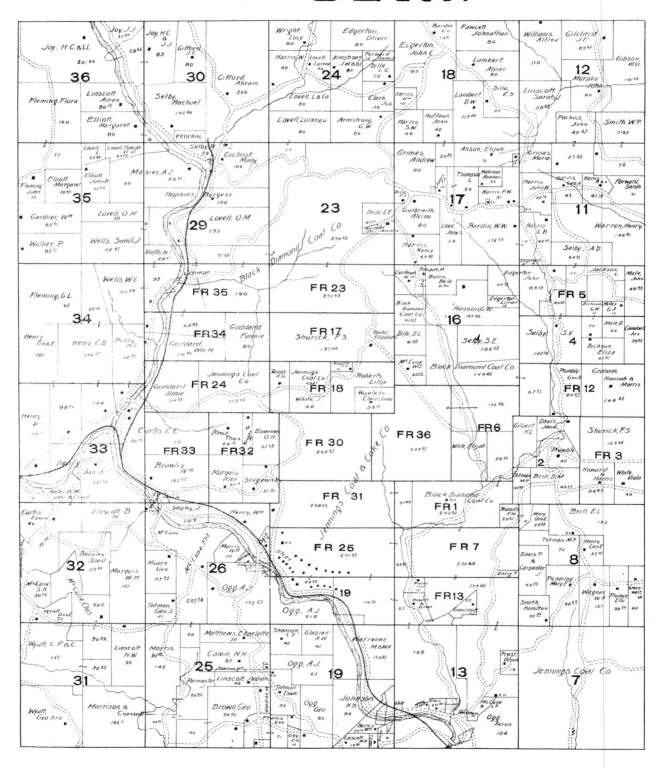

AMES

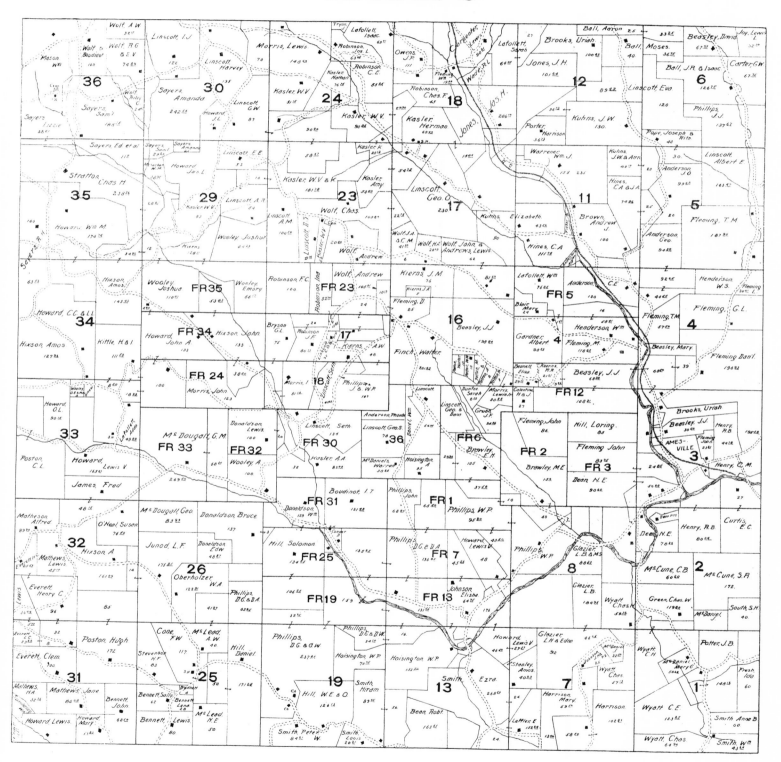

YORK

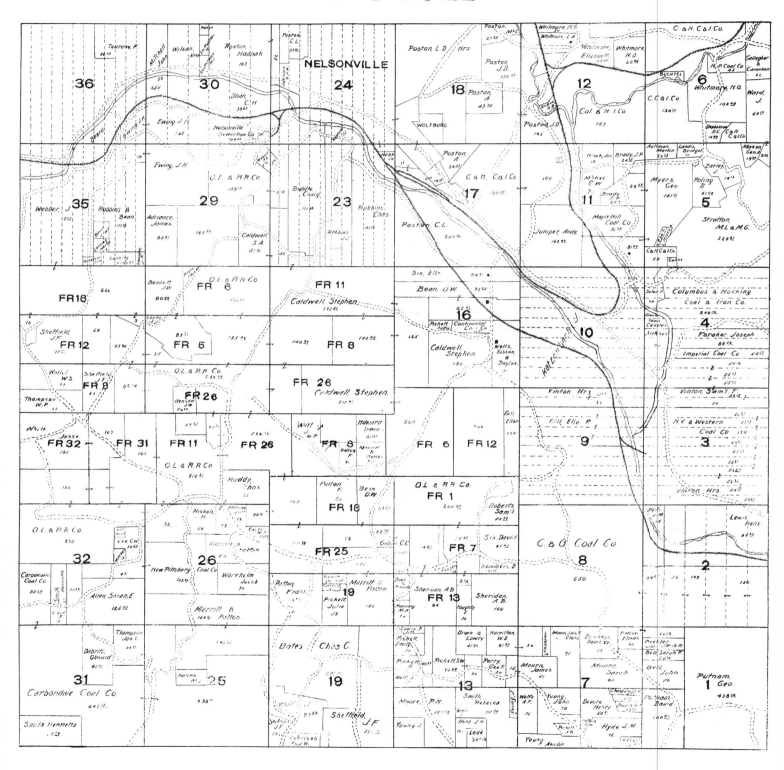

TRIMBLE

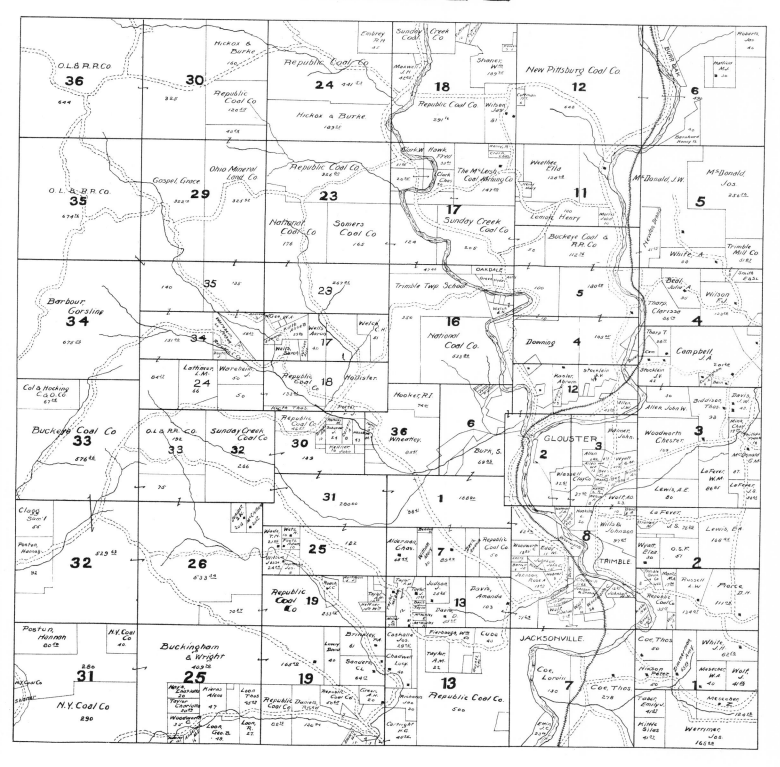

NELSONVILLE

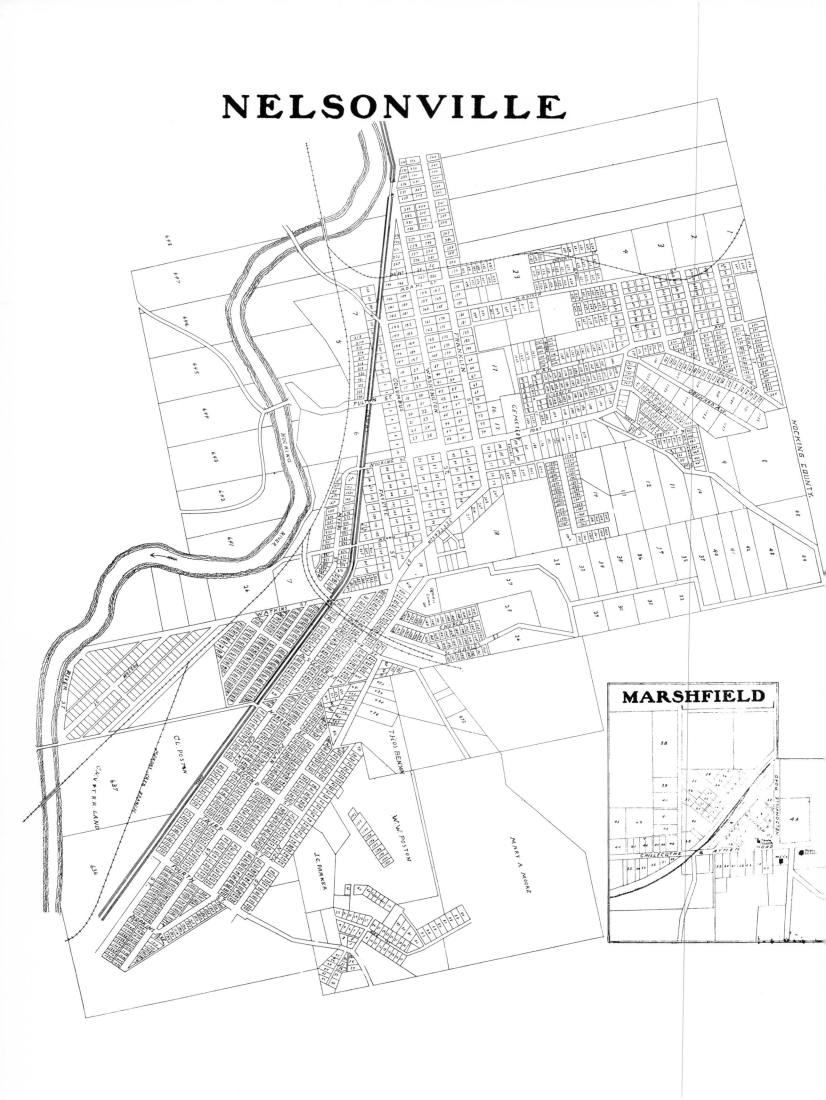

MARSHFIELD

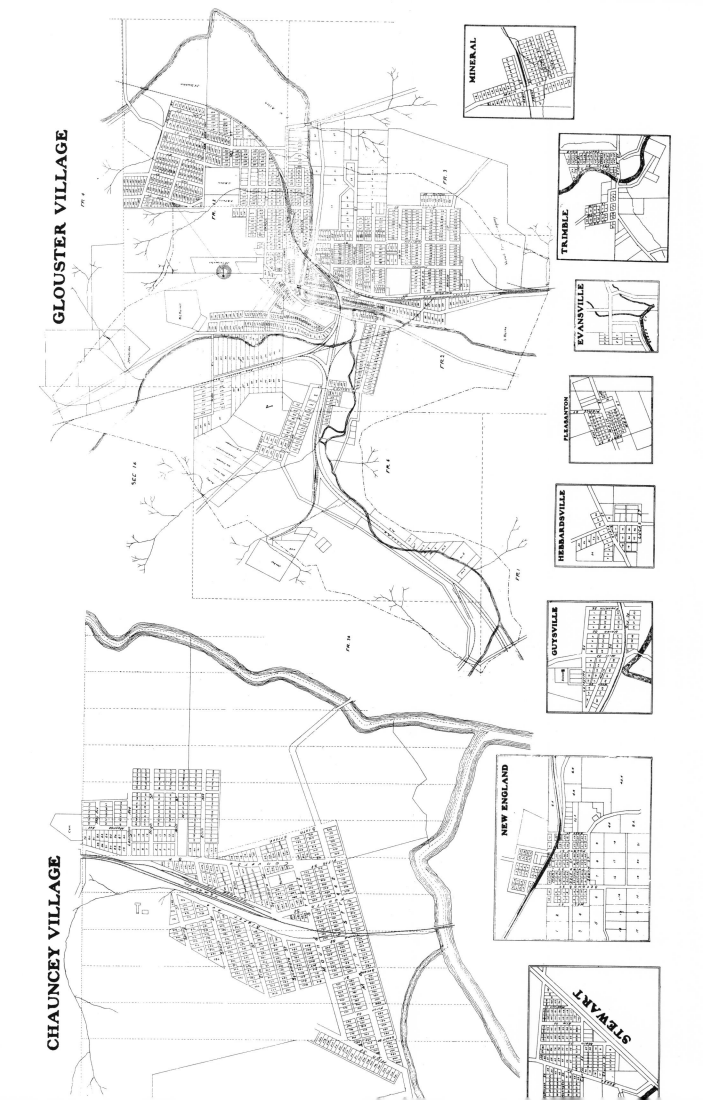

GLOUSTER VILLAGE

CHAUNCEY VILLAGE

MINERAL

TRIMBLE

EVANSVILLE

PLEASANTON

HEBBARDSVILLE

GUYSVILLE

NEW ENGLAND

STEWART

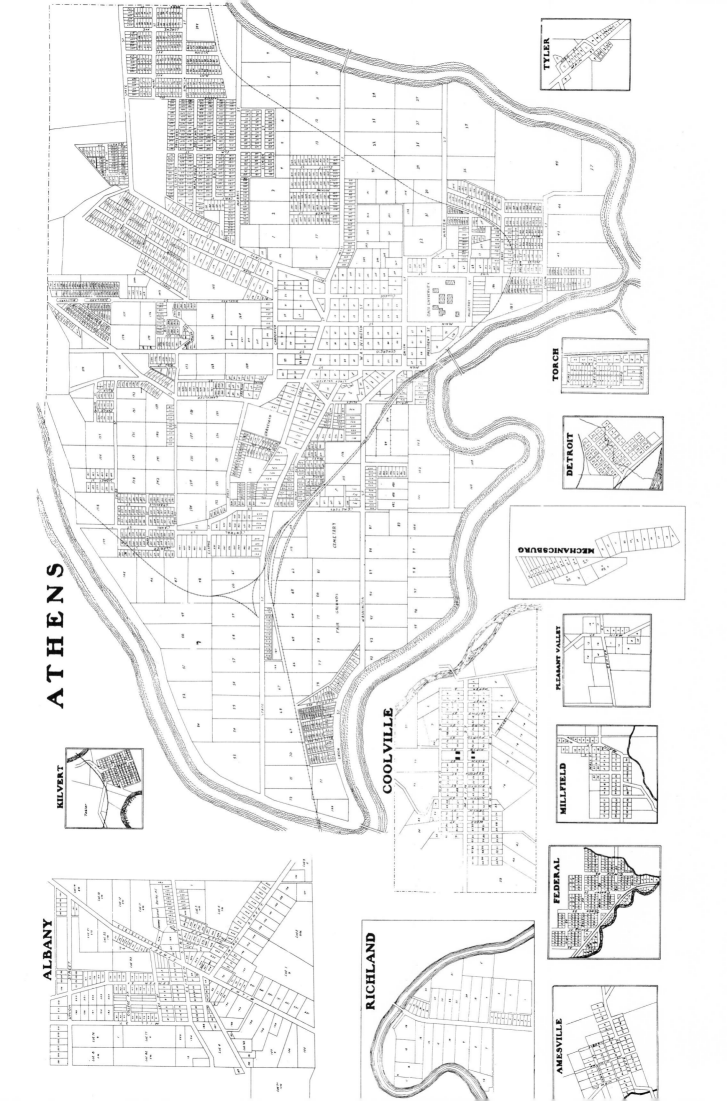

ATHENS

TYLER

TORCH

DETROIT

MECHANICSBURG

PLEASANT VALLEY

MILLFIELD

KILVERT

COOLVILLE

FEDERAL

ALBANY

RICHLAND

AMESVILLE

R. C. M. HASTINGS.

R C. M. HASTINGS, for the past two years successfully engaged in the furniture business, on South Court street, Athens, was born at Hebbardsville, Alexander township, May 27, 1867. He is the son of Professor and Mrs. William M. Hastings, both of whom were natives of Allegheny county Pa. Professor Hastings was well known throughout Athens county. For 14 years he was an instructor in languages at Mt. Lebanon college. Pa. R. C. M. Hastings attended the public schools at Athens, completed a course in Zanesville Business college in 1886, and 1887 and 1888 attended the Ohio University. Two years later he engaged in the general mercantile business at Chauncey where he remained for twelve years. While there he served as township treasurer for several years. He was married to Lizzie Fuller in 1892, daughter of the late Mrs. Mary Fuller. They have two children, Lucile Fuller and Mildred Irene. In the spring of 1902 he disposed of his interests in Chauncey and removed to Athens where he engaged in the furniture business, succeeding C. S. Newsom. From the start his furniture business was placed on a prosperous and successful plane, and he is now enjoying a patronage lucrative and profitable. He has one of the best stocked furniture establishments in Athens county and has built up a deserved reputation for dealing in goods of the finest quality. Through a liberal amount of advertising his patronage extends to all parts of Athens county, which are made easily accessible by the excellent shipping facilities afforded by the railroads entering Athens. He keeps constantly in touch with the best furniture factories in the country and because of this fact he is able to give his patrons the best and the newest designs in "anything in furniture." His determination to give his customers a large stock from which to make their selections has made it necessary to enlarge his storage capacity which will be provided with the completion of his new storage room between Court and Congress streets. He is a member of the Christian church and belongs to several secret organizations.

FURNITURE STORE OF R. C. M. HASTINGS.

ATHENS COUNTY'S FIRST BANK.

The first bank in the county was organized in 1848. State banks were the only kind known, and the bank established here was a branch of the Ohio State Bank. Forty-nine local capitalists put up the capital stock of $100,000 which was the minimum allowed by law. The directors chosen were John Ballard, John Welch, Ezra Stewart, A. B. Walker, Joseph M. Dana, Leonidas Jewett, Douglas Putnam, Samuel Pickering, and Joseph K. Will. John Welch was elected president; Charles H. Cornwell, cashier; Enos Stimson, teller; The bank was located in the brick building opposite the court house and flourished until 1863 when State banks were abolished. The bank organized under the new law and became the First National Bank of Athens with a capital stock of $50,000 and is doing business in the same old stand to-day.

HARDWARE STORE OF FRANK E. GOLDSBERRY.

FRANK E. GOLDSBERRY.

F RANK E. GOLDSBERRY who conducts one of the leading hardware stores of Athens, is a young business man who startd out in life endowed only with a common school education, plenty of pluck, ambition and good health. He has been in business for himself but ten years and to-day carries one of the largest stocks of hardware in the county.

Mr. Goldsberry was born near Pratt's Fork, Ohio, March 2, 1868, and is the son of Mr. and Mrs. John V. Goldsberry. At the age of 16, he began to clerk for George Burson at Pratt's Fork and drove a huckster wagon over Athens and Meigs counties. After six years service with Mr. Burson, he sought his fortune in the west but returned after two years absence and accepted a position as clerk with George W. Ullom April 7, 1890. In 1893 he was appointed assignee for L. O. Tullis who failed in a Men's furnishings store. In 1895 he was made assignee for his employer, George Ullom. In December of the same year he bought the remainder of the Ullom stock and started into business for himself. A little later the firm was know as F. E. Goldsberry & Co. In January of 1901, George Coe bought an interest in the business and the new firm moved to the present location in the Moore-Russell block. On June 15, 1902, Mr. Goldsberry purchased Mr. Coe's interest and has conducted the business himself ever since. In 1901, the harness business was added and has proved quite a success. W. H. Ring and Judiah Higgins both practical harness makers have had charge of this department. E. A. Russell, an efficient clerk has been with Mr. Goldsberry for nearly two years.

Mr. Goldsberry and Miss Alice Grimm, of Burlingham, Ohio, were married May 31, 1890. They have two bright, active boys, Blaine Randolph, age 12, and John Russell, age 8.

Mr. Goldsberry is a prominent Knight of Pythias, passed through the chairs and has served as Colonel. He is also a member of Paramuthia Lodge F. & A. M.

COUNTY COMMISSIONERS

FROM THE ORGANIZATION OF THE COUNTY.

1805—Silas Dean, William Howlett, John Corey.
1805—William Barrows, William Howlett, Samuel Moore.
1806—Alvin Bingham, William Howlett, Samuel Moore
1807—Alvan Bingham, Caleb Merritt. Samuel Moore.
1808—Alvan Bingham, Caleb Merritt, Ebenezer Currier.
1809—Asahel Cooley, Caleb Merritt, Ebenezer Currier
1810—Asahel Cooley, Zebulon Griffin, Ebenezer Currier.
1811—Asahel Cooley, Zebulon Griffin, Seth Fuller.
1812—Ebenezer Currier, Zebulon Griffin, Seth Fuller.
1813—Ebenezer Currier, Caleb Merritt, Seth Fuller.
1814—Ebenezer Currier, Caleb Merritt, Robert Linzee.
1815—Daniel Stewart, Levi Stedman, Robert Linzee.
1816—Caleb Merritt, Asahel Cooley, Daniel Stewart.
1817—Caleb Merritt, Asahel Cooley, Levi Stedman.
1818—George Walker, Stambro P. Stancliff, Levi Stedman.
1819—George Walker, Stambro P. Stancliff, James Gillmore,
1820—George Walker, Stambro P. Stancliff, James Gillmore.
1821—George Walker, Edmund Dorr, James Gillmore.
1822—George Walker, Edmund Dorr, James Gillmore.
1823—George Walker, Edmund Dorr, James Gillmore.
1824—George Walker, Edmund Dorr, James Gillmore.
1825—George Walker, Daniel Stewart, James Gillmore.
1826—George Walker, Daniel Stewart, Justus Reynolds.
1827—George Walker, Harry Henshaw, Justus Reynolds.
1828—George Walker, Harry Henshaw, Justus Reynolds.
1829—George Walker, Harry Henshaw, Justus Reynolds.
1830—George Walker, Absalom Boyles, Justus Reynolds.
1831—Joshua Hoskinson, Absalom Boyles, Justus Reynolds.
1832—Joshua Hoskinson, Absalom Boyles, Justus Reynolds.
1833—Joshua Hoskinson, David Jones, Justus Reynolds.

1834—Joshua Hoskinson, David Jones, Justus Reynolds.
1835—Joshua Hoskinson, David Jones, Frederic Abbott.
1836—Joshua Hoskinson, Alfred Hobby, Frederic Abbott.
1837—Joshua Hoskinson, Alfred Hobby, Frederic Abbott.
1838—Joshua Hoskinson, Alfred Hobby, William R. Walker.
1839—Joshua Hoskinson, Elmer Rowell, William R. Walker.
1840—Joshua Hoskinson, Elmer Rowell, Benj. M. Brown.
1841—Joshua Hoskinson, Elmer Rowell, Benj. M. Brown.
1842—Joshua Hoskinson, Arnold Patterson, Benj. M. Brown.
1843—Silas M. Shepard, Arnold Patterson, Benj. M. Brown.
1844—Silas M. Shepard, Arnold Patterson, Alfred Hobby.
1845—Silas M. Shepard, Ziba Lindlay. Alfred Hobby.
1846—Silas M. Shepard, Ziba Lindley, Alfred Hobby.
1847—Silas M. Shepard, Ziba Lindley, Alfred Hobby.
1848—James Dickey, Ziba Lindley, Alfred Hobby.
1849—James Dickey, Ziba Lindley, Alfred Hobby.
1850—James Dickey, Ziba Lindley. Pearley Brown.
1851—James Dickey, Ziba Lindley, John Elliott.
1852—L. D. Poston, Ziba Lindley, John Elliott.
1853—L. D. Poston, Ziba Lindley, John Elliott.
1854—L. D. Poston, William Mason, John Elliott.
1855—John Brown, William Mason, Daniel B. Stewart.
1856—John Brown, William Mason, Daniel B. Stewart.
1857—John Brown, Joseph Jewett, Daniel B. Stewart.
1858—John Brown, Joseph Jewett, Daniel B. Stewart.
1859—John T. Winn, Joseph Jewett, John E. Vose.
1860—John T. Winn, John Dew, John E. Vose.
1861—John Brown, John Dew. John E. Vose.
1862—John Brown, John Dew, G. M. McDougall.
1863—John Brown, Hugh Boden, G. M. McDougall.
1864—John Brown, W. F. Pilcher, G. M. McDougall.
1865—John Brown, W. F. Pilcher, G. M. McDougall.

1866—John Brown, W. F. Pilcher, G. M. McDougall.
1867—John Brown, W. F. Pilcher, G. M. McDougall.
1868—Thomas L. Mintern, W. F. Pilcher, G. M. McDougall.
1869—Thomas L. Mintern, Saml. S. Boyles, G. M. McDougall.
1870—Thomas L. Mintern, Saml. S. Boyles, G. M. McDougall.
1871—E. M. Blake, Saml. S. Boyles, J. F. Welch.
1872—E. M Blake, Saml. S. Boyles, J. F. Welch.
1873—E. M. Blake, Samuel S. Boyles, J. F. Welch.
1874—Alpheus Wilson, Samuel S.Boyles, J. F. Welch.
1875—Alpheus Wilson, E. H. Watkins, J. F. Welch.
1876—Alpheus Wilson, E. H. Watkins, F. Finsterwald.
1877—Elza Armstrong, E. H. Watson, F. Finsterwald.
1878—Elza Armstrong, E. H. Watson, F. Finsterwald. A. S. Tidd
1879—Elza Armstrong, W. H.Curfman, F. Finsterwald.
1880—W. G. Hickman, W. H. Curfman, F. Finsterwald.
1881—W. G. Hickman, W. H. Curfman, F. Finsterwald
1882—W. G. Hickman, W. H. Curfman, J. W. Murphy.
1883—W. G. Hickman, W. H. Curfman, J. W. Murphy.
1884—W. G. Hickman. W. H. Curfman, J. W. Murphy.
1885—W. G. Hickman, C. I. Ham, J. W. Murphy.
1886—W. G. Hickman, C. I. Ham, Joseph S. Higgins.
1887—J. A. Campbell, C. I. Ham, Joseph S. Higgins.
1888—J. A. Campbell, C. I. Ham, Joseph S. Higgins
1889—J. A. Campbell, C. I. Ham, Joseph S. Higgins
1890—J. A. Campbell, C. I. Ham, Joseph S. Higgins.
1891—J. A. Campbell, Jefferson Perry, Jos. S Higgins
1892—J. A. Campbell, Jefferson Perry, John Burson.
1893—Abner Juniper, Jefferson Perry, John Burson.
1894—Abner Juniper, Jefferson Perry, John Burson.
1895—Abner Juniper, Jefferson Perry, John Burson.
1896—Abner Juniper, Jefferson Perry, John Burson.
1897—Abner Juniper, Jefferson Perry, John Burson.
1898—Abner Juniper, Thomas Dupler, John Burson.
1899—Abner Juniper, Thomas Dupler, John O Hill.
1900—J. W. Jackson, Thomas Dupler, John O. Hill.
1901—John F. Biddle, Thomas Dupler, John O. Hill.
1902—John F. Biddle, Thomas Dupler, John O. Hill.
1903—Joseph Wolf, Thomas Dupler, John O. Hill.
1904—Joseph Wolf, John F. Biddle, John O Hill.
1905—Joseph Wolf, John F. Biddle, S. B. Hill.

County Court.

The first Court of Common Pleas was held July 8, 1805, Robert F. Slaughter, President Judge; Sylvanus Ames and Elijah Hatch, Associate Judges.

Since that time the following Judges have been elected:

1806 Levi Belt, President Judge; Sylvanus Ames, Alexander Stedman and Abel Miller, Associate Judges,
   In 1807 Judge Ames became Sheriff and Elijah Hatch became Judge.

1807 to 1812 William Wilson, President Judge; Alexander Stedman, Abel Miller and Elijah Hatch Associate Judges.

1813 William Wilson, President Judge; Jehiel Gregory, Silvanus Ames and Elijah Hatch, Associate Judges.

1814 William Wilson, President Judge; Jehiel Gregory, Sylvanus Ames and Ebenezer Currier Associate Judges.

1815 to 1818 William Wilson, President Judge; Sylvanus Ames, Ebenezer Currier and Elijah Hatch Associate Judges.

1819 Ezra Osborn, President Judge; Robert Linzee, Ebenezer Currier and Sylvanus Ames Associate Judges.

1824 Alvin Bingham, Associate Judge, *vice* Sylvanus Ames, deceased.

1825 Amos Crippen, Associate Judge, *vice* Robt. Linzee.

1826 Edmund Dorr, Associate Judge *vice* Ebenezer Currier, and Thomas Irwin, President Judge, *vice* Osborn.

1827 Elijah Hatch, Associate Judge, *vice* Amos Crippen.

1838 George Walker, Associate Judge, *vice* Alvan Bingham.

1833 Ebenezer Currier, Associate Judge *vice* Edward Dorr.

1834 David Richmond, Associate Judge, *vice* Elijah Hatch.

1840 John E. Hanna, President Judge, *vice* Thos. Irwin.

1840 Samuel B. Pruden, Associate Judge, *vice* Ebenezer Currier.

1841 Isaac Baker, Associate Judge, *vice* David Richmond.

1845 Robert A. Fulton, Associate Judge, *vice* George Walker.

1847 Arius Nye. President Judge, *vice* John E. Hanna.

1847 Samuel H. Brown, Associate Judge, *vice* S. B. Pruden.

1850 Norman Root, Associate Judge, *vice* Samuel H. Brown.

1850 A. G. Brown, President Judge, *vice* Arius Nye

1852 Simeon Nash elected first Judge under new constitution, when associate judges were dispensed with

1862 John Welch elected.

1865 Erastus A. Guthrie, appointed, *vice* John Welch, elected Supreme Judge.

1866 E. A. Guthrie elected.

1872 J. Cartwright appointed.

1872 David Hebbard, appointed.

1873 Joseph P. Bradley, elected.

1873 Samuel S. Knowles, elected.

1882 Hiram L. Sibley, elected.

1885 Rudolph deSteiguer, elected.

1896 Joseph M. Wood, elected.

COUNTY OFFICERS FOR ONE CENTURY

YEARS.	AUDITORS.	CLERKS.	TREASURERS.	RECORDERS.	SHERIFFS	PROS. ATTORNEY.	PROBATE JUDGE	YEARS.
1805....			ALVAN BINGHAM..		ROBERT LINZEE			.1805
1806....		HENRY BARTLETT.	WILLIAM HARPER	ELIPHAZ PERKINS	....do.......	E. B. MERWIN...		.1806
1807....		.........do.......	EBEN. CURRIER	....do	SILVANUS AMES	....do.......		.1807
1808....		....do.......	ELIPHAZ PERKINS	....do	....do	....do		.1808
1809....		....do.......	WILLIAM HARPER	....do....	ROBERT LINZEE	BENJ. RUGGLES		.1809
1810....	The office of County Auditor was created by act of the legislature, at the session of 1820-21.	....do.......	....do	....do	....do	ARTEMUS SAWYER	PROBATE COURT ORGANIZED IN 1852.	.1810
1811....		....do.......	ELIPHAZ PERKINS	....do	....do	....do		.1811
1812....		....do.......	....do	....do	....do	ALEX. HARPER		.1812
1813....		....do.......	....do	....do	....do	ARTEMUS SAWYER		.1813
1814....		....do.......	....do	....do	THOS. ARMSTRONG	....do		.1814
1815....		....do.......	AMOS CRIPPEN	....do	....do	J. L. LEWIS		.1815
1816....		....do.......	....do	....do	....do	THOMAS EWING		.1816
1817....		....do.......	....do	....do	....do	JOSEPH DANA		.1817
1818....		....do.......	....do	....do	ISAAC BAKER	....do		.1818
1819....		....do.......	....do	C. F. PERKINS	....do	....do		.1819
1820....	JOSEPH B. MILES.	....do.......	....do	....do	....do	SAML. F. VINTON		.1820
1821....	GEN. JOHN BROWN	....do.......	....do	....do	....do	....do		.1821
1822....	....do.	....do.......	....do	....do	JACOB LENTNER	THOMAS EWING		.1822
1823....	....do.	....do.......	....do	....do	....do	....do		.1823
1824....	....do.	....do.......	....do	....do	CALVARY MORRIS	THOMAS IRWIN		.1824
1825....	....do.	....do.......	ISAAC BARKER.	A. G. BROWN	....do	....do		.1825
1826....	....do.	....do.......	....do	....do	....do	DWIGHT JARVIS		.1826
1827....	NORMAN ROOT.	....do.......	....do	....do	ROBERT LINZEE	....do		.1827
1828....	....do.	....do.......	....do	....do	....do	....do		.1828
1829....	....do.	....do.......	....do	....do	....do	....do		.1829
1830....	....do.	....do.......	AMOS CRIPPEN.	po	JOHN McGILL.	JOSEPH DANA		.1830
1831....	....do.	....do.......	....do	....do	....do	....do		.1831
1832....	....do.	....do.......	IsAAC BARKER.	....do	AMOS MILLER	....do		.1832
1833....	....do.	....do.......	....do	R. E. CONSTABLE.	....do	....do		.1833
1834....	....do.	....do.......	....do	....do	....do	....do		.1834
1835....	....do.	....do.......	....do	A. G. BROWN	....do	JOHN WELCH.		.1835
1836....	....do.	JOSEPH M. DANA	ISAAC N. NORTON	....do	JOSEPH HEWITT	....do		.1836
1837....	....do.	....do	ISAAC BARKER.	....do	....do	....do		.1837
1838....	....do.	....do	....do	....do	....do	K. E. CONSTABLE		.1838
1839....	LEONIDAS JEWETT	....do	....do	....do	JOS. H. MOORE	....do		.1839
1840....	....do.	....do	AMOS CRIPPEN	....do	....do	JOHN WELCH		.1840
1841....	....do.	....do	ENOS STIMSON	....do	....do	....do		.1841
1842....	....do.	....do	ROBERT. McCABE	....do	....do	....do		.1842
1843....	ABNER MORSE	....do	....do	....do	....do	T. A. PLANTS.		.1843
1844....	....do.	....bo	....do	JOHN BOSWELL	WM. GOLDEN.	....do		.1844
1845....	LEONIDAS JEWETT	....do	....do	....do	....do	J. D. JOHNSON		.1845
1846....	....do.	....do	....do	....do	....do	....do		.1846
1847....	E. H. MOORE	....do	....do	A. J. VAN VORHES	....do	LOT L. SMITH		.1847
1848....	....do.	....do	WILLIAM GOLDEN	....do	J. L. CURRIER	....do		.1848
1849....	....do.	....do	....do	....do	....do	....do		.1849
1850....	....do.	....do	....do	W. H. BARTLETT	....do	....do		.1850
1851....	....do.	....do	....do	....do	....do	SAML. S. KNOWLES.		.1851
1852....	....do.	....do	....do	....do	JOS. L. KESSINGER	....do	JACOB C. FROST.	.1852
1853....	....do.	....do	....do	....do	....do	....do	....do	.1853
1854....	....do.	....do	SAML. PICKERING	FRANK E. FOSTER	....do	....do	....do	.1854
1855....	....do.	....do	....do	GEO. H. STEWART	....do	GEO. S. WALSH.	CALVARY MORRIS	.1855
1856....	....do.	....do	....do	....do	LEONARD BROWN	....do	....do	.1856
1857....	....do.	LOUIS W. BROWN.	....do	....do	....do	E. A. GUTHRIE	....do	.1857
1858....	....do.	....do	LEONARD BROWN	....do	H. C. KNOWLES.	....do	....do	.1858
1859....	....do.	....do	....do	....do	....do	....do	....do	.1859
1860....	....do	....do	JOSEPH M. DANA.	....do	....do	....do	....do	.1860
1861....	S. W. PICKERING.	....do	....do	NORMAN ROOT	....do	LOT L. SMITH	....do	.1861
1862....	....do.	....do	LEONARD BROWN	DANIEL DRAKE	F. S. STEDMAN	....do	....do	.1862
1863....	....do.	....do	....do	....do	....do	R. DeSTEIGER.	....do	.1863
1864....	....do.	....do	A. S. W. MINEAR	....do	J. M. JOHNSON	....do	....do	.1864
1865....	....do.	....do	....do	....do	....do	....do	....do	.1865
1866....	....do.	....do	....do	....do	....do	....do	....do	.1866
1867....	....do.	....do	GEO. W. BAKER.	JOSIAH B. ALLEN	W. S. WILSON	....do	....do	.1867
1868....	....do.	....do	....do	....do	....do	....do	....do	.1868
1869....	....do.	E. M. PHILLIPS.	....do	....do	....do	CHAS. TOWNSEND	....do	.1869
1870....	....do.	....do	....do	....do	....do	....do	L. M. JEWETT	.1870
1871....	ALEX. W. S. MINEAR	GEO. W. BAKER.	WM. S. WILSON	....do	A. J. REYNOLDS	....do	....do	.1871
1872....	....do.	....do	....do	....do	Nehemiah Warren.	....do	....do	.1872
1873....	....do.	....do	....do	....do	....do	....do	....do	.1873
1874....	....do.	....do	....do	....do	....do	....do	....do	.1874
1875....	....do.	....do	....do	....do	....do	....do	THOS. L. MINTUN	.1875
1876....	....do	....do	A. J. FRAME...	....do	Parker Carpenter	L. M. JEWETT	....do	.1876
1877....	....do	....do	....do	....do	....do	....do	....do	.1877
1878....	....do	....do	....do	....do	....do	....do	....do	.1878
1879....	....do	....do	....do	....do	....do	....do	....do	.1879
1880....	A. J. FRAME	....do	JOHN P. COE	J. W. ANDREWS	T. B. WARDEN	EMMET TOMPKINS	WM. S. WILSON	.1880
1881....	....do.	SILAS E. HEDGES.	....do	....do	....do	....do	....do	.1881
1882....	....do.	....do	....do	LAFAYETTE HAWK	....do	....do	....do	.1882
1883....	....do.	....do	....do	....do	....do	....do	....do	.1883
1884....	....do.	....do	HIRAM L. BAKER	....do	JOHN BODEN	....do	....do	.1884
1885....	....do.	....do	....do	....do	....do	DAVID L. SLEEPER.	....do	.1885
1886....	....do.	....do	....do	....do	FRED STALDER	....do	....do	.1886
1887....	....do.	....do	....do	....do	....do	....do	....do	.1887
1888....	....do.	....do	H. H. WICKHAM	LEROY BEAN	....do	....do	....do	.1888
1889....	....do.	....do	....do	....do	....do	....do	....do	.1889
1890....	....do.	....do	....do	....do	J. FINSTERWALD	....do	....do	.1890
1891....	....do.	....do	....do	....do	....do	JAMES P. WOOD	GEORGE KALER	.1891
1892....	....do.	....dn.	W. F. SCOTT.	....do	....do	....do	A. S. BETHEL	.1892
1893....	....do.	....do	....do	....do	....do	....do	....do	.1893
1894....	....do.	....do	....do	....do	M. M. RILEY	....do	....do	.1894
1895....	....do.	D. A. R. McKINSTRY	....do	....do	....do	....do	....do	.1895
1896....	WILBUR F. SCOTT	....do	E. G. BIDDISON.	....do	....do	E. D. SAYRE	....do	.1896
1897....	....do.	....do	....do	....do	....do	....do	....do	.1897
1898....	....do.	....do	....do	ELMER GOLDEN	C. H. PORTER	....do	....do	.1898
1899....	....do.	....do	....do	....do	....do	....do	....do	.1899
1900....	....do.	....do	W. G. HICKMAN.	....do	....do	....do	....do	.1900
1901....	....do.	....do	....do	....do	....do	....do	....do	.1901
1902....	E. R. WALKER	....do	....do	....do	ANDREW MURPHY	....do	....do	.1902
1903....	....do.	....do	....do	....do	....do	I. M. FOSTER	A. W. LYNCH	.1903
1904....	....do.	....do	E. C. WOODWORTH.	....do	....do	....do	....do	.1904

Charles DeMolet, Plumbing and Heating, Athens, Ohio.

AMONG the representative business houses of Athens, there are none that give us more pleasure to hold up to public light than Charles DeMolet, engaged in Plumbing and Heating. Mr. DeMolet came here from Cincinnati as an employe of B. F. Witman in 1895. Mr. Witman had to advance his fare to get him here. Leaving ten dollars, all the money he had, with his wife Mr. DeMolet came to Athens and went to work. One year after his arrival, he started into business for himself, and today has one of the best paying businesses in the town. He confines himself to plumbing and heating, employs regularly six men and has the confidence and respect of a large and increasing number of patrons.

The secret of his success is honesty, fidelity to the interest of his patrons and close attention to business.

The accompanying illustration is an excellent picture of his place of business at No. 45 South Court street. Mr. De Molet was born in Cincinnati April 2, 1872, attended the public schools of that city and at the age of 14 years was apprenticed with the Thomas Gibson Co. the oldest and the largest plumbing firm in the city. He was married to Miss Margaret O'Connel in 1892, a resident of Cincinnati. Mr. and Mrs. DeMolet are the parents of five children: Charles age 11; John age 9; Margaret age 6; Dorothy age 2. Robert died at the age of one year in 1898. Both are prominent members of St. Paul's church and are highly respected citizens.

Socially, Mr. DeMolet is one of the leading spirits of the Assembly Club, one of the best social organizations of the town, and has been its treasurer ever since he has been a member.

Mr. and Mrs. Elijah F. Poston.

ELIJAH F. POSTON was born on the 7th day of February. 1863, in Canaan township, Athens county, Ohio. He was reared as a farmer boy and in 1897 purchased the farm that he now owns, which consists of 107 acres. He is a practical farmer and the improvement on his farm shows his merits as an agriculturist.

On the 9th day of March, 1898, he married Emma E. Earich, daughter of Joseph

Earich, of Zanesville, Ohio. Mrs. Poston was born on the 4th day of August, 1869, at Millfield, Athens county, Ohio.

They have one child, a son, Ray Earich Poston, who was born on the 22d day of January, 1899.

The accompanying illustration is an excellent picture of the beautiful country home of Mr. and Mrs. Poston, who are shown sitting on the veranda. The neat appearance of house, yard and surroundings tell more than words of the scrupulous care with which Mr. and Mrs. Poston conduct their farm.

E. C. Woodworth, Athens, O.

E C. WOODWORTH, who is serving his first term as Treasurer of Athens county, is a product of the Sunday Creek Valley. He was born near Millfield, Dover township December 29, 1872. He is the son of Mr. and Mrs. L. S. Woodworth, who occupy a fertile, well cultivated farm on the banks of Sunday Creek. Until his early teens, E. C. Woodworth remained on the farm performing all the work incident to the life of the husbandman. He attended the district school with a sort of studied irregularity brought about chiefly by the fact that he found more interest and genuine enjoyment in trapping the wily animals that infested the woods at that time, in snagging the mercurial mud cat then abundant in the

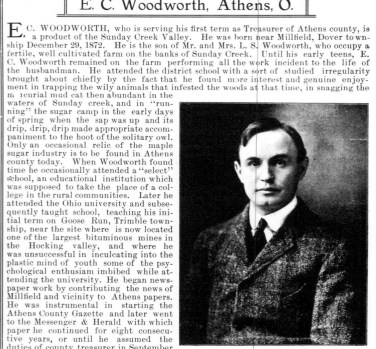

waters of Sunday creek, and in "running" the sugar camp in the early days of spring when the sap was up and its drip, drip, drip made appropriate accompaniment to the hoot of the solitary owl. Only an occasional relic of the maple sugar industry is to be found in Athens county today. When Woodworth found time he occasionally attended a "select" school, an educational institution which was supposed to take the place of a college in the rural communities. Later he attended the Ohio university and subsequently taught school, teaching his initial term on Goose Run, Trimble township, near the site where is now located one of the largest bituminous mines in the Hocking valley, and where he was unsuccessful in inculcating into the plastic mind of youth some of the psychological enthusiasm imbibed while attending the university. He began newspaper work by contributing the news of Millfield and vicinity to Athens papers. He was instrumental in starting the Athens County Gazette and later went to the Messenger & Herald with which paper he continued for eight consecutive years, or until he assumed the duties of county treasurer in September 1904, with the exception of eight months in 1898, when he was a member of Company B, Seventh regiment, O. V. I. in the Spanish-American war. His regiment, however, saw no active service and the time was spent on the sterile, pine-capped knobs near Washington, D. C., and on the meadowed plateaus of Harrisburg. Pa. Since he has reached his majority he has taken more or less part in practical politics. He has served frequently on the Republican central and executive committees, and has preached Republicanism from the stump in every township in the county. He was elected treasurer in November, 1903, and took charge of the office nearly a year later. For two years he was a member of the city council of Athens. He was married in 1900 to Miss Mary P. Fuller of Chauncey and with their two children, Ellis and Elizabeth, live on West Carpenter street. He is a member of several secret societies.

HISTORY OF ATHENS COUNTY

ATHENS County was established by act of the legislature Feb. 20, 1805. It was taken from the territory known as Washington county, the first county of the state. When first established Athens county contained one thousand and fifty-three square miles or about thirty regular surveyed townships, and included five townships now belonging to Meigs county, viz: Columbia, Scipio, Bedford, Orange and Olive townships; two now belonging to Morgan county, Homer and Marion; three now belonging to Hocking county, Ward, Green and Starr; and seven now belonging to Vinton, Brown, Swan, Elk, Madison, Knox, Clinton and Vinton townships; and a strip of land about ten miles long and one mile wide now belonging to Washington county. By an act passed January 30, 1807, entitled "an act to alter the boundary line between the counties of Athens and Gallia," a strip about ten miles long and one mile wide, was added to the southeast corner of Athens county as it then existed. By an act passed February 18, 1807, entitled "an act altering the line between the counties of Washington and Athens," the boundary of Athens was changed so as to take in the portion of Troy township lying east of the Hockhocking river; and the same act detached a strip one mile wide and fifteen miles long, lying along the eastern border of Rome, Bern, and Marion townships, from Athens county, and added it to Washington. By an act passed February 10, 1814, sections thirty-one and thirty-two in township number six, range eleven (Rome) were detached from Washington and added to Athens, and sections eleven and twelve in township number eight, range twelve (now Marion township, Morgan county), were detached from Athens and added to Washington. The creation of the county of Jackson by act of January 12, 1816, took township number ten, range seventeen (now Clinton township, Vinton county), from Athens. The creation of the county of Hocking by act of January 3, 1818, took part of three townships (Green and Starr, of Hocking, and Brown, of Vinton county), from Athens; and by act of March 12, 1845, entitled "an act to attach part of the county of Athens to the county of Hocking," the residue of these townships was stricken off. The creation of the county of Meigs, January 21, 1819, took five townships from Athens and reduced our southern boundary to its present limits. By an act passed March 11, 1845, the townships of Homer and Marion were detached from Athens and added to Morgan county. Finally the erection of the county of Vinton by act passed March 23, 1850, took the remainder of our out-lying possessions in that direction, and the same act detached Ward township from Athens and gave it to Hocking, thus reducing our boundaries all around to their present limits. The present boundaries of the county include about four hundred and eighty-four square miles.

THE OHIO COMPANY.

The territory embraced in the original and consequently present boundaries of Athens county was part of The Ohio Companies Purchase and a brief history of that organization which took such an active and effective part in the early settlement of this territory, cannot be omitted. The Ohio Company resulted from the plans of two Massachusetts men, heroes of the Revolutionary war, General Rufus Putnam and General Benjamin Tupper. The war had naturally engendered the spirit of adventure and its close found many soldiers reduced to poverty or bankruptcy by the result of the seven years' struggle, ready to embark in any scheme that promised to retrieve their shattered fortunes. The time was ripe for western colonization, a subject that had attracted the attention of many Revolutionary leaders during the closing years of the war and was especially favored by Washington.

In 1784 Virginia ceded to the general government all her claim to the territory northwest of the Ohio river, excepting only that tract since known as the Virginia military District, lying between the Scioto and the Little Miami. At this juncture the plan of buying a tract of land was conceived and presented to Congress by Generals Putnam and Tupper, the hope of having congress present each revolutionary patriot with a tract of land having been abandoned. General Tupper was one of the government surveyors appointed by congress to lay out in townships and ranges that part of the Northwest territory which is now southeastern Ohio. He had visited the western country in the performance of his duties in 1785, and doubtless that visit and his favorable report of the region had its influence on the subsequent purchase of the tract of the Ohio Company.

In January, 1786, General Tupper visited his friend General Putnam and as a result of their conference they united in an advertisement which appeared in the newspapers of the state on January 25, setting forth briefly the natural inducements of the Ohio country to settlers and suggesting that all persons who might be interested should meet at designated places in their respective counties on the following February 15 for the purpose of choosing delegates who would assemble at the Bunch of Grapes Tavern, in Boston on Wednesday, March 1, 1786, "then and there to consider and determine upon a general plan of association for said company."

In response to this call, county meetings were held and delegates chosen, who convened at the place and on the day appointed. The delegates were all prominent New England men. Gen. Rufus Putnam was chosen chairman and Major Winthrop Sargent, secretary. As a result of the convention, articles of agreement were entered into and an association was formed by the name of the Ohio Company. The preamble was as follows: "The design of this association is to raise a fund in continental certificates, for the sole purpose and to be appropriated to the entire use of purchasing lands in the Western Territory belonging to the United States, for the benefit of the Company, and to promote a settlement in that country." These articles of agreement were adopted March 3, 1786, and subscription books were opened at once. A year passed before a sufficient number of shares were subscribed to justify further steps. On the 8th of March, 1787, a called meeting was held in Boston and Samuel H. Parsons, Gen. Rufus Putnam and Dr. Manasseh Cutler were appointed directors to make proposals to congress, "for a private purchase of lands and under such descriptions as they shall deem adequate for the purpose of the Company." The directors employed Dr. Manasseh Cutler to make a contract with congress for a body of land in the "Great Western territory of the Union." Dr. Cutler left his home in June 1787, for New York where congress was sitting. The constitutional convention, engaged in framing the Federal constitution, was sitting at the same time in Philadelphia, and Dr. Cutler bore letters of introduction to leading men in both cities. His journal of his trip is reproduced in full in Walker's History of Athens County, and from it, we learn that the art of lobbying was not altogether unknown even in that early period of our history. The journal can not be reproduced here but let it suffice to say he wisely and adroitly made his wants known to congress and while there was much opposition, he finally succeeded in obtaining the tract desired, amounting to nearly five million acres of land of which only one million and a half were for the Ohio Company; and owing to certain embarrassments in its affairs, the Company finally became possessed of only nine hundred and sixty-four thousand two hundred and eighty-five acres. Athens county was embraced in this grant and the two townships within the grant that were reserved for university purposes were Athens and Alexander.

THE FIRST SETTLEMENT.

On the 7th of April 1788 the first party of pioneers, 48 in number landed at the mouth of the Muskingum. They at once set to work to build a block house and provide other means of defense, well knowing that though their savage neighbors were quiet at that time their friendliness could never be relied on. Washington who knew many of them personally, boasted that never was a colony settled by such a high class of men—nor men better calculated to promote the welfare of such a community."

The first settlement which was on the present site of Marietta was called Adelphia, meaning literally "brethren." This seemed to the founders to fittingly express their hopes of the peacefulness and success of the new enterprise. The name Marietta, however, was early suggested as a compliment to Marie Antionette, who had steadily befriended the states through the Revolutionary war. When the subject of a name was put to vote of the people, the old soldiers predominating, expressed their gratitude for the helping hand of the young French queen and Marietta won. A governor and three judges were appointed by congress and the entire government of this country was vested in them, the people having no word in it. A part of the expenses were borne by the United States, but a greater part by heavy taxation of the people governed. Ohio's first provisional territorial government was however, successful for the ten years it was maintained as the power happened to be in the hands of honest, upright men, whose sincere and united aim was for the betterment of the community. The first law enacted was for the regulating and establishment of a militia.

In spite of privations and dangers, a few emigrants arrived during the summer, so that at the beginning of 1789 the population was 132 including some women and children. At this time there was not a single white family in the present bounds of Ohio, save in this settlement, although the settlement of Cincinnati began soon after.

TROUBLE WITH THE INDIANS.

Little by little civilization was making its advance—crops and families began to be raised—small settlements at short distances into the interior were made and roads opened. The Indians had continued friendly to these new comers, who showed a desire only for peaceful and kindly relations. But the frontiers men in Virginia were of a different kind; hunters, who considered every red skin lawful game, to be shot on sight. This continued ill-treatment wakened the slumbering fires in the savage breast and they laid aside tribal feuds to unite in the extinction of the white man from their hunting grounds. Thus began a four years war during which all the horrors of savage butchery united could not drive out these intrepid New Englanders, determined to make this fertile new region their own. However, the stories of Indian massacres which found their way back east kept the tide of immigration restrained until the final treaty of Greenville in 1795. This was an agreement of all the tribes of Indians in Ohio and adjoining country to betake themselves to regions more remote and leave the white man in peaceful possession of their fertile country, in return for which, boundary lines were established and annual allowances of money to Indians assured, and certain hunting privileges granted and provisions for trading agreed upon. The hitherto delayed immigration now began coming steadily from all parts of New England, also New York and Pennsylvania. Wonderful reports of the luxuriant fertility of this new country spread all over the east and the new comers looked to find it a land overflowing with milk and honey.

But enemies of this settlement hoping to bring such desirable settlers into the Cincinnati settlement were also busy reporting the wondrous fertility of the Miami valley and the sterility of the "Huckleberry Knobs." Thus half the immigration at this date went by the Ohio Company's purchase, laughing at anyone for stopping where it was all hills and hollows. But plenty of good energetic homeseekers stopped here—men and women of indomitable courage and persistence, whose sterling worth has made this country what it is today and whose descendants have lived to see these same barren hills bring forth far greater riches from their innermost parts than could ever be gained from any agricultural country. And these same descendants bless the ancestors who stopped and made their homes in the "mountains" of southeastern Ohio, then known only as the Northwest Territory.

ATHENS SITE CHOSEN.

Gen. Putnam who had been instrumental in getting the assignment of the university lands from congress was anxious for the settlement of those two townships, that the building up of a fund for educational purposes might begin. As the surveyor for the Ohio Company he had been all over this ground and selected the location for the university. From all descriptions of the site chosen it is supposed to have been a place three miles west of the present Athens, known as "The Plains." This had been the site of an Indian village and was one of their choice meeting places, also where they buried their honored dead. It was one of their signal stations and choice hunting grounds to which they returned for many years, until as late as 1810 and 1811. There is every reason to believe that a professional surveyor and a man of as much experience and travel as Gen. Rufus Putnam would be keen to note the advantages of such a beautiful level plateau as "The Plains" for the site of a city and as he hoped a great seat of learning in this new western empire, for this university plan was of his conceiving and the pride of his heart.

In 1895 two or three parties came up the Hock-hocking hunting. They were urged by Putnam to locate a settlement on the site chosen by him. These men camped at various places. At the mouth of Federal creek, one Peter Boyles by name, remained. Later in the same year he settled in Canaan township and became the father of the first white child born in Athens county, George Boyles by name. Another favorite camping ground of these early hunting parties was the riffle where Herrold's mill now stands. The story still lives of a man named Gillespie shooting a buffalo on the site of the present fair grounds. He followed the wounded animal as far as the present site of the court house and there killed it.

These early expeditions were not equipped for remaining in the wilderness and finding evidences of Indians on all sides, returned to Marietta.

ATHENS' FIRST SETTLERS.

Early in the spring of 1796 about fifteen men urged by Putnam to locate on the college lands, again returned up the Hockhocking. When they reached the place where Barth's mill and the east bridge now stand, they were attracted by the high bluffs of the present site of Athens.

It is generally supposed that they mistook this for the high plateau to which Putnam had directed them and they came ashore. A few settled on the attractive bluff but most of them sought their farm lands in the surrounding bottoms. Among these were Isaac Barker, Alvan and Silas Bingham, John Chandler, Edmund, William and Barak Dorr, William Harper, Robert Linzee, John Wilkins and Johnathan Watkins.

(Continued on page 13.)

Residence of Elijah H. Brown, Athens Township.

THE ACCOMPANYING ILLUSTRATION shows the home of Elijah H. Brown, in the South-west corner of Athens Township, near Wingett's Chapel, as well as a picture of Mr. Brown himself and his faithful wife, who died August 16, 1903. Mr. Brown was born October 20, 1831, in Green county, Pennsylvania, and came to this county with his parents in 1832. He was the eldest of five children, two boys and three girls. His father, Henry Brown, died in 1839. At the age of sixteen he took charge of the farm of

130 acres and in 1869 bought the old homestead, and his mother who lived to the age of 93 years, and died in 1898, made her home with Mr. Brown. In 1862 he was married to Martha A. Dickerson, who was born and reared in Alexander township. To this union there were born eight children, two of whom died in infancy. Those living are W. H. H. Brown, who is running the old farm; Herma A. Oxley, Cora A. Brown, of Columbus; Altha J. Hunter, Athens; Eva M. Watts, Columbus; and Osee Vore, Athens. Mr. Brown is a member of the Presbyterian church, an ardent Republican, an excellent neighbor and an upright and straightforward citizen.

Mr. and Mrs. John M. Hibbard.

THE HIBBARD FAMILY is one of the oldest families in the county. Elisha, Alanson, James and John, four brothers, came to this county from Vermont in 1816, and settled in different parts of the county. Alanson settled on Sugar Creek and was the father of four sons, Alanson, Jr., Peter, Henry and Sabina. Alanson Jr. moved to Alexander township and was the father of W. A. Hibbard, now living in Athens. Peter lives in Athens township and Henry lives on border of Athens township. Sabina and Alanson are dead.

John M. Hibbard, the father of John M. Jr., whose picture is here presented, died July 15, 1889, aged 90 years. John M. Jr. was born September 21, 1832 in Athens township on the old Henry Hibbard farm. He was married to Betsey Keth January 27, 1854. Seven children were born to them—John M. 3d, James, Nathaniel, Randolph, Lizzie, Corena, Joseph C. and William.

Athens County's Court Houses

IN 1807 the first Court House was built. For two years previous a room had been rented of Leonard Jewett and Silas Bingham for the purpose. This court house was a very substantial one of logs, two stories high, with an immense chimney of brick instead of the usual one of mud, stone and sticks. There is still in existence the elaborate contract for the erection of this chimney. This temple of justice was a very useful addition to the town, being used for the purpose of school house, meeting house and for all public gatherings. Here court was held a number of years until the growing demands of the county required a larger building. In 1814 contracts were let for a new court house to be of brick. In 1818 this was finished and was a substantial brick edifice, very fine for those days and did service for more than sixty years. The 100,000 brick were furnished at $6 a thousand; for laying of brick $500; shingles for roof, $67; laying the floors, $4.50 a square; building the stairs, $60. Although quite expensive for that time, much of the money was raised by subscription and there was no debt on it when finished. Those who remember the building now think of it as painfully plain, unornamental, but though it had undergone changes inside and out as long as it stood it gave evidence of the sturdy honesty with which workmen labored in the early days. Great effort has been made by the publishers of this atlas to find a photograph of the old court house, but the search has proved to be in vain. The present commodious structure ranks above the average county Court House, is modern in its appointments and of an imposing archectural design. The building was completed in 1880 and was contracted to cost $44,705.

Wild Animals of Early Times.

There were few buffalo and elk remaining when white families began to settle in this county, but the bear, wild cat and panther in small numbers still roamed in the forests.

Red deer were frequently found and wild turkeys were plentiful, while the rivers contained an abundance of fish of many kinds, which "could be drawn from the Hocking with brush drags in wagon loads."

Wolves were a constant menace to the sheep. The County Commissioners offered at various times different amounts as bounty for wolf scalps. From $2 to $3 was the usual price. As high as $30 for wolf scalps was paid at a single meeting of the Commissioners.

Residence of Alfred Bailes, Lee Township.

Alfred Bailes was born in Newark, Wirt county, West Virginia, on December 21, 1856, came to Ohio with his parents, Mr. and Mrs. Thomas Bailes, April 7, 1865. In 1880, Mr. Bailes went to Kansas where he lived one year, returning to his Ohio home he

married Miss Louisa Mace, youngest daughter of Milton H. Mace, and who died March 15, 1893. In 1895 he married Miss Anna Chase, eldest daughter of Ausmer Chase, who is yet living.

In 1887, on the farm where he now lives, he took up breeding of fine Delain sheep. By close study and observation he has produced one of the best flocks in the state, having showed his sheep many times at county fairs where he always gets his share of the premiums offered.

The picture shows a pair of poll rams, three and one-year old respectively. The three-year-old produced a 23-pound fleece, fine wool, in eleven months. His nephew, Newton Knowlton, an orphan, is seen in the picture holding, Mr. Bailes' fine family, four-year-old Tilford Wilkes driving horse which Mr. Bailes prizes very highly. Mr. Bailes is also a breeder of Scotch Collie dogs, imported stock, all registered or eligible to register. At the right in the picture, the collies are shown lying down.

Chester White hogs is another breeding specialty of Mr. Bailes. He breeds nothing but the best stock and to this his success is largely attributed. At his Sugar Grove stock farm of 107 acres, he keeps over one hundred head of sheep. The public can always get carefully bred stock of Alfred Bailes.

Residence of Jacob Crossen, Lee Township.

The subject of this sketch, Jacob Crossen, was born in Fayette county, Penna,, in a little town, at that time called Springfield October 18, 1843. He was of Dutch descent and the son of John and Katherine King Crossen. His father whose occupation was that of shoemaker, emigrated with his family to Ohio in 1851. During the autumn of the next year the family suffered from an epidemic of typhoid fever from which the mother died.

The family was then scattered and our subject was left to make his own way in the world. At the beginning of the rebellion, when the first call for three-year men was issued, he enlisted in Co. D. 4th W. Va. regiment on June 24, 1861, was wounded in an assault on Vicksburg, May 19, 1863, He lay unconscious for some hours from gunshot wounds in face, hand and thigh. When consciousness returned he crawled to an old house, and lay there with many others till night when the house was fired by rebel shells. He here escaped death by burning, through the assistance of a comrade who was captured with him and taken inside the confederate lines. Not being able to walk alone he was supported into the lines by two confederate soldiers. He, with eleven others, was sent into the city next morning, where they were assigned to the colored quarters on a rich slave holder's plantation. Here his only attendants were convalescent confederate soldiers, who were unable to give the care needed and the flies blowed his wounds. The bones of his face were so badly shattered he could not move his jaw and was obliged to force what food he ate between his teeth with his finger. He was held a prisoner in the city from May 19 till June 1, 1863, when he was paroled and sent across the river to the convalescent camp at Youngs Point. He was then sent north to Memphis with the first contingent of paroled prisoners and then sent to St. Louis with a boat load of Federal wounded where he remained from the 28th day of June till the 16th day of October, 1863, when he was discharged.

After convalescence he worked as a farm hand eighteen months, then spent six months at school. On February 16, 1867, he was married to Mary C. Patterson who died in 1869, leaving him one son. He was again married in 1871 to Minerva Knight who died in 1874. In 1875 he was married to Samantha Clendenin; to this union was born a daughter and a son. He has served in offices of trust as trustee of Lee township for nine years. In 1893 his health failed and he left the farm going to Albany where he served as one of the towns-councilmen till 1900 when he was honored by the citizens of Albany electing him mayor, which office he filled till the spring of 1902 when he went back to the farm. He is a member of the C. P. church at Albany and of Albany lodge 156 F. & A. M.

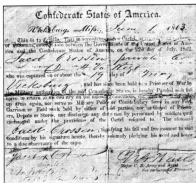

Mr. and Mrs. John M. Stewart.

JOHN M. STEWART, whose home in Waterloo township is here represented was a civil war soldier that saw much service and but few soldiers live to tell the story of so many engagements. He was born in Washington county, Pennsylvania, December 27, 1844. He came to Athens county with his parents when but a year old. At the age of 17, he inlisted in Company D., 75th O. V. I., and participated in the following battles: Monterey, Shaw's Ridge, McDowell, Franklin, Strasburg, Cross Keys, Cedar Mountain, Freeman's Ford, Sulpher Springs, Waterloo Bridge, Second Bull Run, Aldie, Chancellorsville, Gettysburg, Hagerstown, Fort Wagoner, S. C.; Johns Island, S. C.; Camp Baldwin, Florida; Gainsville, Florida. He was captured at the latter place on August 16, 1864, and was taken to Andersonville prison, where he was kept four months, then taken to Florence prison, N. C., and after three months incarceration was paroled at Goldsborough, N. C., when he returned home. He was married to Emeline Beverage, October 18, 1866, and to this union three children were born, two sons and one daughter. Mr. Stewart is a farmer by occupation.

Duffee Bros., Marshfield, Ohio.

The firm of Duffee Brothers, engaged in Hardware. Furniture and Undertaking is one of the enterprising business firms in Marshfield. The accompanying illustrations show their

two business rooms and give a very fair idea of the prosperous condition of their business as to the quantity of stock carried in each line.

George W. Duffee was born in Amesville Sept. 22, 1853, and in early childhood his father, James Duffee, moved to Trimble and engaged in general blacksmithing. Here George attended public school and worked as an apprentice in the shop with his father. In 1877 he was married in marriage with Miss Augusta Allen. In 1881 they moved to Marshfield where Mr. Duffee opened a blacksmith shop and successfully continued at his trade until 1891, when at started a hardware and furniture store. Mr. Duffee is a member of the Masonic Lodge at Marshfield, having passed through the different offices to Master. He is a charter member of Marshfield lodge Knights of Pythias and the Modern Woodman of America. He and Mrs. Duffee occupy their own home and are highly respected citizens. They have two daughters, Janette and Lucile living, one child having died in infancy.

Thomas W. Duffee, the senior member of the firm, was born at Union Furnace, Hocking county, July 3, 1849. He, like his brother, learned the blacksmith trade with his father. The history of the lives of the two brothers are very similar. Thomas started out for himself about the same time as did George. He first located at Hebbardsville, but soon afterward moved to Albany, where he conducted a blacksmith shop until 1901,

when he moved to Marshfield and went into business with his brother. He was married to Harriet Milton, a native of Morgan county in 1873. To this union were born six children, four of whom are living—Ray, James, Hattie and Ora. Mr. Duffee is also a Mason and has passed all the chairs of his lodge.

In connection with Hardware and Furniture, Duffee Bros. do quite an extensive Undertaking business, for which they are fully equipped. This part of the business is looked after almost exclusively by George W.

RESIDENCE OF MR. AND MRS. JOHN M. STEWART, WATERLOO TOWNSHIP.

11

FARM RESIDENCE OF J. L. MANSFIELD, CANAAN TOWNSHIP.

J. L. MANSFIELD, farmer and stock raiser, was born in Canaan township, Athens county, Ohio, Dec. 23, 1848, son of George and Catherine Mansfield. He was born and reared on the farm he now owns. After receiving a common school education he entered the pursuit of farming which he has followed all his life.

Mr. Mansfield was united in marriage Sept. 21, 1872 to Linda J., daughter of Josephus and Eliza Tucker. By this union there is one child, Merwin.

Mr. and Mrs. Mansfield are both members of the Christian church.

Merwin was born Nov. 26, 1876. He received a district school education and at the age of 17 entered Hiram college and finished the preparatory course. After his return home he assisted his father in farming.

He was united in marriage May 22, 1901, to Mabel L., daughter of Orange H. and Anna C. Butts. Both are members of Free-will Baptist church.

Mr. Mansfield owns 200 acres of land well adapted to stock raising, also one of the best grazing farms in the township. At present he is breeding registered short-horn cattle, his herd being one of the best in the county.

He also is a breeder of fine wooled sheep. This farm has been in the Mansfield family for over one hundred years.

E. R. Lash's Drug Store, Athens, Ohio.

THE accompanying picture shows the interior of E. R. Lash's drug store in the Phoenix block on Court street, Athens, Ohio. This is the oldest drug establishment in the county. About 1848 John Perkins established this well-known drug store near the court house and in the 57 years succeeding, the firm has changed names but once. In 1873, Mr. Lash became the sole owner of the business and in 1879 removed his store to its present location. His stock of goods embraces everything usually found in a first-class drug store and the fact he has been conducting the business for over 32 years, is sufficient evidence of his success.

Mr. Lash is the son of Mr. and Mrs. Jacob Lash and was born November 20, 1848. His grandfather, William Lash came here from Pennsylvania in 1814 and settled in Alexander township on the farm yet known as the Lash homestead. He received his education at the Ohio University, leaving that institution in his sophomore year and entered a school of Pharmacy where he was prepared for his vocation of life. He married Miss Alice Johns in 1875 and to them were born E. Rey Jr. and Mrs. Florence Lash Williams of Rochester, N. Y.

Mr. Lash has always been an uncompromising Democrat and while not seeking political preferment, he has been honored several times by his party. For two years he was a member of the Board of Trustees of Athens State Hospital, being president of the board, having received his appointment from Governor Campbell. In 1894, he was Democratic candidate for Congress in the 11th congressional district and in 1896 and 1904 was chosen Presidential elector. He is a prominent member of the Masonic order and has held the highest office in all the Masonic bodies here from Master of the Blue Lodge to Eminent Commander of Athens Commandery No. 15. He is also a charter member of Athenian lodge K. of P. His son, E. Rey Lash, Jr. has been associated with his father in business since 1898. He was also educated at the Ohio University and left that institution in his junior year. He graduated from the Ohio Northern University with the degree of Ph. G. in 1903 and has since devoted his entire time to his father's business. He is a competent Pharmacist and has brought many modern ideas to this well established business. Mr. Lash is a Mason and a member of the Elks Lodge at Nelsonville.

YEOMAN SERVICE NECESSARY.

Labor is the foundation of progress; it is the road to wealth, health and happiness, therefore labor is a necessity. Labor has wrought out of the great wilderness which once shrouded Athens county, sunny fields and happy homes. The hills covered with their dense forests which suggested only endless labor to denude and render valuable clearings, now interest capitalists because of the unlimited wealth buried beneath, for the soil of Athens county is as nothing when compared with its mineral products. Labor has brought forth churches and schools, one to guide and guard the moral welfare, the other to prepare the rising generations that they may labor more intelligently among the fertile resources by which they are surrounded.

Arduous labor on all sides met the first settlers; the material obstacles they must overcome were great. They did not, like the Spaniards, come in search of gold, better for them perhaps had they begun to dig.

But no one then suspected where the real wealth of southeastern Ohio lay. They did not, as the pilgrim fathers, come seeking freedom, driven from home by tyranny. They came, however, of the same sturdy stock and few turned back because labor—unceasing toil—met them on every side.

As there are no bounds to the flights of imagination, so there seemed to be no limit to the marvelous richness of Ohio soil as reported and generally believed throughout the East. This was believed to be literally a land flowing with milk and honey; made richer by nature than could be by art; providing in its lowlands support for millions of cattle, summer and winter; over run with the small fruits of all kinds, berries, wild cherries and wild plums.

Doubtless the comparison between the barren soil of New England and the fertile valleys of Ohio gave some foundation for these luxuriant crops grown in the imagination of the Yankees. Sore must have been the disappointment of the hardy frontiersmen, but bitter they do not seem to have been for no trace of complaint comes down to us.

LOG CABINS.

The heavy timber covering alost every foot of ground greeted the pioneers who first essayed to conquer the wilderness of Athens county. The first business of each was to clear a space and build a cabin. Each man possessed a saw. In the party there was one auger and a cross cut saw. Everything about the structure must be made of wood, even wooden pins being used instead of nails, clumsy wooden hinges swinging the doors. A wooden latch and catch fastened them with a leather string for pulling latch. This hung outside, safe at night when drawn in for security, and anyone could "lift the latch and walk in," which gave rise to the old saying of hospitality "the latch string is always out."

The chimney was left open in the original building and afterwards built of sticks laid up corncob fashion plastered over with mud. In some neighborhoods where soft sandstone outcropped or near rocky streams, stones furnished the foundation of these chimneys. After the logs were chopped the desired length, notched and saddled, the few neighbors available assembled and had a "house raising." Then with mud and sticks, all the interstices were "daubed" to shut out rain and cold. This process it was necessary to repeat each fall, as the rains washed out much of the improvised mortar.

No glass being available in earliest days greased paper or greased deer-hide was used in the windows. A large bed was built into one corner of the room with a "trundle bed" for the youngsters which in the daytime was pushed underneath the high bed. A rude cupboard built in another corner, a rough heavy table at one side with hewn slabs for seats about completed the furniture.

Later as the women began to come, spinning wheels, large and small, split-bottomed chairs, a few stools, a little blue-edged China, so much sought to-day, and a few conveniences for cooking, which was all done in the great open fire place. Of the earliest cabins no traces remain although in various parts of the county are old log cabins. These, however, were

(Continued on page 15.)

BOWER BROTHERS LIVERY, ATHENS, OHIO.

WILLIAM AND CHARLES BOWER, Liverymen and proprietors of the Athens Omnibus & Transfer Co., are two Athens' young men who have won their way to success by dint of hard work, good management and keen foresight. They are the sons of Capt. J. C. Bower, one of the best known men in the county, but who now lives at Groveport, O. J. C. Bower and sons came to Athens from Albany in May 1877, and purchased the farm adjoining the State Hospital grounds on the south. They secured the contract for supplying milk to the State Hospital and continued the contract without interruption for seventeen years. In 1894 William S. and Charles bought their father's interest in the farm and dairy and continued the milk contract at the Hospital for seven years, when they voluntarily gave up the business.

In 1902, they built the large and commodious livery barn shown in the illustration, and engaged in general livery and transfer business. They started right and kept up the pace, and today have one of the largest and most complete liveries in the state. Good horses and good vehicles, along with courteous treatment of the public has won for them a large trade.

No town in the country has better facilities than has Athens. Carriages, coupes and handsome turnouts of all descriptions are found at Bower Brothers. They employ over one hundred horses, and their employees are experienced men at the business and courteous treatment is always assured.

Charles Bower, the junior member of the firm was married to Miss Mary Wilson, of Marshfield, March 2, 1901. They make their home on the Bower Homestead south of town.

William S., the senior member, is a popular young man and has given more or less attention to local politics, not however allowing it to interfere with his business. He has served as central committeeman and is now a member of the village council. Mr. Bower has been many times solicited to stand as a candidate for important county offices but has always refused to consider the proposition.

Dr. Charles Secoy, Veterinary Surgeon and Horse Shoer

DR. CHARLES SECOY, Veterinary Surgeon is another of Athens' young men who has literally "forged" his way to the front, and whatever progress he has made and whatever success awaits him in the future he has accomplished by dint of hard work and great personal effort, fighting the battles of life unaided and alone.

Dr. Secoy, the son of the late Daniel Secoy, was born in Pleasanton, Ohio, April 12, 1868. He picked up a good common school education in the village school and came to Athens when about sixteen and began work for the Athens Foundry. He had picked up the trade of blacksmithing while with his father.

He started into blacksmithing and horseshoeing for himself in 1895 and soon established a large patronage as a horse shoer.

During the first six years he saved enough money to start to college and matriculated with the Indiana Veterinary College at Indianapolis, from which he graduated in 1904. Since which time he has been successfully practicing his profession, and at the same time conducting his modern horseshoeing establishment, a picture of which is here shown.

Mr Secoy was married to Miss Belle Oxley of Pleasanton November 12. 1889. They have two children, Ina aged 13, and Charles Walter aged two months.

YE OLDEN TIMES—BUILT IN 1800.

DR. CHARLES SECOY'S OFFICE—NORTH COURT STREET.

Residence of Solonous F. Beverage.

Solonous F. Beverage, whose photograph is here shown along with his residence in Marshfield, is one of the substantial citizens of Waterloo township, and is well known over the county which he served acceptably as Infirmary Director for six years, making one of the best officers the Infirmary ever had. Through his efforts and direction he practically reorganized the institution and put it on a business basis.

Mr. Beverage was born in Athens township, April 11, 1850. He is the son of John Beverage and grandson of Henry Beverage, who came from Virginia to Athens county in 1800. He is of Scotch descent, his great grandfather having come to Virginia from Scotland.

His parents moved to Waterloo township when Solonous was a small lad. He was educated in the common schools and Miller's Seminary and taught school more or less for 18 years.

Mr. Beverage has been married twice. His first wife was Miss Rebecca Boden. They were married in 1871 and three children were born to them, Leonora, now Mrs. Norris; Lorena, now Mrs. Vorhis, and Herbert C. He was married the second time to Miss Callie Banks. They have one child, Garnet Frances.

He has twice been elected Justice of the Peace since 1900, is a charter member of Marshfield K. of P. Lodge No. 692, member of Athens Company U. R. K. of P., and served two years as 2nd Lieutenant.

SOLONOUS F. BEVERAGE.

J. S. Basom D. D. S., Athens, Ohio.

Dr. J. S. Basom, whose office is in the Phoenix Block on Court street, is the oldest resident dental practitioner in Athens, having begun the practice of his profession here on September 5, 1884, succeeding the late Dr. Edmundson. Dr. Basom was a native of Carthage township, having been born on a farm near Coolville, in 1861. He attended the public schools of Coolville and Tuppers Plains, graduated from a two-year course in dentistry in 1883 and began the practice of his profession in Coolville. He came to Athens the succeeding year and soon secured a clientage that has ever since made him a busy man.

Dr. Basom has always kept abreast of the advancement of his profession and is thoroughly modern in all his work. He has successfully completed work that has been declared impossible by dentists of large cities. In 1891, he took a reviewing course in Philadelphia.

George I. Putnam's Book and Jewelry Store.

George I. Putnam is at the head of one of the oldest business stands in Athens. For twenty-five years he has been connected as clerk, partner and proprietor, selling books, stationery and jewelry. The accompanying illustration is an excellent picture of his place of business.

Mr. Putnam was born in Marietta, December 28. 1857, and is a direct descendent of the Israel Putnam family so prominent in the history of the early settlement of Ohio. His parents on leaving Marietta settled on a farm in York township. They came to Athens when George was but 12 years old and it was here he received his education.

He began as clerk for Kurtz & Norris and afterwards with Kurtz & Minear. In 1884, he and Charles Fletcher purchased the business and continued under the name of Putnam & Fletcher until 1897 when Mr. Putnam became sole owner and has successfully managed the business ever since.

Mr. Putnam was married to Miss Ida Lamb in Elgin. Illinois, in 1884. They occupy their own home on West Carpenter street.

ORGANIZATION OF ATHENS . . .
. . . COUNTY'S TOWNSHIPS.

THERE were originally but four townships in Athens county—Alexander, Ames, Athens and Troy. The county was thus divided by the first board of County Commissioners in 1805. Alexander township was located and surveyed in 1795.

Ames township was settled as early as 1797.

Athens township was surveyed in 1795.

Bern township, originally a part of Ames was organized in 1828.

Canaan township was organized in 1819.

Carthage township, originally a part of Troy, was organized in 1810.

Dover township, originally a part of Ames, was settled in 1799 and separately organized in 1811.

Lee township, originally a part of Alexander, was organized in 1819.

Lodi township, originally a part of Alexander. The eastern half was included in Carthage. Organized as a separate township in 1826.

Rome township was organized in 1811 from Troy.

Trimble township was stricken off from Ames and separately organized in 1827. Named for Governor Allen Trimble.

Troy township one of the original four, was settled in 1798.

Waterloo township, originally a part of Athens, was organized in 1826.

York township, originally a part of Ames, was separately organized from Dover, in 1818.

ATHENS COUNTY HISTORY
CONTINUED.

built when civilization began to bring many conveniences and comparative luxuries within reach of the energetic man. Window frames, glass lights, door knobs and latches and nails rendered these log cabins very fine as compared with their older neighbors.

The log cabin shown on page 13 was built in 1800 by Reuben J. Davis and located on Sugar Creek. It is still standing and is occupied as a dwelling. Jonas Rice bought this property in 1828, and it was in this old log house that Mrs. John Harvey, who is yet living with her son in West Athens, was born April 22, 1827. The late John Harvey bought this place in 1862 and after the destruction of his home in 1903, occupied it for some months before moving to Athens. J. R. Harvey a son, who was born in this house, bought the property in 1900 and in 1903 sold it to Poston & Smith, who still own it.

FIRST WHITE WOMAN.

Early in 1798 several more emigrants arrived at Athens, some bringing their families. Among these was Joseph Snowden for whose wife "Margaret Creek" was named. It is generally supposed that she was the first white woman to penetrate into this vast wilderness. Accompanying Snowden were the Brooks and Haning families, John and Moses Hewitt, Cornelius Moore, Robert Ross, Solomon Tuttle, Christopher Stevens and John Simonton.

Alvan Bingham was appointed by the powers in Marietta, magistrate for this district and Silas his brother was sheriff. Their duty was to prevent the illegal occupation of lands and they were kept busy, for the hardy frontiersmen were rather more inclined to believe in might than right when the courts were at such great distances. These officers, however, through firmness and justice succeeded in impressing all marauders with the uselessness of their attempts and were highly honored by all in the locality. Alvan Bingham was later made the first treasurer of Athens county.

In 1800 the town of Athens was laid out. Only five or six families settled here, the rest being scattered over the luxuriantly fertile bottom lands.

At this time the present location of the college grounds was selected and for town use, that of the Court house and jail was set aside. Also the same amount of ground on the diagonal corner now occupied by the Presbyterian church was given for church purposes.

EARLY GRIST MILLS.

Among the many hardships which the pioneers had to face, not the least was the procuring of bread. For the first year they had to carry flour from the nearest settlements. Even after the first crops supplied grain in abundance there were no mills to grind it. This necessity created many ingenious kinds of hand mills for preparing corn. The best of these seemed very slow when the family was large and corn bread being the principal fare was needed three times a day to fill the hungry mouths. The nearest mill for the Athens settlement was on the Ohio river close to Marietta while the nearest for the Ames settlement was on Wolf Creek in Morgan county and Lowell on the Muskingum in Washington county. Hence the first grist mill in this county was eagerly welcomed when it was built by John Hewitt in 1800. This was on Margaret Creek about where Beasley's stock farm now is and was so extensively patronized that Charles Shepard with an eye to business soon after started one in Alexander township on the place now known as the

(Continued on page 21.)

Residence of Mr. and Mrs. Hiram Crossen.

THE country home here shown is the residence of Mr. and Mrs. Hiram Crossen in Lee township. Mr. Crossen was born in Somerset, Pennsylvania in 1843 and came to this county with his father, Abraham Crossen in 1845 and settled on the farm which he now owns and has lived on ever since 1866. His wife's maiden name was Lucinda Allen and they were married in 1866. They are comfortably located and are enjoying the rewards of an active, industrious and well spent life.

JESSE THROCKMORTON, deceased was born in Greene county, Pa., Nov 30th, 1838, and came to Ohio with his mother and eight brothers and three sisters. His father, Wm. Throckmorton, was killed by a fall while Jesse was in infancy. At the age of 18 years he united with the F. W. B church. and was a faithful member until death. When the civil war was declared he was among the first to inlist. He was a member of Co. C., 36th Regt., O. V. I. At the close of the war he returned to Ohio and on Nov. 25, 1865, was married to Miss Laverna, daughter of Madison Cline, a resident of Meigs county, O. Mr. Throckmorton and his wife lived for six years in Columbia township, Meigs county. In February, 1871, they moved with their daughter Jennie, who was born Dec. 25, 1866, to Athens county on what is known as the Jimmie Luckey farm where he followed farming and stock raising.

He died Aug. 18, 1894, aged 55 years, eight months and 18 days. Since the death of Mr. Throckmorton the farm has been operated by his wife and son, William Madison, who was born Aug. 6. 1872, and was married to Mattie J. Graft June 29, 1894. To this union was born two children, Mary Laverna and Jessie Cline. Their mother died August 1, 1900,

Residence of Dr. F. P. McVay.

The history of the life of Dr. Frank P. McVay is one of accomplishing much under adverse circumstances, his only inspiration being an indomitable disposition to hew success from the rocks of adversity. Like many successful men he recieved his early training on a farm having been born near Newport, Ohio, March 10, 1853. In 1878 he started a small general store at Hulls P. O., this county and was appointed postmaster. He had but cleverly gotten started in business when his store was consumed by fire and he was left penniless.

He secured employment at the Athens State Hospital as attendant and found plenty of time for study and began the study of medicine. In 1883, he entered the Medical Institute in Cincinnati and graduated in 1885. Began the practice of medicine at Alfred, Meigs county, shortly went to Hulls and after one year went to Guysville where he practiced for three years before coming to Athens. June 1, 1889, where he has been practicing ever since and has built up a large and lucrative practice. He is the oldest resident physician in Athens today. He graduated from the Columbus Medical College in 1890, thus having the benefit of two different schools of medicine.

Dr. McVay is a prominent lodge man having passed the chairs of several organizations. He is a Past Master of Paramuthia Lodge No. 25, F. & A. M; Past High Priest of Athens Chapter 39; a Royal Arch Mason; Past Thrice Illustrious Master of Athens Council No. 15; Royal and Select Masters; Past Commander of Athens Commandery No. 15 Knights Templar; member of Syrian Temple of Nobles; Mystic Shrine, Cincinnati; member Sereno Lodge I. O. O. F., Athens; Past Chancellor Athenian Lodge No. 105; Knights of Pythias; Deputy Grand Chancellor of K. of P; member of Athens Company No. 54, 5th Rgt U. R. K. of P; on Brigadier Gen. Minshall's staff with rank of Major; Past Commander and Record Keeper of Athens Tent No. 467, Knights of Maccabees; member Rathbone Sisters Lodge; member of Rebecca Lodge I. O. O. F; at present Worthy Patron of Athens Chapter No. 175 Order of Eastern Stars; member of Athens Village Council for nine years and always member of important committees.

Dr. McVay has always been a liberal giver to charitable causes and lends his skill and medicine to the unfortunate poor without even expecting compensation. He was married to Miss Jessie B. Hull in 1874 at Eldorado, Kansas. They have two bright boys, Frank H., aged 15, and Charles Don, aged 12. The accompanying picture shows their elegant home on East State Street, Athens, Ohio.

MR. RUFUS M. BEVERAGE,
WATERLOO TOWNSHIP.

MR. RUFUS M BEVERAGE whose residence is shown in the accompaning picture, is one of the early residents of Athens county. He was the son of Henry Beverage Sr., and was the youngest of a family of ten children, six boys and four girls. He was born in Alexander township, January 13, 1823, and moved with his father to Athens township, when about five years old. His father rented a farm from Isaac Barker, one mile west of Athens, the old Harper Ferry place. Athens was at that time quite a small town. The merchants had to haul their goods from Hockingport or Pomeroy. The Hocking canal completel in 1841 was considered a great convenience as they could then get goods by boat. At that time there was no Infirmary and paupers were sold to the lowest bidder.

Mr Beverage is of Scotch decent, his grandfather being born in Scotland and settled in Virginia. His mother, Mrs. Jones was of Welsh decent, his grandfather Jones being a Welshman who married an English woman and settled in Virginia about the same time as did the Beverages, The two families closely intermarried. Mr. Beverage's father married a Jones and a Jones married a Beverage. Mr. Beverage was a soldier in the civil war being a member of 63rd Regt. O. V. I and served fourteen months.

✳ ✳ ✳ ✳ ✳ ✳

MR. WILLIAM CLENDENIN
LEE TOWNSHIP

WM. CLENDENIN was born in Mason county, W. Va., February 9th, 1826. He removed to this county in 1868 and settled near Mineral City where he lived for six years when he removed to the farm where he has ever since resided. When he moved to this farm in Lee township there were no improvements but by dilligent effort he became one of the foremost farmers in the Southern part of the county. In 1880 he engaged in the raising of fine sheep and was a successful contestant for a number of years at the county fairs in his own and adjoining counties. But in the decline in the value of sheep and wool he let his flock decrease in number, though he still keeps a small flock.

He was married to Miss Sarah A. Squires who died in 1874. He was afterwards married to Mrs. Elizabeth Patterson McVay. His three sons who grew to manhood all settled in Idaho. One of them, Redmond L., died there in 1892. His three daughters and a step-daughter are all residents of this county.

✳ ✳ ✳ ✳

Residence of James O. Maxwell on Rock Riffle, Canaan Township.

JAMES O. MAXWELL was born near McConnelsville, Morgan county, Ohio, August 29th, 1843. He was the son of Wm. Maxwell and Louisa Mayhugh Maxwell. His father moved to Athens county when he was a small child. He enlisted August 4th, 1862 in Co. A of the 92nd O. V. I. and served until the close of the war, being in 20 or more battles, among them the battles of Chickamaugee, Missionary Ridge and Lookout Mountains. He was with Sherman in his famous march to the sea and was in the Grand Review at Washington.

On March 23, 1866 he was united in marriage to Hannah M. Robinson. This union has been blessed with seven children, four of whom are still living.

In the fall of 1868 he bought a farm in Canaan township, where he now resides. He served as trustee of Canaan township for twelve years in succession, and has always been considered a prominent and prosperous farmer.

County Jails.

THE first County Jail was built in the first year of the county's existence. It was a log building then and adjoined the jailer's house. It was only 24 ft. long and 13 ft. wide. and seems never to have been very secure. In a few years this was replaced by a brick structure much more substantial but from the number of escapes it evidently did not offer a sure confinement for desperate characters.

The present jail is a very handsome cut stone building the contract price of which was $9238, although the cost greatly exceeded that. It adjoins the court house and connects with the Sheriff's house in the rear, is 30x47 feet and contains twelve iron cells.

IMPORTANT EVENTS

IN THE HISTORY OF ATHENS COUNTY, OHIO, ARRANGED IN CRHONOLOGICAL ORDER.

1787   Ordinance providing for University in the Northwest.

1795   First survey of Ohio Company's purchase on the upper Hock-hocking.

1797   The first settlers came to Athens county, about a dozen in number.

1798   The first house on the town plat was built by Captain John Chandler, near where the Catholic church now stands. The second lot of settlers arrived bringing a few families.

The first white woman to penetrate this wilderness, Mrs. Margaret Snowden.

1799   The last buffalo was seen in the county on a branch of Racoon creek.

The first preaching in the county by a Methodist missionary, Rev. Quinn.

1800   The first ferry established near where South bridge now stands, called Coates ferry.

Methodist society organized and visited at intervals by circuit rider.

First grist mill in county on Margaret creek, about 3 miles from Athens.

First Grist mill in Alexander township built by Chas. Shepard.

1801   The first school was established on Higgins homestead three miles south of Athens.

1802   First election of township officers in Ames.

First person buried in the old cemetery in Athens.

First post route through from east.

Legislature passed act establishing the University.

First grist and sawmill in Rome township built by Barrows Bros on Fedreal Creek.

1803   First professional tourist, traveling for his health visits Athens.

1804   First election of township officers in Athens, commisioners.

First meeting of trustees of University called by governor.

Gov. Tiffin visited Athens to see about starting university.

First postoffice established at present site of Barth's mill.

First survey of town plat into lots.

First sale of town lots in Athens, ranging from $10 to $132 in price.

Founding of first library in the northwest territory named the western library association but commonly known as the "Coon-skin Library.'

First schoolhouse built in Amesville.

1805   First court of common pleas convened.

First board of county commissioners offered bounty for scalps of wolves and panthers.

Athens county established, containing 1053 square miles.

Athens township organized.

First grand jury sat in the county.

Aaron Burr visited Athens in the interest of his scheme for imperializing the southwest.

First dam on the Hocking, where Barth's mill now stands east of Athens.

First road tax levied in the county.

1806   First school house in Athens, built where city hall now stands.

Second sale of town lots in Athens, ranging in price from $7.50 to $72.

First apple nursery in the county, planted by Josiah True in Dover township.

First mill on Hocking built by Gregory at Barth's mill east of town.

Peter Cartwright, celebrated Methodist divine preached in Athens.

1807   First court house erected of rough hewn logs.

1808   First lawyer arrived in Athens.

First university building erected.

1809   First Presbyterian church organized.

1810   Census of Athens county, 2787.

First camp-meeting in the county held near Athens.

Last of the bears exterminated.

First orchard of the county planted in Rome township. It consisted of 3000 trees, peach and apple.

1811   Flouring and grist mill built by Cooley Brothers at Coolville.

Town of Athens regularly incorporated.

1812   Methodists built a brick church where Mrs. Henry Wright now lives on Congress street.

1814   Masons charter Paramuthia lodge No. 25 F. & A. M.

Athens county visited by the "cold plague." Only epidemic which ever ravaged the county.

1815   First graduate from University, Hon. Thomas Ewing, given degree of Bachelor of Arts.

The first flouring mill built in Lodi township by Cyrus Blazier.

1816   Corner stone of central building on University laid.

1817   Brick court house built on site of present one.

1820   Population of Athens township, 1114.

Census of the county, 6439.

First successful salt well, by the Nyes in Dover township.

1821   First postoffice established in Ames township.

First postoffice established at Nelsonville called English-town.

Census of Ames township 721.

Joseph Brookson built the first grist and saw mill in Waterloo township.

1822   Postoffice established at Coolville by Jacob S. Miller.

Athens County Bible society founded.

Organization of university completed with faculty of five.

1323   First library organized in Nelsonville called "York township Amicable Library society.''

1825   The pioneer newspaper of the Hocking valley, Athens Mirror established by A. G. Brown, now Athens Messenger.

Methodist brick parsonage built, being part of house where Mrs. Henry Wright now lives on Congress street.

1826   Town election, votes cast, forty-three.

1828   First Presbyterian church incorporated.

First Agricultural society formed. First exhibit made by them. Prizes awarded amounted in all to $75.

First bridge built across the Hocking at Nelsonville, completed in October carried away by flood May, 1829.

1829   First postoffice established at Albany, known as Lee P. O.

First Temperance Society formed.

1830   Census of the county, 9763.

The Mirror becomes the "Western Spectator", edited by Isaac Maxon.

1832   Great spring freshet, when the waters covered the bottoms east of Athens half way up the hill to present site of Catholic church, largely destroyed the crops for that year.

1834   East bridge at Barth's mills built, by J. B. and R. W. Miles.

First postoffice in Canaan township established by Stephen Pilcher.

1836   Bridge west of Athens near present B. & O. bridge.

The east and west wings of University built.

The Western Spectator bought by Abraham Van Vorhes, and name changed to Athens Messenger & Hocking Valley Gazette.

1837   Methodists built their present brick church.

1839   South bridge built—all bridges were toll bridges.

Rev. Wm. H. McGuffey became president of the University. The attendance numbered 250 students.

1840   Census of county, 19,109.

Gov. Tom Corwin at Athens during Harrison campaign. Great barbacue on rear of campus.

First salt furnaces built at Chauncey for extensive salt manufacture and shipment.

1841   First boat went up the Hocking canal.

1846   Catholic church organized.

One hundred volunteers from Athens county for Mexican war.

Coolville Seminary established under auspices of M. E. church. Flourished twenty years.

1847   Great flood, occasioned loss of many thousand dollars to county in destruction of crops.

1848   First telegraph line in the county, called New Orleans & Ohio Telegraph, company.

First State Bank organized in the county, capitalized at $100,000.

1850   Census of Athens county, 18,215.

Athens county having been gradually reduced, became its present size.

Union School System adopted in Athens.

Population of Athens township, 2360.

1851   First Agricultural Fair organized under state law of assistance to county agricultural societies.

Albany Manual Labor Institute opened to all "regardless of color caste or sex.'' Later bought by the Free Will Baptists and name changed to Atwood Institute.

1853   Amesville Academy built. Rev. J. P. Weethee, first principal.

First Teachers' Institute in the county. Held in the court house.

1854   Destruction of old Eagle House on southwest corner of Court and Union streets, known as the "great Taylor fire.''

1855   First railway passenger train on the Marietta & Cincinnati, now the B. & O.

1857   County Infirmary located in Dover township.

Athens county's vote for Salmon P. Chase for governor, 1723.

During this year two million bushels of coal mined in immediate vicinity of Nelsonville. Shipped by canal boat.

Great fire in Nelsonville, C. Steenrod's flouring mill burned, loss $20,000.

1858   Present public school house opened for use.

Great and disastrous flood swept down the valley.

1859   First trotting races ever held in the county made the Fair a great success, 12000 persons in attendance.

Telegraph line between Pomeroy and Athens established.

Postoffice establishd at Marshfield.

1860   "Wells Library founded by Mr. Henry Wells at Albany

Census of Athens county, 21,364.

Ladies of Athens present Home Guards with beautiful silk flag which was carried to war in 1862.

Population of Athens township, 2852.

1861   Whiskey insurrection. Drunken soldiers from Camp Wool create stir in town. Officers with the 18th infantry overhaul all the grog shops, take possession of the whiskey and lock it up.

Great meeting at Athens five days after firing on Fort Sumpter, to encourage patriotism.

Great patriotic rally at Chauncey to organize Home Guards.

Fund of $2000 subscribed in 24 hours to defray expenses of recruits.

Within three months after firing on Fort Sumpter, Athens county raised 1000 men for Union army.

Methodist church remodelled and added to and given perpetual endowment.

Enterprise Institute established at Albany for colored people only.

1863   Catholic church was built on Congress street near Washington.

First National Bank was organized with a capital stock of $50,000.

Gen. John Morgan's raid passed through Athens county. Stopped at Nelsonville, filling tne town and compelling the inhabitants to give them dinner.

Six thousand men encamped at Camp Wool.

1864   Athens Cemetery Association was incorporated and bought present burial grounds.

1865   April 14, great celebration over surrender of Lee.

April 15, town sunken in gloom over news of assassinationof Lincoln.

1866   Great barbacue for returned Union soldiers on college campus, 15000 people present.

1867   Bank established in Albany by John Brown and J. D. Brown.

Coal works at Carbondale, the first opened in southeastorn Ohio.

1868   Athens County Pioneer Association organized by A. B. Walker.

1868   Women admitted as students to University.

Corner stone of State Hospital laid by Masonic order, 1000 Masons from all over the state participating.

1869   Athens Journal started, edited by Hiram C. Martin.

1870   Population of Nelsonville 1080.

Census of Athens county, 23,768.

First train on the Hocking Valley railroad.

1872   First newspaper started in Nelsonville called Nelsonville Times.

1873   First bank opened in Nelsonville.

Miss Margaret Boyd, the first woman graduate of Ohio University.

Great flood which destroyed most of the canal from Logan to Athens. Gas works flooded and Athens in darkness.

First lighting of the streets of Athens by gas.

1874   Athens State Hospital for insane completea and ready for inmates.

Women's famous Temperance Crusade.

1875   Greatest flood ever known since the settlement of the county.

1876   Present rough stone jail built.

1877   Great fire destroyed Ballard block, northeast corner Court and Union street, burned half way to Washington and half way to College street.

Continued on page 19.

Modern Meat Market of Ben Fauser, Jr.

Ben Fauser, Jr., came to Athens from Parkersburg on May 1, 1901, purchased the meat market of C. L. Poston, under the management of Chas. E. Moore, and has given the town a modern and well equipped meat market ever since. Cleanliness, neatness, close attention to the wants of his customers are the secrets of his success. Fauser is the leader in his line. He knows the business from A to Z. He buys good stock and personally supervises his slaughter house.

Mr. Fauser was born in Wuttenburg, Germany, January 1, 1874. Came to this country in 1892 and on October 8, 1901, he was married to Miss Mille R. Larch, a resident of Columbus, Ohio. Mr. and Mrs. Fauser own their own home, on the corner of Washington and College streets, formerly the old Brown home and later the residence and office of the late Dr. Steele.

Home Furnishing Company, Athens, Ohio

In January of 1902, M. E. Twiss and W. V. Dagget, two hustling young business men of Chillicothe, bought the furniture store of Hibbard & Wickham in the Nelson building on south Court street and began business under the name of The Home Furnishing Company. To the already large stock of furniture always carried at this old stand they immediately added a large stock of stoves, carpets, rugs, druggets, etc., in fact everything for the home in the way of furnishings.

This firm has been more than ordinarily successful and they carry one of the largest stocks in the county. They are good buyers and strong competitors and have merited the large and increasing business they enjoy.

Residence of Mr. and Mrs. P. G. Moler.

Pearl G. Moler was born Feb. 23, 1869 in Vinton county, Ohio, and is the son of J. H. and Mary Coe Moler. The Coes and Molers, grandparents of the subject of this sketch, were among the pioneer settlers of Ohio, each family being immigrants from Pennsylvania. Pearl came with his parents to Lee Township, Athens county, when quite small, where his father purchased a farm of 320 acres, and engaged in farming and breeding Short Horn cattle and Delaine Merino sheep. Pearl was the principal shepherd of the flock and exhibited them at different fairs from year to year. His success in caring and exhibiting this flock created a love for the sheep, and when his father retired, Pearl continued the flock of Delaines and herd of Short Horns. He spares no pains in keeping the flock up to their former well earned reputation by adding the best blood obtainable from time to time. Mr. Moler has lately become a chicken fancier, the Buff Plymouth Rocks being his favorites.

In 1892, he was married to Etta M., daughter of R. S. and Rebecca Carpenter, Mt. Blanco, Meigs county, Ohio, and began housekeeping on a part of his father's farm. He has since purchased 118 acres of the farm and remained there until 1902 when he purchased his present home in the corporation of Albany, one half mile north of town, on the road leading to Marshfield, his farm being located on the same road 1½ miles farther north. Mr. and Mrs. Moler are the parents of two children, Robert Glen and Beryl Rebecca. Robert died at the at the age of 18 months.

Mr. C. F. Hummel

Now one of Athen's most successful tailors---was born on a farm in Morgan county. Here he was taught the lesson of self reliance which was his sole capital when he determined at the age of 19 years to learn a trade. He went to Cincinnati and without any assistance succeeded not only in maintaining himself but in attending the Cincinnati Cutting School from which place he graduated in 1893. This accomplished, his ambition led him to McArthur where he established a successful tailoring business.

By seven years of persistent work he attained such success that a broader field became a necessity. For this reason he came to Athens in August of 1900, where steadily increasing business has forced him to abandon his old "stand", for the present handsomely appointed quarters in the Hotel Athens building where he caters to the best trade of the city and satisfies the most fastidious dressers.

Mr. Hummel is a member of the Knights of Pythias and Paramuthia Lodge No. 25 of Free and Accepted Masons.

IMPORTANT
.... EVENTS.

(Continued from page 17.)

1877 First newspaper in Albany "The Albany Echo" published by D. A. R. McKinstry.

1878 Organization of Athenian Light Guards.

1880 Census of Athens county, 28411.
New Court House completed.
Thirtieth Annual Fair, gate receipts $2000.
Population of Nelsonville 3095.
Athens county vote for Garfield 1420 majority.
Soldiers' Memorial association organized at Athens.
Farm of 178 acres one-half mile east of Athens, purchased for Children's Home.

1881 First train on the Ohio Central.
Negro lynched at Athens for attempted murder near Albany.
Grand Army of Republic established at Athens, called Columbus Golden Post.
Children's Home founded.
Pike from Athens to Canaanville built.
Athens County Republican started at Athens by Jas. A. Miller and Chas. Logan.

1882 Hocking Valley railroad hauled daily an average of 700 cars of coal from mines about Nelsonville.
D. B. Stewart's woolen mills burned throwing 30 men out of employment. Loss $15,000.
Chas. P. Reid buys Athens County Republican, moves it to Nelsonville; now the Valley Register.
Enlargement and improvement of Stewart's opera house, Nelsonville.

1883 Razing of the old Brown corner in Athens, the oldest domiciliary landmark in Athens. Erected in 1812.
Gas superseeds oil lamps for street lighting.
Dedication Mt. Zion Baptist church in Athens.
Reunion 75th and 116th O. V. I. at Athens. Great meeting on College Campus, 240 members present.

1884 Great riot among miners at Buchtel.
Cassius M. Clay addresses immense gathering on College Campus during Blaine and Logan campaign.
Incendiary fire in Nelsonville destroyed the school house. Loss $20,000
Great flood in February. Ten inches higher than highest point in July, '75 flood. Tremendous loss down entire valley. Hockingport nearly wiped out Several thousands of dollars in money and provisions raised all over the country and sent to the sufferers of this valley. Half the bridges in the county washed out. No trains for ten days.
Great Blaine meeting about 15,000 people in Athens. Jas. G. Blaine, Gen. Gibson and Hon. E. F. Noyes were the speakers

1885 Great miners' strike in Hocking Valley. Loss to Hocking Valley R. R. Co. $1,000,000. Loss to miners themselves $1,-500,000. Value of property destroyed by rioters, $300,000.
Reunion of 18th O. V. I. at Athens. George W. Towsley found to be the youngest man mustered into the service during war of the rebellion. He was eleven years and 5 months.

1886 Earthquake felt all over the county at 9 o'clock p. m. Sunday, May 2.
Coolville flouring mill destroyed by fire. Loss $20,000.
Greatest peach crop ever produced in Athens county.

1889 Streets of Athens first lighted by electricity.

1891 Major McKinley accompanied by Gen. Goff of West Virginia, and Gen. Harris addressed 8,000 people on College Campus during his first gubernatorial campaign.
Athens Brick plant started.
Openly advertised prize fight in Nelsonville in which one contestant is killed.

1892 Athens county began the building of pikes. The first was from Amesville to Athens.
Savings & Loan Association organized.

1892 First street paved in Athens. West Union between Court and High streets.

1895 St. Paul's Catholic church on North College street built in Athens.

1898 Athens oil fields opened.
July 21 celebration over fall of Santiago.
Flag raising on Campus of Ohio university. Staff erected by the trustees Flag presented by the faculty.
Hudson School Furniture Company in Athens partially destroyed by fire. Heavy loss, no insurance.
Company B 17th reg. O. V. I. first Athens county boys to enlist in Spanish war, started for the front.
Center wing of Athens state hospital for insane burned. Loss $25,000. No lives lost.
Amesville Centennial celebration Aug. 18th.

1899 Present T. & O. C. station built.

1900 Mob surrounds Athens jail demanding Richard Gardner who is spirited away by Sheriff Porter.
Three men lost lives in mine explosion at Glouster.

1900 Desperate battle between officers and Pomeroy safe blowers at Canaanville. Twenty shots fired.
First rural mail route established in county.

1901 Franchise granted Athens and Nelsonville Traction company.
Crusade against expectoration on the streets begun by Athens ladies.
Free mail delivery established in Athens.
Morgan Syndicate buy all coal mines in Hocking and Sunday Creek Valleys.
Amesville's masonic lodge dedicated.
Great peach crop in Athens county. Estimated 1,500,000 baskets marketed.

1902 Messenger & Herald installs type-setting machine. The first in the county.
Marshal Finsterwald shot in battle with Athens burglars in Gallipolis. Williams and Lisle both killed.
Small-pox epidemic at Athens, Nelsonville and Marshfield.

1903 Athens votes for municipal electric light plant. Same at Glouster and Nelsonville.
Athens Presbyterian church dedicated.
Thirty-three voting precincts created in Athens county under new law.
Pest houses for small-pox patients established in Athens and Nelsonville.
State Normal College established at Athens and building erected.
Athens county Infirmary destroyed by fire.

1904 Andrew Carnegie donates $30,000 to establish library. Athens county builds a $41,420 Infirmary.
Mild small-pox epidemic in Buchtel.
Gen. Grosvenor nominated for the tenth term in Congress.
Athens has a Home-Coming celebration. Geo. A. Beaton of New York, a former Athenian banquets 3,000 at one time.
Ohio University celebrates its one hundredth anniversary.
8,000 National guards and 1,000 regulars have a ten day maneuver near Athens.
National guardsmen clash with regulars on streets of Athens. One man killed and three others wounded.

Will E. Moler's Herd of Herefords, in Lee Township.

ONE of the busiest men in the county is Will E. Moler, the hustling young merchant of Albany. Running a general store and taking in produce is enough usually for one man, but Mr. Moler is not an ordinary man. He owns and operates a 200 acre farm near Albany, a 300 acre farm in Vinton county, deals in farm stock and makes a specialty of breeding fine Hereford cattle, one herd is here shown in the picture. He breeds nothing but registered cattle and sells to stockmen who want to start a herd of registered stock. He takes great pains with his cattle and has been in the business for eight years.

He is president of the Athens County Telephone Company and is one of the principal stockholders. He owns and operates a general store at Hebbardsville. Mr. Moler is the son of John H. Moler and was born in Vinton county in August 1866. When a baby in arms he came with his father and settled on a farm near Albany, where he worked until he was 21 years of age. He was educated in the public school of Albany and the Atwood Institute. He worked in the general store of A. Vorhes & Son in Albany for four years, and for Mr. Shively in McArthur for one year. He traveled for E. E. Shedd & Sons of Columbus, O., for seven years and made a decided success as a traveling man. He went into business for himself in 1891.

Mr. Moler was married to Viola Robinett in 1889 and three children were born to them: Arthur Lee 14, Harley Edwin 9, Frank Austin, 7. His wife died in April, 1902, and he was married to Mrs. Cora M. Watson of Byer, O., in 1903. They live in their own home in Albany.

Mr. and Mrs. George Ewing Clark.

MR. AND MRS. CLARK, whose pictures are here shown are well-known people of Amesville and vicinity. They have lived in Ames township over a half century, residing on a farm until 1890 when they moved to Amesville, where they now have a first-class restaurant and grocery.

Mr. Clark was born in Lancaster, O., in 1844, and was the son of Henry Clark, who was reared by Hon. Thomas Ewing, so well-known in the history of this country. The father, Henry Clark, sought his fortune in California at the time of the gold excitement in 1849, and died enroute.

Mr. Clark was married to Lydia A. Beasley, daughter of Isaac and Adaline Beasley in 1868. They are the parents of eight children, three of whom died of diphtheria in infancy, and five are yet living: William E., Thomas E., Lizzie Wilcox, Charles and Anna Smith.

Mr. Clark was Assessor of Ames township for eight consecutive years; member of the village council, of which he was president and acting mayor during the administration of Alonzo Weed.

Judge A. S. Bethel

Elected by the people of Athens county to serve for ten consecutive years as Probate Judge bespeaks the esteem in which Judge A. S. Bethel is held by his fellow citizens. Born in Cambridge, Guernsey county, O., June 19, 1846, he was brought to this county as early as 1855, where his parents settled in Trimble township. Here the Judge was reared and remained until he was 28 years of age. He then became one of the firm of Bethel Bros. in York township. Ten years later he left the farm to take charge of the Brooks Store, one of the largest stores the Hocking Valley and held the position four years. Then he founded the real estate and insurance business under the firm name of Dew & Bethel, now conducted by his son, George Bethel in Nelsonville, Ohio.

In 1892, Mr. Bethel was elected Probate Judge which office he held until 1902. As an office holder he brought to bear upon his work all that good business sense and ability which has been noticeable in all his transactions. Never at any time did he endeavor to make the public interest subservient to self; his efforts have been praiseworthy always.

Having retired from office, he in accordance with his characteristic energy, has successfully developed several thousands of acres of coal lands and marketed them to active coal operators.

That one's endeavors should be so entirely successful as have been the Judges, is perhaps, a more powerful and appealing characterization of the man than any one might draw. The judge now occupies on west Washington street, Athens, O., one of the most handsome homes in the city. a photograph of which is shown in the accompanying illustration. Public spirited, straightforward in all his dealings, friendly and fair with all, Judge Bethel enjoys the highest esteem and confidence of all.

He is prominently identified with the Masonic order and is a member of Athens Commandery No. 15 Knights Templar.

The Athens County Telephone Company.

THE first Independent Telephone line entered the county at Albany, Ohio, the winter of 1897-8 and was conducted by the Chillicothe & McArthur Telephone Co., of McArthur, Ohio. During the spring it was extended to Marshfield and Daleton, and that summer it was run into Athens via Hibbardsville and Fisher. For two years following the terminal or pay station telephone was operated in the dental office of Dr. C. L. Jones, and offered the people of Athens practically the only rural service in existence in the county, at that time; however, there were about one hundred telephones in operation by the Bell company in Athens.

During the summer of 1901, this Independent line and franchise were taken over by a company of local people, composed of Dr. A. F. Holmes and W. E. Moler, of Albany; G. W. Duffee, of Marshfield and Dr. C. L. Jones of Athens.

About this time a canvass was made of the county and some seven or eight companies formed to accomplish a quick and thorough development so that every postoffice in

the county could be reached by a business man without going to central. This rapid development stands a credit to the companies that carried it through, and has placed Athens county foremost of all the other southern counties in the number of Independent telephones in operation, which recent statistics show to be by actual count 2965 telephones. These telephones are handled on eleven exchanges, connected by trunk lines, and reach practically all the cities in the state by copper long distance lines.

On January 1, 1905, the Athens exchange had in operation over 500 telephones, reaching practically every business house in the city. Eight modern lead covered cables enter the office from different parts of the city, and improvements and extensions are daily being made giving employment to fifteen men and girls through this home industry.

The success of this enterprise has demonstrated that the average business man needs extensive local and county service, and a system offering Chicago and New York service does not fill the needs. Much more could be said about the exchanges at Nelsonville, Glouster and Albany, and the 800 farmers that have telephones on this system in the county, but space will not permit.

Residence of A. J. Frame, Athens, Ohio.

THE accompanying illustration shows the handsome and comfortable residence of Mr. and Mrs. Agustus J. Frame, on East State street, Athens, Ohio, one of the prettiest locations in the town.

Mr. Frame is a native of Athens county, having been born at Coolville August 21, 1834. He engaged in the mercantile business in that village in 1856 and continued with varying success until 1874, when he was elected county treasurer. He was inducted into that office in 1875 and served two terms, statutory provisions barring him from renomination.

In 1880 he was elected auditor of Athens county and on account of efficiency and courteous treatment of the public, he held the office for sixteen consecutive years. It has been said that Mr. Frame was the best auditor the county has ever had, and the state auditor has declared him to be one of the best county auditors in the state.

Retiring from the auditor's office in 1896, he was elected treasurer of the Ohio University in 1897, which office he still fills to the satisfaction of the Board of Trustees.

What higher commendation could be offered demonstrating the sterling, manly qualities of this man than that he held two of the most important offices in the county for twenty consecutive years?

Mr. Frame has always been an uncompromising Republican, a prominent Mason and a member of Athens Commandery, Knights Templar, of which order he is also treasurer.

RESIDENCE OF A. J. FRAME, EAST STATE STREET, ATHENS, OHIO.

Mayor J. R. Hickman, Nelsonville.

THE picture here shown is that of J. R. Hickman, mayor of the city of Nelsonville who is now serving his second term. Mr. Hickman was born in Somerset, Ohio, March 5, 1856 and came to Nelsonville with his father, the late Wesley C. Hickman in 1867. He clerked in the drug store of his uncle W. G. Hickman for a time, studied law with his father and was for 15 years employed by the Hocking Valley railroad. He served for nine consecutive years as clerk of York township; was for two years clerk of the city of Nelsonville, and for two years was a member of the council.

He was married February 28, 1882 to Miss Vesper Carnes. They have seven children: Florence, aged 20; Harry, 18; Marie, 16; Elsie and Effie, 14; Carrie, 11, and Carnes 6.

Mr. Hickman has held many positions of trust and has always deserved the confidence reposed in him. He is a stalwart Republican, and has been prominently mentioned as a candidate for Probate Judge.

ATHENS COUNTY HISTORY
CONTINUED.

Armstrong place and occupied by Elza Armstrong. Later Timothy Goodrich built the first saw mill in the county at the same location as the Hewitt grist mill on Margaret Creek.

The miller was those days regarded as a public benefactor and permitted to locate on any land where a desirable site was found.

ATHENS FIRST SETTLEMENT.

Ohio is a great state to which all ''Buckeyes'' love to turn with pride whatever part of the world they may inhabit, It is second to none in all that goes to make a live and prosperous community.

But little over a century has passed since the white man began to exercise dominion over this region; the erstwhile home of the red man, yet within these years have grown up a population of 4,157,545 people. On every hand rise the dwellings and spires of a highly civilized community. It was but little over a century since the wolves, bears, buffalo and deer made this the paradise of hunting grounds for the Indian where now steam carries away thousands of car loads daily from our busy mines and manufactures.

But little over a century since the red skin pitched his wigwam or built his rude hut where now we see in all directions evidences of wealth, comfort and luxury. But little over a century since the first pioneers, unmindful of peril, full of adventure, fortitude and heroic self-sacrifice encamped and built the first house in Athens. This was erected in 1798 just back of where St. Paul's Catholic church now stands and was the home of Capt. John Chandler. This spot also bears the distinction of having the first brick house in town built upon it by Joel Abbott in 1804.

Among the first cabins built was that of John Havner on Mill street immediately back of H. H. Wickham's present home. On the southwest corner of Mill and College streets, William Dorr built a double log house using one side as store the other as residence. This later became a tavern, and it was here that Aaron Burr stopped on his visit to Athens in 1804; also here Gov. Tiffin, the first governor of Ohio, was entertained when he came to attend the first meeting of the trustees of the University in 1805. Later Judge Barker built his large house, a mansion for those days, on this same site which was for three generations known as the Judge Barker corner. This was torn down in 1903 to make room for the handsome double house of W. B. Lawrence and Dr. T. J Merwin. John Johnston built his log cabin on the corner, now occupied by Raw's department store.

(Continued on page 23.)

Shadow Rocks.

This interesting freak of nature is found on the Frank Patton farm near Beebe, in Rome township. The rocks may be seen from the B. & O. S-W. railroad, and are always objects of interest to passengers. The rocks, or the big rock and its shadow, stand nearly thirty feet high on the extreme and almost precipitous summit of the hill. The foundations are gradually wearing away but children now unborn will be old men and women before these silent witnesses of many past generations shall have tottered and tumbled to the river below.

George H. Maxwell's Dairy Farm and Residence, Near Fisher's Station.

GEORGE H. MAXWELL was born in Waterloo Tp., Athens Co., O., Jan. 15, 1867. He was the son of John M. Maxwell and Melvina Story Maxwell, and the grandson of William Maxwell and Louisa Mayhugh Maxwell. When he was about eight years old his parents removed to Canaan township where he grew to manhood.

He worked on the farm and attended the district school until he was about 18 years old when he obtained a teachers' certificate and began teaching. He attended the Ohio university at Athens for several terms, teaching part of the time to pay expenses at school. He followed teaching for fourteen years. On July 25, 1889, he was married to Miss Minnie Moore and to this union four sons were born.

He began keeping house in Chauncey where he taught the school at that place for the year 1889 and 1890.

When he finished the school at that place he returned to Canaan township and engaged in farming and teaching.

In October, 1891, he removed with his family to Shelby, Iowa, where he taught school. In March, 1903, he returned to Canaan township, Athens county, Ohio, and purchased a farm of C. L. Bean. Here he resided over seven years when he sold this farm and bought what is known as the Clem Hooper farm in Alexander township. In about two years he sold again and then purchased the William Dean farm at Fisher, Ohio, which is here shown in the illustration. When he moved to this farm he entered into the dairy business and is still engaged in said work, selling his milk to the people of Athens.

Mr. and Mrs. Charles Delnow Hopkins' Residence, Athens, Ohio.

CHARLES DELNOW HOPKINS was born on a farm near Marshfield, Ohio, July 28, 1869, and is a descendent of John Hopkins, who settled at Cambridge, Mass., in 1616; from whom so many illustrious and distinguished scholars and patriots trace their ancestry.

He is the eldest son of George W., and Rachel Cline Hopkins, and grandson of Rev. James H. Hopkins, one of the pioneer Methodist ministers of southern Ohio.

Mr. Hopkins attended the district and village schools and at the age of sixteen began teaching school, employing his leisure time in preparing himself for college.

In 1888 he entered the Ohio Wesleyan University at Deleware, O., which his grandfather had assisted in founding, and received the degree of B. A. therefrom in 1891.

The succeeding year he was principal in the public schools of the city of Delaware, occupying his spare moments and vacations in studying law with Judge Freshwater, of that city.

In the fall of 1892 upon examination entered the Senior Class of the Law Department of the Ohio State University, and graduated therefrom in 1893, receiving the degree of L. L. B. Immediately afterwards he formed a law partnership with Hon. C. E. Peoples, at Pomeroy, Ohio. In the following year he removed to Athens and formed a partnership with the late Hon. Charles Townsend, Ex-Secretary of State.

Mr. Hopkins is now actively engaged in a lucrative law practive and is also engaged in other business enterprises.

October 8, 1895, he was united in marriage to Miss Adda Carpenter, only daughter of Judge Rufus and Elizabeth Cornell Carpenter, who had been a classmate at college and a member of the Class of 1893, Ohio Wesleyan University. They have two children, Rufus Carpenter and Rachel.

Mr. Hopkins is a member of the F. & A. M., the I. O. O. F., and other social as well as political organizations.

Home of Mr. and Mrs. Lewis Richardson, Near Frost, Ohio.

LEWIS RICHARDSON, farmer of Frost. Ohio, was the second child of a family of ten children, of Thomas and Miranda Richardson. His mother was the daughter of William and Saloma Barrows Frost. Lewis was born on the farm where he now lives, on August 17, 1839. He has a record few men can show, having lived on the farm for sixty five years, where his father was born and lived for seventy-four years, and where his grandfather lived and died, he having settled here in about 1800. The homestead contains 330 acres, 230 acres under improvement.

Mr. Richardson was married to Miss Nettie A. Browning, in December, 1892. This union was blessed with four children: Clyde A., born March 29, 1894; Guv Afton, born Sept. 13, 1895; Cecil Vane, born April 14, 1898; Wade Atlee, born Feb. 4, 1900. All are at home with their parents.

Mr. Richardson took an active part in the war for the suppression of the rebellion, inlisting in Co. K., 39th regiment O. V. I., in July, 1861, and served three years as a private. He was discharged August, 1864.

He is a member of H. G. Frost Post, No. 341, being at present commander. He is also a member of the Masonic Fraternity, and votes the Republican ticket.

The Richardson home shown in the illustration is as comfortable and convenient as it looks and is one of the most picturesque homes in the county.

MR. THOMAS RICHARDSON.

Residence of Mr. and Mrs. Robert Smith, Jr., Canaan Towhship.

———

THE beautiful country place here represented, is the home of Mr. and Mrs, Robert Smith, Jr., located on the Canaanville-Amesville road in Canaan township. It is one of the best farms in the township, thrift and prosperity being in evidence on every hand.

Mr. Smith was born in Ireland at Londonderry in 1859. He sought his fortune in America in 1880 and located in Illinois where he remained for three years returning to Ireland. He again came to America in 1886 and located in Canaan township. He was married to Rebecca McDaniel of Canaan township in 1891 and located on the farm where he now lives. The residence shown in the illustration was built in 1901.

Mr. Smith has prospered by dint of hard work, close attention to business and shrewd business judgment. He is one of the prominent and most public spirited men in his township, is a stalwart Republican and has served as a member of the county Republican central committee.

ATHENS COUNTY HISTORY
CONTINUED.

Jared Jones built on the present Dorr lot on Court street near Washington. Dr Perkins in 1800 purchased a log cabin on State street near Congress—builder unknown—and moved his family here from Marietta where they had spent the winter enroute from New Haven, Connecticut.

Dr. Leonard Jewett, who came to Athens in 1804, bought a hewed log house built by Capt. Silas Bingham on the lot now occupied by H. D. Henry on College street.

The second brick house erected in Athens was built in 1804 for the double purpose of store and dwelling, near the corner known since 1812 as "Brown Corner," having been built on at that time by Brown and now since 1868 occupied by the Bank of Athens.

ATHENS COUNTY ESTABLISHED.

In 1805, when this county was separated from Washington and given its own government and the name of Athens county, the settlement in its midst became the county seat bearing Athens as its name. At this time Athens had always been spoken of as the Middletown, meaning that it lay in the center of the Ohio Company's purchase until the name of Middletown had become fastened upon it.

In 1800 the first post route crossed the county at Amesville going from Marietta to Zanesville. The carrier was supposed to make the trip every two weeks but frequently three and four weeks intervened. In 1802 the first reguarly established route crossed Athens township from Marietta to Chillicothe making a stop in Athens. Chillicothe was at this time the seat of territorial government.

THE FIRST POST OFFICE.

In 1804 the first postoffice in the county was established by Jehiel Gregory who kept it at his house across the river east of town, where Barth's flouring mill now stands. Prior to the coming of this post route the mails were gotten every two or three weeks from Gallipolis, where the boats from Wheeling to Cincinnati exchanged mail bags.

The second postoffice in the county was established in Ames township in 1821, Loring B. Glazier being the postmaster and keeping the mail at his house.

In 1900 there were sixty-one offices in the county. In 1905 sixteen of these had been dropped owing to the rural routes established in the intervening time. Twenty-nine of these routes make an almost complete net work over the county and with a few additional routes soon to be opened will carry mail to every farm house in the county.

The list of these offices with routes are as follows: Athens 9, Albany 4, Amesville 1, Coolville 4, Glouster 2, Guysville 2, Marshfield 1, Millfield 1, Nelsonville 3, Stewart, 1 Pratt's Fork 1, total 29.

Athens is the only office doing sufficient business to make it a second class office and entitle it to free city delivery. This was established in 1902.

(Continued on page 26.)

BENNETT & MILLER, BARBERS, ATHENS, OHIO.

AMONG the many enterprising young business men of Athens, Bennett & Miller, the proprietors of the City Hall Barber Shop, should be numbered among the first. These young men purchased the shop and business they now own on October 1, 1904, of Bennett Bros., who succeeded W. E. Koon. This was the first successful white barber shop in Athens and for several years the only one.

The present owners came here from Amesville and enjoy a splendid trade numbering their patrons among the best people of Athens. The accompanying illustration shows that theirs is a model shop in every particular, and the enterprise manifested by these young men make them worthy of the patronage they have at all times.

Residence of Mr. and Mrs. Mason Andrews in Alexander Township.

RESIDENCE OF MR. AND MRS. MASON ANDREWS.

BARN AND BARNYARD OF MR. MASON ANDREWS.

MASON ANDREWS was born in Ames Township Athens county Ohio May 27 1845. He is a son of David and Christiana (Mowery) Andrews. The subject of this sketch was reared on a farm, and received only a common school education. He lived with his mother until manhood. the father having died while he was yet young. He was married Dec. 29 1863 to Miss Eva Howard. daughter of Lloyd and Elizabeth Howard. To them were born, six children, all living, Lloyd R. Emma W. William M. Ira E. Hulda E. and Jay C. Mr. Andrews. has held places of trust at the hands of the people. He was twice elected Trustee of York Township, while yet a resident there. and is now a member of the board of trustees of Alexander Township. He is known to be a public spirited man, yet giving his voice to an economic and just administration in public affairs. Farming is his occupation, and he is located on a beautiful farm. in the central part of Alexander Township. Mr. and Mrs. Andrews are members of The Cumberland Presbyterian Church at Hebbardsville.

George A Kurtz's Hardware Store.

ONE of the leading hardware stores in Athens is shown in the illustration and is owned and operated by Mr. George A. Kurtz who knows the business and the wants of the people from A to Z. No more complete stock of hardware is found in Southern Ohio.

Mr. Kurtz was born on a farm near Albany in 1853 and came to Athens in 1865. He was identified with the mail service for eight years, four of which in Athens post office and four years on the road as postal clerk. He went into the hardware business as clerk for Bartlett & Kurtz in 1887 and has been identified with that business ever since. In 1893 the business was sold to A. W. Connett & Son and in 1899 again sold to L. H. Glazier, Mr. Kurtz remaining with the business in each change until March of 1904 he purchased the business, put new life into it and is today doing the leading business of the town.

Mr. Kurtz was never married and makes his home with his aged mother, on North Congress street.

Drug Store of Frank W. Gibson, Amesville.

FRANK W. GIBSON was born near Athens, July 11, 1851. Attended the public school till 16 years of age when he entered the Ohio University for two years. He was compelled to stop school and go to teaching expecting to return the following year. He continued teaching. however, for twelve years in the public schools and the Academy at Amesville. O. In 1878 he purchased a stock of drugs in Amesville and has continued the business in that village ever since, gradually enlarging his stock till today he has one of the largest and best stock outside of the city in the country. In 1879 he married Luella Curfman, daughter of W. H. Curfman. They have five children, two sons and three daughters.

He has been postmaster for two terms, and Justice of the Peace ten years.

THE NEW CLINE BUILDING. ATHENS, OHIO.

THE NEW CLINE BUILDING, located on Court Street, Athens, Ohio, one door south of Athens county's court house, here shown in the illustration and contrasted with the picture of the old Perkins' home and "Medicine Store," the original building that occupied this prominent business location, gives one a very good idea of Athens today contrasted with the Athens of fifty to sixty years ago.

Mr. J. H. Cline, who now owns this property is one of Athens' most enterprising and progressive business men. He is a native of Meigs county, and is the son of F. Marion and A. L. Cline. He received a good general education as a boy and early went into the drug business, serving an apprenticeship for five years with E. Davis & Co., of Middleport, Ohio. He graduated from the Philadelphia College of Pharmacy in 1889 and afterwards was employed as head clerk in L. C. Funk's store in Philadelphia.

In June of 1893, he purchased the drug store of W. A. Hibbard, in what was then known as the Perkins Block. This room has been occupied as a drug store ever since John Perkins started a medicine and general store here

THE F. L. PRESTON CO.   CLINE'S PHARMACY.

in 1828. In 1848 he made it exclusively a drug store.

On purchasing the store Mr. Cline at once put the business on a modern basis and has ever since given the people of Athens as good accommodation as can be found in any city. The illustration, showing the interior of the drug store is prima facie evidence that it is a model in its class. George E.

OLD PERKINS BUILDING

Whipple, a graduate of the Pharmacy Department of the Ohio Northern University in June, 1901, is Mr. Cline's head clerk and has charge of the detail of the store.

Mr. Cline bought the building in which the store is located, August 1, 1903, and began at once to remodel it, putting in a new pressed brick front with modern entrance and windows, and added a third story making it one of the handsomest modern blocks in Athens.

The building is tenanted by Cline's Pharmacy, part of the F. L. Preston Department store which also occupies a large part of the second floor. On the second floor also are the offices of Dr. H. T. Lee; Drs. C. H. and Edna Thompson's dental parlors; L. H. Clark, lawyer; C. L. Wilson, broker; and C. McLean, jeweler.

On the third floor are suites of rooms and a large dancing hall, leased by the Athenian Club, one of the most exclusive social clubs in the city.

Mr. Cline gave Athens its first high class soda fountain. He built up a large trade and "Cline's Soda" has become known as a synonym for the best. On account of his rapidly growing trade, he built an ice cream factory in the rear of his building in the spring of 1904, and equipped it with complete modern machinery for making the product for which his soda fountain is so famous. Although this industry is but a year old the enormous quantity of this popular delicacy that is sold here and shipped to neighboring cities indicates that the enterprise is a long felt want. Neopolitan ice cream in fancy shades and ices are kept on hand at all times.

While Mr. Cline has done much for Athens in the way of a modern store, and its accompanying conveniences, he has prospered himself and is reaping the reward of his zealous devotion to business. His careful attention to the wants of his patrons, and the neat, attractive appearance of his store, speak more than words of the secret of his pronounced success.

J. H. CLINE'S MODERN PHARMACY.

The Lawrence-Worstell Building.

THE handsome three-story business block here shown in the illustration is located on Court St., Athens, Ohio, and is known as the Lawrence-Worstell building. W. B. Lawrence and L. G. Worstell built this building in 1902 on the site of the old Hoyt homestead. Shortly after the building was completed, Mr. Lawrence disposed of his interest, and the building is now owned by L. G. Worstell and Miss Lillian E. Michael.

The building is tenanted by Thompson & Scott, clothiers and furnishers; Johnson's restaurant; the Athens Journal; Junod & Roberts, lumber dealers; and the third floor is divided into rooms and a dance hall furnishing an elegant home for the Assembly club, the largest social organization in Athens.

L. G. WORSTELL'S RESIDENCE.

The residence here shown is the home of Lawrence G. Worstell and is beautifully located on University Terrace, south. Mr. Worstell is one of Athens' most prominent young lawyers, and has led a busy life from the first day he was admitted to the bar, in 1894. He read law with the firm of Grosvenor & Jones and was taken into the firm as soon as he was admitted to practice. He has ever since been a member of the firm, which is known as Grosvenor, Jones & Worstell.

Mr. Worstell was born at Tappan, Harrison county,

August 21, 1863. He attended Hopedale College in 1881-82 and matriculated in the Ohio University in 1883. After attending one term, he taught school until 1885 when he returned and graduated with the class of 1888.

After graduating he taught mathematics in the Toledo, Ohio, High school for one year when he went to Salt Lake City, Utah, where during his four years connection with the public schools of that city he organized its first high school. He quit the public schools in 1893 and began to study law.

In 1889 he was married to Miss Lenore M. Michael.

Mr. Worstell is a public spirited citizen and has been a member of the school board of Athens since 1900 and is now its president. He has been identified with the Republican politics of the county in many ways although he has never been a candidate for office.

ATHENS COUNTY HISTORY
CONTINUED.

PRIMEVAL FORESTS.

It is almost impossible for the present generation, familiar with our acres of cleared fields and blocks of brick buildings, to conceive of the wonderful exuberance of the primeval forests which met the pioneer. Every spot where a tree could stand was occupied and what immense labor was required to consume these primeval forests, to fell and clear sufficient space to build a cabin and raise crops. This magnificient forests growth proclaimed the luxuriant fertility of the soil and invited settlement.

Over thirty varieties of trees sixty feet or more in height are known to have been found here in early days. One hundred and three varieties of trees and herbaceous plants were found growing by Dr. Drake the botanist in 1803. The bottom lands contained immense sycamore, poplar, black and white walnut,

black and white ash, buckeye, beech, soft and hard maple, black, white, yellow and red oak. So dense was the shade that the sun could scarcely penetrate and at noon the light was near that of twilight. The hills were covered with dense growths of oak, hickory and ash with here and there a few pines, poplars, and maples.

The white oak grew to enormous size often measuring four to five feet in diameter with straight trunks, the first limbs often 50 to 75 feet from the ground. These are nearly all gone. Many have lived their natural life or been affected by the cutting down of their neighbors. The age of these giants is conjectural. Their very slow growth would indicate that they had seen centuries come and go while they attained to their immensity and that they must have ben of considerable size when the pilgrims landed at Plymouth Rock.

In all parts of the country grew the sugar maple and these trees were carefully protected from the woodsman's ax. From these were obtained the most of the sugar and molasses needed during the first half century though now pure maple sugar is seldom seen. The process of making the sugar was of the crudest. Like other large tasks the neighborhood assisted. Often the children could aid to empty and replace the buckets at the trees. It was great fun to gather at the sugar camps the evening they were to "stir off." The ground covered with snow, lights scattered here and there, trees tapped and with the "drip, drip," of the sugar water, filtering through the spile into a hewn trough from a convenient sized log, made a picture of primitive life that is unknown to the present generation.

It was rare sport to follow the sled loaded with barrels and with a gourd dip up sugar water to fill them. Then it was hauled to where they were boiling off the sugar. All were treated to a "sugar egg" to take home. If the young folks had stayed too late, the "sugar egg" was made to serve as a peace offering with the mothers.

The wanton multilation and destruction of these primeval forests by the pioneers seem to-day inexcusable; acres and acres of fine timber were burned simply to get rid of it when if it could have been sawed, stored and protected it would have supplied the needs of generations yet unborn.

Droughts, floods and tornadoes are some of the results of the wholesale destruction of these forests. If we can learn the lesson thus taught we will carefully protect the few remaining acres of woods and plant more whenever and wherever possible. This is the most reliable crop that can be grown on much of the hilly, run down land in this county.

The bureau of forestry is demonstrating this and it is to be hoped that our farmers will yet recognize its value and be benefited thereby.

PIONEER HARDSHIPS.

While their life was hard and their work was onerous the hearts of the early settlers were not hardened by it, neither did they follow the example of their Puritan fathers and frown upon fun and frolic. They frequently dropped work for a gay time at a neighbor's and made joyous sport out of work, which must be done. To hire help was almost impossible, but houses must be built, fruit gathered and preserved for winter use, corn husked, barns built, harvest gathered and hogs killed. So the neighbors assembled as each ones need came and word was sent. Let it be a "quilting bee," "a corn husking," "apple paring," "log rolling," "house raising" or "hog killing" many willing hands made light work and happy hearts found

(Continued on page 29.)

RESIDENCE OF MR. AND MRS. L. G. WORSTELL, ATHENS, OHIO.

THE BANK OF ATHENS.

ATHENS, OHIO.

J. D. Brown, President.   W. B. Golden, Cashier.

Capital, $50,000.

Surplus—Full Individual Liability.

J. D. BROWN, President.

W. B. GOLDEN, Cashier.

ORGANIZED by John Brown and James D. Brown in 1867. During nearly forty years it has carried on legitimate, conservative banking and has steadily increased in capital and patronage. We propose in the future, as in the past, to offer every facility to our customers consistent with safety to them and ourselves.

We will be glad to have you favor us with your business and you may rest assured the interest and security of our patrons will have our first and best attention.

Ask your neighbor.

J. D. BROWN'S BLOCK ATHENS, OHIO.

ATHENS COUNTY'S WAR RECORD.

DURING the terrible four years, from 1861 to 1865, in which the government waged a tremendous war to preserve its own existence, and the union of the states, Athens county was not behind any portion of the loyal north, in the promptness and zeal of her responses to every call. According to the United States census report, of 1860, the number of male inhabitants of the county in that year, between the ages of fifteen and fifty, both inclusive, was five thousand and eighty-nine.

The county furnished to the government during the war, in all, two thousand six hundred and ten soldiers, or more than fifty per cent. of her men able to bear arms. In other words, of the able bodied men in the county, every other one left his business and his family to assist in suppressing the rebellion.

This is a record of which the county may well be proud—a record which no county in the state of Ohio, and we dare say, few counties in all the northern states, can surpass. And it should be added that no draft was ever made in the county. What she did was done voluntarily, and stands as a lasting monument of her patriotism. During this trying period, the mass of her people, women not less then men. were profoundly stirred, and a loyal zeal pervaded all.

Abstract of Soldiers in the United States and State Service, furnished by Athens County, in the War of the Great Rebellion.

Townships.	No. in U. S. Army.	No. of 100 Days' Men.	Total
Athens,	267	96	363
Alexander	162	58	220
Ames	142	—	142
Bern	108	—	108
Carthage	112	—	112
Canaun	117	10	127
Dover	154	30	184
Lee	117	68	185
Lodi	143	39	182
Rome	156	54	210
Trimble	143	27	170
Troy	181	—	181
Waterloo	172	—	172
York	226	38	264
Total,	2,190	420	2,610

ST. PAUL'S CATHOLIC CHURCH, ATHENS, OHIO.

IN point of years St. Paul's Catholic Church, the present handsome edifice which is here shown in the illustration comes third in the list of the churches in Athens and like all other religious organizations, its progress for years was slow. Beginning with a mere handful, the organization has grown in numbers and importance until today it is one of the substantial religious bodies in the city.

The history of the Catholic Church of Athens, properly begins in 1846 when an organization was formally effected. For several years thereafter, the members did not enjoy the convenience of a church edifice and meetings were held in the court house. Father Albrick, of Pomeroy, came up regularly every month to hold services. During his pastorate, the church flourished as well as could be expected under the disadvantageous conditions and many new members were added. Father Albrick was succeeded by Father McGee, a Dominican, from Somerset, Ohio. He was followed by Father Gell of Pomeroy and in turn succeeded by Father Tenerie, of Vinton county.

At this time the membership of the church had increased to about seventy-five and all realized the necessity of an edifice of their own in which to conduct religious services. It was during Fhther Tenerie's pastorate that the question of erecting a church was discussed, and before he severed his connection with his Athens charge, preparations for building a church were consummated. The site chosen was on Congress street. Father Tenerie left however before the church was completed and was succeeded by Father Madzell who was later on followed by Father Curtzen. In 1863 the Congress St. church was completed and ready for occupancv. Since the completion of the church, the following pastors have been in charge: Fathers O'Reily, Slavens, Campbell, Hartnedy, Love, Madden, McGuirk, W. F. Boden and J. B. Mattingly, to whose untiring efforts and skillful management, more than any one else, is the present handsome church and parsonage due.

For a period of thirty-two years services were held in the Congress street church, and during that time the membership had increased to approximately two hundred. It became evident in the latter part of 1904, that the facilities for accommodation were inadequate, and a movement was inaugurated by the pastor, Father Mattingly, looking to the erection of a more commodious structure. The work of raising funds was necessarily slow, but in the early part of 1895 ground was broken for the present edifice which stands on College street. It was erected at a cost of $14.000 and has been used for church purposes since late in the autumn of 1905. The church is one of the handsomest houses of worship in Athens, and stands as a beautiful monument to the industry and enterprise of the Catholic people of Athens and the untiring zeal of Father J. B. Mattingly·

The structure is one hundred and ten feet high; it is finished with hard wood, adorned with stained glass windows and with white and golden al:ars and modern pews making a most attractive appearance,

The cornerstone of the church was laid with impressive ceremonies on May 12, 1895 in the presence of several thousand people. Rt. Rev. Bishop John A. Watterson, of Columbus, officiated assisted by Father Mattingly, the pastor, and Father Cush of Dresden.

The handsome parsonage also shown in the illustration was erected in 1901 under the pastorate of Father Mattingly. Father James T. Banahan succeeded Father Mattingly as pastor of St. Paul's church on November 15, 1904. He came here from Wheelersburg, Ohio, his first pastorate. He is an exceptionally able young man, kind, courteous and popular both in the church and out. His boyhood home was in Providence, Rhode Island. He was educated for the priesthood in Mt. St. Marys College at Emmettsburg, Md., and at St. Marys Seminary, in Baltimore, Md. The church is flourishing under his pastorate and the membership now numbers about 300.

PARSONAGE OF ST. PAUL'S CHURCH.

ST. PAUL'S CATHOLIC CHURCH.

REV. JAMES BANAHAN, PASTOR.

J. W. Johnston's Residence Near Carbondale.

THE subject of this biography is a native of Waterloo township, where he was born in 1849. He was reared on the farm which in many respects accounts for his sturdy character and scrupulous integrity. He attended the common schools and received a thorough grounding in the branches taught at that time. He was married in 1872 to Amelia Gabriel. Two children, Harrison and Elizabeth are the result of this marriage. Four years after his marriage, his wife died, and in 1877 he was married to Mrs. Eliza Weatherspoon to whom has been born one son, Silas. Mr. Johnston early in life learned the trade of blacksmith which he has successfully followed, locating at different times at Carbondale and Zaleski. For the past fifteen years he has been a permanent resident of Waterloo township and is the owner of three small farms. He is a member of Constitution Lodge No. 426, F. & A. M., and of the Knights of Pythias.

fun in the work and companionship. A picnic supper in orchard or barn wound up the days work and sent them home rejoicing.

Possibly the younger members stayed for a dance on the barn floor by the swinging light of lanterns or flickering candles and the festivities lasted until morning dawn.

The pioneers all stopped work at noon Saturday for every one felt that a week of hard labor earned them the holiday. The men usually tried to take a wagon load of produce to town or found need for certain things obtainable only in town that they might spend the afternoon among old cronies gathered there.

There were no blue ribbons worn in those days, "whiskey flowed like water." It cost only 12½ cents a quart; thirty-five cents a gallon. It entered largely into all arguments and discussions which frequently ended in all round fights. Bandaged black eyes and plastered cuts worn to worship next day attested to the goodly gathering, the emphasis of some one's remarks the night before. But little attention was paid to such incidents by officers of the law. "Drinking a little too much" was taken as a matter of course but we have the testimony of pioneers that "drunkenness was much less frequent than in this day of high license and "fighting whiskey.""

HUNTING WILD ANIMALS.

The history of pioneer life generally turns on the dark side; but the hardships of the early settlers were not a series of unmitigated tribulations. They contrived to do many things to break their monotonous round of duties. Whatever was to be done whether work or play they called in all the congenial spirits of the neighborhood and made of it a great romp. One of their wild recreations, most exciting because of its dangers and withal most necessary, was the wolf hunt.

In those days more mischief was done by wolves than by any other wild animals. Rarely did they attack persons but stock of all kinds furnished them many free lunches. However besides causing sad havoc in the barnyard, they managed to keep the families awake at night with their constant barking. This is said to be most terrifying in sound and like the ever present mosquito their noises were about as dreadful as their depredations.

The most effectual way of ridding the country of these pests was the "circular hunt." A number of men and boys with their dogs met on the appointed day and were stationed in a circle covering several miles. They would gradually close in on their center of operation gathering not only wolves but deers and many smaller animals. Often thus a dozen wolves were killed in a single day. Guns were rarely allowed on these days for fear of danger to others, the dogs were the efficient means of death.

(Continued on page 31.)

The Imperial Barber Shop, Athens, Ohio.

THE Imperial Barber Shop, the interior of which is here shown, was the enterprise of three mail carriers: F. C. Dean, H. J. Long and Clade Logan, who purchased the shop February 1, 1904, and employed three first-class barbers. June 1, 1904. Mr. Logan purchased the interest of the other two carriers and at the time this picture was taken, was the sole proprietor. In March of 1905, the building in which the shop was located, was

sold to The Athens National Bank, who removed the building and are now erecting a fine four story structure on the old site. The Imperial shop will have an elegantly appointed room in the new building where Mr. Logan will command the excellent trade he has always enjoyed.

Mr. Logan is the son of Mr. and Mrs. A. L. Logan, of Amesville, and was born July 13 1880. He attended the public schools of Athens and graduated from the Commercial Department of the Ohio University in 1903. He was one of the first free city delivery mail carriers, having won the position by competitive examination.

Residence of Dr. and Mrs. Clarence L. Jones.

The residence here shown is the home of Dr. Clarence L. Jones on University Terrace, Athens, Ohio. The subject of this sketch was born in Parkersburg, W. Va., August 23, 1870 and when about 10 years old removed with his parents to Albany where he attended the public schools. He was a student for four years in the Ohio University, for one year in the medical department of the Rose Polytechnic school in Terre Haute, Indiana, then took a three years course in the University of Michigan, graduating from the Dental Department. He began the practice of his profession in 1894 at Glouster, O., where he remained one year, going to Albany he practiced two years before establishing an office in Athens where he has successfully practiced ever since.

In 1900 he became interested in the Home Telephone company and assumed the management, Dr. Perry L. Beal was taken into partnership in the dental office and looks after that business while Dr. Jones divides his time between dentistry and the management of the telephone business which has now assumed great proportions and therefore occupies a great portion of his time. The company was recently reorganized and capitalized at $100,000.

In October, 1899, Dr. Jones was married to Miss Vera M. Stewart of Albany. They have bright little twin boys born December 31, 1902.

The Devil's Tea Table, Near Mineral.

Nearly every county in Southern Ohio has its Devil's Tea Table, and Athens is not behind her sisters in this regard. Athens county's Devil's Tea Table is located a little to the north-west of Mineral and in plain view of that village. It is about thirty feet high, accessible only by ladder. If the devil ever took tea on this rock it was a long time ago, as the good people of Mineral have eliminated the "devil from their midst" even as a temporary guest, and the name if ever recalled is used as an antiquated by-word.

THOMAS G. ROBINSON was born in Ames township, Athens county, Ohio, September 10, 1858, on the farm now owned by Hugh Mathews, he being the eldest son of Mr. and Mrs. F. C. Robinson, and the grandson of John C. Robinson, one of Ames township's oldest settlers.

He was one of ten children, nine of whom are still living. His grandparents on his mother's side were Mr. and Mrs. Joseph Johnson. His grandmother Johnson lived to see her fifth generation.

Mr. Robinson moved with his parents from the farm on Peach Ridge to a farm near New England, Athens county; from there to a farm three miles northwest of Amesville on which his parents are still living, their children being all married and doing for themselves.

The subject of this sketch is a name-sake of Thomas Gardner, one of Ames township's first settlers. Mr. Robinson was married March 24, 1881, to Mary E. Wooley, the eldest daughter of Mr. and Mrs. Joshua Wooley, who was one of Ames township's prosperous farmers. Mr. Robinson and wife and their parents were all born in Ames township. He moved with his family to Alexander township March 12, 1883, on a farm purchased from Thomas Mulligan, on the head waters of Shadecreek, four miles north of Jerseyville. Their farm consists of 167 acres.

Mr. Robinson is one among the best stock raisers in his township, his principal stock consisting of Delane sheep and Durham cattle, with a good horse to sell once in a while. His family consists of his wife, two daughters and one son, Etna, Anna and Cecil.

Residence of Mr. and Mrs. S. Woodyard, in Alexander Township.

THE residence here shown is the home of Mr. and Mrs S. Woodyard, on what is known as the Walnut Grove farm, in Alexander township. Mr. Woodyard is the son of Isaac and Mary Woodyard, who were among the pioneer families of Athens county.

He was left an orphan at the age of nine years, from which time he was cared for by relatives until a young man of maturity, when he engaged in mercantile business, which he successfully followed for twenty-five years. At present he is engaged in the sheep and wool industry.

He was married to Miss Ida Brooks, and they have three children: Blanche, Bliss and Octa.

Residence of Mr. and Mrs. Oliver Ballenger, in Alexander Township.

OLIVER BALLENGER was born June 7, 1848, in Alexander township, Athens county, Ohio. He was the son of James and Susan Ballenger, who emigrated to this country from Michigan in 1828. At this time the country was an entire wilderness. In 1855 his father died, leaving him at the age of seven years to battle the cares of life without the hand of a father to guide him.

In 1870 he went west, returning to this county in the fall of 1872. He was married to Sarah C. Gillett. who was born in Adams county, Ind., in 1851, and moved to this county with her parents, George and Elizabeth Gillett, to Canaan township in 1857, and remained there until she was married.

To them were born eight children, seven of whom are living—four sons and three daughters: George L., Albert F., Clyde B., Alba H., Mrs. Effie Wooley, Mrs. Gertrude Seaman and Eva Ballenger.

Oliver Ballenger has devoted his entire life to farming, having resided on the same farm owned by his father. By close observation and dilligent effort he has become a practical farmer and successful man.

Another peculiar recreation was bee hunting and many sturdy pioneers boasted of this art. It consisted in quietly watching the bee as it gathered its store of sweetness from flower and leaf then following it to its home and marking the spot for future use. The honey was deposited high up in a hollow tree. In the fall when ready the tree was cut down and the honey gathered for family use for the winter. Several gallons were often found in one tree and honey was about the only food which the early settlers had in abundance.

SQUIRREL HUNTS.

Another favorite pastime was the squirrel hunt. This lacked the element of danger which made the others so exciting, but as all the pioneers needed to be expert shots the spirit of rivalry added its flavor to the sport. Two leaders were designated who chose their favorites as in a spelling match. A certain day, usually a month distant, was set for meeting to bring in the returns. Then every hunter hied him to the woods and did battle royal with the modest thrifty little squirrel. The admission fee to enter the race was usually a bushel of corn. On the appointed day the hunters met, produced the scalps, and the lucky side carrying away the corn divided it among themselves.

However, these hunts as the wolf hunts were demanded for protection of the settlers. The squirrels were a great nuisance and were found in countless numbers and unceasing vigilance was required on the part of the settler to protect his corn from their ravages. They were too common to be considered valuable for food and so destructive that the legislature took the matter in hand and enacted a law which had the double object of destroying the squirrels and providing the people with currency.

As elsewhere mentioned the greatest lack of the early settlers was money. While they might not suffer for food or clothing they lacked the cash wherewith even to pay taxes. This law passed in 1807 was entitled "An act to encourage the killing of squirrels" and provided for part of the taxes to be paid in squirrel scalps.

BEAR HUNTS.

The bear hunt was probably the most exciting event of the neighborhood. This was never done on the organized plan of the wolf hunt, but when any one discovered a bear he signaled for help by blowing a horn and started after the animal. All the men and boys within sound of the horn would drop their work and some on their horses with dogs at heels followed the horn. A good young bear would lead them a great chase sometimes lasting the whole day before it would become so exhausted as to take to a tree. There the dogs surrounded it and kept it until the hunter came up and a rifle shot made an end of bruin. The event ended with skinning the bear cutting up the carcass into as many pieces as there were hunters and each returned to his home with a nice supply of fresh meat which was considered quite a delicacy.

PIONEER WOMEN.

"What would the men of olden times have done if the women of olden times had not been with them." Aye! what would they have done without the cheery presence of the mothers in the home, for homes they were, crude as they were. Men had been here before; for fifteen years previous to the earliest settlements white hunters had wandered over this northwest territory. But not until the women came, were there homes and settlements established.

Oh the hardships they endured! Many came from as comfortable homes as America could boast in that day. Many were delicately reared, tenderly nourished; but brave at heart and loving they dared the unknown hardships of the unknown life because those they loved saw best to come.

Pittsburg seemed to be the objective point in crossing the mountains and it was possible to reach there in wagons. But there the wagons were exchanged for boats and after landings were made at the mouth of the Muskingum or Hocking, or at Pomeroy, the rest of the way must be on horseback, often with one baby in the arms and one and two children rode behind. Often in pouring rain everyone wet to the skin they journeyed on. Children taken ill by exposure and fatigue or the strange berries gathered along the way, must be carried in the mother's arms on the horse. Even after death had taken the suffering one, the mother might still cling to the little loved corpse and try to carry it to their destination that the grave might be within sight of the cabin door.

The new comers had no place to stay while their cabin was being built but crowded in with some earlier comer, who remembering her sore need in those days, was glad to help the strangers. Means to pay for such assistance was small and ate great bites in the family purse which contained all they had from the sale of the homestead in the east.

As quickly as the house was raised and some slight attempt at roofing protected them a little from the elements, the new comers were ensconced within their own four walls.

The mother and older children could assist at the "daubing" with mud of the chinks and crevasses. They might be compelled to live there some time before the chimney could be built and often be smoked out of the house by the green logs. Often it might be weeks before the father, busy with so many new duties and hampered by lack of means and implements, could make a door or window for the little cabin. An old quilt

(Continued on page 37.)

Residence of Mr. and Mrs. A. L. Johnson, Athens, Ohio.

A. L. JOHNSON, whose comfortable residence on Morris Ave., Athens, O., is here shown, was born in Ames township in 1862. He sold his farm of 127 acres in 1902 and moved to Athens where he has since been engaged in the livery business. He and his brother-in-law, John Howard, purchased a stable on Congress street, and in the spring of 1904, Mr. Johnson purchased his partner's interest and has successfully continued the business.

He was married to Miss Altha Howard, the daughter of W. M. Howard, March 29, 1883. They have had four children, Harry, who died at four and a half years; Constance, Vernie, Fay and Homer.

Mr. Johnson is one of a family of eleven children, eight of whom are still living. His father died when he was nineteen years old. Mr. and Mrs. Johnson own their own home and a 100 acre farm in Rome township.

⚜ The David Allen Homestead in Alexander Township. ⚜

◎   ◎   ◎   ◎

THE picture here shows one of the prettiest homes in Athens county. It is the late David Allen home three miles south of Athens in Alexander township. David Allen bought this place early in the 60's and after a few years sold it. He bought it again in 1876 and made his home here until his death in June, 1903. His wife whose maiden name was Mary Jane Wilkins, died in September, 1900, they having lived happily together for 61 years. They reared a family of seven children, all of whom survive them: Mrs. Townsend, wife of the late Major Chas. Townsend, ex-Secretary of the State of Ohio; Capt. Josiah B. Allen, recently clerk of the Supreme Court of Ohio; Mrs. C. Dent Gist, wife of Athens Postmaster; John H. Allen, George D. Allen, William A. Allen, and Mrs. Lillie A. Fuller. All of these are shown in the picture with Mr. and Mrs. Allen in the upper corner.

The residence is occupied by Mr. and Mrs. John Allen and family and William A. Allen, unmarried.

◎   ◎   ◎   ◎

The First National Bank, Athens, Ohio

THE First National Bank of Athens is the oldest financial institution in the county and was organized under Federal laws February 25, 1863, being the successor of a state bank organized in 1848. It was the two-hundred-and-thirty-third national bank in the United States and was capitalized at $50,000.

The first board of directors were N. L. Wilson, Judge John Welch, John Ballard, E. H. Moore, D. C. Skinner, Douglas Putnam and A. D. Brown.

E. H. Moore was the first president and was actively identified with its management as president and member of the directory until his death in 1900. A. D. Brown was the first cashier.

In 1870, the late Judge de Steiguer was elected vice-president and the late Thomas H. Sheldon, cashier. Mr. Sheldon served as cashier until 1882 when he resigned and went to Colorado and D. H. Moore was advanced to cashier, a position he holds today.

The First National with its 42 years of business is recognized as among the safe and conservative banks of the state. It has been made a United States depository and is entitled to the fullest confidence of the public. During all the financial storms that have passed over the country within the period of the banks history, no breath of suspicion has ever been uttered against the First National Bank of Athens.

Its present officers are Henry O'Bleness, president; C. L. Poston, vice-president; D. H. Moore, cashier, S. N. Hobson, assistant cashier; George De Camp and John B. Wood, tellers.

The Bank has resources of nearly $600,000.

Barrett Bros. Grocery, on Main Street, Athens, Ohio.

BARRETT BROS. GROCERY, ON MAIN STREET, ATHENS, OHIO.

THE accompanying picture gives one a good idea of the interior of Barrett Bros. grocery, on Main street, Athens, Ohio, one of the leading grocery firms in the city. Barrett Brothers came to Athens March 1st, 1904, and purchased the store of C. O. Moore & Co., who succeeded Cotton Bros. They had not been in business here for a week until they demonstrated to the public that they knew their business. As a result they have enjoyed a thrifty and increasing business, and today enjoy their share of the trade in Athens.

Barrett Bros. have been actively engaged in business for themselves since 1896, when they succeeded their father, J. P. Barrett, in the general store at Tupper's Plains. The store here is under the management of R. W. Barrett, and the store at Tupper's Plains is managed by J. A. Barrett.

Honesty, close attention to the wants of their customers and a good stock of goods have been the elements of their success here and at Tupper's Plains.

Both are young men and are deserving of the generous patronage that has been accorded them.

E. C. WOODWORTH'S RESIDENCE, ATHENS, OHIO.

Residence of Mr. and Mrs. George L. Pake, Marshfield, Ohio.

IN this picturesque country home, widely known for its hospitality, reside George L. Pake and Emma (Streight) Pake, his wife, with their daughter, Louise. At the time that Philip L. Pake lost his life in the Battle of the Wilderness, his son, the subject of this sketch, was about four years of age; the mother, Melissa Hopkins Pake, was left with three boys, the eldest being but six. Mr. Pake spent his early days on a farm in Meigs county, near the village of his nativity. But farming was not his calling, his mother discovered this, often finding him hidden away reading a book, when he had been sent to hoe in the garden. He is still a student having received three years of excellent training at the Soldier's Orphan's Home at Xenia, Ohio, followed by student life at the Atwood Institute at Albany, Ohio, and later at the Ohio Unillersity, from which he graduated in 1884.

Business life began immediately in employment with the B. & O. S-W. R. R., known at that time as the C. W. & B., at Marshfield, Ohio, which still claims him as a resident. In 1903 Mr. Pake represented the Ohio Division in a National convention of telegraphers in St. Louis. Educational work has also engaged his attention, he being joint author of "Aims and Means in Education," a book described by one as "a book from which not a word could be cut, and the work left complete."

Mr. Pake has recently severed his connection with the B. & O. to enter upon service as special Evangelist of the Railroad Y. M. C. A.

RESIDENCE OF MR. AND MRS. GEO. L. PAKE, MARSHFIELD, OHIO

MARSHAL PETER FINSTERWALD, ATHENS, OHIO

FEW men enjoy the honor of holding an office by popular vote for eighteen years, yet that is the record of Peter Finsterwald, whose picture is here shown. He was elected Marshal of Athens in 1881 and excepting six years when he directed his attention to his private business, he has been at the head of the police department of Athens ever since. He has not held the office through favoritism as the public has no favorites except where pre-eminent fitness and great efficiency is manifest.

Peter Finsterwald is one man in ten thousand as a police officer. Fearless, courageous, of iron will and bull-dog tenacity, he has only to be known to be respected. He is also a sleuth in tracking down criminals.

PETER FINSTERWALD

RESIDENCE OF MR. AND MRS. PETER FINSTERWALD, IN ROME TOWNSHIP.

In 1901 Athens was infested with a gang of desperate burglars. Finsterwald had them spotted and finally got onto a scheme of theirs to rob a rich widow in Gallipolis. Finsterwald organized a half dozen officers and stationed them in the widow's home the night the robbery was expected. The robbers came and were met by the officers armed to the teeth. A desperate fight ensued. A score of shots were fired. Williams and Lisle, the two robbers, were shot to death and Finsterwald was shot twice, one bullet piercing his breast just above the heart, and another making a flesh wound in his arm. He recovered, although his life was despaired of for a week or more. This

was the most serious incident of his life, but he has experienced hundreds possibly as dangerous.

Peter Finsterwald is a native of Athens county and served three years in the civil war as a member of Co. A., 92nd Regt. O. V. I., enlisting in 1862. While he lives in his own home on Second street in Athens, the home here shown is on his farm of 170 acres in Rome township, near Stewart.

Home of T. J. Herold, Athens, Ohio

THE rather unique picture here shown is the home and family of Thomas Jefferson Herold, on the corner of Dean avenue and Cemetery street, Athens, Ohio.

Mr. Herold is the son of Joseph Herold, deceased, and was born near Herold's Mill, west of Athens, May 1, 1842. Near the close of the civil war he enlisted as a soldier for five years in 141st Regiment, O. V. I., and served four months, when the war closed. Returning from the army, he went to Monday Creek, afterwards known as Floodwood, where he took charge of the business of his father, running a store, coal mine and farm. In 1877 he went to Armitage and purchased of his father the salt works at that place. After five years he came to town and built the building shown in the illustration, and started into the grocery and meat business, which he has continued ever since.

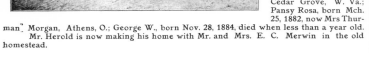

Mr. Herold was married to Miss McGonagle Sept. 2, 1869. One child was born in 1870 and both mother and child died. In '72 he was married to Miss Eunice Reynolds at Henry Herold's home by Rev. E. N. Nichols. They lived happily together until Mrs. Herold's death on August 24, 1903.

Mr. and Mrs. Herold are the parents of six children: Amy, born Aug. 28, 1873, now Mrs. U. M. McCaughey, of Akron, O.; Joseph W. Herold, born April 12, 1875, now agent of the K. & M. Ry., at Charleston, W. Va.; Mabel Maud born April 6, 1877, now Mrs. E. C. Merwin, Athens, O.; Herbert J., born Jan. 21, 1880, now agent of the K. & M. Ry., at Cedar Grove, W. Va.; Pansy Rosa, born Mch. 25, 1882, now Mrs Thurman Morgan, Athens, O.; George W., born Nov. 28, 1884, died when less than a year old.

Mr. Herold is now making his home with Mr. and Mrs. E. C. Merwin in the old homestead.

Residence of Mr. and Mrs. Evan J. Jones, Athens, Ohio.

THE home here shown in the illustration is the handsome residence of Mr. and Mrs. Evan J. Jones, on University Terrace, Athens, Ohio. It is located east of the north end of the historic campus of the Ohio University, the most beautiful natural forest park in Ohio.

Mr. Jones has been practicing law in Athens since 1874, and has been very successful in his profession. He came up from the lowly walks of life and by his own efforts secured his education and made an honored place for himself at the bar and as a citizen of the town.

He was born in Centerville, Gallia county, O., Oct. 3, 1849. His mother died when he was eight years old, and he remained with his father's family until he was sixteen. He attended Ewington Academy, the Normal University at Lebanon, and entered the Ohio University in 1869, and graduated with the class of 1873, maintaining himself in the meantime by teaching. In 1875 he was admitted to the bar, and formed a partnership with the late Hon. Charles Townsend. In 1878 he formed a partnership with Hon. Charles Grosvenor, and has been associated with him ever since, the firm name now being Grosvenor, Jones & Worstell.

Mr. Jones was married to Miss Lucy Johnson, of Pennsylvania, Dec. 17, 1879. They have five children: Helen, who died in infancy; Albert J., Evan, Rodger and Ruple.

Mr. Johnson has held many positions of trust in his profession, and has been a Trustee of Ohio University since 1893.

THIS beautiful country place is the home of Mr. and Mrs. Nathan W. Baker, and is located in Athens township, in what is known as the "Baker Settlement," on Margaret's Creek. The picture speaks more than words of the thrift and special care taken of this ideal farm home.

The "Baker Settlement" was originally made up of the sons of Jacob Baker, but as time passed the boys scattered and are living in different parts of the country. Nathan W., however, the subject of this sketch, still retains his property here although he has not lived on the place since 1896, when he and his excellent wife took charge of the Athens County Infirmary, as Superintendent and Matron.

Jacob Baker, the father, was born here in 1815, on the farm now owned by W. E. Baker. His father, Isaiah, came to this locality in 1814, from Barnstable, Mass., and was thus one of the pioneer settlers of Athens county. Isaiah's father was born in England, and when a mere lad out looking for the cows, he was enticed on board a ship by the sailors and brought to this country.

Ruth Reynolds Baker, the mother of Nathan W., was born Aug. 18, 1816, and after the death of her husband, made her home with her youngest son, W. E. Baker, on the old homestead until her death, Dec. 1, 1904. She was a noble

NATHAN W. BAKER.

Christian woman and much beloved by her family and acquaintances.

Nathan W. was born November 13, 1844. He led the ordinary life of a farmer boy, and growing to manhood he was married to Miss Almira Herron, the daughter of the late William Herron, of Waterloo township, January 28, 1868. They have no children. In 1873, Mr. Baker bought the farm shown in the picture, and while he carried on a general farming business. he began in 1871 to make a specialty of breeding and raising Short Horn Durham cattle. His first cow was purchased in Fayette county and cost him $410 at public auction. With this he started a herd of Short Horns and is in the business today, the illustration showing two of his herd.

Mr. Baker traveled at one time 1200 miles to buy a bull calf that cost him $400. He will introduce into his herd nothing but the best and has been satisfied with nothing but the highest excellence in breeding and therein his success lies. He never maintains a herd of over twenty-five and finds ready sale for calves at $50 to $300. He has exhibited his stock at county and state fairs for the past thirty years, and almost in-

variably captures the first prize. Charles Oxley has had charge of the farm since Mr. Baker left it in 1896, and takes care of the high bred stock.

Mr. and Mrs. Baker have the undisputed record of being the most efficient managers that ever held the position of Superintendent and Matron at the County Infirmary. Their nine years' service at the institution have proven that they are admirably adapted for the place. They did not seek the place in fact the position sought them through the Board of Infirmary Directors. Mr. and Mrs. Baker were reluctant to leave their pleasant home in the country, but after careful consideration they were impressed the more that it was a duty and accepted the trust.

Mr. Baker has served as expert judge of cattle and in sweepstakes at the State fair. He is a member of the State and National Board of Charities and Correction, has been a member of the Board of Directors of the Athens' County Agricultural Society for twenty-five years, and served several terms as President of the Board.

He was recently appointed by Governor Herrick as a delegate to the National meeting of the Board of Charities and Correction at Portland, Oregon.

CALM WOODLAND 6
Picture taken when a year old. At twenty months she weighed 1397 pounds.
Bred and owned by N. W. Baker.

ROYAL NONPAREIL
Age thirty months and weighs 2152 pounds. Bred and owned by N. W. Baker.

D. ZENNER & CO. Athens, Ohio

THE handsome three-story pressed brick building here shown in the illustration is the home of the D. Zenner & Co. store, the oldest commercial business in Athens and is the largest and most progressive retail store in the county. David Zenner, who founded this business, and whose name is yet used, died in 1891, but the principle of strict business integrity, which is the bulwark and corner-stone of the store, still lives in the present management.

David Zenner came to Athens from Cincinnati in the spring of 1853, at the time of the construction of the old Marietta & Cincinnati railroad, now known as the B. & O. S-W. Ry. Mr. Zenner came to establish a temporary store, and opened a stock of goods in the Stewart building standing on the site of the building now owned by the Knights of Pythias lodge. The store was afterwards moved to the Bayard Ullom building, then to the First National Bank building for twelve years and in 1872 moved to the present location on Main street.

In these years there were several changes in the firm. First D. Zenner then Zenner & Golden, then D. Zenner, then Zenner & Golden. and finally Zenner alone 'till 1867 when the firm became known as D, Zenner & Co., when Mr. John Friday went into the firm and continued until 1875. Mr. Leopold Friday became an active member of the firm in 1875. In 1887, Mr. John Friday died and Mr. Henry

RETAIL DRY GOODS AND CLOTHING STORE OF D. ZENNER & CO.

THE LATE DAVID ZENNER.

Zenner the son of David Zenner became a member of the firm. In 1901 Mr. Leopold Friday died and Mr. Zenner became sole owner. In all respect to his predecessors, Mr. Zenner gave the business a new life. introducing modern ideas and is today the recognized leader in retail merchandising in Southern Ohio. In 1902 he bought the business room adjoining to the south, remodeled the entire buildings and added a third story.

Modern fronts and beautiful show windows have displaced the common place, an elevator has been put in for the convenience of customers, the building beautifully lighted inside and out with hundreds of electric lights, a cash carrier system has been installed and in short, every modern convenience and equipment has been added. While his leading lines are Dry Goods and Clothing he has each year added different departments and the store is now more on the plan of a department store. Thirty clerks are regularly employed and in the busy season this number is often doubled.

Residence of Mr. and Mrs. Henry O'Bleness, Athens, Ohio

HENRY O'BLENESS, born in Newport, Ohio, on the Ohio River above Marietta, June 16, 1842, has been a resident of Athens since 1869. Mr. O'Bleness worked at the carpenter trade in home village and in Marietta where he early began contracting. When 26 years of age he secured the contract for the carpenter work of the Athens Asylum and was engaged on this work for five years. Since then he has built entire nearly all the later buildings of this institution.

He has been largely engaged in building construction in Ohio and West Virginia where for a number of years he was erecting public buildings among which is the State Hospital for the Insane at Spencer. Many of the larger buildings of Athens were built by him.

In a business way Mr. O'Bleness has been identified with Athens development. He was an organizer and for several years general manager of the Athens Brick Co., and one of the reorganizers of the Athens Foundry and Machine Company, is president of the First National Bank of Athens, a director of the Peoples Bank of Nelsonville, and a stockholder of the Nelsonville Brick Co.

He served on the Athens Board of Education for 21 years and for 15 years was President. He also was Water works trustee four years during which time the system was installed, and as a member of the present Board of Public Service which installed the municipal electric light plant. In 1901 he was appointed a trustee of the O. U. by Gov. Nash. He served during the Civil War in Co. F. 85th O. V. I. and Co. G. 148 O. V. I.

Mr. O'Blenness was married to Josephine M. Shearer, of Belpre, Ohio, in March 1871, and four children were born to them: Harry C., secretary and treasurer of the Athens Foundry & Machine Co; Charles G., secretary and treasurer of the Nelsonville Brick Co;. Ralph A., deceased, and Mary L. O'Bleness.

h'ang at these openings was all the protection from driving storms and howling wolves. This furnished no obstruction against the immense snakes which sometimes found their way in, attracted by the warmth.

Much labor and unremitting toil have rid the bottoms of their swampy marshes and miasmas but the early comers suffered with the "shaking agu" chills and fever, a sickness incident to all new countries which often attacked the entire family at once. So the faithful mother had the duties of nurse added to all her other cares. A woman's work was never done for continually more hands were needed to plow, to sow, to get in the seed, or to gather the crops at the most propitious time and the mother's hands were always ready to help. Then in the evening while the men rested she stood spinning the material for clothing for all which she made by the flickering candle light after the rest were in bed asleep. They had little clothing save what was carded, spun, woven and made into wearing apparel by her own hands. They had few cooking utensils and little in variety to cook—were often compelled to live on hominy for weeks at a time and the only bread might be made from corn ground in a hand mill or pounded in an improvised mortar, a hole burned in a stump. So with this multiplicity of duties the pioneer woman worked and struggled. Proudly and uncomplainingly she made the rude cabin a home of love and happiness. All blessings and honor to the memories of these heroic women who bravely bore their share of the trials and burdens of those times, and when we praise the pioneers who "blazed" the way to a higher civilization for the sake of generations then unborn, let us always remember the pioneers were not only men but women. God bless them.

HARDSHIP AND INCONVENIENCES.

The hardships of pioneer life to the delicately nurtured young folks of to-day would seem unbearable, but those who endured them thrived. They became our great men and the mothers of our great men in every walk of life. The log cabins were built with the kindly assistance of neighbors who came to the "house raising" and made a gala day of it. In earliest times houses were made without nails or any tools, save an ax, saw and auger and the work was most laborious. No wonder that they consisted of but one room with a loft. Let the family number six or sixteen the single room answered for all purposes, kitchen, dining room, living room, bed room and guest chamber. Friends were always welcome—strangers were rarely turned from the door if seeking either food or shelter.

One bed was built into the walls when the house was built. This being ample, generally supplied the older members of the family. A huge trundle bed which in the daytime rolled under the large bed was filled with all the remaining youngsters packed in as sardines in a box, feet together and heads sticking out both sides. When strangers asked for a night's lodging or friends a few miles distant came to spend a day and night and brought their family, ingenuity was taxed to the utmost to provide for all. The large bed with true hospitality was always given up to the new comers be they one or many.

The young bride of to day equipped by means of linen shower, tin shower, etc., would be at a loss to prepare a meal with the crude accoutrements of those days. The immense open log fire overhung with hooks from which various sized pots could be suspended, sometimes as many as four would be boiling at once. A wild turkey or spare ribs to roast, were hung up by a string with a dish underneath to catch the drippings. Down in the ashes in front, bread, biscuits and cakes were baked. Late the "Dutch-oven" came into use which was a huge iron pot with lid. It was placed on coals and with coals on top of it made a very hot oven for baking quickly. It is said that the flavors of dinners thus prepared are never equaled now with gas ranges and granite wear and the many germicidal protectives and preventives of to-day.

Added to the many cares of the brave women of that early day was the necessity of spinning and weaving the clothing worn by the family. Not few were the women who boast of having planted the flax tended and gathered it, spun, woven, dyed, cut, fitted and sewed the clothing she wore.

Let it not be thought that because clothing was so primitive dame fashion passed by these early settlers. Clothing was still more meager with our first progenitors yet they made it a vital subject of thought and discussion. In 1800 both men and women went bareheaded and barefooted as long as the weather permitted. In the winter the men wore home-made woolen caps and leather moccasins which but poorly protected their feet while pantaloons of deerskins and a home-made garment of "linsey woolsey" belted in, took the place of shirt and coat; an extra cape for protection in storm completed their wardrobe. Later the fur caps of raccoon's skins with the tail dangling behind, fur coats and rawhide boots began to make their appearance.

The young people usually walked to church carrying their shoes and stockings and put them on near the church door.

The women could only seek variety by the various ways in which they applied the few available dyes to their home wrought materials and the manner of decorating their moccasins. No settlement was very old before the traditional peddler began to find his way there from eastern markets with his gay cotton handkerchiefs, glass beads, calf skin shoes, gaudy calicoes and bright ribbons. By 1830 the Kentucky jeans had replaced all else for men's clothing and gradually the Godey, Demorest and Harper's Bazar fashion magazines began to whisper of Paris' latest fashions and pioneer life had moved leagues to the west, we were becoming a much civilized community.

(Continued on page 29)

J. R. HARVEY, General Merchandise.

GENERAL STORE OF J. R. HARVEY, ATHENS, OHIO.

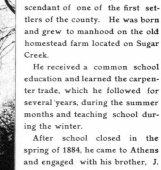MR. HARVEY is a native of Athens county and a descendant of one of the first settlers of the county. He was born and grew to manhood on the old homestead farm located on Sugar Creek.

He received a common school education and learned the carpenter trade, which he followed for several years, during the summer months and teaching school during the winter.

After school closed in the spring of 1884, he came to Athens and engaged with his brother, J. H. Harvey, as clerk which occupation he followed until late in the following fall when he returned to the country to teach a winter's term of school. At the close of the term he returned to Athens and purchased the stock of general merchandise of his brother and began business for himself, where he has been ever since.

The location is one block east of the K. & M. depot on the north side of Dean avenue. He carries a general line of staple and fancy groceries, dry goods, notions, fruits, hardware, boots and shoes, glass and queensware and almost anything found in a general store.

In August, 1904, he rented a room in the Foley & Walsh building, opposite the old stand, and moved his grocery store there, separating it from his general stock, and is now using both stores with quite a degree of increased business.

Mr. Harvey is among Athens' most highly respected citizens, a pleasant gentleman and an honest man. He has served as a member of the city Council and on the board of Water Works Trustees, where he satisfactorily discharged his duties.

GROCERY STORE OF J. R. HARVEY, DEAN AVENUE, ATHENS.

RESIDENCE OF MR. AND MRS. THOMAS J. HAMILTON, IN MARSHFIELD, OHIO.

THOMAS J. HAMILTON was born April 15, 1834, near Pottsville, Pennsylvania, the son of Samuel and Eliza Hamilton. He moved with his parents to Washington county, O. when ten years old. In 1857 he was married to Miss Anna Cox and three years later they moved to Mineral, in Athens county, and have resided since in Waterloo township. His present home, which is shown in the illustration, is in Marshfield. Mr. and Mrs. Hamilton are the parents of ten children, five boys and five girls. Five children are still living: John E., Garrison J., Thomas F., Nancy J. Hysell and Hattie B. Todd.

At the outbreak of the civil war, Mr. Hamilton answered the call to arms and enlisted in Co. C, 18th Regt., O. V. I., and served his country for three years. He participated in the battles of Stone River, Chicamauga, Lookout Mountain, Mission Ridge and numerous smaller engagements. Returning home from the army he took up the duties of a private citizen with as little ostentation as when he offered his life as a sacrifice on his country's altar.

THE residence here shown is known as the Clem Hooper farm in Alexander township, now the home of Mr. and Mrs. John F. Davis. This is one of the best hill farms in the county. Mr. and Mrs. Davis purchased and moved onto this place in 1903, and expect to make it their home.

Mr. Davis was the son of Joseph and Alvira Davis and was born September 4, 1861. Most of his life has been spent on a farm, his experience being varied by several years in the shoe business in Athens.

He was married to Miss Mary E. Armitage, daughter of Hiram Armitage in November, 1873. They lived on the home farm near Nelsonville for two years and then moved to Athens, then back to the farm. Afterwards they resided on the Hiram Connett farm where they lived for about six years, and before moving to Alexander they lived five years on the Joseph Dorr farm, west of Athens.

Mr. and Mrs. Davis have reared an interesting family and are highly respected by their neighbors and friends.

C. E. White, Furniture, Carpets and Undertaking, Coolville, Ohio.

MY father J. L. White, established the Undertaking business here in 1865. At his death in 1878, I took charge of the business and continued the Undertaking business alone until 1882, when I formed a partnership with J. K. Davis and added Furniture and Carpets to the business under the firm name of Davis & White.

Mr. Davis died two years later, and I bought the business and built the building which I now occupy, and have conducted the Furniture, Undertaking and Carpet business since that time under the name of C. E. White.

Dr. J. C. Coleman.

Dr. Coleman is a familiar character, known to every man, woman and child in Waterloo township, where he has successfully practiced his profession for the past twenty-five years. For seventeen years his office and home was in Mineral, but for the past eight years he has lived in Marshfield and enjoys a lucrative practice.

In the dark days of the early sixties Dr. Coleman answered his country's call to arms and enlisted in Co. C., 3rd Regt., O. V. I., under Captain Dana and continued in the service four years. He graduated from the M. E. Institute in Cincinnati. He is a thorough going republican and withal a genial and popular man.

E. B. Clarke.

One of the well-known citizens of Athens county, was employed several years in county offices and postoffice at Marietta. Next he was employed with the Marietta & Cincinnati R. R. as telegraph operator, agent and superintendent of telegraph. Was first superintendent of telegraph of Hocking Valley R. R., and was its Athens' agent for sixteen years. Spent some time in the south by advice of physicians and in 1894 returned to Athens and engaged in Real Estate business, and is now proprietor of Clarke's Real Estate Agency.

Mr. and Mrs. Clarke have a comfortable new home just completed, which they occupy on South College street, Athens, Ohio.

CHAIN OF LAND TITLES.

The lots on which the court house and jail stands were, of course, on the land granted for university purposes. The town of Athens being, in 1811 duly incorporated the trustees of the Ohio university were authorized and directed to lease to the county commissioners on a nominal rent, for ninety-nine years, renewable forever, the lots on which the court house and jail now stand.

The Ohio university derived its title through the board of treasury, authorized by Congress to give two complete townships for the uses of a university near the center of the Ohio Co's purchase. This title from the United States government was signed by George Washington, president, dated Oct. 17, 1787. The United States derived its title from the State of Virginia by deed of cession, signed by Thomas Jefferson, Samuel Hardy, Arthur Lee and James Monroe, delegates from the common wealth of Virginia in the second Colonial Congress authorized by an act of Virginia dated October. 20 1783 "an act to authorize the delegates of the state in congress to convey to the United States in congress assembled all right of this common wealth to the territory northwest of the Ohio river" the deed of cession being dated March 1, 1784. The State of Virginia derived its title from James I. King of England by charter dated May 23, 1609. Great Britain derived its title by right of discovery of Sebastian Cabot in 1498.

EARLY MILLS AND MILLING.

Probably the greatest need which met the first settlers was a mill to grind their corn and wheat. As soon as their clearings were made and planted the virgin soil rapidly produced the harvest, but it could not be utilized for food in that state. The farmer must "sack up" his grist, place it on his horse and ride to mill there to await his turn. All mills had small capacity and sometimes the farmer must preserve himself in patience for two or even several days before he could get his chance at the mill—then grind his own flour and start on his homeward journey.

The need was so great and millers were so weclomed that the settlers for miles around would gladly unite and give their services for erection of both dam and mill.

The earliest comers in Athens county got their grists ground by carrying it horseback down into Washington county to the Ohio or over to the Muskingum river. These were tedious journeys occupying a week or more depending on the load.

The first grist mill to be built in this county was by John Hewitt in 1800 on Margaret Creek about three miles from Athens. This was so successful and so widely patronized that another one was soon built by Charles Shepard in Alexander township.

The first mill on the Hocking was built in 1806. "An act authorizing Jehiel Gregory and John Havner their heirs and assigns to erect a mill dam across the Hock-hocking river" was the first law passed in the state relative to the construction of dams or navigation of any streams. This act demanded that the

DR. ULYSSES P. WHITE, whose beautiful modern home here shown in the illustration, is located on College street, Athens, Ohio, is an example of what a poor young man may accomplish when he sets about it in earnest to do it. His mother, Mrs. Mary J. White, owns and occupies one-half of the house.

Dr. White was born in Dover township, Athens county, on March 3, 1868, and grew to manhood in that vicinity, receiving such education as the community afforded until he was able to merit a certificate to teach school. He attended the Ohio University one year and taught school two years before deciding to study medicine. He became a pupil of Drs. Primrose & Hyde in Nelsonville, in about 1891, and after reading medicine for two years, spent one year in the Medical College of Cincinnati and then two years in the College of Physicians and Surgeons in Baltimore, Md., graduating from that institution in the spring of 1894.

He began the practice of his profession in Chauncey and remained there for five years, the last four of which, however, he was in partnership with Dr. W. T. Sprague. They enjoyed a large practice.

Dr. White came to Athens in September, 1900, and has built up one of the largest clienteles in the city. Since 1901 he has been associated with Dr. J. T. Merwin. Dr. White was married to Miss Ida Sanner, a native of Hocking county, June 18, 1893.

The Athens Concrete Block Company furnished the blocks in the construction of this modern and beautiful home.

---

dam should be made with a lock or apron "coonstructed in such a manner that the free navigation of the river shall not be obstructed." Also required them to pilot all persons or crafts through and forbid accepting a fee for same. This dam was built in 1805, and the mill later known as Gregory's mill built in 1806 east of town, where Barth's mill now stands. This has been a flouring mill site occupied continuously ever since. The earliest mills were very crude affairs, but soon gave way to a better class. In 1832 J. B. and R. W. Miles built a large three-story mill on this site putting in machinery of more modern nature and greater capacity. The Herrold mill, west of Athens, as it is called, was built by Capt. Silas Bingham in 1816. About this time small hand mills began to be seen. A man named Musselman, one of the first men to settle in Vinton county discovered there beds of stone suitable for mill burrs and manufactured these small mills which he peddled over the sparsely settled country.

Until quite recent years the "grist" system of milling prevailed. The farmer took his sack of grain to be ground, waited for it, and paid, as tole, one-eighth, which the miller was allowed by law. The farmer carried home not only the flour, but the bran and middlings as well. Many men, living today can remember how big they felt when as small boys, they were entrusted with the grist and seated on the old horse with bags before and bags behind, they proudly started on their first trip alone. Many also remember the agony of fright when on their way home after dark they heard the howling of the wolves afar coming nearer, and many a boy has drawn up his legs high and

(Continued on page 43.)

Residence of Mrs. Martha Wolfe, Athens, O.

ONE of the prettiest and most comfortable residences in Athens is here shown. It is the home of Mrs. Martha Wolfe and her two sons, Arthur A. and Ned J., and is located on the corner of College and Mill streets, facing College street.

Mrs. Wolfe is the widow of the late Stacy F. Wolfe, who was born in Morgan county, near Glouster, in 1856, and died at his home here March 23, 1898. Mr. Wolf was for a number of years connected with the Trimble Mill Company and Trimble Hardware Company before he came to Athens in about 1902, when he became largely interested in the Athens Lumber company and at the time of his death was president and manager. Mr. Wolfe was a public spirited citizen and his loss to Athens was surpassed only by the loss to his family.

Arthur A. is engaged in the Feed Store business on North Court St., Athens, and Ned is employed by the Glouster branch of the Athens Lumber company.

STACEY F. WOLFE, (deceased)

LODGES AND FRATERNAL ORDERS.

Paramuthia Lodge, No. 25, F. & A. M., Athens, Ohio.

Date of Charter, October 2d, 1814.

Alderman, Wm. N.
Armstrong, Harry O
Armstrong, Will P.
Atkinson, A. A.
Anderson, Arthur
Baird, Augustus
Baker, Fred R.
Bean, C. Leroy
Bean, Elijah
Bentley, W. B.
Bethel, A. S.
Bessor, G. O.
Biddison, Elmer G.
Biddle, Thos. R.
Biddle, David H.
Boldman, C. F.
Brown, Wm. H.
Burchfield, D. M.
Bush, Fred W.
Campbell, John C.
Carpenter, Rufus
Chubb, E. W.
Cline, J. Halliday
Clayton, Jefferson B.
Cotton, Horatio M.
Courtney, A. V. M.
Copeland, Chas. M.
Cornwell, Chas. A.
Covert, B. M.
Doan, Frank C.
Dike, Francis H.
Dunnington, J. E.
Dyson, George C.
Evans, D. J.
Finsterwald, John
Foster, Israel M.
Frame, Agustus J.
Frame John A.
Fulton, James B.
Fuller, Carl
Fuller, Dudley D.
Gibson, Frank W.
Golden, William B.
Goodspeed, Jos. M.
Grosvenor, Chas. H.
Guenther, Fred L.
Goldsberry, F. E.
Henke, Daniel W.
Haning, Harley H.
Harris, C. Watson
Harris, Charles A.
Harris, Curtis V.
Harris, Leander
Hastings, William J.
Headley, Burley A.
Henderson, C. B.
Henry, H. Dow
Hibbard, S., Hadley
Hibbard, William A.
Higley Brewster O.
Higgins, Judiah
Hobson, Samuel N.
Hopkins, Charles D.
Howe Edward W.
Hummel Charles F.
Hutchinson F. W.
Hysell Francis H.
Jennings, Ebenezer
Jewett, Leonidas M.
Johnson, John P.
Jones, James A.
Jones, D. D.
Jones, D. L.
Keller, Frank E.
Kern, Peter
Kern, Clifford G.
King, G. Walton
Kinkead, John P.
Kyle, James
Lash, Eli R.
Lash, E Ray
Leland, Wirt
Lewis, Amanson M.
Logan, Frank H.
McClanahan, James
McClanahan, J. C.
McCune, Samuel L.
McKee, Wilson H.
McLean, Ciny
McVay, Frank P.
Merwin, J. T.
Merwin, E. C.
Mercer, W. F.
Millikan, Charles C.
Mirick, George P.
Moore, W. R.
Newsom, Charles, S.
O'Bleness, Henry
O'Bleness, Chas. G.
Palmer, James A.
Peoples, David W.
Phillips, Harvey F.
Pickering, Bell W.
Pickering, Joseph L.
Port, Luke A.
Potter, Charles W.
Richards, James S.
Richards, Paschal L
Rigg, Parker
Robinson, Harry
Rouse, Eli
Sacket, Lawrence A.
Sands, Joshua
Schrantz, Tod L.
Schrantz, James W.
Scott, Charels H.
Scott, Wilbur F.
Scott, Winfield K.
Sewell, Chas. V.
Secoy, Wilbur M.
Smith, Clarence W.
Smith, David J.
Smith, John W.
Snow, John E.
Snow, C. A.
Sommer, Sam,
Souls, G. W.
Spicer, John
Stalder, Fred
Stalder, Harry G.
Starcher, William E
Sedman, Frank G.
Thompson, C. H.
Thompson, S. David
Townsend, C. H.
Ullom, A. W.
Walker, George R
Warden, Timothy B.
Webster Harry M.
Winters, Samuel G.
Wilson, Charles L.
Wilson, Hiram R
Woodworth, F. L.
Worstell, L. G.
Zenner Henry

Constitution Lodge, No. 426, F. & A. M., Marshfield, O.

Date of Charter, 1869.

Arnold, G. W.
Arbaugh, H. D.
Barron, Joseph
Brown, E. H.
Betts, Frank
Bailey, W. H.
Braley, J. E.
Burt, Charles
Boden, J N.
Barker, F. M.
Barker, Jos.
Boyles, M. A.
Burt, F. J.
Carmichael, R.
Carmichael, R. L.
Cox, Edward
Clark, Joshua
Condiff, J. A.
Cook, Lutulis
Conkey, O. B.
Diver, James
Dixon A. H.
Downard, H. M.
Dumaree, C. H.
Davis, A. S.
Davis, Edward
Davis, R. W.
Dunfee, G. W.
Doolittle, M.
Doolittle, F.
Enderlin, R. P.
Frank, Geo.
Gieseke, Wm.
Gieseke, H. W.
Gould, Wm.
Hunter G. A.
Hunter, L. E.
Hunter, A. O.
Hysell, Rock
Haysen, Jas.
Hewitt, H. N.
Hewitt, J. C.
Hester, C. V.
Harris, G. K.
Herron, W. M.
Imes, R. P.
Jones, J. H.
Jones, Eber
Johnson, J. W.
Knowlton, C. L.
Lowrey, V. C.
Lighfritz, P. B.
Lippenscott J.
Lax, Thomas
Lostro, J. R.
McClure, C. F.
McArthur, C.
Mourne, J. E.
McVay, F. H.
Mallen, Hugh
McLead, I. N.
McHarg, J. M.
Nicholas, Ardy
Perrin, D. A.
Pierce, C. C. Jr.,
Pierce, C. C.
Pierce, W. E.
Pedigo, S. E. G.
Pake, G. L.
Phillips, F. P.
Rhorick, E. L.
Rankin, Jas.
Stewart, F. L.
Smith, C. F.
Sturgill, F.
Sturgill, Wm.
Sherman, J. J.
Stewart, J. M.
Todd, Curtis.
Wilkes, J. F.
Watkins, F.
Wise, Mat
Wilson, P. B.

Trimble Lodge, No. 557, F. & A. M., Trimble, Ohio.

Date of Charter, Oct. 23, 1889.

Allen, J. M.
Allen, A. B.
Andrews, B. A.
Brown, B.
Brown, J. C.
Brown, A. L.
Brown, Iden
Brinning, C. J.
Blackburn, J. C.
Carpenter, J. E.
Cooley, H. E.
Cornwell, G. Fred
Charles, David
Dupler, Harry G.
Danford, H. D.
Danford, S. J.
Danford, E. F.
Danford, S. S.
Danford, V. G.
Duncan, W. H.
Duncan, J. C.
Davis, G. A.
Davis, M. O.
Drury, E. E.
Francis, J.
Fierce, J. H.
Fierbaugh, O. S.
Griffith, D. R.
Hodgson, J.
Hutchinson, H. L.
Harley, Harry
Hilt, W. C.
Hatton, Chas. L.
Hyde. W. H.
Johnson, W. B.
Johnson, S. H.
Jones, E. L.
Jones, Fred L.
James, William
Koons, F. M.
Koons, E. S.
Kantz, John E.
Law, Daniel W.
Lewis, D. R.
Lewis, Thos. D.
Lewis, S. J.
Lawrence, E. I.
Murphey, A.

Trimble Lodge—Continued.

Moorfield, J. H.
Morgan, J. W.
Morris, Elza
Morris R. H.
McElfresh, W. A.
Needy, S. W.
Nelson, Alex
Penrod, J. J.
Payne, Francis
Perry, John
Pettit, H. E.
Pride, C. A.
Rhodes, J. M.
Raber, J. W.
Richards, C. L.
Sands, D. T.
Stahl, W. H.
Spurier, N.
Thomas, D. C.
Thomas, J. D.
Wilson, W. R.
Woodhouse, Fred
Wyper, W. C.
Wolfe, G. H.
Williams, D. H.
Wheatley, J. W.
Williams, Chas.
Woodbridge, H. S.
Young, A. C.
Zimmerman, G. A.

Amesville Lodge, No. 278, F. & A. M., Amesville, Ohio.

Date of Charter, October 1858.

Brawley E. H.
Balderson, Seth
Balderson, F. O.
Baird, Waldo
Beasley, F. J.
Brill, D. W.
Boileau, William
Cellars, W. F.
Curfman, O. A.
Clark, W. E.
Clark, T. E.
Davis, Porter
Davis, Chas.
Deweese, George E.
Dempster L. H.
Ellis, J. F.
Frash, C. I.
Fleming, G. L.
Grandstaff, J. J.
Galbrath, S. A.
Gilligan, Jas.
Glazier, E. F.
Grosvenor, John H.
Holdcraft, R. E.
Henry, Z. L.
Henry, Herbert H.
Henry, Heber H.
Harris, L. W.
Harris, William E.
Hamilton, Ed.
Hill, Olive E.
Hill, Wm. E.
Johnson, J. H.
Keirns, R. R.
Linscott, B. W.
Linscott, Harvey
Linscott, G. Owen
Linscott, G. W.
Linscott, S. P.
McCune, L. P.
McCune, C. B.
McCune, F. M.
McCune, A. L.
McCune, S. R.
McGraw, J. R.
Marquis, J. A.
Moore, Jas. G.
Nice, C. A.
Ogg, C. J.
Ogg, A. L.
Ogg, Arhthur
Ogg, Leonard
Phillips, John
Phillips, W. B.
Rathburn, D. L.
Riggs, J. H.
Rutledge, H. B.
Smith, E. A.
Slowter, William
Stiers, F. J.
Snedeker J. C.
Sager, J. A.
Sprague, J. E.
Totman, Geo.
Totman, M. P.
Totman, S. E.
Townsend, H. H.
VanValey, C. J.
Wells, S. J.
Wickham J. R.
Warrener, W. J.
Wyatt, G. E.
Wilder, J.
Young, H. C.

Albany Lodge, No. 156, F. & A. M., Albany, Ohio.

Date of Charter, September 27, 1848.

Blake, W. W.
Baughman, Jesse
Bartley, F. A.
Biddle, A. C.
Biddle, J. S.
Brooks, T. B.
Brown, J. N.
Coe, T. W.
Chase, J. U.
Carpenter, J. L.
Carpenter, R. S.
Carpenter, Jno. L.
Cline, J. H.
Castor, O. W.
Crossen, J. K.
Crossen, W. E.
Crossen R. J.
CrossenK. T.
Canny, F. G.
Chase, H. M.
Coe, P. V.
Dickson, M. J.
Dickson, D. C.
Dickson, J. W.
Dickson, I. N.
Dixon, M. A.
Dailey, A. C.
Dailey, W. B.
Dailey, E. T.
Dailey, O. D.
Dent, E. A.
Duffey, T. W.
Daines, Frank
Galaway, J. M.
George, J. F.
Holmes, A. F.
Haning, J. P.
Haning H. E.
Irwin W. H.
Irwin T. C.
Kern, G. H.
Knowlton, Elsw.
Lee, T. W.
Lowther, Frank
Moore, J. C. P.
Murphey, O. B.
Murphey, F. R.
Murphey, C. W.
Martin, W. H.
Martin, J. R.
Martin, Lee
Mohler, J. H.
Minear, A. D.
Minear, H. W.
McKinstry, D. A. R.
McDonagle, R. B.
McComas, I. E.
McCarty, J. H.
Matheny, H. A.
Patterson, M. E.
Patterson, R. M.
Pride, W. A.
Rossetter, T. K.
Rossetter, C. M.
Rossetter, L. T.
Rossetter, J. G.
Rutherford, E. W.
Richey, Peter
Robinet, F. M.
Radcliff, H. J.
Robinson, A. C.
Reeder, H. A.
Rathburn, L. D.
Swett, G. D.
Smith, W. B.
Stanley, A. L.
Stanley, A. C.
Stanley, E. I.
Shaffer, D. W.
Shaffer, W. G.
Scott, A. M.
Sharp, D. B.
Sharp, Chas. F.
Sharp, W. L.
Townsend, W. H.
Turner, D. H.
Vorhes, B. C.
Vorhes, W. M.
Vorhes, P. A.
Woodgerd, John
Woodgerd, W. P.
Wells, R. G.
Webb, W. A.
Wood, J. F.
Wood, G. E.
Wible, W. C.
Wines, A.
Zimmerman, M. D.

Coolville Lodge, No. 337, F. & A. M., Coolville, Ohio.

Aigen, James
Buck, C. W.
Baker, Aaron
Barth, Otto
Bailey, J. E.
Brown, W. E.
Brown, H. H.
Burden, R. W.
Carlton, A. D.
Chase, Joseph
Creesy, W. D.
Clarke, B. F.
Coggeshall, J. C.
Curtis, H. R.
Cunningham, H.
Dufer, E. P.
Dinsmore, F. P.
Daugherty, J. B.
Dunfee, D. S.
DeVore, J. T.
DeVore, C. T.
Evans, W. G.
Frame, A. P.
Frost, D. H.
Frame, A. T.
Frost, Zenas
Frame, A. M.
Flinn, A. E.
Frame, Ward A.
Griffin, R. M.
Guthrie, J. E.
Hughes, R.
Hollister, A. A.
Humphrey, Frank
Johnson, J. W.
Kibble, E. M.
Knowles, Horace
Kibble, J. P.
Kinkead, D. N.
Lant, Joseph
Mitchell, W. M.
Monahan, F. S.
Nist, Jacob
Nist, Chas.
Oakes, C. W.
Parker, C. C.
Posey, L.
Patten, W.
Richardson, L.
Russel, Amanuel
Russell, S. E.
Russell, Adson
Russell, J. E.
Rodgers, E. L.
Russell, C. E.
Spencer, W. B.
Shields, J. L.
Sewell, G. W.
Tidd, J. M.
Townsend, J. M.
Tobey, H. F.
Taylor, F. C.
Tidd, F. B.
Wells, A.
Welch, John
Winters, S. S.

Savanah Lodge, No. 466, F. & A. M., Guysville, Ohio.

Adams, C. A.
Atkinson, Paul
Beebe, Owen
Beebe, H. W.
Burden, Hiram
Buck, Simeon
Brewer, Isaac
Bean, Jeremiah
Bean, Parrill
Bean, E. E.
Bean, J. F.
Bean, C. J.
Bean, L. G.
Bishop, Joseph
Copeland, C. H.
Calvert, C. C.
Charlton, M. J.
Coleman, F. K.
Cornell, D. W.
Day, Chas.
Edwards, D. H.
Finsterwald, Lewis
Finsterwall, J. H.
Fuller, E. G.
Fell, E. D.
Gossage, Warner
Halbert, E. E.
Hulbert, C. C.
Hammond, F. I.
Harper, E. D.
Hatch, H. A.
Hill, J. O.
Hill, F. J.
Hoisington, D. W.
Hoisintgon, C. H.
Jarvis, G. P.
Jewett, W. J.
Kelley, Almarine.
Kincade, C. E.
Kimes, F. E.
LeGoullon, H. O.
Lightfoot, Joseph
Marshall, J. H.
Mills, W. H.
Munn, R. B.
Murphy, J. W.
McNeil, P. P.
McVickers, Jas.
Pierce, L. P.
Pierce, C. W.
Parsons, E. H.
Reeder, A. P.
Rice, W. B.
Rice, J. H.
Rodhaver, J. A.
Rodhaver, J. G.
Smith, J. B.
Smith, L. H.
Stalder, J. E.
Stalder, Samuel
Townsend, N. C.
Townsend, A.
Warren, G. W.
Wharff, Amos
Wharff, C. M.
Wharff, G. E.
Wilson, S. A.
Wickham, H. H.
Whitacre, C. A.

Albany Lodge, No. 785, I. O. O. F., Albany, Ohio.

Instituted July 23, 1890.

Allen, W. J.
Baughman, W. E.
Brooks, Frank
Bowers, W. H.
Beasley, Geo. E.
Brown, N. C.
Baughman, Lee
Baughman, L. H.
Billups, A. O.
Canode, P. C.
Coe, T. W.
Canny, L. B.
Clark, O. W.
Conner, A. B.
Chase, T. J.
Cross, Carl
Duffee, J. H.
Dowd, Charles
Enlow, E. M.
Enlow, Luster S.
Fisher, Henry
Gorby, J. C.
Holmes, A. F.
Holdren, Geo.
Hursey, J. H.
Jordan, Abe
Jordan, S. A. D.
Jordan, C. L. V.
Jordan, F. M.
Jordan, Frank
Luckett, S. V.
Lewis, E. E.
Knowlton, A. D.
Leply, T. W.
Knowlton, Ellsworth
Knowlton, W. H.
Knowlton, Lloyd
McCarty, John H.
Mohler, W. E.
McComas, V. C.
Minx, C. O.
McPherson, C. L.
Minear, A. Z.
Neff, W. L.
Nelson, Emmett C.
Nichols, Wm.
Neff, John W.
Richey, John
Robinett, Jasper
Robinett, Charles E.
Rutherford, W. B.
Rickey, F. E.
Roberts, D. F.
Reed, Earl C.
Reeder, H. W.
Smith, C. B.
Smith, W. A.
Sweeney, P. H.
Swearingen, W. E.
Stanley, E. I.
Sharp, W. L.
Sharp, D. B.
Tewksbury, G. J.
Tom, C. H.
Tewksbury, A. F.
Wood, Geo. G.
Webb, S. D.
Wilson, Pearl
Woodgerd, F. E.
Winn, B. F.

Charles Thomas Lodge, No. 739, I. O. O. F., Jacksonville.

Swartz, Wm.
McKelvey, E. C.
Gibbs, Wm.
Gillot, Dessie
Mathews, A. E.
Swartz, Charles
Learned, Frank
Love, Leslie G.
Sayer, John
Muir, Edward
King, B. W.
Wolfe, John M.
Lautz, John E.
Buchman, Nathan
Love, Arthur C.
Brown, B. F.
Collins, M. M.
Dusz Robert
Mansfield, J. H.
King, U. M.
Phillips, W. R.
Wolfe, Geo. H.
Dusz, Charles
Hilyer, W. H.
Raber, J. W.
Hixon, Robert
Kinder, David
Cook, Charles
Selby, Ralph
Anderson, Richard
Selby, Watson
Oldroid, Jerry
Kinder, Clark W.
Rabe, Frank
Kistler, Andrew J.
Kempton, J. F.
Vening, Geo. H.
Swill, Bert.
Stewart, Frank
Chute, J. E.
Fisk, E. W.
Stump, Pearl
Pettit, Bart
Davis, Geo.
Bracken, Patrick
Haskins, Dan
Hooper, Silas
Parker, Wm.
Nail, John W.
Taylor, Hooker
Mingus, J. H.
Raber, Albert
McKinley, J. H.
McGee, Adam
Moore, Geo. L.
Wolfe, A. O.
Hilt, Wm. C.
Cary, Leotus G.
Phillips, Willard D.
Priest, Charles
Sands, Daniel
Gooding, L. R.
Graham, H. W.
Stam, Dr. John
Moore, Mell
Woodhouse, Fred
England, A. H.
Sidenstucker, Hart.
Haunstine, Lewis B.
Nickelson, Clinton
McKinley, Daniel J.
Deal, John
Dunlavy, M. M.
Danford, S. J.
Priest, Rev. D. S.
Householder, S.
Carbaugh, G. A.
Haunstine, Lewis
Hutchinson, H L.
Penrod, John J.
Penrod, H. W.
Wemmer, J. M.
Stacebus, Lewis
Swartz, Lewis
Williams, Geo. C.
Lewis, Samuel
Smith, Elijah
Andrews, J. M.
William, Charles
Shirkey, Richard
McKinley, Peter H.
Srigley, Dr. H. S.
Howard, Eldon C.
Hixon, Dr. Geo. W.
Edwards, Albert
Caldwell, Charles C.
Parker, Frederick
Bryan, Herbert
Parkins, Rev. F.
Rutherford, A. U.
Robinson, Wm.
Weldon, Harry
Earick, Jos. W. Jr.
McAtee, Babe
Seel, Peter
Rambo, Geo. S.
Grossman Isaac
Cole, Peter
Hall, Wm. U.
Kempton, Silas G.
Nickelson, G. C.
Eddy, B. F.
Eddy, Charles T.
Crawford, Carlton
Farris, Geo.
Luther, Geo.
Storts, D. V.
Learned, Herbert
Marquis, C. G.
Householder, Harry
Gooding, Frank
Gilley, Wm. J.
Kettle, Frank
Gilkey, Gilbert E.
Yager, Charles
Roush, J. M.
Metz, Daniel
Coe, James
Cooley, H. E.
Johnston, W. J.

Methodist Episcopal Church, Athens, Ohio.

FOR the first dozen years the Methodist society in Athens had no regular place of worship; then a brick church was erected on the lot now belonging to Mrs. Wright, on South Congress street. A parsonage also of brick was built near by in 1825. All traces of both have long since disappeared.

The present church was built in 1837 and remodeled in 1861. What was probably the most important event in the early history of the local society, was the great revival that occurred in 1827. This revival brought into the church such men as Ames, Trimble, Sehon, Clark, Herr and others who gave their entire lives to its service and became more or less prominent. E. R. Ames subsequently became a bishop; Joseph M. Trimble was later a professor in Augusta college, Kentucky, and Missionary secretary besides filling other responsible positions. Homer J. Clark was for some time president of Alleghany college. Sehon, who was a native of Virginia, held the position of Missionary Secretary in the M. E. Church, South; while William Herr was for more than fifty years in the active ministry during which time he occupied a number of important pulpits and was prominently identified with various religious agencies. The records of the society for a number of years following are exceedingly scanty. Its history, so far as it can be recovered at this late day, now that the pioneers have all passed over to the majority, can be gathered only in a very fragmentary way from the printed records of the few who have left memorials more or less complete of their connection with the local organization.

It is a matter of common knowledge that besides Bishop Ames, three of the present General Superintendents were in their earlier years identified with the society; Cranston, McCabe and Moore.

Possibly the three most important members of the local church since its organization, were Calvary Morris, a brother of the Bishop; D. B. Stewart and E. H. Moore. All three came into the county in the early part of the century, the first named from Virginia, the second from

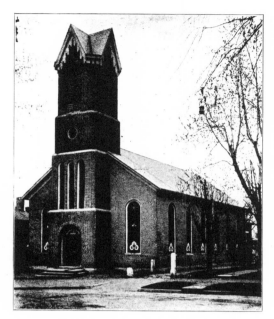

METHODIST EPISCOPAL CHURCH, ATHENS, OHIO.

Connecticut and the last named from Massachusetts. All were prominently identified with most of the larger business enterprises of the county and of South-eastern Ohio.

Mr. Morris was Sheriff of Athens county, five times a member of the General Assembly, three times a member of Congress, twice Probate Judge, besides at different times holding

other offices of minor importance. He died in 1871 at the age of seventy-three.

Mr. Stewart held few offices, preferring to give his time to his own affairs, but such positions as he held he filled to the best of his ability. Mr. Stewart's father whose name was also Daniel, had been at the time of his death in 1859, a member of the church for sixty years. The village of Stewart prepetuates the family name.

Mr. Moore served one term in Congress and held various other positions of trust during his long life. His only son is now bishop in active service. He died in 1900 at the age of eighty-eight.

The membership of the church at this date, 1905, is about 750; the number in the Sunday School is a little above 400; the Epworth League has a membership of quite 150.

OFFICERS OF THE CHURCH:

Bishop—David H. Moore, D. D. L. L. D.
Presiding Elder—Rev. Arthur M. Mann.
Pastor—W. L. Slutz, D. D.
Superannuate—Rev. Edward W. Howe.
Local Preacher—Rev. W. A. Thomas.

TRUSTEES—Henry O'Blenness, Charles W. Super, Eli Dunkle, Dr. W. N. Alderman, Rufus Carpenter, Hull Foster, J. A. Palmer, L. G. Worstell, W. B. Bently.

STEWARDS F. S. Coultrap, C. M. Copeland, E. W. Chubb, C. W. Lawrence, J. L. Pickering, H. L. Wheaton, W. F. Mercer. T. J. Herold, W. B. Lawrence, Eli Dunkle, E. G. Eaton, Dr. H. T. Lee, L. H. Clark.

Sunday School Superintendent—F. S. Coultrap.
Supt. Primary Dept.—Miss Lucy A. Cramner.
Epworth League President—L. M. Clark.
Supt. Junior League—Miss Jennie F. Myers.
Class Leader—W. A. Thomas.
Chorister—Miss Jane Ryan.
Organist—Mrs. Hattie Hines Blackburn.
President W. F. M. S.—Miss Kate Boyd.
President W. H. M. S.—Mrs. Margaret Vickers.

Farm Residence of Mr. and Mrs. James Gilkey, in Alexander Township.

THE appearance of the home and surroundings is the true index of the man. The thrift or lack of it is plainly indicated by the conditions around and about a farm house and the outbuildings. The picture here shown of this pretty country home is a tribute to the thrift and industry of its owners, Mr. and Mrs. James Gilkey, who live in the vicinity of the Bassett Church, in Alexander township.

James Gilkey is the son of the late William Gilkey, who in his lifetime was one of the most thrifty hill farmers in the county. James was born on the farm where he now resides. His youth was spent working on the farm and attending the common schools of the neighborhood. He was born November 22, 1845, and in his lifetime he has turned over every foot of ground that has been broken on his farm of 150 acres.

He was married to Miss Sarah Johnson the daughter of Joseph Johnson, a native of Alexander township, in 1865.

Three children have been born to them only one of whom is now living, Mrs. Luella Beal, the wife of Dr. Perry Beal, now living in Athens, Ohio.

Mr. and Mrs. Gilkey are members of the Methodist Episcopal church and are exemplary citizens. Their farm is well improved and they have residence property in Athens.

LODGES AND FRATERNAL ORDERS.

Stewart Lodge, No. 753, I. O. O. F., Stewart, O.

- Lightfoot Joseph
- Ginn, E. H,
- Ewers, M. I.
- Beebe, Owen
- Johnson, Chas.
- Crippen, G. H.
- Carter, F. C.
- Campbell, Chas.
- Gossage, Warner
- Semons, T. A.
- Semons, Wm.
- Hawk, G. H.
- Bean, Ed.
- Wharff, H. M.
- Townsend, N. C.
- Biggins, W. W.
- Biggins, H. E.
- Biggins, J. A.
- Beebe, H. W.
- Kincade, E. H.
- Parker, D. A.
- Fuller, A. D.
- Rasley, H. W.
- Kincade C. E.
- Castle, L. D.
- Hayes, C. W.
- Evener, G. D.
- Evener, R.H.
- Miller, L. L.
- Minear, W. F.
- Ladd, F. G.
- McAfee, E. S.
- McAfee, Thos.
- Rowell, Theodore
- Burk, J. L.
- Bean, C. J.
- Nicholson Frank
- Hovey, H. C.
- Rice, J. H.
- Rice, W. B.
- McCullough, Herb.
- Norris, D. A.
- King, F.D.
- Fry, S. W.
- Featherstone, John
- Cather, Quincy
- Whitacre, C. A.
- Coleman, W.L.
- Hoisington, W. H.
- Hoisington, S. H.
- Biddison, S. J.
- Oliver, John
- Storer Worley
- Rainey, J.A.
- Buck, B. B.
- Cook, R. B.
- Pickett, John
- Norris, J. C.

Coolville Lodge, No. 527, I. O. O. F., Coolville, O.

- Agin, James
- Anderson, G. W.
- Allen, O. P.
- Brindley, Dell
- Buck, Charles
- Brown, W. E.
- Burmaster, Angest
- Bailey, J. C.
- Buck, Simeon
- Bingman, W. E.
- Bridges, W. R.
- Barrows, J. R.
- Campbell, G. K.
- Welch, McCellan
- Cunningham, C. C.
- Cowdry, H. C.
- Dodderer, Lewis
- Durant, J. L.
- Dewolf, John
- Grimes, J. F.
- Humphrey, Waldo
- Hartnell, Joseph
- Huston, Geo.
- Kaler, J. V.
- Kibble, A. B.
- Lyons, W. H.
- Lowman, R. A.
- Lawrence, A. E.
- Morrison, H. B.
- Medley, James
- McLaughlin, John
- Mills, T. J.
- Nave, E. G.
- Palmer, J. A.
- Payne, F. M.
- Parrish, H. H.
- Russell, William
- Richardson, Harvey
- Ruth, W. A.
- Russell, L. A.
- Runyan, J. G.
- Simms, G. B.
- Smith, Henry
- Spencer, W. B.
- Simpson, R. W.
- Snyder, C. L.
- Shields, J. L.
- Sandborn, C. D.
- Spencer, G. D.
- Smith, S. S.
- Torrence, J. W.
- Walden, W. M.
- White, A. B. Sr.
- Willing, W. H
- Walden, J. S.
- White, A. B. Jr.
- Wise, E. T.

Sereno Lodge, No. 479, I. O. O. F., Athens, Ohio.

- Ackley, E.G.
- Ansee, S. E.
- Ayers, A.E.
- Ayres, Milo
- Burns, Henry M.
- Beverage, D. C.
- Blackwood, W. S.
- Brown, C.H.
- Brown, L. E.
- Bean, C. R.
- Bolin, E. F.
- Brewer, Chas.
- Brooks, Wm. C.
- Brewer, Cassius
- Bellows, Frank
- Brooks, J. E.
- Biddle, D. H.
- Brown, Elias
- Cornwell, D. C.
- Connett, H. G.
- Cooley, Henry A.
- Carnes, Chas. E.
- Casley, W. A.
- Cabeen, J. H.
- Cook, R. S.
- Cramner, M. L.
- Carr, P. C.
- Chappelle, A. A. H.
- Cromley, Wm.
- Carpenter, Roll
- Clifton, W. E.
- Dickason, H. E.
- Dickey, C. L.
- Dunkle. Eli
- Dixon, H. A.
- Dalton, Ralph
- Earhart, G. H.
- Earich, J. W.
- Earhart, Jno. W.
- Ford, G. G.
- Finsterwald, Wm.
- Fryberger, Addison
- Grones, F. S.
- Gregory, T. J.
- Gist, C. D.
- Gillion, Ed
- Gulley, Geo.
- Gift, C. D.
- Graham, J. H.
- Hastings, W. J.
- Henry, Chas.
- Hawk, P. W.
- Hibbard, S. H.
- Hambleton, B. F.
- Henry, J. L.
- Hopkins, C. D.
- Harvey, J.R.
- Hart G. H.
- Hooper, Ralph
- Hooper, C. A.
- Jones, L. F.
- Jones, J. O.
- Jourdan, Joseph
- James, Ray
- Kincade, M. F.
- Lewis, W. A.
- Lawrence, Jno. E.
- Lash, Geo. B.
- Moore, C. O.
- Miner, Jno. C.
- Maxon, A. G.
- Maxwell, E. R.
- Morrison, H. D.
- Martin, C. W.
- Mansfield, Jesse
- Marquis, D. Earl
- McLead, N. E.
- McVay, F. P.
- McLean, H. F.
- McGraner, Patrick
- McKee, Jas. H.
- McHarg, Jas.
- McGraner, Jno.
- McCollister, D. S.
- Newsom, C. S.
- Nye, L. C.
- Nice, H. D.
- Nanna, G. D.
- Osborne, E. H.
- Pickering, T.M.
- Pierce, M. A.
- Porter, Jno. G.
- Pratt, P. G.
- Pickering, A. S.
- Randall, B. P.
- Rose, E. T.
- Reid, R. H.
- Roach, Orr
- Roach, C. H.
- Reid, Harry A.
- Scott, Winfield
- Sommer, Sam
- Strahl, O. L.
- Super, Chas. W.
- Simms, A. H.
- Shirley, P. E.
- Slaughter, Chas.
- Sater, Wm.
- Secoy, Wilbur
- Stewart, Clarence
- Thomas W. A.
- Tresize, B. F.
- Ullom, G. W.
- Walker, G. R.
- Whipple, Geo.
- Wildes, Wm.
- Winning, Thos.
- Walker, E. H.
- Walker, F. B.
- Walker, Leon H.

Lee Rebecca Lodge, No. 523, I. O. O. F., Albany, O.

- Lewis, Mary A.
- Crossen, Edna M.
- Webb, Lizzie V.
- Sweeney, Elizabeth
- Knowlton, Kate
- Robinett, Amanda
- Hursey, Alta
- Winn, Allie C.
- Webb, S. D.
- Knowlton, Ellsworth
- Conner, Amus B.
- Tom, Nancy
- Tewksbury, Mary
- Rose. E. T.
- Radcliff, Cora
- Hoak, Ella
- Winn, B. F.
- Conner, S. Elbert
- Conner, Cora R.
- Jordan, Abe
- Jordan, Agnes
- Holmes, A. F.
- Holmes, Jennie
- Bowers, Nettie F.
- Neff, Mary
- Canny, L. B.
- Canny, Adda M.
- Smith, C. B.
- Smith, Mary E.
- Cline, Mary
- Cross, Anna
- Parker, Tabitha
- Robinett, Ida
- Moler, W. E.
- Moler. Cora

Wahneta Tent, No. 146, K. O. T. M., Glouster, Ohio.

- Antle, Des
- Andrews, Arthur
- Andrews, L. R.
- Allen, A. B.
- Angle, Henry
- Angle, John
- Andrews, Ira
- Allen, W. G.
- Andrews, B. A.
- Andrews, Chas.
- Bryson, Frank
- Brooks, W. H.
- Byers, Albert
- Brown, I. W.
- Buchman, Wm.
- Brinkley, Alex.
- Bailey, James
- Baker, Fred
- Bryson, M. M.
- Brown, Gilbert
- Balderson, Lamp
- Carpenter, W. A.
- Carter, W. G.
- Campbell, G. W.
- Carpenter, S. S.
- Carpenter, W. H.
- Crawford, A. J.
- Cavey, J.E.
- Cunningham, Sam
- Champlin, M.
- Clark, Noah
- Drake, J. M.
- Davis, J. W.
- Duncan, W. H.
- Dyson, Elijah
- Douglas, Geo.
- Drake, A. H.
- Duncan, James
- Dupler, Ed.
- Drury, E. E.
- Davis, J. L.
- Dupler, H. G.
- Dille, Alvin
- Duncan, C. E.
- Dew, Ona
- Eddy, O. D.
- Embry, Wm.
- Earich Elbert
- Eberts, Leonard
- Evans, Willard
- Fisher, C. W.
- Fairs, G. E.
- Gardner, B. A.
- Goldsworthy, John
- Gooding Ed.
- Hart, A. L.
- Higgins, J. F.
- Howard, Jas.
- Harris, R.
- Hesse, J. L.
- Hayden, John
- Hooper, Ben
- Hodgson, Wm.
- Hanson, Harry
- Henry, R. S.
- Hatton, Chas.
- Hoge, Anderson
- Hartley, C. L.
- Howard, John
- Hopes, Thos.
- James, Wm.
- Joseph, Wm.
- Jasper, Geo.
- Jonas, Winnie
- Kistler, Wm.
- Keeth, Jas.
- Kasler, A.
- Kirby, Edwin
- King, W. F.
- Koons, Chas.
- Kasler, Chas.
- LeFever, Everet
- LeFever, E.W.
- Lewis, Thos.
- LeFavor, M. M.
- Lehew, S. B.
- Leighty, W. S.
- Love, Geo.
- McAfoose, L. D.
- McDonald, W. W.
- McLaughlin, A.
- Mason, J. E.
- Morris, John
- Morris, Elza
- Mandt, Wm.
- Mundew, Leslie
- Mingus, Albert
- McCarty, F. D.
- McLaughlin, Henry
- McLaughlin, Joseph
- McLaughlin, Alfred
- Morris, Chas.
- McDoonald, J. L.
- Morris, F. C.
- McNally, Phillip
- Murphy, F. I.
- Oliver, Earl
- Nelson, Alex
- Nelson, Wm.
- Pickering, B. W.
- Peach, Sam
- Price, Geo.
- Reed, C. F.
- Rose, H. S.
- Rose, G. W.
- Rothman, E. S.
- Robinson, Asa
- Robinson, James
- Strohmeyer, F. C.
- Snell, M. D.
- Skinner, Robt.
- Stedman, I. N.
- Stahl, W. H.
- Shilling, Scott
- Snowden, Luster
- Smith, Thos.
- Stedman, John
- Stedman, Frank
- Steffy, Seward
- Unger, I. H.
- Thompson, S. D.
- Truex, Jerry
- Truex, R. C.
- Thomas, Pearl
- Theopolis, Chas.
- Tryon, A. L.
- Vernon, C. A.
- Vercoe, Jas.
- Walters, J. T.
- Witig, Albert
- Warehime, Lewis
- Wilson, Alex
- Wallace, Wm.
- West, Henry
- Warehime, Jacob
- Ward, J. W.
- White, Geo.
- Yarger, Criss
- Zimmers, F. J.
- Zimmers, Henry

Marcellite Rebecca Lodge, No. 401, I. O. O. F., Glouster, Ohio.

- Crombia, Myra
- Bee, Jennie
- Cook, Rebecca
- Carpenter, Jennie
- Duncan, Kate
- Drury, Anna
- Storer, Blanch
- Wagoner, Dora
- Higgins, Martha
- Harris, Mary
- Hall, Lou
- Jasper, Lillie
- Kasler, Emma
- Mason, Dora
- Morris, Clara
- Skinner, Maggie
- Stahl, Maggie
- Andrews, Lizzie
- Bryson, Cora
- Brown, Blanch
- Hemsley, Maggie
- Rose, Adda
- Dupler, Adda
- Cherrington, Vesta
- Davis, J. W.
- Dupler, E. E.
- Dupler, Irene
- Embry, William
- Fisher, Mary
- Faires, Eliza
- Griffith, Rachel
- Stedman, I. N.
- Smith, Tom
- Higgins J. F.
- Harris Richard
- Hooper, Jennie
- Jones, Sarah
- Jones, Miss Sarah
- James, Mary
- King, Hannah
- Keith, Alice B.
- Kerby, Fanny
- King, R. S.
- LeFavor, Ella
- Lewis, Maggie
- McAfoose, Alice
- Morgan, Mary A.
- Andrews, L. R.
- Morris, Charles
- Embry, Edna
- Stahl, Lillian
- Stahl, W. H.
- Steffy, Lillie
- Mason, Stella
- Bryson, Emma
- Oldroyd, Alice
- Wilson, Cassie
- Suvers, Emma
- Vernon, Minnie
- Wareham, Clara
- Gibson, Dora
- Wareham, Bertha
- Wheatley, Lucy
- Zimmers, Selina
- Butler, Hannah
- Mingus, Albert
- Pickering, Bessie
- Peach, Maria
- Hutchison, Lillie
- Faires, Emma
- Gooding, Hannah
- Cobb, Anna
- Campbell, Valelia
- Auers, Mary
- McLaughlin, Jennie
- Murphy, Lizzie
- Edwards, Jessie
- Lehew, Hannah
- Andrews, Sarah
- Eddy, Agnes
- Hatton, Rhoda
- Hesse, Alice
- Balderson, Jennie
- Balderson, Mayme
- Davis, Clara
- Oliver, Earl
- Howard, John
- McLaughlin, J. A.
- Andrews, Mary
- Wittig, Yetta
- Price, Adda
- Price, George
- Swisher, Tillie
- Wheeler, Etta
- Duncan, Anna
- Lattimer, Lena
- Morris, Eva
- Vercoe, Hannah
- Culver, Thea
- McAfoose, Alta
- Wagoner, Ada
- Andrews, B. A.
- Murphy, T. I.
- West, Polly
- Dyson, Mary
- McDonald, Jennie
- Matthews, Susan
- McDonald, Will
- Nelson, Polly
- Oliver, Lizzie
- Peach, Jane
- Palmer, Martha
- Rose, Mrs. H. S.
- Robinson, Mary
- Reaney, Jessie
- Roush, Lillian
- Strohmeyer, T. C.
- Strohmeyer, Lucy
- Skinner Robert
- Skinner, Maggie
- Skinner, Maggie E.
- Leighty, Epsy
- Williams, Mary
- Dillie, Alvin
- Dillie, Mrs. Alvin
- Clark, Lucy
- Angle, Mary
- Angle, May
- Lett, Ivy
- Vernon, Alice
- Hanson, Harry
- Wareham, Lewis
- Henry, Roy
- Leighty, Wilber
- Lehew, S. B.
- Angle, Henry
- Andrews, C. H.
- Robinson, James
- Dulaney, Agnes
- Andrews, Eva
- Yarger, Chris.
- Yarger, Mary
- Brown, Maggie
- Andrews, Ira
- Hipsher, Gertrude
- Dentener, Jennie
- Simes, Bertha
- Latimer, Hetta
- Antle, Des
- Hesse, J. L.
- Clark, Noah
- Latimer, Ida
- Wilson, Dora

Nineveh Rebecca Lodge, No. 296, I. O. O. F., Jacksonville, Ohio.

- King, Emma
- Williams, Ada
- Love, Ella
- Almond, Addie
- Chute, Anna
- Brown, Clara
- Dunlavey, Martha
- Stacks, May
- Williams, Minnie
- Oldroyd, Mary
- Parker, Kate
- King, Maggie
- Kempton, Emma
- Wolfe, Nettie
- Gibbs, Anna
- Anderson, Mayme
- Hooper, Cora
- Wolfe, Lotte
- Watkins, Lydia
- Dusz, Bertha
- Oldroyd, Patience
- Parker, Nora
- Selby, Anna
- Hawk, Edna
- Dusz, Freda
- Shirkey, Anna
- Hellyer, Alice
- Hilt, Amanda
- Johnson, Della
- Williams, Linda
- Anderson, Cass
- Williams, Nellie
- Chute, Stella
- Stamm, Ida
- Cook, Lena
- Cook, Minnie
- McKinley, Mary
- Carter, Mary
- Penrod, Celara
- Penrod, Jane
- Lantz, Jennie
- Bell, Iva
- Kempton, Margaret
- Rambo, Hettie
- Dusz, Amanda
- Hooper, Cora
- Strawn, Manda
- Sidenstricker, Lydia
- Shirker, Mary
- Lantz, Viola
- Brannon, Mary
- Cary, Luella
- Hilt, Vena
- Druggan, Elza
- Raney, Mildred
- Nail, Stella
- Smith, Mary
- Bracken, Mary
- Sivil, Mina
- Markus, Maud.
- Eddy, Zella
- Carpenter, Viola
- Edwards, Lizzie
- Williams, D. S.
- Nicholson, C.
- Swartz, Chas.
- Brannon, John
- Gillott, Deresa
- Gooding, L. R.
- Gooding, Frank
- Gilley, Gilbert
- Collins, M. M.
- Weldon, Harry
- Markus, C. G.
- King, B. W.
- Williams, Chas.
- Chute, J. E.
- Brown, B. F.
- Parker, Wm.
- Kempton, J. F.

Pinninah Rebeccah Lodge, No. 142, I. O. O. F., Buchtel, Ohio.

- Snyder, Mrs. Nettie
- Barstoe, Mrs. Nora
- Sears, Mrs. Mary
- Barstoe, Mrs. Minnie
- Sears, William
- Berry, George.
- Sohn, Mrs. Polly
- Whetzel, Sopha
- Wade, William
- Shingler, Bertha
- Kitzman, Bertha
- Twiner, Mrs. Mary
- Russel, Mrs. Maude
- Sohn, Edward
- Shrieves, Susan
- Williams, Mrs. Lulu
- Cline, Mrs. Maggie
- Bruce, Mrs. Hallie
- Schentz, Minnie
- Rife, Mrs. Mabel
- Mitchell, Mrs. Iota
- Oakley, Robert
- Stephenson, Mary
- Conner, Webb
- McKee, George
- Shrieves, Nantie
- Inman, Elizabeth
- Schentz, I.
- Mason, George
- Mason, Mrs. Addie
- Berry, Mrs. Minnie
- Grimm, Mrs. Ida
- Grimm, Charles
- Rittenberry, Grace
- Zarley, Mrs. Osie
- McQuaid, Mrs. Jane
- Braidy, Mrs. Ella
- Phillips, Mrs. Flora
- Hagg, Mrs. Sopha
- Newman, Mrs. Susie
- McKinney, Jennie
- Hunter, Mrs. Ida
- Hartley, Oliver
- Zarley, Charles
- Snowden, William
- Cunningham, Wm.
- Radcliffe, Miss Jessie
- Pospichel, Mrs Anna
- Lindsey, Miss Etta
- Hayden, Blanch
- Marks, Mrs. Rose
- Jonas, Mrs. Mary
- Young, Mrs. Levisa
- Smith, John
- Smith, Mrs. Emma
- Whetzel, Mrs. Cora
- Evans, Mrs. Kate
- Barstoe, Mrs. Alice
- Grimm, Miss Leona
- Keeney, Manerva
- Little, Mrs. Sylvia
- Lovett, Mrs. Bess
- Grimm, Mrs. Andy
- Radcliffe Miss Nelle
- Eddy, George
- Inman, Miss Leona
- Robinson, Mrs. Anna
- Whitmore, Mrs. Ida
- Bruce, Mrs. Annie
- Brickner, Mrs. Mary
- Wade, Mrs. Lizzie
- Whetzel, Mrs. Mazy
- Andrews, Mrs. Stella
- Whitmore, Lelia
- Hayden, Miss Lizzie
- McDonald, Mrs.
- Spary, Nora
- Stratton, Lizzie
- Graham, Maggie
- Schentz, Tudie
- Colians, Blanch
- Garlinger, Laura
- Hartley, Rebecca
- Hartley Clarinda
- Whitmore, Lillie
- Wade, Mrs. Della
- Yates, Mrs. Mary
- Stevenson, Olive
- Diddy, Mrs. Mary
- Cline, Mrs. Alice
- McKinney, J.
- Thompson, C. H.
- Hartley, Bert
- Ewers, Emert
- Bartoe, William
- Eddy George
- Lee, Mrs. Sarah
- Schentz, Mrs. A.K.
- Batcheler, Haniliah
- Shingler, Mrs. Mary
- Garlinger, Lucinda
- Hilger, Mrs. Settee
- Wade, Mrs. Lizzie
- Hallam, Mrs. Mary
- Ilderton, Mrs. Mary
- Kinner, Mrs. Ollie
- Nervan, Mrs. Rosa
- Oakley, Mrs. Sarah
- Taylor, Mrs. Maggie
- Stewart, Mrs. Nettie
- Whitmore, Carrie
- Thompson, Mrs. Ollie
- Ewers, Mrs. Maggie
- Lenox, Mrs. Mary
- McKee, Mrs. Mattie
- Lewis, Miss Nora
- Hawk, Mrs. Addie
- Lewis, Miss Ora
- Hayden, Mrs. Mary
- Hite, Mrs. Lowell
- Thompson, Goldie
- Sears, Mrs. Elizabeth
- Linton, Margaret
- Milligan, Miss Ella
- Barstoe, Mrs. Emma
- Keeney, Miss Lizzie
- Linon, Miss Clara
- Williams, George
- Newton, Mrs. Sylvia
- Pummell, Mrs. Addie
- Chambers, Jennie
- Dixon, Mrs. Mary
- Grimm, Miss Maude

Philippine Lodge K. of P., Chauncey, Ohio.

- Sanders, Walter
- Partlow, Charles
- Fisk, C. M.
- Hastings, R. M.
- White, U. P.
- Ellis, M. T.
- Halbert, Jno.
- Smith, Will
- Pitko, John
- Titko, Steve
- Martin, Owen
- Keaton, Riley
- Rade, J. R.
- Wade, G. P.
- Collins, Will
- Daines, D. N.
- Wade, F. E.
- Preston, D. A.
- Sanders, J.
- McManaway, Wesley
- Willis, Saumel
- McKnab, James
- Druggan, C. S.
- Winefordner, Wm.
- Roberts, O. C.
- Donley, William
- Shaffer, C. W.
- Sprague, W. T.
- Riley, Frank
- Cook, O. Maurice
- Walker, C. W.
- Druggan, Peter H.
- Smith, Dave
- Gabriel, George
- Collins, James
- Brown, Edward
- Schoonover, Lee
- Stalder, Harry
- Lehman, Lewis
- Telman, James
- Schoonover, Will
- Lewis, Frank
- Cuninghame, Carl
- Cuninghame, Harry
- Leffler, Charles
- Layhugh John
- Cunnighame, E. W.
- Tittle, John
- McHarg, I. M.
- Courtney, H. S.
- Clester, J. P.
- Jackson, Andrew
- Dukeman, Mike
- Keesey, Sherman
- Gearhart, Wright
- Birge, Ele
- Smith, D. L.
- Schoonover, John
- Blavcett, Will
- Fisk, John
- Cunninghame, Hom
- McKibben, Parker
- Minister, Edw.
- Foraker, Steve
- Dodds, Harry
- Tippell, Lucius
- Rackenn, James
- Cunninghame, Vint
- Leffler, Ed
- McDaniels, S. G.
- Nye, Robt. E.
- Nye, G. W.
- Watkins, A. E.
- Berge, A. W.
- Six, Geo. A.
- Wieles, W. R.
- Rily, W. E.
- Wooley, John
- Smith, Thos. J.
- Seevees, Homer
- Ferriss, W. C.

Residence of Mr. and Mrs. R. M. Patterson, Alexander Township.

ROBERT Milton Patterson was born in Alexander township, Athens county, Ohio, January 1, 1850. His grandfather, Robert Patterson, being of Scotch-Irish descent, came to America from Ireland in 1790. He located first in Massachusetts, where he married Nancy Tilton, of a leading Quaker family.

They removed to Washington county, Pa., where they spent the remainder of their lives.

William Patterson, the father of the subject of this sketch, was the eldest of a family of ten children. He was raised on a farm in the hills of Washington county, Pa., getting his education as best he could in private and subscription schools. He engaged in teaching and surveying, and in 1830 he married Elizabeth Cooper, whose parents came from the New England family of Coopers and Atkinsons.

In 1833, he with his little family removed to this county, driving through in a covered wagon, in the month of April, and settled on wild and uncultivated lands in the College township of Alexander, where he engaged in farming and lived the balance of his days.

The subject of this sketch was the youngest of a family of eight children, and at the age of 14, by the continued bad health of his father, and the enlistment of his only brother in the service of his country, brought upon him the active care of his father's farm and family. Not having the opportunity of school—only three months in the winter, the last two of which was spent at the Albany Atwood Inststute under the tutorship of Professors Chase, Peden and Spencer, along with Judge and Perry Wood, Dick McKinstry and a host of others.

At the death of his father he was named as executor in the will, and was compelled to cancel other aspirations and return to the farm to care for his aged mother and invalid sister; and in September of the same year he was married to Lizzie R., only daughter of John C. Cuckler, of Alma, Ross county, O., but who resided at that time with her grandfather, the venerable John R. McCune, of Athens.

Locating on the farm then recently purchased from C. D. Long, known as the Ami Condee farm, he engaged in the breeding of and dealing in thoroughbred Merino sheep, until he had the reputation of having one of the best flocks in southern Ohio.

Politically Mr. Patterson is a stalwart Republican, having been active in the interests of his party. He served eight years as clerk of his home township and in 1890 he assessed the real estate, and was re-elected without opposition for the same place in 1900, being the only appraiser that the County Board did not change his work.

In the fall of 1900 he was nominated and elected a member of the State Board of Equalization for this, the 9th-14th Senatorial district, and in the following December the Board commenced its sessions in Columbus.

Mr. and Mrs. Patterson have raised a family of nine children, seven girls and two boys: Birdie E., wife of Chas. R. Bean, who died Sept. 29, 1893; Alice G., wife of Harry D. Hooper, of Athens; Edna C., wife of Julian Gift, of Hibbardsville; Nellie E., Mary Forestine, Lena Estelle, Willie R., Attie Winnifred and Guy W. Both of the boys died when quite small.

Mr. Patterson is a member of Albany Lodge, No. 156 F. & A. M., and he and family are all members of the Cumberland Presbyterian church at Hibbardsville. He now has a farm of 340 acres located on east Margaret's Creek, and known as one of the best farms in the county.

ATHENS COUNTY HISTORY
CONTINUED.

ridden in that cramped position for miles, fearing the wolves might get him. Another experience many recall is having the bag become over balanced and fall from the horse when the youngster too small to lift it or get it on the horse must wait until some passing traveler could help him.

In early times all grinding was accomplished by passing the grain between two immense circular millstones or burrs. The degree of fineness must be regulated by the miller who was of necessity well skilled in his business. He needed to be expert not only in making flour, but also in attending to the burrs and machinery. About thirty years ago the roller process began to supplant the old method and now burrs are obsolete in the milling business. Few mills from earliest time could run during the summer season owing to scarcity of water, so gradually steam began to crowd out the water mill while the picturesque water wheel is entirely a thing of the past.

ROADS AND WAGONING.

Roads were not needed in the earliest days of the settlements for vehicles of any kind were scarce, all traveling being done on foot or horseback. All produce and merchandise was carried on pack horses, and paths winding among the trees met these demands.

As the settlements began to grow and crude home made, wagons and sledges began to appear, public roads were made connecting the principal settlements.

By making of roads was not meant grading, graveling or bridges, simply cutting down the trees to leave a path wide enough for a team and wagon. Owing to the dense shade through which these roads ran and all lack of drainage they were almost impassable ten months of the year. Often eight to twelve days were occupied in making what would be one short days journey to-day. One of the earliest acts of Ohio after it became a state was to pass a law providing a fund for construction of roads. Three per cent of the proceeds of all public lands sold were to be applied to roads built under the direction

(Continued on page 45.)

GROUP OF SOLDIERS

FROM WATERLOO TOWNSHIP IN THE CIVIL WAR, TAKEN MAY 30, 1903.

Dr. J. C. Coleman,   C. C. Pierce,   Lafe Hawk,   J. H. Jones,   William Townsend,

J. H. Dowler.   John Adams,   J. L. Cooper,   F. M. Barker,   J. O. Imes,

R. M. Beverage,   Louis Hysell,   Thomas Johnson,   Stephen Allen,

Thomas King,   Alexander Russell,   E. W. Gilbert,   Joel Lowther,

A. W. DeVore,   P. Jones.

Residence of Mr. and Mrs. Isaac Nice, Near Athens, Ohio.

THIS home and family group represents all of a temporal nature that is near and dear to Mr. and Mrs. Isaac Nice, who live about four miles south of Athens, on the Jerseyville pike. The house and barn is located on a bluff overlooking the pike and a picturesque valley, not possible to be shown in the picture.

Isaac Nice was born December 7, 1842, at Big Run, Athens county, Ohio, and is the son of Philip and Rebecca Nice, who came to Big Run from Virginia in about 1838. At the outbreak of the civil war Isaac answered the call of his country and enlisted in Co. G., 92nd Regt., O. V. I., and served three years, or until the close of the war, being mustered out of service at Chattanooga, Tennessee.

The most remarkable thing in Mr. Nice's life is that he is living today, or that he lived through the service as a soldier. In the battle of Chicamauga, on September 19, 1863, he was struck in the right temple by a ball from the enemy, and the missile passed in a downward course clear through his head and came out under the jaw on the left side of his head. He was carried to the rear and in a few hours regained consciousness and walked sixteen miles to Chattanooga. He was wounded on Saturday and his wound was not dressed until the following Saturday, when, after a tramp of thirty-six miles from Chattanooga he arrived in Nashville. He took a sixty day furlough and in six months joined his regiment at Ringgold, Georgia.

He returned from the army to his home in Big Run, and on May 19, 1867, was married to Miss Minerva Devore, daughter of Henry Devore, and went to housekeeping in York township, where he carried on farming and worked at the carpenter trade until 1890, when he purchased the Will Angel farm of 200 acres, in Alexander township, where he has since lived.

Mr. and Mrs. Nice have five children: Etta M., Hattie A., Stella A., now Mrs. C. L. Creamer, Harley E. and Henry D., all of whom are shown in the picture. Mr. Nice's mother, Rebecca, died January 26, 1905, in her 86th year. At the time of her death she had two great great grand-children, seventy-one great grand-children and ninety-one grand-children. She was the mother of eighteen children, fourteen of whom are still living.

Mr. Nice has occupied positions of trust and for the past six years has been a trustee of Alexander township.

Farm Residence of Mr. and Mrs. William Hooper, in Alexander Township.

THE comfortable farm home here presented is the residence of Mr. and Mrs. William Hooper, near Bassett's Church, in Alexander township. Mr. Hooper is the son of Ashur Hooper, who came to this county in 1819, from Belmont county, and settled on a farm near Pleasanton, where William was born January 11, 1841, and spent his boyhood and early manhood.

In 1865 he was married to Miss Ellen Elizabeth Lash, the daughter of

Abram Lash, one of the early settlers of the county, and one of its prominent and highly respected citizens.

In 1868 Mr. Hooper purchased and moved on the farm near Bassett's, and has made his home there ever since.

Mr. and Mrs. Hooper are the parents of three children, one having died in infancy, and the others are Emma Jane and Frank J. Frank is married and lives on an adjoining farm to his father.

No more hospitable home can be found in the county, and the occupants enjoy a large circle of friends among their many acquaintances.

They are among the stalwart citizens of their neighborhood, and enjoy to the highest degree, the confidence of the people with whom they live and associate. Kindly and generous to a fault, Mr. and Mrs. Hooper are enjoying the result of honorable and well spent lives, always standing up for whatever is best in manhood and womanhood in the various problems that must be confronted in the course of human life.

COOLVILLE CAMP GROUNDS, COOLVILLE, OHIO.

SOON after the Civil War, the subject of the location of an old fashioned camp ground for the Marietta District of the M. E. church, was agitated from time to time, which ultimately took shape in the year 1880, while Rev. Henry Gortner was Presiding Elder of the Marietta District. The first meeting held to consummate such organization as an Association was on Wolf's Plains, west of Athens. Then and there a committee was appointed on location—Revs. M. V. B. Euans, G. A. Marshall and Henry Gortner comprising such committee, with instructions to report at Ministerial Association to be held in Zaleski later on in the same year. At this meeting a committee consisting of Revs. H. B. Westervelt, M. B. V. Euans F. C. Ross and H. Gortner were appointed to draft a Constitution and By-Laws for the Association; also to report at the Zaleski meeting.

Zenner's grove and Humphrey's grove were the prominent sites considered. The former was offered for lease for a term of ten years at rate of $50.00 per year, and the latter for ten or more years free of charge. The question of water supply was a leading question, but happily all doubt on that point was removed, and the committee reported favorably in behalf of Humphrey's grove, midway between Coolville and the railroad. At this meeting held in Zaleski, September, 1880, the organization was perfected, and a President. Vice President, Secretary, Treasurer and Board of Trustees were elected.

At a meeting of the Association May 17, 1881, the Board accepted Brother Shepherd Humphrey's lease of his grove with the proviso, "that in the event the grounds ceased to be used by the M. E. church for religious worship, they would become the property of the Parent Board of the Missionary Society of the M. E. Church and not revert to his heirs or estate." A lot was reserved for himself and one for each of his four sons. He was elected a member of the Board of Trustees, which position he has ever since held. His untiring efforts in behalf of the Association knew no bounds. Health permitting, he attended every meeting of the Board. His donations and assistance in time of need were worthy of the man, and will long be held in grateful remembrance by the friends of the Association. Bro. A. S. Tidd was a loyal supporter of the Association from the time of its inception to the date of his death. Bro. J. A. Palmer, of Athens, was a zealous co-worker with Mr. Tidd, and to their labors the Association is indebted for the plans of the grounds and especially the water supply system—the best found on any camp ground in the country; pure, fresh spring water being furnished at the door of each cottage. Mr. D. B. Stewart was an honored member of the Board continuously until old age and infirmity compelled him to retire. His services were invaluable. Calvin Leseur of Belpre, was a "bow of strength" to the Association throughout its history. Joseph Lant and G. K. Campbell, who came into the Board later, have held official relations for over twenty years.

The grounds are located on the left bank of the Hocking river and five miles from its mouth, on an elevated plateau about 250 feet above the river. The unobstructed views, both up and down the river, and the village on the south, form a very pleasing landscape.

This place of religious worship has been honored by the presence of some of the most noted men of the age, including the President of the United States, Senator of the United States, Governors of Ohio, Members of Congress, several of the Bishops of the M. E. church and many noted divines of this and other denominations, and the best evangelistic talent in the country.

Mr. C. E. White is now and has been in charge of the finances for many years, and is wide awake to the best interests of Association

MR. SHEPHERD HUMPHREY

ATHENS COUNTY HISTORY
CONTINUED.

of the general assembly. These were known as state roads. Only one of them crossed this county going from Marietta to Chillicothe. This was not macademized in any way being only a dirt road with little if any grading on it.

Athens county did not begin to build macademized roads or pikes until 1892, when through the efforts of Hon. D. L. Sleeper, Athens countys' representative in the general assembly of Ohio, a special act was passed, known as the "Sleeper law," which authorized Athens county to issue bonds to the amount of $300,000 to be used for pike construction.

SPELLING AND SINGING SCHOOLS.

The principal public entertainment of the nighborhood in early days was the spelling school. This attracted young and old alike who gathered from far and near to fight for the honored but much disputed position of "best speller" in the locality.

These were carried on in several different ways of choosing heads, sides, words, etc., but usually closed by one "spelling down" the entire gathering and a grand frolic and ride home in the moonlight. The old fashioned speller a book now found only on a few old book shelves containing a variety of words, and one who knew them all well deserved the awe and admiration of the community. Though sometimes a good speller would inadvertently miss a word early in the contest and have to sit down in mortification, while a comparatively poor speller might happen to stand till nearly or quite the last and carry off the honors.

No wonder that the lads and lassies of those days who are the grandfathers and grandmothers of to-day are rare spellers and look rather contemptuously upon those who with all the superior advantages of school and education to-day can not begin to spell with those of the old spelling school days.

Another opportunity for fun and frolic was the singing school. These were organized by a teacher who went from

Continued on page 48.

✣ ✣ ✣ ✣ ✣ ✣ ✣ ✣ ✣ ✣

Residence of Mr. and Mrs. John Kale, Athens, Ohio.

JOHN KALE, whose home in Athens is here shown, was born in Loramie, France, August 10, 1841, and came with his parents to this country in 1849, and landed in Cincinnati.

When about fifteen he located in Vinton county and soon went to work in the railroad shops at Zaleski, where he worked as a car builder for twenty-seven years.

In 1861 he enlisted in Co. D. 2nd Regt., W. Va. Cavalry and served throughout the civil war. He was in the battles of Cedar Creek, Lynchburg, Lewisburg, Wythville and a score of others, but he was in at the grand review at Washington at the close of the war and never received a scratch in his four years' service, and was mustered out in Wheeling.

Mr. Kale was married to Miss Mary L. Black on May 15, 1869, and five sons have been born to them: Tun F., A. H., P. H., J. R. and H. W. Kale. All are engaged in railroad work but Tun, who is a dry goods clerk in Athens.

F. L. PRESTON COMPANY DRY GOODS STORE, ATHENS, OHIO.

F. L. PRESTON COMPANY CLOTHING STORE, ATHENS, OHIO.

THE beginning of the Preston Stores in Athens, Co., O., was in March, 1882. L. P. Preston and F. L. Preston, his son, opened a clothing store in Nelsonville, Ohio, under the firm name of L. P. Preston & Son. L. P. Preston, the senior, was well advanced in years at that time, having spent a life time in the business of buying and selling merchandise, and with varying fortunes; at one time a leading merchant and banker at Columbus. Ohio, as well as one of the pioneer merchants of the Capital city. Coming to Columbus from Vermont in 1839, he formed a partnership with his brother, "S. D." the firm doing business in Columbus and Indianapolis as S. D. &

L. P. Preston. They were also interested with William Neil, of Columbus, in the banking business. Success followed their efforts for many years, but they were doomed to fail at the high tide of supposed prosperity, owing to a money panic that first caught the bank, extending to the other ramifications of their, at that time, extensive business. About 1867 Mr. Preston, Sr. came to Nelsonville to manage a "Company Store" for W. B. Brooks, who, at that time, was a leading coal operator, bringing his family with him, and was in this service about eleven years. Therefore, at t e beginning of the business in Athens, Co., O., (Mr. L. P. Preston being advanced in years), the manage-

L. P. PRESTON & SON CLOTHING STORE, NELSONVILLE OHIO.

F. L. & S. D. PRESTON, DRY GOODS STORE, NELSONVILLE, OHIO

F. L. PRESTON'S RESIDENCE, ATHENS, OHIO.

ment fell upon his son, F. L., the present senior partner with his brothers in the Preston stores at Nelsonville and Athens.

From beginning the first store with a modest capital, the stores under the leadership of F. L. Preston have prospered, enjoying the full confidence of the public and a large patronage. The management has always been energetic and aggressive, and the Preston stores have earned the reputation for up-to-date merchandise at reliable prices. Today after adding one store after another as the opportunities presented themselves, the combined business of the Preston stores is no doubt the largest in the county, in the line of Dry Goods and Clothing. The equipment being two large Dry Goods stores exclusively devoted to Dry Goods and two Clothing stores carrying extensive lines and doing a large trade in clothing, while each are separate and distinct stores, they are all under the same general management and belong to the same owners, being S. D. Preston. Manager of the Nelsonville Dry Goods store of F. L. & S. D. Preston ; L. S. Preston Manager of the Nelsonville Clothing store of L. P. Preston & Son ; F. L. Preston Manager of the Athens stores of The F. L Preston Company.

Recently the Preston's have opened another dry goods store at Belle Center, Ohio, which will add to their already large outlet for merchandise, thereby assuring buying facilities possessed by few outside the large cities, and enabling them to promise to their customers every inducement in return for their liberal patronage.

F. L. Preston, the subject of this sketch, was born at Delaware. Ohio. January 10, 1854. being reared and educated in the Columbus schools. At the age of 17 he entered the store of W. B. Brooks, at Nelsonville, his father being manager. Soon young Preston was given a confidential position in the coal office of the firm in Columbus, keeping their wholesale books and being private secretary and correspondent to Mr. Brooks. This was one of the largest coal operating firms in the Hocking Valley. After two years Mr. Preston was made secretary and office manager for Brooks & Baker, the firm being a creation of Mr. Brooks for the purpose of manufacturing enameled stove hollow ware. Mr. Preston spent about three years with this firm as office manager and traveling salesman, when Mr. Pendleton resigned his position at the Nelsonville office and young Preston, now 22 years old; was given charge of the Nelsonville office business, remaining in this capacity up to the time when he engaged in business for himself, having served the Brooks interests about ten years. His experiences with this firm were extensive and always

considered by him valuable, especially at Nelsonville, as he had the oversight there of the accounts of about 400 men, and other business transactions with them. This created a close friendship between the young bookkeeper and the several hundred employees which was destined to remain abiding. This association and experience gave him the necessary equipment in the knowledge of human nature and how to deal with people to qualify him for his splendid and successful business career since.

March 31, 1879, Mr. Preston was married at Nelsonville to Ella Herrold, eldest daughter of John and Nancy

Herrold. To them three children were born. L. Perry, Jr., John H. and Fred Dix. Perry dying February 11, 1901. Mrs. Preston died February 1, 1893. Mr. Preston married Mrs. Jennie Wheeler, of Logan, October 10, 1894.

Mr. Preston has never been a candidate for any public office, confining himself to the business of the firm of which he is senior partner and other business enterprises in which he is interested. And thus it can be said that he is one of the best, most enterprising, and successful business men of Athens county. His new home shown herewith is one of the finest in Athens, the city of fine homes.

RESIDENCE OF MR. PETER OXLEY, IN LODI TOWNSHIP.

❉ ❉ ❉ ❉ ❉ ❉ ❉ ❉ ❉ ❉ ❉ ❉

PETER OXLEY is one of the pioneer citizens of this county. He was born in Belmont county, February 4, 1828, coming to Athens county in 1842, having lived here ever since. He has cleared and helped to clear two farms, on one of which he still lives with his son Charlie and family. By dint of industry and enterprise he has possessed himself sufficient of this world's goods to be in comfortable circumstances, notwithstanding that fire destroyed his home a few years ago.

For some time before the breaking out of the war he was a member of a private military company in Athens, and during hostilities was ready to go to the front, but the serious illness of his wife, finally resulting in her death, prevented him exercising his loyal desire till in the spring of' 64 when he enlisted in Company B., 141st Regiment. Even this short service so injured his eyes that he is drawing a pension for their injury.

Mr. Oxley was married twice, his first wife being Lusetta C Moore, to whom he was married February 27, 1857, Mrs. Oxley dying in 1864. His second wife was Lucinda Thompson, to whom he was married March 19, 1867. she dying January 9, 1880.

Mr. Oxley is the father of six children, all of whom are living.

district to district and for a small fee gave the most elementary instruction in reading music. Sometimes this teacher could play the violin and found pupils for that also but as a rule the only equipment he had was a strong voice and a tuning fork. Bright swinging attractive glees were not then known and the pupils were kept in the tiresome a b c of music until near the close of the term when a few Sunday school songs or hymns were worked up in two-part style and rarely was an anthem attempted. As the young men came largely for fun and to go home with the girls it was often an impossibility for the singing master to keep order and attention in his class but even in this primitive way a love for music was awakened and developed which, in many, brought fine results in later years, those who found our great music centers and carried the fork on to success. Also these schools developing a general love of music were the forerunners of the organ or piano now to be found in almost every home in the country, no matter how poor or obscure.

STREAMS AND THEIR NAMES.

Many interesting legends cling about the early names of a country, but in later years they are so often lost sight of that one seldom pauses in the busy rush of the 20th century to ask where did this rivulet get its name, who gave it, what event did it commemorate or what did the word mean.

The Ohio Company being composed largely of classical students from Yale and Harvard we are not surprised to find them affixing classical names such as Adelphi, which later became Marietta, to the first settlement, and Athens, to the University settlement which they hoped to make the seat of learning for this whole "Northwest Territory." In very few respects did they adopt the Indian name they found awaiting them, but preferred to civilize the names as well as the country, of which they had taken possession.

The name of Hock-hocking they left however very much as it was though tradition tells us it was more like "Hochocen" meaning to the Indians, bottle like. This had reference to the shape of the river just above the falls near Logan, which viewed from the overhanging cliffs still resembles a long necked bottle.

Federal creek was so named by one of the first exploring parties which left the Marietta settlement, because they discovered that thirteen branches composed the main stream. It must be remembered that these sturdy hunters were revolutionary soldiers, to whom that magic number thirteen must always mean the federal state.

Margaret Creek was so name in honor of the first white woman to penetrate this wilderness and settle hereon. Margaret Snowden by name.

There is a tradition that another party of adventurous hunters out on an exploring expedition crossed the hills instead of following the river because of the swampy condition of the valley. They encamped on Saturday evening on a creek and spent Sunday there naming the creek Sunday. The next evening coming to another stream they encamped there and named it Monday Creek. Most of the small creeks in the county are named for the early settlers who first made their clearings near by.

Continued on page 51.

ATHENS PUBLIC DRINKING FOUNTAIN.

This beautiful add artistic drinking fountain is located on the Court House esplanade and is a monument to the generosity of the Young Women's Christian Temperance Union of Athens, and was presented to the city of Athens on May 30, 1895, with appropriate ceremonies. The statuary that adorns this fountain is a faithful copy of the famous Greek statuary representing Hebe, the Goddess of Youth. She was the cup-bearer in Olympus and always retained the power of restoring the aged to the bloom of youth and beauty.

On the fountain are two inscriptions as follows:

"For God and Home and Every Land."
Erected by the Young Women's Christian Temperance Union and presented to the city of Athens May 30, 1895.

Truth forever on the scaffold,
Wrong forever on the throne,
Yet that scaffold sways the future,
And behind the dim unknown
Standeth God within the shadow,
Keeping watch above his own.
—LOWELL.

F. C. Strohmeyer's Residence, Glouster.

F C. STROHMEYER, whose beautiful home is here illustrated, is one of the good citizens of Glouster. He was born Nov. 30, 1858, at Pomeroy, Ohio, removing with his parents to Syracuse, Ohio, in 1866, where his parents still reside.

His father, F. G. Strohmeyer, was born in the northwestern part of Germany on January 28, 1833, but came to the United States with his parents in 1843, settling at Pomeroy, O., where he was married to Caroline L. Bartels, born in Westphalia, Germany, January 16, 1835, she coming to the United States at the age of 20, and locating at Pomeroy, Ohio. Thus Mr. Strohmeyer comes of sturdy and industrious German stock.

The subject of this sketch was first married to Zelda Hartley, daughter of John C. and Myra Hartley, of Syracuse, Ohio, Nov. 16, 1879. To this union were born ten children, six of whom are living, Bertha, born September 7, 1880; Clarence, born October 13, 1882; Charles, born April 8, 1886, Carrie, born June 24, 1890; Grace, born December 9, 1893, and Hazel, born October 8, 1895.

In April, 1887 Mr. Strohmeyer removed with his family to Elenwood Kansas, but returned to Syracuse in October of the same year; coming to Glouster the following month, where his wife died January 10, 1899.

On June 6, 1901, he was married to Lucy, daughter of A. H. and Isabell Winebrenner, of Syracuse. To them two children were born, Virgil, April 7, 1902 and Harold, March 27, 1905.

Mr. Strohmeyer has a delightful home and an interesting, industrious family, honored and respected by all. The father is employed most of the time at mining.

FARM RESIDENCE OF MR. AND MRS. C. P. CLESTER, DOVER TOWNSHIP.

C P. CLESTER, the picture of whose beautiful home we herewith present, was born in Dover township, October 2, 1848. and and has lived here continuously ever since. His father was born in Bedford county, Pa., December 17, 1814, and his mother at Hagerstown, Md., January 6, 1818. His father died August 14, 1869, but his mother still enjoys good health. The subject of this sketch was married to Miss Carrie McAffee, November 10, 1869. To this union two children were born: Sadie, March 5, 1871, and Carrie May December 7, 1875. Sadie is now the wife of G. H. Junod, President of the Athens Lumber Company, while Carrie is now Mrs J. D. Martin, who is associated with the Athens Lumber Company. Mr. Clester received his education at Weethee College, at the feet of Prof. Weethee, its founder, while Mrs. Clester is a product of Athens High School, she having been born near Athens October 15, 1848. The parents of Mrs. Clester were born in Scotland, but came to this country about seventy years ago, first settling at Wooster, Ohio. Mr. Clester has been a director of the County Infirmary seven years, assessor three years and land appraisor two terms. Both he and his wife are members of the Methodist church, while Mr. Clester has been Sunday School superintendent for a long term of years. They have lived in this lovely country home for over fifty-one years, where their children and grand children make them many happy visits

THE HISYLVANIA COAL COMPANY, TRIMBLE, OHIO.

THE Hisylvania Coal Co., whose splendid and prosperous plant is represented above, is one of the substantial industries of Athens county, and is located at Trimble. The company is composed of professional and business men of Ohio and Pennsylvania. Its officers are J. H. White, Pittsburg. Pa., President, who is one of the ablest attorneys of that great city, with W. H. Hopewood, a leading physician of Uniontown, Pa., as Secretary; J. W Blower, of Trimble, its Treasurer and General Manager, is one of the most capable and successful coal operators in the country, with a splendid record as a coal developer. His brother, E. M. Blower, also of Trimble, is Superintendent. To the splendid business ability and skill of these two brothers is largely due the enviable success of the plant which is known as Mine No. 23. This mine was purchased from the William Job Coal Co. when it was only partly developed. The present company began to ship coal in December, 1901, although its tracks and tipple were not completed until in January, 1903; the

delay being caused by the railroad company not making its switch connections until the latter date; since which time the plant has been in almost continuous operation, giving steady employment to about one hundred and twenty-five men.

There is great demand for their product, not alone because of its excellent quality, but also because of the good feeling and mutual interest of employers and employes guaranteeing against strikes and all internal disraptions. Buyers therefore can depend upon the prompt shipment and upon the rapid increase and development of the mine.

The seam worked is the well-known Hocking or No. 6, the quality of which is considered the best in the Sunday Creek Valley. The lease is for 830 acres of coal owned by A. E. Lewis, of Sabina, O., and the heirs of the late William Palmer, of Glouster, O. The main opening is a slope eight feet high and sixteen feet wide, driven thro the solid rock to a distance of 550 feet; with a dip of

twenty-five per cent. At the foot of the slope a tunnel was sunk to the depth of 650 feet before a seam of nominal thickness was reached.

The machinery installed in this plant is of the latest and most approved kind, and consists of two 100 horse power Atlas Tubular boilers, one pair of 16 x 24 Mansfield hoisting engines for hauling the coal from the slope. The power plant consists of 100 K. W. Jeffrey generator and an 150 horse power McEwan automatic engine. The coal is mined by two Jeffrey electric chain machines and two Goodman machines of the same kind, all making an under cut of seven feet.

This company has never built any miners' houses and none are required, as ninety per cent of its employes own their own homes, thus guaranteeing the best class of workmen, dwelling in peace and prosperity.

Its very name suggests peace and enterprise, being a combination of the names of the two states, which have done so much toward these glorious ends in government.

RESIDENCE OF MR. AND MRS. JAMES McCLANAHAN.

JAMES W. McCLANAHAN, whose residence and farm property on Coolville Ridge in Canaan township, is here shown, has earned the title of "successful man." He was born on Wolfe Creek, in Morgan county, March 24, 1842, and came with his parents, Mr. and Mrs. Matthew McClanahan, to Alexander township, this county in where he lived until the outbreak of the civil war.

The life of a farmer boy was too mild for him while the country was in need of men. He enlisted July 25, 1861 in Co. C., 30th Regt., O. V. I., and served practically through the war, being mustered out of service August 29, 1864, near Atlanta, Ga. He participated in the battles of Antietam, South Mountain, Vicksburg, Mission Ridge, etc.

Returning from the army he settled down to the ways of peace, and on December 2, 1865 was united in marriage to Miss Maria Sams. He purchased 90 acres of the farm he yet owns and began to dig his profits out of the soil. So well has he succeeded that today he owns 430 acres, three dwellings on Mill street in Athens and is now prepared to enjoy the fruits of his economy and labor, and with his wife, who is yet living, enjoy a peaceful and happy old age, surrounded by a family of ten children—five girls and five boys—whose names follow: Mary J. Rodgers, Alexander township; Epsa A. Leighty, Glouster; Arminta M. Maxwell, Canaan township; Blanche Dinsmoore, Valiparaso, Ind.; Elsie Philipps, Jerseyville; James S., John C., Robert, William M. and Elmer E.

Mr. McClanahan is a member of Paramuthia Lodge, F. & A. M., of Athens, O.; is a clever neighbor and upright citizen, and numbers his friends by the score. Few men have amassed so many acres, raised so large a family as has Mr. McClanahan.

LODGES AND FRATERNAL ORDERS.

Athenian Lodge, No. 104, K. of P., Athens, Ohio.

Caldwell, J. E.
Haney, Scott
Finsterwald, Sam
Kidwell, J. W.
Webster, Dana
Walker, E. Raymond
Beckler, H. S.
Feth, Jacob
Cotton, T. C.
Charlton, M. J.
Junod, Geo. H.
Buxton, Frank
Lash, E. R.
Calvert, Wm.
Gabriel, A. L.
Selby, John
Roush, T. B.
McKee, Geo.
Peoples, D. W.
Beal, P. L.
Moorhead, Fred
Morrow, J. S.
Morse, B. E.
Brown, C. F.
Smith, C. W.
Thompson, C. H.
Cotton, E. H.
McVey, F. P.
Beam, C. L.
Carscadden, Bert
Merrill, L. D.
Goldsberry, F. E.
Fuller, Carl
Pierce, C. H.
Biddison, E. G.
Armstrong, H. O.
Carscadden, E. C.
Cochran, Alex
Peters, Geo. H.
Patterson, W. R.
Heisner, Fred
Hastings, W. J
Brooks, H. W.
Sutton, Asa
Warner, C. J.
Beasley, Geo.
McCune, John K.
Pickering, T. M.
Henry, J. J.

Moore, D. H
Moore, C. O.
Blackburn, Wm.
Woodworth, E. C.
Zenner, Henry
Finsterwald, Peter
Sayre, E. D
Martin, J. D.
Webster, H. M.
Logan, Earl
Sickels, Lester E.
Harris, C. C.
Mansfield, Fred
Hankie, D. W.
Brown, Guy H.
Lawrence, W. H.
Johnson, J. H.
Haning, H. H.
Vaughn, W. J.
Roach, A. C.
King, Rev. G. W.
Cline, J. C.
Hallm, T. O.
Herrold, J. W.
Blackwood., J. P.
Newsom, C. S.
Stalder, H. G.
Finsterwald, Frank
Duncan, John S.
Merrill, F. M.
Burke, Wm.
Basom, Dr. J. S.
Day, Jesse C.
Foster, I. M.
Jourdan, W. F.
Linscott, A. P.
Finsterwald, Henry
Cuckler, Ray
Harris, C. A.
Kelley, L. W.
Radcliff, L. D.
Roberts, L. W.
Bower, Charles J.
O'Bleness, Harry C.
Lowe, T. L.
Eaton, E. G.
Martin, C. J.
Gibson, E. G.
Russell, J. E.

Walden J. S.
Walden, G. H.
Russell, W. E.
McLaughlin, John
Barrows, U. M.
Chevalier, O. E.
Jones, Dr. C. L.
Besser, Geo.
Clayton, Earl S.
Russell, E. A.
Biddle, Dr. D. H.
Ramsey, Harvey
Atkins, E. L.
Nawman, A. I.
McMasters, H. H. K
Robbins, C. E.
Tribe, Clifton
Rink, A. O.
Cabeen, Robert
Cooley, R. V.
Myers, R. V.
Weatherbee, A.
Mercer, L. L.
Hope, J. T.
Bethel, Webb G.
Cornwell, C. A.
Logan, C. L.
Twiss, M. E.
Gillespie, Dr. R. P.
Parker, W. C.
Mills, Prof. E. M.
Higgins, J. M.
Figley, H. M.
Hooper, Ralph
Wilson, Prof. H. R
Jones, W. C.
Edgar, Addison
Clark, H. C.
Bean, Allen
Miller, Wm. A.
Fulton, Harry
Copeland, T. A.
Blackburn, D. E.
Howard, John
Wilson, H. L.
Sutton, R. E,
McKinley, H.
Robbins, J. F.
Nye, L. C.
Sheldon, C. R.

Glouster Lodge, No. 336, K of P., Glouster, Ohio.

Achauer, B. F.
Antle, Des
Atlas, E.
Alexander, Robt.
Andrews, Frank
Andrews, Loran
Andrews, C. H.
Andrews, L. R.
Bell, Peter
Bryson, J. W.
Bodach, Geo.
Beavin, John P.
Bryson, Frank
Blanchard, W. R.
Brown, Gilbert
Bateman, Wm.
Barnes, Charles
Biddison, T. G.
Benedum, O. S.
Clark, John
Crumbie, Wm.
Cox, John
Carpenter, S. S.
Carter, J. W.
Cox, J. T.
Curfman, C. V.
Chamberlaine, Wm.
Cuckler, S. L.
Crew, Solomon
Criswell, Harve
Coffman, G. E.
Campbell, W. S.
Creig, A. J.
Cavey, John
Creachbaum, Lewis
Cooper, Robert
Crawford, Sam'l
Crawford, A. J.
Davis, D. B.
Davis, Thomas
Dunnett, Robt
Daugherty, H.
Evans, D. J.
Ellis, Thomas
Evans, Thomas
Embrey, Wm.
Eberts, S.
Emrich, G. W.
Gunther, Howard
Gatchel, John
Gibson, Daniel
Gatchel Clarence

Hamilton M. Sr.,
Hamilton, Wm.
Hopes, Thomas
Hanson, P. E.
Higgins, J. F.
Hamilton, M. Jr.,
Hemsley, Thomas
Hopkins, Theo.
Henderson, J. F.
Hemry, R. S.
Hanson, H. M.
Harris, Reese
Hoodlet, Walter
Hanson, R. S.
James, Wm.
Johnston, Thomas
Jones, J. E.
Jacob, Henry
Jones, John
Jonas, August
Jones, Lewis
Kistler, Wm.
Kay, Benj.
Kelley, C. W.
Kiskbride, Charles
Kendall, W. M.
Kasler, Wm. M.
Kasler, Abram
Kasler, Charles
Lawrence, E. I.
Lloyde, Philip
Love, David
Love, Wm.
Leonard, Herbert
Lyman, Joe
Lookenotte Frank
Love, Albert
Love, Walter
Linscott, N. W.
Lunsford, Wm.
McCarty, W. E.
Miller, Frank,
McLain, Carlos
Murry, David Jr.
Murry, David Sr.
Mathieson, John
Morris, Abe
Morris, Wm.
Morris John
Morgan, W. H.
Morris, Geo.
McClellen, James

Mohler, R.
McDonald, W. W.
Morgan, J. W.
McLaughlin, Wain
Myers, J. G.
Nixon, S. H.
Nichols, E.
Nelson, Alex.
Powell, W.
Packer, Worthy
Parker, J. S.
Powers, Thos
Oliver, Earl
Orndorf, C. D.
Rose, H. S.
Rothman, E. S.
Ray, John
Reese, Moses
Ripass, J.C.
Runther, John
Stroehmyre, Fred
Steinmitz, L. R.
Stedman, I. N.
Skinner, Bert
Thomas, W. C.
Thomas, S. D.
Theophilus, W.
Thomas, J. D.
Vernon, C. A.
Vermaaton, Ed.
Vermaaton, Anthony
Vermaaton, Geo.
Williams, Richard
Williams, D. H.
Winning, Thomas.
Walters, Walter
Williams, Benj.
Williams, Wm.
Williams, E. E.
Welch, M. B.
Williams, Thomas
Waldie, M.
Wade, N. P.
Walters, Thomas
Wilburn, A. C.
Williams, John
Wilson, Albert
Weaver, I. H.
Yaw, J. V.
Zarley, F. M.

Sunday Creek Lodge, No. 248, K. of P., Jacksonville, O.

Philips, J. T.
Roby, Wm.
Venning, Charles H
Watkins, Wilson
Laferty, Archibald
Burnley, Isaac
Kempton, Curtis
Lantz, John E
Nutter, Richard
Brown, Robert
Hiser, Wm.
Herbst, Geo.
Hiser, Otto
Rankin, Robert
Bartram, Wm.
Exenkemfer, Herm'n
Wade, Charles
Rutledge, Geo. A.
Mingus, Joseph S.
Brookins, Martin
Cochran, Charles
Booth, Snyder

Border, S. E.
West, Joseph
Lott, Charles E.
Burns, Eugene
Cooley, Sylvester
Mulfas, Raymond
Stephenson, Elmer
Gibbs, Wm.
Stephenson, Joseph
Brookins, Howard
Taylor, John D.
Reak, Wm.
Byers, Geo. A.
Householder, Sylves
Gilley, Gilbert E.
Beiderman, Nathan
Goodrich, Earnest A
Adair, Frank A.
Allen, Charles
Allen, John
Bee, John
Chute, Justus E.

Edwards, Albert
Elswick, William
Elswick, John
Gibbs, John
Hope, James
Hiser, Charles
Hipshire, Charles
Johnson, James
Kistler Andrew
Koons, Frank P.
Muir, Edward
Rasp, George
Stewart, Frank
Sehoenian, C. G.
Taylor, Thomas
Dusz, Charles
Baker, Charles
Johnson, Julius
Gillet, Wm.
Branon, John W.

Athens Conclave No. 9, S. W. M., Athens, Ohio.

Hoisington, Geo.
McKibben, Richard
McKibben, Harry
Goff, W. D.
Nicholson, W. H.
Woogered, James H.
Woogered, Vivan L.
Bobo, G. H.
Bobo, Harry
Hoisington, Fred R
Ruston, William
Farrell, W. H.
Tucker, Chas.
Woogered, H. B.
Sutton, F. F.
McKibben, W. F.
McKibben, Albert
McLaid, Ray

Stephenson, Frank
Martin, Aaron
Dille, C. A.
French, Wm.
Halsey, A. L.
McKinstry, Ralph
Baker, R. D.
Fenzel, Fred
Brooks, W. J.
Beasley, L. D.
Strawn, Clarence
McWhorter, J W.
McKibben, Harrison
Mace, Alonzo
Sams, Grove
McKinstry, G. B.
Bobo, Frank
Simmons, Geo. F.

Bobo, J. C.
Bobo, R. G.
Gabriel, Geo. Jr.,
Duncan, J. S.
Hutchison, Samuel
James, Alvah
Burke, Samuel G.
Salters, W. F.
Sams, Harry
Kyle, W. W.
Simmons, Albert
Mitchell, Geo.
Kelley, Louis
Ashworth, Chas.
Gibson, J.H.

Court Dove, No. 117, Forresters of America, Chauncey.

Wilson, Geo.
Six, S. D.
Willis, Samuel
Henry, Wilford
Powell, Clarence
Smith, Thomas
Smith, Sylvester
Rackham, John
Carter, Chas.
Sprague, W. V.
Sprague, W. T.
Watkins, A. C.
Gabriel, Den
Parfits, James
Hawk, Fletcher

Campbell, John
Smith, A. C.
McLead, John
Waunacott, Harry
Jackson, Chas.
Watkins, Frank
Linscott, D. H.
Carter, Fred
McKee, Emric
Keasey, Sherman
Shaffer, John L.
Wakeley, Wm.
Matheney, John
Ragan, Daniel
Lehmon, Bert

Hawk, Roy
Campbell, Chas.
Smith, D. J.
McDainel, S. G.
Barker, H. M.
Carter, L. B.
Keasey, Peter
Harvey, Floyd
Fry, C. C.
Powers, Thos.
Brown, Walter
Ragon, Wesley

The Knights of the Maccabees of the World, Tent No. 147 Nelsonville, Ohio.

Lamb, R. T.
Courtney, L. A.
Washburn, C. E.
Rittgers, E. E.
Standford, Ed
Sanders, J. D.
Davis, Wm.
Tippie, W. E.
Beverage, J. C.
Howe, J. R.
Welch, C. E.
Evans, Ed. C.
Clayman, M.
Aumiller, C. L.
Richards, Morgan
Rosser, T. S.
Williams, W. H.
Morris, R. D.
Sickels, L. E
Gilbert, E. M.
Wallace, C. C.
Finley, L. R.
Shaffer, E. E.
Hyde, J. M.
Longstaff, Thos.

Gibson, C. W.
Cook, N. S.
Hickman, J. R.
Gerrard, Edward
Groves, Nolan
Edington, John
Evans, W. B.
Crane, L. E.
Wilson, John M.
Smiley, C. E.
Redd, C. H.
Hoch, Carl
Keeton, C. D.
Hempton, A. C.
Hempton, C. E.
Ingels, Chas.
Morrison, Walter
Wilson, S. J.
Woodard, M. L.
Forrset, Hiram
Webb, Oscar
Betts, P. C.
Coakley, Fred
Wells, E. T.
Hall, Harry

Coakley, Alonzo
Maxwell, R. L.
Thompson, A. E.
Ely, A. R,
Davis, Frank
Coakley, G. W.
Poirier, Harden
Ballard, C. L.
Coakley, Bert
McClurg, Chas.
Brooks, Chas.
Donnelson, John
Hartman, Jas.
Coleman, Edward
Cope, Geo.
Rosser, Eugene
Morgan, Hiram
Cordel, Geo.
Brooks, Jacob
Key, John
Lowery, Jas.
Nease, S. N.
Brown, C. L.
Saxon, J.
Sayler, Chas.
Linton, Earnest

Chauncey Hive, No. 274, L. O. T. M., Chauncey, O.

Courtney, Minette
Courtney, Elizabeth
Campbell, Emma
Cunningham, Ella
Cunningham, Sarah
England, Ella
Faires, Hattie
Fulton, Ella
Franz, Alice
Gardner, Susan
Hixon, Rinda
Hudnall, Luella

Henry, Nettie
Jackson, Minnie
Katzenbach, Annie
Katzenbach, Fanny
McHarg, Ella
Martin, Linnie
Nye, Sarah
Pendergrass, Ida
Pendergrass, Maud
Sprague, Floride
Sprague, Royal
Shields, Lucinda

Shields, Annie
Shields, Etta
Stalder, Addie
Six, Daisy
Thomas, Bell
Tippett, Emma
Watkins, Myra
Wilson, Elizabeth
Welling, Clara

Charity Conclave, No, 8, S. W. M., Marshfield, O.

Barrows, Joseph
Six, P. B.
Stanley, Pearl
Hunter, C. B.
Hutchins, W.
Snedden, Annis
Lewellen, A. E.
Robinett, S. E
Tremain, Albert
Philips, G.
James, John
Nice, M. W.
Miller, Marion
Dodds, John
Six, Harrison
Walker, G. W.
Sturgill, W. R.
Townsend, Robt.
Clark, W. C.
Ely, J. D.
Stanley, Clarence
Nichols, G. T.
Mitchel, W. Jr
Six, W. G.
Doll, G. P.
Bust, Ray
Gabriel, H. C.
Quick, Chas.
Quick, Jas.
Clark, P. G.
Cooper, Chas.
Cooper, John
Smith, John
Johnston, J. F.
Burkett, T. A.

Bagley, Chas.
Sweeney, James
Haines, Joseph
Carter, C. E.
Burkett, S. M.
Stanley, Peter
McCoy, J. O.
DeWees, H. T.
Cox, W. D
Young, Clifford
Nichols, Mason
Six, D. H.
Creighton, S. E.
Snow, A. M.
Ross, W. L.
Penrod, J. W.
Perry, J. N.
McDaniels, J. W.
McLead, Chas.
Martin, F. M.
McLead, Hall
Lowry, Don.
Knowlton, Levi
Hoodlett, Fred
Cox, Wallace
Pedigo, Dr. S. E. G
Beckley, Marion
Robinett, W. H.
Downard, L. E.
Crossen, Ira
Carter, Harvey
Beverage, James
Barnes, Ira
Bobo, C. F.
Andrews, Oscar

Bobo, C. P.
Stewart, Dan
Frank, Robt.
Beverage, O. C.
Cox, Elsworth
Cundiff, Austin
Six, Wesley
Moshier, Floyd
Doolittle, Robt.
Todd, Henry
Gabriel, W. G.
Grim, John
Davis, W. J.
Schmitt, John A.
Sherman, Geo.
Chester, Chas.
Quick, Elmer
Martin, Frank
McLead, Vance
White, Sherman
Quick, W.
Mashetter, John F.
Maco, G. W.
McPherson, W.
Cox, C. H.
Penrod, A. J.
Willison, K. C.
Shingler, Thos.
Strinmeyer, Frank
Graft, Abe
Dixon, M. W.
McVay, L. L.
Myrtle, Chas.

Nelsonville Hive, No. 210. L. O. T. M., Nelsonville, O.

Aumiller, Gay
Anderson, Bessie
Butt, Rose
Betts, Geneve
Betts, Stella
Betts, Dora
Bland, Lillian
Brown, Lillie
Barron, Tillie
Cook, Emma
Coakley, Rachel
Dowler, Ira
Edington, Ellen
Edgell, Jennie
Evans, Lula
Howe, Oril
Howe, Sarah
Howe, Jennie
Hill, Clara
Hoodlett, Hattie
Harrold, Isabella

Graham, Fanny
Frame, Gertrude
Jacoby, Gertrude
Johnson, Lula
Johnson, Carrie
Kaelin, Lizzie
Katzenbach, Sarah
Love, Adda
Love, Selma,
Lee, Caroline
Linton, Callie
Lancaster, Rachel
Minner, Mary
Minner, Ida
Mender, Jennie
McNabb, Blanch
Patton, Lillian
Power, Ella
Powell, Jennie
Richards, Susan

Rhoads, Nellie
Rhoads, Maud
Robinson, Rilla
Slater, Anna
Socie, Frances
Sickles, Irma
Sweeney, Elizabeth
Stratton, Mary
Saylor, Sarah
Shrader, Allie
Tomlinson, Alice
Vore, Margaret
Williams, Katherine
Washburn, Rowena
Wyman, Ida
Wallace, Clyde
Warner, Lizzie

Athens Hive. No. 272, L. O. T. M., Athens, O.

Andrews, Lillie M.
Allen, Attie B,
Blackwood, Emma
Baker, Faye A.
Brooks, Ruth
Beasley, Ella
Barker, Dora
Burt, Margurite
Bean, Hattie
Beal, Luella
Butts, Thedocia
Brown, Mary M.
Cook, Anna A.
Cochran, Elizabeth
Cotton, Isabelle
Coleman, Antoinette
Chappelle, Vesta
Chappelier Emma E
Cameron, Ella
Connett, Hattie
Dill, Jennie R.

Droze, Emma, A.
Eaton, Della
Fulton, Esther R,
Gillilan, Bertha
Higgins, Elizabeth
Hastings, Elizabeth
Haney, Emma E
Hill, Ida
Hooper, Kate A.
Johnson, Elizabeth
Jordan, Bertha
Kern, Nelle
Lawrence, Etta
Lawrence, Helen
Logan, Laura V.
Miller, Verna
Miller, Setepta
Munn, Retta C.
Munn Carrie
Moore, Luella
Moore, Ida M.

McVay Jessie B.
Mourne, Mary
McNutt, Catherine
McKinstry, Caroline
Paul, Elma
Nicholson, Ida
Osborne, Ella M
Pratt, Margaret
Richey, Hattie
Reid, Nora L.
Reeves, Minnie
Secoy, Mary B.
Smythe, Garnet
Thompson, Clara
Tresham, Anna D.
Warren, Flora
Wright, Malisa
Wilson, Lula

K. O. T. M. Lodge, Chauncey, O.

Gardner, M. J.
Gardner, Ray
Courtney, H. S. A.
Cradelbaugh, Chas.
Cook, O. M.
Curtis, M. G.
England, A. H.
Hixon, Robert
Harve, J. C.
James, C. M.
Martin, J H.
Pendergrass, Pete
Sprague, Dr. W. T.
Sweeney, Chas.
Swart, Geo.
Tippett, L. C.

Welling, Ed.
Robinson, Vick
Linscott, Harry
Chappelear, Isaac
Courtney, Hoyte
Brown, Ed.
Devore, E. C.
Faires, W. C.
Henry, Wilfred
Koons, G. M.
Katzenbach, Geo.
Katzenbach, John
Lowe, G. W.
Six J. W.
Sears Ed.
Gardner, Guy

Wilson, Isaac
Perry, Thos.
Stalder, R. C.
Pendergrass, Lloyd
Pendergrass, F. J.
Welling, A. O.
Harvey, Floyd
Welling, Wesley
Nye, Carl
James, Robert
Wanless, Fred
Welling, J. R.
Watkins, Bert

ATHENS COUNTY CHILDREN'S HOME.

SUPT. ELZA ARMSTRONG. (deceased.)

MRS. ELZA ARMSTRONG. (Supt. and Matron.)

THE Childen's Home is the result of conditions, physical, moral, and financial, existing in the '80's when John S. Fowler, a philanthropist Quaker, formerly of Washington County, found that the dependent children of the county were inmates of the Infirmary. together with the adult inmates. This was recognized as being undesirable, and almost criminal to the child. But a flood of the Hocking river had destroyed much of the Infirmary property, and there was an urgent necessity for a new Court House and Jail, all of which would impose a heavy tax upon the county. With these conditions before him. Mr. Fowler deemed it unwise to attempt to constitute a Children's Home out of a general tax fund ; he therefore spent some four years in making a systematic canvass of the county for private subscription with which to create this eleemosynary institution. His efforts were crowned with a subscription list to the amount of $13,031.61. In 1880, by act of the Legislature, this work, together with it subscription list, was placed in the hands of the Commissioners, who the same year, purchased the present site of 125 acres, paying therefor $6.600. The list of subscribers obtained by Mr. Fowler was turned over by the County Commissioners to the county auditor who realized $9,500 thereupon. The site purchased was improved and ready for occupancy in the fall of 1881, the County Commissioners appointing a Board of Trustees, by whom and their successors, the Institution has since been governed.

Mr. and Mrs. J. M. Nourse were the first Superintendent and Matron, who were in charge till January 1st, 1883, being succeeded by Mr. and Mrs. W. A. Thomas, who held the positioms for three months' being suceeeded by Mr. and Mrs. Elza Armstrong, who took charge April 23d, 1883, since which time they have been its efficient Superintendent and Matron till Mr. Armstrong's death, February 22d, 1905,

since which time Mrs. Armstrong has filled the double office of Superintendent and Matron, most creditably and to the satisfaction of all. There are now 60 children in the Home, ranging in ages from two and one-half months to fifteen years. Since its opening to the present there have been 629 children cared for, many of whom have made noble men and women. The plant consists of 13 buildings, and is modern and up to date. with a complete water system, and heated and lighted by gas. On the farm is raised most of the living of of vegetables, meats, grains, &c., and the surplus, amounting to nearly $400 a year, is sold. The cost per capita for each inmate is about $80 per year, and the total annual running ex-

penter, who was born in Meigs County, Ohio, October 26, 1829. Mrs. Armstrong was a teacher for nine years, two terms of which were in Albany Academy. To Mr. and Mrs. Armstrong was born one son, who died at the age of eighteen years. Mr. Armstrong died February 22d, 1905, the last of his company of California 49ers.

No more efficient public servants can be found than those who have had charge of of Athens county's dependent children for over twenty years. Mr. and Mrs. Armstrong seemed to have but one aim in their work, and that was to train these children for good citizenship, and they have succeeded nobly, as is attested by many living witnesses. Mrs.

penses is about $4,000. The children help in the work of the Institution, and thus are prepared for self help, being well schooled for ten months of the year.

Elza Armstrong, for so many years Superintendent, was born at St. Mary's, Ohio, January 6, 1827. His father dying when Elza was a mere child, he remained with his mother till he was 12 years old, when he came to his grandfather's at Hebbardsville, Athens County, where he made his home till a young man, when he joined a company of 49ers for California, where he dug gold with some success for about three years. Returning to Hebbardsville, he engaged in stock business till 1883 when he assumed management of the Children's Home. November 17, 1857, Mr. Armstrong was married to Miss Lydia M. Car-

Armstrong is continuing the work with eminent satisfaction and success, to which they both had given their lives, and thus they have created a model institution, of which the county is justly proud.

The present Board of Trustees are

J. D. BROWN,
A. H. WELLS.
JOSEPH JORDON,
FRED W. BUSH.

ATHENS COUNTY HISTORY
CONTINUED.

EARLY PRICES.

A hard working and energetic man soon improves his circumstances and lays the foundation for a competence wherever he may be placed. But the generation of today marvels how it was done in this country a century ago, when the prices then paid are noted from 1815 to 1830.

It was nothing unusual for a young man to work for 31 1-4 cents a day, and on Saturday night to receive in pay something like this: Two tin cups at 25 cents each, a

quarter pound tea 50 cents, one pound coffee 50 cents, 37 1-2 cents in money, making in all $1.87 1-2 and walk home ten miles with his valuables.

A common price paid about the same time to a school teacher was $1.50 a week. Mail carriers carrying mail 200 miles a week and enduring the greatest hardships were rewarded with the munificent sum of $6.00 a month.

Pork and salt were about the only things produced in such quantities and of sufficient value for the country merchant to attempt to ship. Every country store had its "pork house," where most of the hogs of the neighborhood were brought, cut up and packed for sale.

This gave employment to a good many men and boys about the village who were paid by being given all the spare ribs, tenderloins, pigs feet and pigs heads. they

would carry away. These parts were not considered of any value and much of them were hauled off and dumped out of town. Any poor or unfortunate family could thus obtain free all the pork they could salt down for the winter.

While those might be called hard times, each and all were accommodating and suffering for actual necessities was rarely heard of. On the other hand every article not produced here was very high ; coffee at 50 cents a pound, tea $2, pins 25 cents a paper, cashmere $3 a yard, ribbon $1 a yard, calico 75 cents, cotton stockings 50c and 75c.

All these articles were carried from the east on pack horses, and nearly all the manufactured stuffs were imported from England.

Continued on page 53.

Farm Residence of Albert Johial Allen, Glouster, Ohio.

ALBERT JOHIAL ALLEN, is one of the old and representative citizens of Glouster, having been born in Trimble township November 1, 1834. He is of New England stock, his father having come from Woodstock, Mass., about 1810 and settled near where Chauncey now is. His grandfather on his mother's side was one of the Revolutionary heroes, and was a member of the Ohio Purchase company.

Mr. Allen married Hannah E. Hadley, December 7 1857. Mrs. Allen was born June 7, 1838, her parents coming from Massachusetts and New Hampshire. Her great grandmother was the historic Hannah Eastman, whom history recounts with such a thrilling experience with the Indians. Her father was a Colonel in the civil war, and was one of the earliest settlers of Athens county.

In 1857, Mr. Allen bought a farm out of the "Arnold land," Mr. Putnam, a younger brother of the famous Revolutionary General of the some name, being the agent at Marietta.

On part of this farm a part of Glouster now stands. Mr. Allen enlisted in the civil war, being mustered into services at Gallipolis, May 2 1864, and being discharged in September of the same year.

In his family were six children, the three older having died. Mr. and Mrs. Allen still reside in their nice comfortable home in Glouster.

Residence of John W. Davis, Glouster.

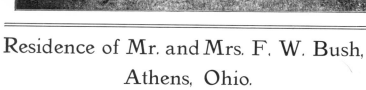

JOHN W. DAVIS, the son of Elder F. J. Davis, was born Aug. 27, 1861, in Trimble township, near the present residence of J. W. Jones, pension agent, in Glouster, O. He was married to Clara E., daughter of J. J. Allen, December 24, 1887. They have six children, three boys and three girls, all living in Trimble township, in and near Glouster. Mr. Davis has been a house builder and contractor for twenty years.

His father F. J. Davis, was the son of Isaiah Davis and was born May 14, 1838, near Chauncy. Isaiah was the son of Nehemiah Davis who emigrated to Washington county from Maine in about 1800, and was the first Baptist Minister in Ohio. He established the first Baptist church in the north-west territory.

Residence of Mr. and Mrs. F. W. Bush, Athens, Ohio.

THE illustration shows the residence of Mr. and Mrs. Fred W. Bush on College street, Athens, O. Mr. Bush is a native of Noble county, O., the son of Rev. and Mrs. W. S. Bush, now living at Pleasanton, Athens county.

He was born September 3, 1867, at Renrock, and received a sufficient education in the common schools to enable him to get a teachers' certificate. After his first term he matriculated in the Ohio University and taught school in the meantime to meet his expenses. He graduated with the degree of B. Ped. in 1892. After teaching three years, he purchased an interest in the Athens Messenger and Herald, and in 1896 succeeded Charles E. M. Jennings as editor and manager, a position he holds today.

On January 1st, 1900, he was married to Miss Georgia Hall Jones, of New York city. They have two children, Marian Claiborne, born January 11, 1902, and Gordon Kenner, born April 21, 1903.

Mr. Bush, greatly assisted by Mrs. Bush, has compiled and edited this Athens County Atlas and History, in connection with his regular newspaper work.

ST. ANDREW'S CATHOLIC CHURCH, NELSONVILLE, OHIO.

REV. W. F. BODEN.

NOT many years ago the Catholics of Nelsonville having no church, held divine services in different halls in that city as often as a priest stationed in Athens, Ohio, visited them. From about 1870 up to 1893, the following Rev. Fathers visited Nelsonville: Fathers Campbell, Hartnedy, Lane, Madden, McQuirk and W. F. Boden. In the year 1888 Father McQuirk made the arrangement to have regularly, twice a month services in a hall in the city. On the 1st of January, 1889, Father Boden succeeded Father McQuirk as pastor of St. Paul's Church in Athens, Ohio, and he also visited Nelsonville twice a month on Sundays. At this time the membership of the church had increased to over one hundred. Father Boden and the Catholic people and even a good many who were not of the same faith, desired to have a Catholic church in Nelsonville. In 1890 Father Boden began to collect money in the mines at Nelsonville, Buchtel, Murray City, Jobs and New Pitts burg. for building a church. All the men in the mines contributed to the building fund. November 27, 1891, two lots were bought for church property—lot No. 84 on East Washington street, for $2300 and lot No. 85 on corner of East Washington and Jefferson streets for $2050. In 1892 the contract for building the present church on Jefferson street for temporary purposes was let. As soon as the congregation is large enough the real church will be built on lot No. 84.

ST. ANDREW'S CHURCH.

INTERIOR OF CHURCH.

November 30, 1893, Thanksgiving day, Rt. Rev. J. A. Watterson dedicated the new church and appointed Father Boden as its first resident pastor. On December 23rd of the same year, Father Boden took charge. The church property of St. Andrew's is a fine property, and has a value of about $12,000. The membership has increased to about three hundred and fifty.

ST. ANDREW'S RECTORY

ATHENS COUNTY HISTORY
CONTINUED.

DISTANCE FROM MARKETS.

Owing to the isolation of the settlement at Athens and the lack of easy communication with the outer world there was little market for the products of the settlers. Each family endeavored to raise that which supplied their greatest needs. Their neighbors did the same; thus, there was little or no local demand for the surplus. The settlers on the Ohio river sometimes attempted to ship their over production to eastern and southern markets, but this was a tedious and dangerous experiment. They must go by boat to New Orleans, a trip of one hundred days, and sell their goods for whatever they could get. It was then shipped by vessel to New York. They must then return through unbroken wildernesses with the money realized from the sale of the produce, on their persons, thus becoming an easy prey to robbers.

These assassins found no trouble in disposing of the body in the nearest stream and escaping on the horse. In this way many men in those days simply vanished from the face of the earth, their friends never knowing whether they reached New Orleans with their boats and were murdered on the return route or whether their boats sank in the Mississippi with all on board.

Many who were mourned as dead finally after months of silence appeared in the settlement with tales of various accidents and misfortunes which had caused their long delayed return.

EARLY MAIL FACILITIES.

The first mail route from the east to cross the mountains in 1802 stopped at the Ohio river, where if anyone went from the Athens county settlements down to Marietta or Hockingport, on their return they would bring back all the mail for their neighborhood. This might be once in three weeks or once in six or eight weeks.

In 1803, an enterprising fellow whose name is lost to history established a route through the various settlements of southeastern Ohio, which circuit he made every three weeks and for the support of which, all who received mail were very glad to pay.

In 1804, first postoffice in the county was establishd at Athens by Jehiel Gregory who was the first postmaster. The office was kept in his house east of Athens where Bartn's mill now stands.

The contract for carrying the mails was let to reliable men who usually carried it themselves although often compelled to employ assistance, for in their trips through unbroken and uninhabited country they met with great hardships. The duties of the mail carrier on the route including Athens was to carry 200 miles from Marietta to Chillicothe and back in a week. When mail routes were first established through the county the dangers from wild animals was largely past, but the numerous streams which, of course, were without bridges would fill quickly from hard rains and become raging torrents. The carrier, however, must go over, or through, for even in those days Uncle Sam would brook no delay.

During the war of 1812, the bags were largely filled with government dispatches alone, making a very heavy load. The mail was required by contract to be carried at the rate of five miles an hour. This was most rigidly watched and enforced. At this time three men were employed on this route, each making the round trip once a week, regardless of weather or obstacles. If they had to swim a creek they must stop, dry the mail bags, then on again through the night. It certainly was money well earned, those $6 to $10 a month.

There were stations along the way where they were allowed from one to four hours rest and the carriers who were hunters often spent this time in hunting. Thus they paid the board for themselves and horse. The mail continued to be carried by post riders until 1825 when stage lines were started.

The postage on letters often cost more than the freight on a barrel of flour the same distance. The rates were governed by the number of sheets within. This certainly tended to the repression of volubility for few were the letters that could be condensed into one sheet of paper. The postage on a letter written on only one sheet and sent on any regular route in the state was in early days 25 cents. Later that was reduced to 10 cents and 5 cents while 25 cents would carry a letter to New Orleans. There were no stamps and this charge was collected from the recipient. Rarely was a letter prepaid even when from a young gentleman to his lady love. Letters frequently lay in the office weeks because of the insufficient finances of the receiver.

The mail facilities of today, our rural routes, free delivery and special deliveries would have seemed Utopian to the pioneers as would also the price of a letter which can go from here to California for 2 cents.

There are today nine rural routes going out of the Athens office bringing daily delivery to nearly every farm house within a radius of ten miles. The first route in the county was established December 1, 1900; the second within two months. In December 1901 four more routes were sent out from the Athens office; one more in 1903; two more in 1904. On February 1, 1902 city delivery was established in Athens and it is still the only office in the county doing sufficient business to be entitled to free delivery. That is, it is the only second class office. Nelsonville and Glouster are third class offices and the remainder in the county belong to the fourth class.

DIFFICULTIES OF EARLY TRAVELERS.

The only means of getting about in early days was on foot or on horseback. All paths were narrow windings in and out through the dense forests. There were no bridges and a horse must needs be a good swimmer as well as a good traveler. It is surprising how frequently regardless of difficulties the journey was made from here to Washington, Baltimore, Philadelphia and New York. Much of the way lay through almost unbroken paths and across the Alleghenies. The Ohio was crossed by ferry but the mountain torrents and streams must be forded or swum.

All corn and wheat was taken to mill on horseback. All salt, hardware and merchandise brought to the settlement was brought on horseback. The emigrant came to his new home bringing all his worldy goods and wife and children on horseback. These journeys were probably more trying on the strength and endurance of the horse even than on the rider, but the horses were seldom required to put forth any speed.

Starting from the east the trip to the foot of the mountains was not so hard, and congenial parties taking it slowly in pleasant weather could make a continuous picnic of it. But a few days of mountain climbing was most tiresome to man and beast and by the time they reached the Ohio all were so exhausted that they were illy prepared for the hardest part yet to come.

The Massachusetts and Connecticut farmers were not accustomed to such roads, their wagons were not built for such work; they lacked utterly the heavy brakes needed, but the sturdy drivers learning to be ready for any emergency would chop down small trees and attach them to the rear of their wagons to act as a break coming down the steep mountain sides.

Continued on page 61.

FARM RESIDENCE OF HIRAM L. BAKER, ATHENS TOWNSHIP.

HIRAM L. BAKER was born near Athens, September 2d, 1839. His great grandfather Nicholas Baker, was born in London, England. But when a small boy he was kidnapped by the crew of a pirate vessel bound for America and was landed at Barnstable, Massachusetts, where he became engaged in business and where later he married Elizabeth Merchant. To them one son, Isaiah, was born. They subsequently emigrated to Athens County, Ohio, the journey being made in an ox cart, and consuming six weeks. Isaiah Baker married Eunice Smith, and to them eight sons, one of whom was Jacob L., and three daughters, were born.

Jacob L. Baker was one of the pioneers of Athens County, being born March 12th, 1815. By the death of his father he was left an orphan at nine years of age. After securing the limited education possible in the log school houses of those days he started in life with a full determination to win, which was his only capital, and began the slow accumulation of the acres comprising the region ever since known as the "Baker settlement." When twenty-one years of age he married Ruth Reynolds, and to them were born nine sons and one daughter; the third son being Hiram L., the subject of this sketch. His birth place is almost in sight of his present home, where he has devoted the greater part of his life to agriculture and stock raising. He received his early education in his home school and later attended the Ohio University at Athens, and was for a time teacher in the district schools.

He married Mary A. Brown, also a decendent of one of the county's early settlers. To them were born four sons, Harley, Hadley, Emmett Earl, and Henry Herbert, the first two of whom died in their youth. In 1884 his wife died and five years later he married Eliza Friend. To them one son, Olin Oris, was born.

In August, 1862 he answered his country's call for volunteers and was mustered in at Gallipolis, O., September 12th of the same year, becoming a member of Company I of the 116th O. V. I. Nearly his whole term of service was spent on detached duty, principally as wagon master. After seeing some of the most famous battles of the Civil war he was mustered out at Richmond, Virginia, June 14th, 1865.

Mr. Baker also entered, for a time, the field of politics and in 1883 was elected County Treasurer, which office he held for two terms.

His farms are located about five miles south-west of Athens. where he has long given attention to the raising of high grade stock, notably Shorthorn cattle.

For many years he has been identified with the Methodist Protestant Church, holding his membership at Union, four miles west of Athens.

Robert Love's Residence, Millfield, Ohio.

ROBERT LOVE was born in Athens County, Ohio, November 16th, 1844. On the breaking out of the war he enlisted in Company K, 116th Regiment, and was in active service to the close of the war. Most of the time he was acting corporal. He never spent a day in a hospital or prison, though passing through many exciting, trying places. In the battle of Ft. Grade, Petersburg, when the color bearer was shot down Mr. Love rushed into the dangerous spot and raised the flag of his regiment.

He received an honorable discharge, and returned home with nothing more from the rebel arms than a slight bayonet wound.

Mr. Love has always been a farmer, and owns a fine one in Dover township. At present he and his wife live in Millfield, where they enjoy life in its simplest and truest sense. Mr. Love's army experiences qualify him to give much interesting history of those terrible days of blood and strife.

Some of Mrs. Love's relatives appear in the little picture in the corner, the baby being her grandchild, a bright, winsom child indeed. Mr. Love is looked upon as a man of sturdy qualities, a good business man, and a successful artisan of the soil, which business he greatly enjoys.

RESIDENCE OF MR. AND MRS. FRANKLIN P. PHILLIPS, ATHENS.

THE beautiful residence here shown is the home of Mr. and Mrs. Franklin P. Phillips, at 102 East State street, Athens, Ohio. Mr. Phillips is the son of E. H. Phillips, of Waterloo township, and was born near Amesville, December 11, 1853. He grew to manhood on a farm, attended common schools and the Atwood Institute, at Albany. Arriving at his majority, he sought his fortunes in the west, and worked at the carpenter trade in a half dozen western states as far west as Oregon.

He was first married to Miss Emma Jameson, of near Council Grove, Kansas, with whom he lived happily for five years or until her death, which occurred while they were living near Edgar, Nebraska. To them one daughter was born, Miss Jennie Clyde Phillips, who is living at Laramie, Wyoming.

After sixteen years Mr. Phillips returned to Athens county, and in 1900 was married to Mrs. America L. Goodwin, of Mineral, Ohio, where after about one years residence, they moved to Athens, and Mr. Phillips engaged in general contracting and lumber dealing.

He is the general manager of the Sunnyside Lumber Company, is a member of Athens Commandery No. 15, Knights Templars and a member of the U. R. K. of P.

: : : : Residence of Dr. Warren V. Sprague, Chauncey, Ohio. : : : :

DR. WARREN V. SPRAGUE, born June 3d, 1873, at Millfield; graduated at Lebanon, Ohio in 1892; entered Starling Medical College in 1898; graduated April 10, 1902; member of Starling Loving Medical Society; member "Old Northwest" Genealogical Society; a resident of Chauncey since 1902.

The Sprague family, of English descent, was among the earliest in Ohio. Major Joshua Sprague, [1729-1816] a Revolutionary soldier, son of Captain William and Alice [Browne] Sprague of Smithfield, Rhode Island, arrived at Marietta in June, 1788. He helped build the block houses at Campus Martius and Waterford. His wife was Abigail Wilbur. James, his third son, born 1761, served three years in the Connecticut line, Revolutionary War; settled at Otsego, Muskingum County; first wife, was Mary, daughter of Ebenezer Spooner, a Revolutionary patriot. James, eldest son Anson, [1781-1856] arrived at the Waterford garrison, [Ft. Frye] about 1795. His wife, Susannah Sprague, was born in that fort. After the Indian troubles he engaged in farming. In 1832 he removed to his farm near Reynoldsburg, Ohio. His third son, William P., [1819-1887] was a farmer and stock-raiser. He married Mary, daughter of Joseph Turner. His third son, Levi A., was born December 24, 1844, educated in the Reynoldsburg and Columbus high schools; married Sarah, daughter of Austin True, and removed to Millfield in 1870. Their children are Florence (deceased); Dr. Wiley; Dr. Warren; Myra, wife of Albert Watkins; Jennie, a graduate of Ohio University, and Dr. John.

Dr. Warren married December 25th, 1894, Miss Floride Kistler, of Lancaster. Their children are, Lenore A., born October 9, 1895, and Lindley V., born April 7, 1900. Mrs. Sprague is a charter member of the local chapter D. A. R. of Athens. Her father was Samuel A. Kistler, a graduate of Ohio University, 1858, and a member of the Athenian Society; admitted to the Bar in 1860, practicing his profession at Lancaster. His parents were Samuel, Sr., and Eliza-beth [King] Kistler, of Carroll. Samuel, Sr., was an extensive farmer, a Mason, and a captain of the State Militia in 1841. He came about 1810 from Kutztown, Pa., with his parents, Henry and Hester [Kramer] Kistler. Henry's father was George Kistler, Jr., a Revolutionary patriot.

Mrs. Sprague's mother was Floride J., daughter of Colonel Ziba and [Mary Bartlett] Lindley, of Alexander Township, Athens County. His father, Col. Ziba Lindley, Sr., a pioneer, came from Morristown, N. J.

He was a Revolutionary soldier and Colonel in War of 1812. Mary Bartlett Lindley was the daughter of Henry Bartlett, prominent in early Athens, whose father, William Bartlett, a sea captain, served in Revolutionary War. On one occasion while at the home of Captain Bartlett, General Washington named the baby. Captain Bartlett's wife was Zoanna Herrick, daughter of Colonel Henry Herrick, patriot, and graduate of Harvard and descendant of Sir William Herrick, of England.

L. A. WHITMORE'S GREEN HOUSE PLANT, BUCHTEL, OHIO.

A FEW THOUSAND CARNATION PLANTS.

FERNS, ROSE PLANTS, ETC.

THE industry shown in the illustrations herein represented, is situated two miles east of Nelsonville, and one mile west of Buchtel, Ohio, occupying a location between the picturesque hills of the Monday Creek Valley, one of the most beautiful valleys of Athens county. Surrounded, in fact, almost buried, in the great coal region of South Eastern Ohio. Under the careful management of Mr. Whitmore, this industry has become the largest and most profitable of any of its kind in this part of the State.

L. A. Whitmore, the promoter and owner, was born March 13, 1858, being the son of Oliney and Elizabeth Whitmore, of Buchtel, O. His father, Oliney Whitmore, has been instrumental in developing much of the mineral resources of York township. His grand parents, Aaron and Betsy Whitmore, came to Athens county in the early pioneer days, in 1821, from Connecticut, when railroads and modern methods of travel had not yet been dreamed of within the confines of Athens county. This journey by wagon occupied eight weeks. Mr. Whitmore was married October 10, 1883, to Miss Carrie Ziesler. He has a family of six children, viz: Egbert, William, Robert, Howard, Leila and Flora. For several years he has been identified with

RESIDENCE AND GREEN HOUSES.

Athens county's progress in various ways. Not only an active and valuable citizen of the community and county, he has become foremost in his special industry. Starting on a very small scale, adhering strictly to the development of his business, the Buchtel Greenhouses began to grow until they have reached a supremacy enjoyed by no other of its kind in this section of Ohio. It supplies all kinds of vegetable plants, cut flowers of all kinds, potted flowers, seeds of all varieties of plants, flowers and vegetables, especially garden seeds, while design work is made a specialty.

During the year just passed, sales of four inch pots of Geraniums have amounted to over six thousand, and eight thousand pots of Pansies were sold, besides a general sale of all other plants, flowers and seeds. Sales from this plant for the year 1904 amounted to nearly four thousand dollars.

Mr. Whitmore is generous and courteous in his business, and a visit to the Whitmore Greenhouses is always pleasant and instructive.

One would scarcely select a mining village for the location of a greenhouse, but Mr. Whitmore has demonstrated that a successful business does not necessarily depend upon location if what the general public want is produced in first-class condition.

HOUSE OF ROSES.

THE LETTUCE BEDS.

Residence of Mr. and Mrs. John Finsterwald, Athens, Ohio.

JOHN FINSTERWALD.

JOHN FINSTERWALD, whose picture is here presented along with his beautiful modern home on East State street, Athens, Ohio, is a man that has come up from a modest beginning, with his hands as his only capital, to a place among the well-to-do people of the community. He is the son of John Finsterwald, Sr., deceased, and was born in Athens township April 1, 1859. He spent his boyhood on the farm but early became dissatisfied with the humdrum life on the farm and went to mining coal with a pick. Farming and mining occupied his time till 1885, when he became deputy sheriff under Fred Stalder, and in 1889 was nominated and elected sheriff, and served four years. He was one of the best sheriffs the county ever had, and displayed wonderful ability and success in running down criminals.

On September 22, 1889, he was married to Miss Mary Weihr, a popular school teacher of Athens. They have four children, Freda, age 15; Nelle, 13; Edwin Sayre 11 and Russell 9.

On retiring from the sheriff's office he moved to the Mansfield farm, about three miles east of Athens. which he had purchased two years before. Here he and his family lived until 1902, when he sold out and moved to Athens. He bought the Towsley property on east State street in 1901, where he yet makes his home.

Mr. Finsterwald is an enthusiastic Republican, and has been identified with county and district politics for many years, having served as county chairman and other important offices. He has been Deputy Revenue Collector for six years, and his efficiency has been rewarded by placing him in the best salaried district in the service.

Residence of Mrs. Mary Patton in Rome Township.

FRANCIS B. PATTON, whose late residence is here shown, was born October 20, 1838, and died May 1, 1900. He enlisted as a private in the Civil War, in Company A, 92nd O. V. I., and served two years and ten months; was in the battles of Hoover's Gap, Chickamauga, Chattanooga, and with Sherman to the sea. He came home via Washington and was mustered out at Columbus, Ohio. Mr. Patton was married September 11, 1877, to Mary Johnson, a native of Rome township, born June 28, 1846. He was a member of Coolville Lodge, No. 337, F. & A. M. and Columbus Golden Post No. 89, G. A. R., Athens. His parents, Joseph and Parmelia Patton, were both natives of Ohio. His father was born April 24, 1815, and his mother April 24, 1818. They had five children,—Francis B., Preston I., Martha, Oscar, and Mary. Mrs. Patton's parents, J. W. and Catherine (Beebe) Johnson were both natives of Athens county. They had six children,—Eliza, Mary, William, Sarah and John.

H. D. HENRY, one of Athens county's most successful business men, was born on a farm in Bern township, 42 years ago. Till 1878 his business was farming and and attending school, teaching his first term in 1878. In 1881 he formed a partnership with J. P. Owen, in a general merchandise store at Millfield, continuing the same till the fall of 1883, and then reengaged in farming. June, 1889 he married Effie L. Woodworth, and continued living at Millfield till 1891, when having sold their coal land, they moved to Athens. In 1896 he associated himself with the Athens Lumber Company, taking the presidency and general management of the same in 1898. Selling his interests in the spring of 1905, Mr. Henry became one of the organizers of The Athens National Bank, and was elected one of its vice presidents. Mr. and Mrs. Henry have four children, all girls, Virgene W., Lucile R., Alice M. and Doris I. Mr. Henry is prominently identified with the business interests of Athens. and is one of its most enterprising citizens.

H. DOW HENRY.

Mr. Henry's father, H. C. Henry, was born in Athens county, March, 1829, of Scotch-Irish descent, his father, John Henry, coming from Ireland to Pennsylvania, thence to Athens county, Ohio, where he took up a large tract of government land. He married Sarah J. Smith in 1850, she dying some years later. Mrs. Hattie Antle, Mrs. Eva Gifford and Mr. Henry, her children, are all living in Athens county. Mr. Henry is enjoying the peace and quiet of a happy old age incident to a well-spent and industrious life, at his beautiful country home shown in the illustration. He has been a successful man, and learned the lessons of frugality in hewing out his fortune in the heart of a virgin forest, which surrounded him when he started out in business for himself. The secret of his success is, "he learned to do well whatever he undertook." and he applied that principal to every act of his long and successful career. Mr. Henry is one of the most highly and respected men in his community.

H. C. HENRY.

H. C. HENRY'S RESIDENCE, AMES TOWNSHIP

Chester Woodworth, father of Mrs. Henry, was born in Williamsfield, Ashtabula county, Ohio, in 1827, being one of seven sons and two daughters. His earliest known ancestors were of Dorchester, N. H., and from here his father, together with six other families, emigrated to Ohio in 1814, settling at Williamsfield. When Chester was but thirteen years old his father came to Athens county, settling on Green's run. Later he made his home at Millfield, where he married Rebecca Johnson, who died in 1875. leaving two children, Lydia A., born in 1854 and died in infancy, and Effie L., born in 1868, who married H. D. Henry in 1889. In October, 1876, Mr. Woodworth married Minerva J. Pratt, with whom he lived happily till he died in the triumphs of Christian faith, December 26, 1900. and was buried in the cemetery at Chauncey. He was largely identified with land interests in his locality, and did much to develop the coal interests of Sunday Creek Valley.

RESIDENCE OF MRS. CHESTER WOODWORTH, MILLFIELD, OHIO.

CHESTER WOODWORTH (Deceased.)

Residence of Mr. and Mrs. Albert H. Wells, Kimberly, Ohio.

A LBERT H. WELLS, the son of Samuel J. Wells, was born in 1848, and lived on a farm in Athens township, near Salem church, till he was twenty-one years old. Five years of that time he taught school of winters. He spent one year in the west. Mr. Wells eventually made Electa J. Boyles his wife, and to them have been born one son, Samuel J. Wells, who is the father of three children, Catherine. Beatrice and Albert. Of these grand children their grand parents are very proud and fond, as well they may be indeed.

In the corner of the home picture are shown the photographs of Martin and Judith Davis Boyles, the grand parents of Mrs. A. H. Wells. These people were of the pioneer days and conditions. and helped to make the earliest history of the county. They were married in the old log house on Sugar Creek, an illustration of which is given in this book, which was built in 1800, and is yet in a perfect state of preservation. Today it is better known as the old Harvey home.

In about 1834 Mr. and Mrs. Boyles bought a farm on Meeker run, but soon thereafter sold it to their son, Thomas Milton Boyles, father of Mrs. Wells. July 3, 1836, Thomas Boyles married Sarah A. Merritt, and they occupied this old home for fifty years. In August, 1886, Mr. Boyles dying, Mrs. Boyles continued her residence here till her death in March, 1900, making sixty-four years that Mrs. Boyles occupied a home on this same farm.

In 1901, A. H. Wells and his wife purchased this old homestead and landmark, and are thus preserving and cherishing up the works of their pioneer ancestors.

Residence of Dr. and Mrs. W. T. Sprague, Chauncey, Ohio.

D R. WILEY TRUE SPRAGUE, son of Levi Allen and Sarah (True) Sprague, was born March 6, 1871, at Millfield, graduated at Lebanon, 1890, and at Starling Medical College, 1895; has practiced his profession at Chauncey for the last ten years. He married August 23, 1893, Royal daughter of R. S. Dent—whose history appears elsewhere. Their children are Allen Dent, born June 13, 1897, and Gerald True, born March 13, 1899. The paternal ancestry is delineated in an article on Dr. Warren Sprague. The maternal ancestors, the True's of English stock, were also pioneers in the Northwest Territory. Captain Henry True, early of Salem, Mass., married Israel Pike, of Salisbury, Mass. Their fifth son, Captain Henry True; (1644-1735), married Jane Bradbury, and lived in Salisbury.

Their fifth son, John True (1678-1754), married Martha Merrill. Their second son, John True, Jr., born in 1703, or 4, married Mary, daughter of Abner Brown. Their tenth son, Ephraim True, a Revolutionary soldier, born December 21, 1756, in Salisbury, went to Saybrook, N. H., and married Martha , daughter of Thomas Eaton. He emigrated about 1793 to Washington county, Ohio, and died August 17, 1835 at Lower Salem. His first son, Josiah True (1776-1865), early settler of Dover, came out to Sunday Creek about 1799. He was a man of much enterprise, managing almost all township affairs for many years. He was a mason, also a soldier under Captain Gregory, in the war of 1812. He married Almira, daughter of Captain Solomon (1753-1830), and Deborah (Strong) Tuttle, the first settlers in Trimble township, coming from Brandon. Vt., the captain having served throughout the Revolution as one of Colonel Ethan Allen's Green Mountain boys. Solomon's father was Captain Thomas Tuttle, also of the Revolution. Josiah True's children were John, Cyrus, Lydia, Romana, Josiah, Austin, Mason, Almira, Lucy, Mary, Deborah and Thomas. Austin True, of Millfield, was born March 6, 1818, and married Jane. daughter of Resolved (1780-1850), and his second wife, Nancy (Bachelder) Fuller. The Fuller's came from Thompson, Conn., to Marietta about 1794, and later to Dover township. Resolved's father, Job Fuller, a Revolutionary soldier, married Susannah Russell. Mrs. Fuller's grandfather, Captain Benjamin

Bachelder, a seaman, removed from Kingston, N. H. to Swan Plantation, Belfast, Maine, about 1797. She came about 1818 with her parents, Benjamin Jr. (1773-1859) and Olive (Layton) Bachelder, to a farm near the mouth of Sugar Creek, but later the parents removed to Goshen, Ind. Sarah, daughter of Austin True was born June 27, 1848.

GOING on the principle that the dependent population should be cared for, Athens county, early in 1857, put herself on record as being ready and able to care for her imbecile classes. At this early date the county purchased the Seth Fuller farm of one hundred and forty-seven acres in Dover township, near Chauncey, paying therefore $14,700. It had old farm buildings erected back in the 40's, but these buildings were repaired and enlarged to accommodate one hundred inmates, though as many as one hundred and seventy-five had been cared for in a single year, about eighty, however, being the yearly average. James Tinkum was the first inmate, being admitted May 6, 1857.

The old plant was destroyed by fire September 19, 1903, but temporary quarters were devised till the present fine and complete building could be finished.

The present plant consists of different buildings, but the one used for strict Infirmary purposes has a capacity for about one hundred and fifty inmates, and is one of the finest county charitable institutions in the State. Its cost was $45,496.43. Its appointments are scientific and sanitary. It has some fifty rooms for all purposes, including surgical rooms, baths, etc., and the entire plant covers a half acre of ground.

THE OLD INFIRMARY DESTROYED BY FIRE IN 1903.

It is lighted with electricity, generated by its own plant. Its floors are of tile and hard wood. The arrangement is such as to separate the sexes entirely, even as to separate dining rooms, porticoes, etc. The farm is so productive and so well managed as to make the institution almost self-supporting.

Mr. and Mrs. Baker are in their tenth year as Superintendent and Matron.

The Directors, whose pictures are shown herewith, are William James, of Glouster; R. S. Dent, of Millfield, and John McLaughlin, of Coolville.

Too much praise cannot be given the Board of Directors for their splendid management, economical and business-like manner, in handling this institution, and the county can be assured that her poor and her property are well cared for by these trustworthy public servants.

Mr. and Mrs. Baker, as Superintendent and Matron, have long since proven their worthiness and ability. No more suitable people could be found for the places they have so eminently and satisfactorily occupied for nearly ten years. The neatness and system of the place are to be highly commended.

Such an institution, so managed, is a saving to the individual and a saving to the county. A saving of the individual from loss and a saving to the county in all its best aspects.

Athens county can well and proudly adjust and adapt herself to this new institution, inasmuch as it has no superior in any county of the State, if indeed any equal. And it is so constructed as to endure for many generations. The tax levy is so slight for its maintenance as not to be noticeable upon any one's return. Its work is charitable in the truest and most scientific sense, in that it inculcates and intensifies habits of self-help, which today is the recognized standard of charity. This has a tendency to remove the odor and distaste attached to institutions of a charitable character, and gives the individual inmate a degree of self-consciousness that he is yet a man. We congratulate ourselves in our high attainment and degree of efficiency in caring for our dependent classes.

PRESENT BOARD OF INFIRMARY DIRECTORS.

R. S. DENT.   WILLIAM JAMES.   JOHN McLAUGHLIN

ATHENS COUNTY'S CHILDREN'S HOME.

ATHENS COUNTY HISTORY
CONTINUED.

MOUNDS OF ATHENS COUNTY.
By CLARENCE MATHENY.

As one explores the mounds and various other ancient earth works of the prehistoric race so long extinct, there comes over him some such a feeling as when he stands on some great battle-field and calls to mind the almost unimaginable struggles that have made sacred that field. He takes in his hand the bones of one of those who perished centuries ago or the stone and cop-per articles made by hands with no assistance except such tools as could be shaped from stone and examines them with as much solemnity as would characterize one engaged in the most sacred ceremonies of modern religion. It is a true reverence for that ancient race, a genuine desire to reach a knowledge of their state of civilization or of barbarism, that impels men of scien-tific propensities to spend time and money and energy to ex-amine the numerous mounds and other ancient foundations. All the knowledge obtainable is contained in these earthworks. More than this is most certainly beyond the grasp of human en-deavor. However, the work of the various societies of Archae-ology has brought to light much valuable information that will at least enable us to form some idea of their condition. It is with profound interest that one studies these discoveries and learns what implements they toiled with and to what extent they had mastered the art of living well and comfortably.

As to the origin of the mounds but little can be said and even that is wrapped up in a cloud of uncertainty. From all in-dications they were built many centuries ago by a race of peo-ple who had attained to some degree of civilization, at least,

they were far beyond the American Indian, found inhabiting this continent when European adventurers first placed foot on this soil. Some have attempted to establish the now recognized fallacy or mistake that the Mound Builders and the American In-dians were one and the same race. This can not be very well defended since the Indians were absolutely ignorant of the origin

of the mounds, and the various articles and remains unearthed point to a more distant race, having better habits and more indus-trious ways than have characterized the American Indian. The best authorities agree that the Mound-Builders were a very numerous race entirely separate and distinct from those first

found in various parts of the Western Continent. From the vast number of earthworks and the fact that all tools were very primitive, that mysterous race must have been no less numerous than the present population. The fact that the country presented early a roughness of appearance and gave small indications of previous habitation does not destroy this view. For should our own race be swept entirely away by some dire epidemic and two-thousand year pass over our country, very little would remain to show that so progressive and abundant a race as ours had ever gained sustenance from this soil.

The age of the mounds is likewise uncertain. The only means by which a plausible conjecture might be made would be to study the state of preservation of the remains, and also the trees and other vegetation found growing on these artifical eleva-tions. Bones under less favorable conditions than those present-ed by the mounds have been known to have been preserved for a period very litle less than two-thousand years. Consequently we are quite certain that the mounds are at least that old. How much older they are than this no one cares to conjecture.

As mounds vary in form and dimensions, so do they vary in the purposes which they served. Some were for purposes of burial; some were used for altars or religious rites; others were for residences; and still others were for means of defense and signal stations. Those of Athens county were simply places of burial, the size of the mound probably being in proportion to the importance of the deceased chief or leader. The position of the mounds as well as their form and size clearly shows them not to have been for purposes of war.

Ohio has ten-thousand mounds and fifteen hundred circum-vallations. Athens county ranks fourteenth, having fifty-one mounds exclusive of other earthworks. The explorations of the mounds of this county by the various Archaeological Societies

Continued on page 77.

E. Logan & Company's Shoe Store, Athens, Ohio.

A MONG the many enterprising business houses of Athens, E. C. Logan & Co., will rank near the head. This store, a picture of which is here shown was started in No-vember of 1895, and from a small beginning it has increased in every way until it now enjoys the leading business in footwear in the town. Mr. Logan has had charge of the busi-ness since the beginning. It was his first venture in business for himself but he had associa-ted with him his brother, F. H. Logan, as a silent partner and they have proven themselves wideawake and energetic business men.

On account of increased business the store has moved twice, the last moving to the commodious room in the Phœnix Block on Court street. This room is light and airy and makes ideal quarters for the business.

THE : OHIO : UNIVERSITY : OF : ATHENS : OHIO.

The Famous Old Beech.

THE history of the Ohio University is set among matters and events of great moment. Contemporaneous with its origin, we find the master intellects of our ancestors bringing forth the great Ordinance of 1787 and the supreme law of the land embodied in the Constitution of the United States. From this ancient institution have emerged eminent executives, masters of feeling and sentiment, and intellects of priceless worth, like the fabled spirit of beauty and love which rose out of the foam of the ever-troubled ocean. To trace the history of the Ohio University, we must necessarily inquire into the history and workings of the Ordinance of 1787.

The chief source of the Ordinance of 1787 was contained in the Land Ordinance of 1785. At this time, both State and Federal treasuries were depleted by

the creditors were left no alternative in the matter, and their claims must either be laid on this virgin territory as full satisfaction of their debts, or they would be left with a mere claim on a bankrupt government, which had neither currency nor credit and which was loathe to renew even the promise of payment. Both creditor and debtor were viewing this territory as practically worthless, and it became the *rejected stone* in the structure of our great governmental edifice whose proportions were soon to develop and arise almost as harmoniously as if to the music of the lyre. The future history of this territory fully exemplified the statement that "The stone which the builders refused is become the head stone of the corner."

It has been stated that no event has a separate existence, and certainly is this true of the Ordinance of 1787. Some of the most basic historic principles of our government are interwoven in its provisions, and out of it have emerged many judicial interpretations and state constitutions, and other govermental docu-

to the principles of morality, education, and religion. In time of peace or war, its policy has been always in support of a strong central government and in fostering the welfare, happiness, and culture of its inhabitants. Its five great States held the balance of power during the trying times of the Civil War; these were loyal States, and at the suggestion of Ohio, with an Ohio University man as governor, a conference of the "war governors" of Ohio, Indiana, Illinois, Wisconsin and Iowa was held, and as result of this conference, 85,000 new troops were placed in the field, Ohio furnishing 30,000 of this number.

More than 20,000 people have received the whole or a part of their education at Ohio University. Space will not permit the names of even the alumni. The institution now has a faculty of 44 members, an enrollment of more than 1000 students, and an annual revenue of about $125,000. Connected with it is the State Normal College, established by act of the Legislature passed in 1902. On the beautiful campus of

OHIO UNIVERSITY CAMPUS.

the ravages of the Revolutionary War, and this fact of commercialism prompted both State and Federal authorities having control of western public lands to dispose of them and discharge a portion of the burdensome debt imposed by a long period of war. When the question of raising revenue confronted them, naturally, they first determined to dispose of their waste lands. These lands had never brought any revenue, yet the idea was prevalent that they would be a source of income at this time. Virginia imposed a tax of two cents per acre on her public lands, but was never able to collect it; and later whole states were disposed of without affording any appreciable public revenue; yet while the public domain consisting of these waste lands had never yielded any enormous income, both State and Federal governments looked forward to these as a means of replenishing their treasuries, or rather of discharging a portion of the war indebtedness to soldiers and officers by giving them grants of these over-mountain lands to relinquish their claims. It was an act not more of desperation than repudiation; and this choicest of territory was considered as waste lands by debtors, while

ments; and when we think of the numerous and fortunately vain attempts to amend the compact, and of the bulwark of strength hurled against it at various times by would-be reformers and fanatics, we rejoice that its magnanimity was ever preserved and unhesitatingly look upon it as one of the "Three Title Deeds to American Constitutional Liberty." Bancroft, in prophetic language, thus describes the grandeur of its origin,

"Before the Federal Convention had referred its resolutions to a committee of detail, an interlude in Congress was shaping the character and destiny of the United States of America. Sublime and humane and eventful in the history of mankind as was the result, it will take not many words to tell how it was brought about. For a time wisdom and peace and justice dwelt among men, and the great Ordinance, which could alone give continuance to the Union, came in serenity and stillness. Every man that had a share in it seemed to be led by an invisible hand to do just what was wanted of him; all that was wrongfully undertaken fell to the ground to wither by the wayside; whatever was needed for the happy completion of the mighty work arrived opportunely, and just at the right moment moved into its place."

That the great Northwest has "shaped the character and destiny of our republic" goes without demonstrating. Its early settlement secured it unreservedly for the Union. The laws by which it was to be governed made it forever free territory and dedicated it

the University may be seen the first building in Ohio erected at state expense designed for the training of teachers for service in the public schools. The building is a model of its kind, and was finished and made ready for occupancy at a cost of $52,000.

Ohio University now includes the College of Liberal Arts, the State Normal College, the Commercial College, College of Music, the Department of Electrical Engineering, the Department of Civil and Mining Engineering, the Department of Drawing and Painting, and the State Preparatory School.

The summer school last year at the Ohio University was the largest in the state, and numbered 557 students. The summer term beginning June 19, 1905, enrolled 650 students. The increased appropriation given by the State Legislature has added a stimulus to every department, and this fact, together with the prestige given it by the faculty give assurance of success for the institution in which every friend of liberal culture can have just pride.

VIEW ON HOCKING, NEAR CAMPUS.

OPPORTUNITIES FOR BOATING.

THE CARNEGIE LIBRARY ON SOUTHWEST CORNER OF CAMPUS.

LADIES' DORMITORY, CORNER COLLEGE AND UNION STREETS.

Dr. Alston Ellis is president of Ohio University. During his administration. the enrollment has rapidly increased, and two new buildings have been erected. Dr. Ellis is possessed of strong executive ability, and every department of the institution reflects his energy, enthusiasm and infinite resourcefulness.

Thomas Ewing was the first graduate of the Ohio University, and he best illustrates the excellence of that intellectual strength. which prompted and directed our governmental movements for the major part of the nineteen century. A noted contemporary of this eminent jurist. said of Mr. Ewing: "How instructive is the life of such a man, and with what force does it commend itself to every young American, not only arousing him to exertion, but admonishing to fix his ambition high, and to gratify it only in the path of virtue, integrity and honor, and thus to win that reputation that abides and outlasts the corrosive rust of time."

Ewing was the son of an pioneer. and his early life was one of industry and hardship. He received a common school education, and by teaching and working in the Kanawha salt works, he managed first to see his father's family out of debt and later to attend the Ohio University, from which he graduated in 1815. Certainly from the richness of his future career, the knighthood of the Fifth commandment, "Honor thy father and mother," was never more exquisitely revealed and its promises more copiously filled than in the later life of Mr. Ewing.

What magic is there in the light of hickory bark, and what a charm or enchantment in the glow of the pine-knot and the feeble flicker of the tallow candle! To be born in a log cabin, to be reared amid hardships, to be educated with great difficulty—form a combination of qualities, which designate fame, fortune, power and prestige—as is instanced almost universally in the lives of our early Ohio statesmen. This is our political doctrine of manifest destiny. It is like the "open sesame" of the Arabian Nights, by whose magic command, all resistance immediately vanished; or like the loosening of the Gordian knot, the secret of which our aspiring youth, would give their future in exchange to know. What a criterion! In logic, how absurd, yet in fact how true. But when we penetrate more deeply into the lives of these monarchs of mind, we learn that they were truly able, home loving, patriotic and righteous, and they thus possessed all the marks of nature's noblemen.

PRESIDENT ALSTON ELLIS.

After graduating from the University, Thomas Ewing studied law in Lancaster, and soon was admitted to the bar. He began practicing at the age of twenty eight, verifying the maxim "that the law has hope for those who come to it late." His broad practical experience and his keenness of logic soon brought him to the front, and his counsel and advice was sought for in the leading cases of his day. From his force of logic and masterly presentation of facts, he was called the "Great Logician of the West."

Samuel Sullivan Cox, "Sunset Cox," was born at Zanesville in 1824. He received his early training in the common schools, and after taking such high school work as was then afforded he attended the Ohio University for a period of years. He left the institution during the presidency of Dr. W. H. McGuffey, entering Brown University, from which he graduated in 1846. Cox was a wit, an humorist and a writer of great ability. He was indeed a bundle of nerves, and was keenly alive to everything about him. He

was an example of fine sentiment and feeling, and his tender sympathy for all the humanities endeared him to his fellow men and at once made him a veritable fountain of sensibility and emotion. In his speech on the Life Saving Service Bill, he said: "Humanity, more beautiful than art and more profound than science, has bent over her tempestuous seas her grand ethereal bow, unfolding its hues of promise as an everlasting covenant with heaven."

During his stay at Athens a lawsuit between the college and the town was decided in favor of the latter, much to the displeasure of the students. Party spirit ran high, and the division lines were as marked as in fights between "townsmen" and "gownsmen" in an English university town. A celebration most distasteful to the college boys was decided on; a bonfire was to be built, speeches were to be made, and a cannon was to be fired. The bonfire blazed, the speeches were made, but the boom of the cannon was not heard, for the "great gun" of the town, a six-pounder, had been prudently spiked the night before by a daring college boy. It was not known till long after that the youth who so effectually silenced the voice of the cannon for that and for many succeeding nights was "Sunset" Cox, a man who was destined to live not only in immortal type, but in the hearts of a grateful posterity as well.

In the same year in which the Ohio University was founded there came to Ohio the family of John Brough, Sr., from Maryland, who settled in the valley of the Little Muskingum in Washington county. It was here that John Brough, the eminent war governor of Ohio, was born in 1811. Brough was a born executive; strong in physique, resolute of countenance, he possessed that thorough-goingness and accurate execution which characterized his administration as governor of Ohio. His type was that representative of a strong and determined will, and it is in this particular that he distinguished himself in early life, in college at Athens, in the field of journalism and in the governor's chair.

Gov. John Brough, a Student in the University and Ohio's War Governor.

THE OHIO STATE NORMAL BUILDING.

Brough attended such common schools as were afforded at that pioneer period, and early in life, like Ben Franklin, was apprenticed as a printer. It was his experience in the print shop that gave him such a comprehensive view of human nature, and many facts here acquired by his absorbent mind gave him a stock of information which stood copious draughts during his future career. He was not a theorist; his clear logic, apt perception, and open and frank disposition moved him to apply promptly and well his new acquisitions of knowledge. While a student at the university his work was characterized by zealous effort and dilligent research. He worked in the office of the Mirror during his leisure hours and thus defrayed his expenses. He was a great athlete, and while at Athens, tradition has it, that he accomplished his greatest feat by kicking a football over the main building of the university.

MODERN OHIO UNIVERSITY.

The Ohio University to-day is one of the most stable, thorough, and progressive institutions of the Central States. Situated in the midst of the romantic scenery of Athens, it is easily accessible by the Baltimore and Ohio Railroad and its branches, by the Ohio Central Lines, and by the Hocking Valley Railroad and its branches. By these routes it is about one hundred and sixty miles east of Cincinnati and seventy-five miles south-east of Columbus. Approaching the town on the early morning or late evening trains, the lover of natural scenery cannot fail to be charmed with its picturesqueness. Following the meanderings of the Hockhocking through its graceful curves and varied scenery broad panoramic views give way to narrow passes and jutting precipices, while in the distance deep rows of wooded hills form a background to the entire picture, and rising to lofty heights in their verdant majesty cause the sun to appear to rise or set as the case may be more than a dozen times in as many miles. The Hockhocking with its tributaries drains one of the most beautiful parts of Ohio, and the town of Athens having the happy destinction of occupying the preterred portion of this charming valley, gives to the Ohio University a local habitation worthy of the ancient institution and a name that links with it the choicest associations of learning and literature in the distant past.

FACTS FOR PROSPECTIVE STUDENTS.

Would-be students of any institution are called upon to consider these facts before selecting a particular college or university under whose guidance they may take their work:

1. What courses are offered, and are they in harmony with the life profession or work I have selected?

2. What time is required for the completion of these courses?

3. What does it cost and what will be my necessary living expenses in such an institution?

Endeavor will be made to answer these questions briefly and plainly. First, as the work offered, much may be said. Young ladies and gentlemen who have not completed the equivalent of the work done in a first class high school, here have an opportunity of taking this work in the State Preparatory School. This will give them Freshman rank in not only this but in any college in the State. Those having had such work may pursue the regular college courses in arts, philosophy, or science; for these courses, the work done at the Ohio University is of the very highest type, and it is recognized and accredited by the more prominent eastern colleges and universities.

Aside from the above work the student may avail himself of a full commercial course, a course that gives him an insight into practical business, one which is first class in every particular. In selecting this course at the Ohio University, a student will save from $25 to $50 per year in the amount of tuition charged by independent commercial schools. The work is thorough and the graduate students of the Commercial College of the Ohio University are in demand among business men.

A course in the College of Music may be chosen. By way of equipment and instruction, the strength of this department should appeal very forcibly to musi-

cally inclined students. This being a College of the University, its students are given an opportunity to acquire a liberal education which is necessary for a complete rounding out of a musical course. Too much stress cannot be laid upon this peculiar advantage—to the college student, that of the culture and refined taste which must come from the association with a School of Music, its recitals, concerts, lectures, etc—to the student of music, that of the intimate connection with a great seat of learning, having its libraries, laboratories and lectures, its learned men and its classic traditions.

The school of Engineering, civil, electrical, and mining, is of most practical value to young men desiring work in either of these fields of effort. The mechanical equipment of these several departments is all that could be expected or desired; and the increasing demand for students who have finished this work illustrates the practical utility in establishing these courses. The equipment for practical work includes a complete outfit of electrical apparatus. A fine set of surveying instruments of the most approved kind is found among the apparatus for civil engineering.

If students are inclined toward teaching the State Normal College, in connection with the Ohio University, offers the very best of advantages. The building and equipment are new, and the members of the Faculty are school men of varied experience and are

THOMAS EWING.

particularly adapted to their respective departments of work. The profession of teaching is rapidly progressing and is increasingly recognized as one of the most pleasant and helpful of vocations in which young people may engage.

It must be admitted that a person who has learned how to do a thing can do it better than one who has not learned how. The scientific purpose of the normal school is to teach persons how to teach, but such knowledge must presuppose a knowledge of what to teach. The teacher who is to be capable of the best service should have both scholastic and professional training. It must not be forgotten that normal training is not necessarily all professional, so called. The school that can combine these two essentials in the teacher's preparation should certainly be sought. Each of the courses offers collegiate training in academic and culture studies in addition to the training along distinctively professional lines. All studies in the several courses in the College of Liberal Arts are open to the students of the Normal College. To be admitted to any of the regular courses in the Normal College a student must have made preparation equal to that required for admission to any other regular

college course. Normal College students are taught in the same classes by the same professors, and have access to all the privileges of the University.

AS TO TIME REQUIRED.

This depends very largely on the ability and advancement of the pupil. There are three preparatory courses, Classical, Philosophical, and Scientific, each requiring three years for completion, and each leading to a corresponding course in the collegiate department.

Four college courses are given in the collegiate department, equal in educational value. Four years are given to each course.

Graduates of high schools having a four-year course will be admitted to the Two-Year Collegiate Commercial Course without condition.

IN THE NORMAL COLLEGE.

In the Normal College, the five year course in Elementary Education is designed for those who have less education than that obtainable in a high school of the first grade, under statutory classification. Students are admitted to that year or class in this course for which their previous attainments qualify them.

The two-year course in Elementary Education is designed for those who have graduated from high schools of the first grade or who possess equivalent scholarship. Both courses in Elementary Education lead to a diploma from the Normal College.

The four-year courses in Secondary Education are the equals in scholastic requirements of any other courses in the University.

A one-year course is also offered to college graduates. Those who complete this Course of Study will be granted a diploma with the degree of Bachelor of Pedagogy.

WHAT WILL IT COST?

Board can be obtained within a reasonable distance of the University at $3.25 per week. By forming clubs, students may board at from $1.75 to $2.25 per week. Those students whose circumstances require it, are allowed to board themselves, but this plan is not recommended, because likely to be prejudicial to health and good scholarship.

The actual cost of an education at Ohio University will depend very much on the habits and disposition of the student. The necessary cost is very low—as low as that of any institution affording equal advantages.

The following table may serve as a guide of the actual necessary expense of a student for one year of forty weeks:

LOWEST.

Registration fee	$15.00
Board in clubs, average	80.00
Room	20.00
Books	10.00
	$125.00

HIGHEST.

Registration fee	$15.00
Board in private family	140.00
Room	30.00
Books	15.00
	$200.00

This estimate is for three terms of forty weeks, and includes all necessary expenses except laundry, and a small fee for membership in the Literary Societies, the Athletic Association, and subscription to the college paper, "The Mirror" Additional charges are made when students take electives in Chemicals and special work in Electricity. No laboratory fee exceeds one dollar per term.

There is no charge for admission in any of the regular preparatory or collegiate classes, but all students pay a registration fee of five dollars per term. Besides this, instruction in the following branches is to be regarded as extra and must be paid as follows:

Piano, elementary	$12.00
Piano, advanced	15.00
Voice culture	15.00
Use of pinano, one hour daily	2.00

The fee in Music include the registration fee of five dollars.

FEES IN COMMERCIAL COLLEGE.

All students pay a registration fee of $5.00 per term. Besides this, there is an extra fee of $5.00 each, per term, for Stenography, and Typewriting. The fee for Typewriting alone is $2.00 per term. There is no extra fee for Book-keeping. The fee for the diploma is $5.00; for certificate, $1.00.

SILAS COE was born in Washington County, Pennsylvania, December 1, 1814. He was married February 21, 1839, to Emily Porterfield, who was born January 11, 1819, in Belmont county, Ohio. To this union were born ten children, seven of whom still live. Margaret J., John P., Mary M., Will M., Sarah E., Joseph A., and Travis W. Those deceased are David S., who died January 19, 1849; James, September 28, 1849; and Susannah C., November 13, 1878. The father died October 29, 1864, the mother February 16, 1890. The family came to Athens county in January, 1848, settling on a farm near Albany, Ohio. The above group represents the descendants of Silas and Emily Coe. The views here represented are taken from the farms owned by John P. Coe.

He was born October 5, 1841. October 11, 1866 he was united in marriage to Lucy A. Blake. She was born February 6, 1847, near Albany, Ohio. They are the parents of eight children. Flora A., Will W., Perry G., Frank E., Mary E., Gus B., J. Howard, and a daughter, who died in infancy. Mr. Coe spent four years in the service of his country, enlisting in Company C., 36th Ohio Regiment, in August, 1861. Since returning from the war he has been actively engaged in farming and other various industries. From 1880 to 1884, he served as Treasurer of

Athens county. At present. he, together with his wife and youngest son, reside on a farm one-half mile north of Albany, Ohio.

Mr. Coe is one of Athens county's most highly respected citizens and enjoys to the highest extent the the esteem of the entire community. The hospitality of his home is so well known as to be proverbial.

JOHN P. COE'S FARM NEAR HEBBARDSVILLE, OHIO.

RESIDENCE OF MR. AND MRS. JOHN P. COE, IN ALBANY, OHIO.

HON. HENRY LOGAN, the pictures of whose home, corner of Washington and Congress streets, Athens, and himself, are presented above, is one of Athens County's older citizens. He was born in Alexander Township, November 21st, 1832, where he resided till September, 1885 Though born and raised to the farm, he was a merchant in Pleasanton for twenty-five years, and was appointed Post Master for that place in 1862, serving in that capacity for twenty-three years He was Township Clerk six years Trustee three years, and has been Justice of the Peace for over a quarter of a century. While his technical education was confined to the common schools, he received a liberal training in the great university of practical experience. For some time after his moving to Athens, poor health deprived Mr. Logan of active duties in life, but finally engaged in farm impliment and buggy business with Judiah Higgins, which he continued for about ten years. He then engaged in securing leases for gas and oil. His father, John Logan was a native of Alexander Township, as was also his mother, Elenor Lattimer Logan. She died when Henry was about six years old. For a number of years after his removal to Athens, Mr. Logan's father made his home with him, where he died May 15th, 1889, at the age af 87 years His grandfather, William Lattimer, had moved to St. Marys'. Mercer County, where he died at the age of over 90 years. Mr. Logan is of Irish descent, and he has many of those traits which belong specifically to that people. He has always been a busy and industrious man.

June 9th, 1853, married to Caroline, daughter of Dr. George and Ann Bean, of Alexander Township. She was born in Canaan Township, May 29th, 1833. To Mr. and Mrs. Logan seven children have been born, Rettie, Reppie, W. G., Ella, Flora, Earle, and Frank, all living but Flora. They have thirteen grand children and three great grandchildren. Mr. and Mrs. Logan are consistent and active members of the Methodist Episcopal Church.

In April, 1902, Mr. Logan was elected Mayor of Athens, and is at present occupying that office. Athens feels that her interests and affairs are in good hands so long as Mr. Logan is her chief officer. He enforces the laws, and tries to give the city such government as it deserves, and is splendidly upholding her honor and dignity.

Residence of George H. Lowden, Nelsonville, Ohio.

GEORGE H. LOWDEN was born at Emporia, Kansas, September 22d, 1871. With his parents he came to Ohio, settling in the southern part of Athens County, where he resided for sixteen years, when in 1890 he removed to Nelsonville with his parents. Mr. Lowden has been engaged in school work for seven years as Principal of the East Nelsonville Public Schaols, resigning this position to accept the Superintendency of York Township Schools. This is indicative of Mr. Lowden's ability. He is regarded as one of the progressive and successful teachers of the county, and the end of his promotion is not yet reached.

His residence shown in the accompanying illustration is one of the prettiest home sites in the city of Nelsonville and is an evidence of the general thrift and progressive tendencies of the owner.

GEORGE H. LOWDEN.

Mr. Lowden interests himself in politics as a diversion and is a thorough going Republican, active both in primaries and general elections. He has frequently been mentioned as a candidate for important offices but has always preferred to give his attention to his profession.

LIST OF EARLY POSTOFFICES AND WHEN ESTABLISHED AND THE FIRST POSTMASTER.

Athens, 1804, Jehiel Gregory; Amesville, 1821, Loring B. Glazier; Coolville, 1822, Jacob S. Miller; Nelsonville, 1825, Daniel Nelson; Federalton, 1829, Elijah Hatch; Lee, now Albany, 1829, Jacob Lentner; Canaanville, 1834, Stephen Pilcher; Hebbardsville, 1834, A. Stearns; Millfield, 1834, John Pugsley; Calvary, 1838, Sylvanus Howe; Chauncey, 1838, Henry Clark; Guysville, 1839, Guy Barrows; Hockingport, 1839, Ferdinand Paulk; Shade, 1839, J. M. Waterman; Trimble, 1841, Samuel Porter; Hulls, 1851, Isaac B. Dudley; Lottridge, 1851, Edward Lawrence; Pleasanton, 1851, Franklin Bernham; Torch, 1851, Nicholas Baker; Woodyards, 1851, Robert Figley; Garden, 1853, John O. Fox; Hartleyville, 1853, Martin Shaner; New England, 1857, T. R. Rider; Rock Oak, 1857, S. D. Workman; Marshfield, 1859, Hugh Boden; Salina, 1866, George T. Gould; Big Run, 1866, Thomas Lucas; Kings, 1866, Irwin R. King.

The following postoffices have been established since 1866:

Beaumont, Beebe, Broadwell, Buchtel, Burr Oak, Carbondale, Chase, Derthick, Doanville, Fisher, Floodwood, Frost, Glouster, Hollister, Jacksonville, Kimberley, Latrobe, Luhrig, Mineral, Modoc, Oakdale, Olbers, Pratts Fork, Sharpsburg, Stewart, Utley.

The following postoffices have been discontinued since the advent of Rural Free Delivery:

Armadale, Anthony, Garden, Glen Ebon, Grosvenor, Hixon, Judson, Kilvert, Linscott, Lyda, Lysander, Marchmont, Vanderhoof, Youba, Zelda.

The following postoffices have been changed:

Lee to Albany, Rawndale to Luhrig, Salina to Beaumont.

LODGES AND FRATERNAL ORDERS.

Nannie Ullon Rebeckah Lodge, No. 553, I. O. O. F., Athens, Ohio.

Ayers, A. E.	Grim, Katie	Pratt, Margaret
Bellows, Jennie	Graham, J. H.	Porter, Freida
Brooks, Kate	Hambleton, F. B.	Parker, Cora
Boelzner, Emma	Hambleton, Abbie	Roach. Jessie
Blackwood, Winifred	Huls, Wm. L.	Reeves, Minnie
Blackwood, U. S.	Huls, Margaret	Robertson, May
Buck, Mildred	Hixon, Rinda	Rickey, F. E.
Bartlett, Rhoda	Harvey, J. R.	Rickey, Mary
Beverage, D. C.	Henry Chas.	Reid, R. H.
Bean, Della	Hart, G. H.	Reid, Margaret
Bean, C. R.	Hart, Kate A.	Reid, Nora L.
Bolin, Flossie	Hall, Edna	Roach, Orr R.
Bolin, Edward	Jordan, Lillian	Roach, Eva May
Cook, Amanda A.	Jewell, Grace,	Reed, Lillian
Cook, R. S.	Kline, Margaret E.	Shirley P. E.
Connett C. G.	Lafferty, Etta	Shirley, Anna
Connett Lizzie	Mills, Clara	Stewart Mary E.
Carr P. C.	Mills, Margaret B.	Stewart, Anna
Carr Nell	McKinstry, Caroline	Stewart, Clarence
Cochran, Elizabeth	McKinstry, Effie	Sater W.
Carty, Effie	McVay, F. P.	Sater Margaret
Carty, F. B.	McVay, Jessie B.	Smythe Garnet
Casley, W. A.	Martin, Mattie	Strawn, Ida
Casley, Addie	Murdock, Mary	Thompson, Minnie
Dalton, R. A.	Mansfield, Jesse	Tresize, Maud
Earich, J. W.	Mansfield, Clara	Ullom Geo. W.
Earich, Hattie	McFaden, Maude	Walker, Lelia
Earhart, Geo.. H.	Nice, H. D.	Wise, Alice
Edmundson, Edith	Nice, Mabel	Woodgered, Emma
Edmundson, Josie	Nye, Mary	Watkins, Bessie
England, Ella	Nanna, D. G.	Watkins, Mayme
Fauser, Ben. Jr.	Nanna, Dora	White, Elizabeth
Fauser, Millie	Osborne, Ella M.	Wildes, Mabel
Fryburger, Mary	O'Dell, Mary	Webster, Cynthia
Foster, Daisy	Paul, Elma	Webster Delpha
Francis, Emma	Pratt, P. G.	

L. O. T. M. Lodge, Albany, Ohio.

Cline, Mellie R.	Reeves, Libbie T.	Holmes, Mabel
Chase, Mary A.	Swett, Victoria	Jones, Minnie
Cline, Blanch	Thorn, Sidney	Lewellen, Maud
Coe, May M.	Chase, Eunice	Louther, Nellie
Dailey, Bertha R.	Cross, Anna	McWhorter, Rebecca
Dailey, Amelia N.	Dailey, Eva	Vorhes, Gertrude
Hurse, Alta M.	Duffee Anna	Wible, Viola
Moler, Cora	Graham, Maggie	Woodard, Janie

Glouster Lodge, No. 336, K. of P., Glouster, O.

Achauer, B. F.	Gessell, A. A.	Needham, P. G.
Armstrong H.	Green, A, H.	Penman, M.
Anderson J. O.	Hanson, P. E.	Palmer, C. E.
Antle, Des.	Haskins, J. M.	Pickering, B. W.
Aldrich, A. I.	Jennings, Ezra	Pedicord, J. A.
Andrews R. A.	Johnson, Al	Pride, C. A.
Archer, J. H.	Kinney, G.W.	Pope, J. A.
Bryson, M. M.	Kinney, Perry	Sanders, C. M.
Butler, G. E.	King, W. G.	Strinmetz, L. R.
Birtcher, F. B.	King, C. L.	Stedman, L. L.
Biddison, C. A.	Lookenott, Frank	Stedman, J. S.
Blower G. C.	Lawrence, E. I.	Sawyer, G. E.
Campbell, J. E.	Lilley, J. C.	Sellars, C. E.
Cavey, G. W	LeFever, B. T.	Shaner, D.
Carpenter, W. H.	LeFavor, M. M.	Suver, F.
Coryell, M.	Lewis, S. J.	Stahl, W. H
Duncan, C. E.	Lewis, T. A. R.	Thompson, S. D.
Duncan, G. E.	Roush, J. M.	Thompson, F. P.
Druggan, R. P.	Rothman, E. S.	Vercoe, W. F.
Druy, E. E.	Roberts, D. M.	Wallace, C. F
Druy, W. R.	Rodgers, C. E.	Wise, W. F.
Dawson, M. E.	Myers, J. G.	Wallace, G.
Danford, F. A.	Matson, John	Wyatt, T. L.
Dentner, J F.	Morris, Thos	Wells., J. H.
Dulaney, M. L.	McCloud, P. H.	Wolf, J. R.
Ellis, T. E,	Mingus, A.	
Ellis, David	Morris, C. D.	
Gormley, Hugh,	Nelson, Alex.	

Thea Chapter, No. 192, O. E. S., Glouster, Ohio.

Allen, A. B.	Pride, W. A.	Hatton, Chas.
Allen, Gwennie	Pride, Gertrude	Hatton, Rhoda
Andrews, Elzabeth	Perry, John	Johnson, W. B.
Bryson, Mary	Rothman, E S.	Johnson, Ella
Brooks, Catherine	Rothman, Rellie	James, Mary
Crawford, A. J.	Thomas, D. C.	Jones, Fannie
Crawford, Ella	Thomas, J. D.	King, Ida
Culver, Edward	Thomas, Emeline	Koons, Adelaide
Culver, Nettie	Thomas, Sadie	Lefavor, Alice
Culver, Thea	Thomas, Margaret	Lewis, Maggie
Clark, Louvina	Tippet, Emeline	Morgan, Mary
Cox, R. C.	Wyper, William	McDonald, Ella
Cox, Flora	Wyper, Margaret	Nelson, Alex.
Cheadle, Georgia	Wyper, Anna	Nelson, Mary
Cornwell, Fred	Wilson, Chas.	Pickering, B W.
Drury, E. E.	Williams, Minna	Pckering, Susie
Drury, Anna	Young, Alice	Pickering, Julia
Eddy, O. D.	Young, Tena	Pickering, Ethel
Eddy, Agnes	Goulding, Anna	

Nelsonville Lodge, B. P. O. E., No. 543, Nelsonville.

Sharp, James	Angell, E G.	Logan, Frank
Kelch, Larence	Armstrong, W. P.	Carpenter, L. F.
Hawkins, Harry	Foster, I. M.	Cooley, Frank
Howe, H. E.	Eberle, L. J.	Shepard, Jas. T.
Evans, Ed. C.	Bowers, W. S.	Sharp, James
Eberle, Louis J.	McBride, Peter	Kaelin, Mauris (dec
Bort, Wm. F.	Hanning, W. P.	Howell, J. N.
Lefever, B. E.	Iler, Harvey	Haughee, James
Wilson, Eben	Haning, H. H.	Wilson, Eben
Scott, C. E.	Knight, A. D.	Howe, Sam J.
Baird, Chas. L.	Bates, C. H.	Pritchard, Jas. I.
Rosser, E. J.	Murphey, Jas. S.	Aumiller O. L.
Pritchard, Jas. I.	Warner, Isaac	Leslie, C. E.
Woodworth, E. C.	Johnson, Geo.	Howe, H E.
Preston, Len	Welch, C. E.	Pemberton, H. W.
Pickett, Jas. E.	Rosser, E. J.	Bethel, George
Palmer, John	Tennyhill, Will G.	Morgan, F. A.
Crawford, A. J.	Shepard, Farnk S.	Murphey, Wm.
Rose, J. B	Ginnan, James	Webb, Geo. M.
Walker, E. R.	Gross, Morris	Cox Jno. M.
Vorhees, Ed. M.	Gordon, Jno. J.	Schafer, George
Moore, D. H.	Ley, H. J.	McLean, W. E.
Stalter, R. R.	O'Donnel, W. P.	Dailey, O. D.
Shepard, Chas.	Mason, Ralph M.	Juniper, Ed.
Comstock, A. C.	Denison, Jno. M.	Monahan, W. H.
Poston, W. C.	Moore, A. E.	Kelch, L. R.
Josten, James	Baird, J. C.	Irvin, Frank
Rhoads, W. S.	McVicker, James	Hawk, Harry
Armstrong, H. O.	Thacker, Fred.	Cummins, C.
Hallum, T. O.	Stuart, W. J.	Shellhamer, Geo.
Craig, T. W.	Stalter, J. A.	Wallace, D. L.
Burns, Tom	Ryan, R. E.	Frazee, Harry
Alderson, R. P.	Hickman, P. W.	Roberts, Geo. R.
Scott, C. E.	Poston, L. D.	Webb, Reuben
Owens, Ed.	Kessinger, E. J.	Krizer, Chas. B.
McDowel, Lee	Pritchard, A. L.	Zimmerman, M. D.
Dusz, Wm.	Ridenour, G. D.	Juniper, J. G.
Cable, Don C.	Henderson, Geo.	Rice, L. P.
Hyde, J. M.	Shugart, R. L.	Lefever, B. E.
Dew, C. G.	Slater, Joseph	Vorhees. Chas.
Bland, Jno. P.	Coe, C J.	Rauch, Frank
Minner, Frank	Preston, S. D.	Moore, A. M.
Donaldson, J. E	Murphy, Andy	Morris, P. C.
Wilson, Harvey, D.	Evans, Ed. C.	
Stalder, H. G.	Lash, E. Ray	

Athens, Aerie, F. O. E., No. 529, Athens, Ohio.

Andrews, Wm. M.	Fulton, Clif	Moran, J. H.
Armstrong, H. O.	Gabriel, Elmer	Mowry, F. B.
Barnhill, Bert	Gabriel, Ezra	Mulligan, J. A.
Barnhill, W. A.	Gardner, Wm. E.	Munn, Amos
Barth, Otto	Graham, Guy	Munn, O. G.
Bartlet, H. G.	Graham, Jno.	Munn R. B.
Bean, Murn	Grim, Chas. A.	Murhy, H. W.
Beasley, G. E.	Gross, C. W.	Myers, R. V.
Beasley, L. D.	Gross, F. R.	Nern, F. F.
Bell, J. B.	Haftner, M. W.	Phelps, C. W.
Boelzner, P. C.	Hall, Karl T.	Pickering, C. O.
Bower, C. J.	Haning, H. H.	Poff, Mervin
Bower, W. S.	Haning, Jesse E.	Pontius, L. P.
Bowers, Mathias	Hatch, A. P.	Port, George W.
Brown, Justus	Hedges, Fred	Porter, C. H.
Buck, H. W.	Hibbard, W. A.	Quick, J. S.
Burch, Dorsey	Higgins, J. M.	Quick, R. E.
Burgoon, W. A.	Hill, G. W.	Quinlan, T. J.
Cameron, H. C.	Jones, D. E.	Reiske, P. P.
Cameron, W. A.	Jones, Dan E.	Robbins, C. E.
Campbell, J. C.	Jordan, O. G.	Roush, P.E.
Chambers, Herb. L.	Josten, C.	Roush, T. B.
Clark, C. W.	Josten, James	Russell, Joe
Coleman, W. W.	Josten, Walter	Rustin, Wm.
Cooley, E. D	Jourden, H. E.	Sanders, H. L.
Coots, W. N.	Joyce, W. H.	Sams, D. G.
Coss, J. C.	Junod, E. D.	Scanlon, E. M.
Coss, L. A.	Kale, T. F.	Sigler, Wm.
Crippen, C. T.	Kempleman, L.	Slaughter, I. W.
Crossen, J. H.	Klingenberg, J. F.	Steward, E. M.
Davis, DeValson	Laird, A.	Steward, F. H.
Davis, T. E.	Laughlin, Carl	Traglio, P.
Dean, F. C.	Laughlin, E. R.	Walker, E. H.
Dew, Silas	Lehrer, Jas.	Walker, E. R.
Donaldson, J. E.	Leidel, E. E.	Walker, Fred
Drake, P. G.	Long, H. J.	Warren, Jesse
Duffy, J. P.	Malone, John	Watkins, C. W.
Farrell, Frank	Mansfield, Frank	Watkins, Frank
Farrell, Jas. A.	Mansfield, H. F.	Watkins, Wm. W.
Farrell, L. J.	Martin, Henry	White, Arthur
Farrell, W. H.	McDougall, C. S.	White, U. P.
Fauser, Ben.	McKinstry, Ralph	Winning, Thomas
Fenzel, Geo. L.	Meighen, Hugh	Wolfe, A. A.
Figley, C. C.	Milligan, B.	Wood, Ed. E.
Finsterwald, Jesse	Mills, W. A.	Wood, Ira
Frost, M. F.	Moore, G. H.	Woodworth, E. C.

Euphemia Chapter, U. D., O. E. S., Amesville, Ohio.

Henry, Myrtle J.	King, Gertrude	Johnson Phoebe
Wyatt, G. E.	Gibson, Maud	Troutfetter, Jennie
Patterson, Emma	Gibson, Luella	Henry, Z. L.
Henry, Herbert H.	Henry, Blanche	Johnson, James
Snedeker, Belle	Henry, Rea P.	King, R. V.
Dunbar, Lucy	Gifford, Eva	Dyson, George C.
McCune, Effa	Ogg, Fannie	Henry, Heber H.
Cellars, Rev. W. F.	Carpenter, Etta	Gibson, F. W.
Beasley, Jennie	Snedeker, J. C.	

Valley Lodge, No. 169, K. of P., Nelsonville, Ohio.

Allen, R. E.	Gibson, Chas	Powell, Wm.
Allen, F. R.	Gruesner, Mathew	Powell, Ed. C.
Allen, John	Hanning, Chas.	Powell, Harry
Allen, Jesse	Hanning, Walter	Pratton, Frank
Adamson, Geo.	Hartgrove, R. C.	Porter, Joseph
Aumiller, O. L.	Hartgrove, Sheldon	Perry, Wm.
Asbell, Chas	Hatch W. H.	Powers, A.
Andrew, Pearl	Haybron, W. J.	Potts, Chas.
Anthony, R. F.	Haybron, Ira	Pugh, Henry
Anthony, A. D.	Harrold, Jas. L.	Pugh, Enoch
Barker, W. E.	Harrold, A. E	Raine, Percival
Barker, W. L.	Harrold, Lientelles	Raine, Thos.
Bayles, James	Hawk, Wesley	Rardin, Sam
Barron, T. S.	Hall, Harry	Reynolds, Chas.
Barron, Albert	Harbarger, James	Reynolds, Brad
Bateman, Ralph	Hickman, J. R.	Rider, John
Bateman, Carl	Hickmann, P. W.	Rider, Frank
Bateman, Pearl	Hinman, Harry	Riddle, Wm.
Bateman, Daniel	Hill, N.	Riddle, Thos.
Batteman, James	Higgins, F. E.	Richards, Morgan
Baird, Chas. L.	Howe, Samuel	Ringhiser, Henry E
Baird, John	Howe, Hiram	Rice, Lewis
Barnecut, Chas. P.	Howe, J, R.	Robb, Calvin
Bailey, Benjamin	Howl, J. N.	Robb, Mell
Brandenburg, P. H.	Huddy, John	Rosser, Sherman
Brandenburg, H.	Hysell, Rock	Robertson, S. F.
Bartoe, Jacob	Iler, H. H.	Robertson, W .O.
Bartoe, F. W.	Jack, J. L.	Robson, W. R.
Blakeley, Oat	Johnson, G. K.	Ross, Clark
Blackburn, J. W.	Johnson, Geo. E.	Ross, John U.
Blackburn, S. S.	Johnson, H. N.	Roscoe, John
Brown, J. H.	Johnson, Wm. T.	Runnion, Scott
Brown, Admiral	Johnson, Alva	Shepard, James T.
Brickles Joseph	James, C. C.	Shugart, R. L.
Butt, S. E.	Juniper, Clarence	Sherman, Jacob
Burnell, Wm.	Juniper, J. G.	Stack, Warren
Butterworth, W C.	Kreig, H. D.	Slater, Clarence
Butterworth, Ed	Krizer, Emmett	Schidt, G. Fred
Buchannan, H. E.	Krizer, Chas.	Scott, Earl L.
Beattie, Dave	Krizer, P. R.	Saltz, J. H.
Beattie, James	Kelch, H. A.	Shannon, Wm.
Beard, E. B.	Kelch, L, R.	Shaw, Samuel
Beard, John C.	Keeney, Granville	Shaner, J. W.
Bean, Wm.	Key, Samuel	Swain, R. E.
Bethel, Geo. E.	Kenney, Herbert	Stilwell, Samuel
Beard, J. S.	Krepple, Frank	Shafer, Harvey
Bland, Wm.	Kennedy, Chas.	Starret, C. W.
Beckler, S. H.	Kontner, C. S.	Shellhammer, Geo.
Beckler, P. D.	Kourt, E. R.	Sisson, C. H.
Carr, A. J.	Kloz, John	Sisson, W. B.
Cable, C. W.	Kerman, Emmett	Slicker, Geo.
Canterberry, Chas.	Lancaster, Henry	Six, David
Chambers, I. E.	Lamott, Wm.	Smith, Chas.
Casey, W. W.	Landis, J. L.	Smith, Jas. C.
Chambers, Jno.	Levering, Geo.	Smith, Daniel
Carter, M. E.	Levering, Henry	Smith, Elva
Clark, Joshua	Lee, Asa P.	Smith, J. G.
Clark, Wm.	Lightfritz, P.	Stocklein, Ed.
Cavanaugh, Jas.	Linton, Carl	Stack, Steve
Call, Jas.	Lowden, John	Stevenson, J. W.
Childs, F. C.	Lowden, Geo. H.	Stoneburner, Clar.
Cotton, A. G.	Longley, Samuel	Shooner, Joe.
Coleman, Chas.	Lloyd, E. H.	Stedman. Bert
Conoway, Chas.	Lynn, Sherman	Socie, Lewis
Coleman, Jas.	Malone, John	Storch, John
Coe, C. J.	Malone, H. K.	Sweeney, Michael
Cook, Chas. W.	Malone, C. A.	Taylor, John
Chute, Isom	Mallen, Hugh	Tannehill, Wm G.
Cummins, Edward	Maze, Madison	Theiss, Julius
Cummins, C C.	Matheney, Jerry	Tedrow, W. C.
Davis, A. W.	Myers, Wm.	Tipton, Harry
Davis, C. J.	Mellinger, E. M.	Tomilson, C. B.
Davis, W. E.	Mitchell, T. C.	Thompson, Dudlass
Dilcher, Fred	Mink, Lewis	Vorhes, V. H.
Daugherty, John	Minner, Frank	Vorhes, A. B.
Devore, Primrose	Martin, L. D.	Wallace, J. S.
Devore, Earl	Monks, Chas.	Wallace, Wm.
Dew, C. Guy	Monks, John W.	Wallace, Burrel
Dewhurst J. E.	Morgan, Wm.	Wallace, Cliff.
Dixon, W. J.	Monce. Edward	Warheim, Homer
Dishon, Morris	Moore, A. M.	Warner, Isaac
Downhour, Chas	Moore, Frank	Washburn, Geo.
Dowler, Thaddeus	Monahan, W. H.	Wend, Lewis
Dowler, F. B.	Munn, James	Wend, Geo.
Duffy, Chas.	McNabb, Aaron	Welch, C. E.
Edwards, Joseph	McCauley, Wm.	Welch, Harry
Emish, Frank	McGaines, Pratt	Webb, Babbett
England, Chas.	McDowell, Lee	White, R. A.
Evans, Wm.	McCullon, Joseph	Wells, J. D.
Eddy, Robert	McVickers, James	Wilds, Jas.
Evans, Wesley	McCullough, J. H.	Wilson, Ebon
Frank, Henry	McGill, A. J.	Wilson, J. L.
Farrow, C. E.	Neace, Thos. J.	Wilson, Fred
Figgins, Alonzo Sr.,	Nelson, Alex.	Williams, Net
Figgins, Alonzo, Jr.	Nelson, W. E.	Wildes Jacob
Fillinger, Noah	Narthop, Martin	Williams, Wm.
Furniss, Harry	Patton, W. A.	Williams, David
Graham, Monte	Parks., W. T.	Woody E. W.
Graham, P. A.	Place, B. Austin	Woody A.
Gear, John	Pearce, G. W.	Woodring, M'Clel'nd
Gettell, H. W.	Pritchard, J. I.	Woorley, K. L.
Gettell, Chas.	Pritchard, A. L.	Woorley. Wm.
Gleason, Jacob	Pidcock, James	Woolett, D. A.
Gillilan, H. R.	Price, L. H.	Wolf, F. H.
Groves, Amos	Parfitt, Tom	Wolf, Willis
Groves, J. B.		
Gibson, W. W.		

. . . . THE CARPENTER HARDWARE COMPANY. . . . .

CARPENTER BLOCK, NELSONVILLE, OHIO

THE CARPENTER HARDWARE COMPANY was organized in May, 1904, with a capital stock of Fifty Thousand Dollars, with the object of conducting stores at Athens, Glouster and Nelsonville, Ohio, in the wholesale and retail of general hardware, furniture and household supplies. The stock of the Nelsonville Hardware Company at Nelsonville, Ohio, and the stock of Glouster Hardware Company at Glouster, Ohio, were taken over by this company and a wholesale and retail store was established at Athens, Ohio. The object in merging the stores was for the purpose of buying in larger quantities, securing the lower price, thereby serving customers with the very lowest price possible. They buy in large quantities direct from the factory. The car load purchases are shipped to Athens, then distributed to the stores at Glouster and Nelsonville. They also wholesale goods to the merchants in their territory from the store in Athens. They carry a complete line of general hardware, stoves and ranges, and make a specialty of builders hardware. In this line they carry P. & F. Corbin's goods, the largest and finest line manufactured in the United States. They also carry in stock a complete line of paints, oils and varnishes. In mixed paints they handle the O. D. & B. high grade paint, every gallon guaranteed.

The management of the Carpenter Hardware Company is thoroughly familiar with goods sold in mining towns and are always prepared to furnish anything required pertaining to the miner's equipment. Their long experience and knowledge of the kind of coal mined enables them to intelligently endorse the best.

The store at Nelsonville is the largest of its kind in Southern Ohio, the building which was constructed in 1902 under the management of the Nelsonville Hardware Company, has a fifty foot front built of Union furnace speckled brick. With full plate glass front on first floor. The length of the building is one hundred feet. The first floor has the appearance of one large sales room being partially partitioned, one-half being stocked with a fine line of furniture, the other with everything common to the hardware trade. The basement and second floors are used for storage of duplicate stock. This building is furnished with an elevator from basement to second floor. They drive their dray in the basement and unload goods on the elevator and distribute to the floors above.

Their store at Glouster occupies four floors, and they carry in stock a complete line of heavy and light hardware, stoves and ranges, paints, oils and varnishes. A complete line of furniture, also buggies, wagons and farm implements.

In the year 1892 the Glouster Hardware Company was organized by J. W. Bryson, Frank Bryson, Des Antle, J. E. Carpenter and W. A. Garpenter. In the year 1896 W. A. Carpenter and S. S. Carpenter bought the interests of the Messrs. Bryson's and Antle, and in the year 1900 J. E. Carpenter W.A. Carpenter. L. F. Carpenter, S. S. Carpenter and Harry Furniss organized the Nelsonville Hardware Company, and in 1904 the Glouster Hardware Company and the Nelsonville Hardware Company were taken over by the Carpenter Company. The present officers are W. A. Carpenter, President and General Manager; J. E. Carpenter, Vice President; L. F. Carpenter, Secretary, S. S.

INTERIOR OF STORE IN GLOUSTER.

INTERIOR OF STORE IN ATHENS.

Carpenter, Treasurer; M. R. Crooks and F. Keintz, Directors. The combined floor space of the company is twenty-six thousand square feet, making the largest stores of its kind in Southern Ohio.

That the merger of the several hardware companies into The Carpenter Hardware Company will prove a great success to the stockholders of the company as well as a boon to purchasers of hardware, etc., in both valleys and in the county seat is assured when the character of the men composing the company is considered. Practically every one of them are experienced in the line—past masters as it were—and in the words of that great statesman and president maker, Marcus A. Hanna, "they know their business." Their stores stand out in a class of their own. A casual glance into any one of these three great concerns, located in the three most densely populated centers in the county will convince the observer that there is good management behind the enterprise and each store is a model. The gigantic scale on which the purchasing is done will readily convince the purchaser that the man that buys the most buys the cheapest and making an ordinary profit, still sells cheaper than the little fellow.

A. H. CARNES' BUSINESS BLOCK AND STORE, NELSONVILLE, OHIO.

A. H. CARNES was born in Loudoun county, Virginia, August 10, 1824, and with his parents came to Morgan county, Ohio. in 1832, removing to Nelsonville in 1841. Here his parents, James and Mary Carnes, both dead, they both having been born in Virginia. After the

A. H. CARNES.

death of his parents young Carnes worked at any honorable employment his hands could find to do, digging coal being his principal business for about fourteen years. His business ability being discovered, he was persuaded to go into the

store of W. B. Brooks, in whose employ he remained til the fall of 1871, making a service of about fifteen years. He then bought the old Lewis Steenrod place of business, being the same location where Mr. Carnes now is, and where he has been doing business ever since the fall of 1871.

Mr. Carnes enlisted in the Mexican War in June, 1846, and served but a few months because of failure of health. He was in the hospital at New Orleans for some time, where he received his discharge.

After a lapse of forty years he received a pension as a Mexican War Veteran, he being the only surviving veteran of that great struggle in the county.

April 1, 1850, Mr. Carnes was united in marriage with Sarah A., daughter of John Cruthers, as a result which union five children were born, two of whom are yet living. The eldest son, Charles, died at the age of eighteen years, a daughter, Effie, dying at the age of thirty-one years, and Zephyr, at the age of forty-four years.

May 23, 1860, Mr. Carnes married Miss Emily Bridge, of Nelsonville. To this union two children were born, both now living. Mr. Carnes has twenty-two grand children and three great grand children now living. These, together with the host of other relatives and friends, Mr. and Mrs. Carnes are enjoying in their old age.

Thus in these few words is recorded the chief incidents of a long and useful life. It would require a great deal more space than is at command to recite the many personal incidents that were characteristic of the man that gave him abundant success. From nothing he has won a competency by manly conduct, persistent honesty and broad-minded generosity in all his dealings with his fellow man.

MRS. A. H. CARNES.

MISS CALLIE A. CARNES.

INTERIOR VIEW DRY GOODS, NOTIONS, ETC.

INTERIOR VIEW QUEENSWARE DEPARTMENT.

CHARLES AUGUSTUS SNOW.

C. A. SNOW'S RESIDENCE ON EAST STATE STREET, ATHENS, OHIO.

CHARLES AUGUSTUS SNOW was born in Athens Township, November 26, 1852, and has been a very busy and successful citizen of the county ever since. When a young man he attended Ohio University to the Sophomore year, teaching school in the meantime and after he left the University till he had put in fourteen years of professional life.

For a time he was manager of a branch office for the Singer Manufacturing Company at Mt. Vernon. In 1885 he bought the William T. Dean farm of one hundred acres near Fisher's Station, and in 1890 engaged in the dairy business, marketing his product in Athens. In 1897 he left this farm and bought the A. Norton farm of two hundred and fifty acres, one mile east of the city of Athens, and enlarged his dairy herd and business to one of the finest in the country. With this fine herd of over seventy cows, Mr. Snow was able to take such contracts as the Athens State Hospital for the Insane, which he has been supplying since August, 1901. His is an ideal dairy plant. The farm is divided between first-class grazing and farming land. Oil and gas wells are on the farm of sufficient capacity to supply all home needs of fuel and lighting. The farm is abundantly supplied with never failing springs, and their waters are piped to every place of domestic and herd use.

August 3, 1876, Mr. Snow was married to Miss Dassa Clutter, and to this union three children were born: Grace L., January 19, 1878, she being married April 9, 1901 to Fred L. Hammond, Mrs. Hammond dying September 15, 1902. Dalton C. Snow, their second child, was born April 10, 1879, he marrying Anna Winner, March 18, 1903, to them being born a girl, now nearly one year old. Herbert L. Snow was born October 8, 1880, and married Anna Balis, February 20, 1900, they now being citizens of Chillicothe. Mr. Snow is an employee of the B. & O. S-W. railroad. Dassa Clutter Snow died September 13, 1883, and in March, 1884 Mr. Snow married Mrs. Cina E. Fisk Patterson, of Nelsonville. They have one son, Robert B., who was born August 28, 1886. Mr. and Mrs. Snow are most pleasantly located in their fine city residence in "Sunny Side," a picture of which is herewith shown. Mr. Snow gives general oversight to his farm and dairy business, but his sons have immediate charge of the dairy and farm. Each day they deliver 150 gallons of milk to the State Hospital, and the feed for maintaining a herd that will supply that quantity of milk is raised on this farm, hence Mr. Snow & Sons do quite a little farming along with the dairy business.

The Snow farm residence shown in the background of the picture has nearly all the conveniences of a home in the city, yet its surroundings is that of the country. It is in the city school district, while it lies outside of Athens corporation. One can scarcely picture a more nearly ideal farm site—fertile bottoms, upland pasture, and close to market.

C. A. SNOW'S FARM AND HOLSTEIN HERD NEAR ATHENS, OHIO.

LODGES AND FRATERNAL ORDERS.

Athens Tent, No. 467, K. O. T. M., Athens, O.

Ashworth, Milton
Boelzner, Clifford J.
Brown, W. E.
Barth, Otto
Brown, Edmund E.
Cotton, E. H.
Cotton, T. A.
Campbell, E. G.
Carscaden, E. C.
Cramner, M. L.
Cramner, Clyde
Droze, Selden, E.
Daggett W. V.
Eaton, E. G.
Ford, Chas. E.

Gibbs, Isaac A.
Griffen, W. C.
Gillespie, Roy P.
Hill. S. B.
Hill, Pearl, D.
Johnson, J. H.
Leasure, E. T.
Laughlin, Waldo
Lawrence, A. E.
Logan, Clade L.
Maxwell A. L.
McVay, F. P.
Mansfield, Clyde C.
Mansfield, Frank M.
McCartey, Jonas J.

Nanny, D. G.
Oxley, Doll
Perry, Charles
Perry, Albert
Radford, W. H.
Sams, Peter Y.
Taylor, F. C.
Weatherbee, Albert
Wilson, Ralph B.
Woodworth Franz L.
Warren, C. S

Adelphia Temple, No. 91, Rathbone Sisters, Marshfield

Beverage, Callie
Beckle, Elizabeth
DeWees, Mattie
Doll, Anne
Hamilton, Jennie
Jackson, Maggie
Pake, Emma S.
Pierce, Christena
Phillips, Lucy
Rhorick, Joanna
Swaney, Kate
Barker, Jannette
McCoy, Sarah
Beckler, Nora
Clendenin, Mina
Martin, Callie
Martin, Mary
Kelley, Arcella
Kelley, Anna
Cox, Sophia
Devore, Lida
Vansky, Elizabeth
Jones, Stella
Loper, Rose
McCoy, Mabel

Duffey, Jannette
Martin, Clara
Riser, Nellie
Cox, Birdie
Russell, Anna
Martin Zona
Albaugh, Rose
Hoffner, Susanna
McBride, Ella
Russell, Mabel
Williams, Kate
Russell, Martha
Wilson, Emma
Baird, Sarah
McGraer, Kate
Carter, Maggie
Withers, Nora
McHarg, James
Rizer, C. O
Pierce. C. C.
Russell, J. O.
Thomas, W. A.
Sherman, Jacob
Fyler, James
McBride, Jos.

Hoffner, Conrad
Cox, Harrison
Morarity, Geo.
Lostro, J. R.
Martin, A.
Williams, W.
Russell Milfred M.
Pake, Geo. L.
Wilson, Elmus
Rhorick, Edward
Hamilton, John
Davis, Edward
Morse, Birt
Beckler, B. F.
Beckler, P. D.
Henry, Dr.
Pedigo, Dr. S. E. G.
Duffee, W. F.
Dumaree, Chas.
Doll, Geo.
Beverage, S. F.
Halliday, W. M.
Hewitt, J. C.
Jackson, R.
McVay, F. H.
Ryan, John

Pleasant View Temple, No. 135, Rathbone Sisters. Chauncey, Ohio.

Willis, Lizzie
Harvey, Lizzie
Martin, Emma
Preston, Rose
Walker, Mealie
Collins, Clarinda
Collins, Mary
Bracken, Mary
Collins, LizzieC
Grabel, Frank
Hickson, Rinda

Smith, Maury
Braker, Matilda
Jackson, Mertie
McDaniel, Sadie
Willson, Elizabeth
Elliott, Alice
Shield, Anne
Dodds, Mamie
Sprague, Floride
Foraker, Edith
Combs, Martha

Minister, Florence
Fisk, Elizabeth
Schoonover, Abbie
Lebman, Myrta
Fisk Maud
McHarg, Ella
Shafer, Dora
Lefler, Sarah
McKibben, Mame

Athens Lodge, No. 973, B. P. O. E., Athens. Ohio.

Wood, J. M.
Lynch, A. W.
Stedman, F. C.
Allen, J. B.
Brannan, J. C.
Preston, F. L.
Thompson, C. H.
Morgan, T. L.
Wolf, B. F.
Biddle, D. H.
McDougall, C. S.
Kurtz, Geo. A.
Golden, W. B.
Zenner, Henry
Bower, C. J.
Brown, Guy. H.
Finsterwald, Jno.
Henderson, C. B.
Phillips, W. R.

Cline, J. H.
Biddison, C. L.
Worstell, L. G.
Earhart, G. W.
Pickering, F. S.
Edmundson, J. C.
Webster, H. M.
Wolfe, A A.
Wood, J. P.
Junod, Geo. H.
Fuller, Carl
Roach, C. W.
Higgins, J. M.
McKee, W. H.
Bessor, Geo.
McVay, F. P.
Murphy, Hal. W.
Alderman., W. N.
DeCamp, Geo.

Scott, W. K.
Thompon, S. D.
Harris, C. V.
Henry, J. L.
Wood, J. V.
Jewett, L. M.
Enlow, E. M.
Fulton, J. B.
Reynolds, G. W.
Bonifield, R. E.
Peoples, D. W.
Moore, C. O.
Beasley, G. E.
Price, A. E.
Alderman, F. L.
Bryson, C. H.
Demolet, Chas.
Berry Carl C.
Jones, C. L.

Mohawk Tribe, No. 174, I. O. R. M., Athens, Ohio.

Miller, James A.
Henry, J. L.
Deau, W. E.
Connett, L. L.
Newsom, C. S.
Rassmussen, Martin
Scott, Win
Harris, C. C.
Carr, P. C.
Fenzel, Fred
Pickett, J. W.
Henry, Charles
Davis, T. E.
Cook, J. E
Cramner, Morris
Dickinson, H. E.
Dell, T. H.
Jones, U. G.
Webber, Charles
Lewis, W. A.
Farrell, W. H
Dalton, F. H.
McKinstry, C. A.
Dickson, H. A.
Slaughter, Eber
Hull, Arch
Jackson, Owen
Hibbard, R. A.
Baker, B. F
Secoy, Charles
Secoy, R. D.
Cook, C. S
Munn, R. B.
Webster, Frank
Beasley, L. D.
Brickles, David
Bean, Allen

Milligan Branch
Carr, I. M.
Bennett, B. A.
Kelley, Jacob
Cameron, Wm
Watkins, C. W.
Fulton, F B.
Wendelkin, G. W.
Hunter, John
Farrell, Frank
Cameron, Henry
Pidcock, John
Davis, Walter
Carter, W. E.
Burley, Frank
Day, Gilbert
Burch, H. O.
Lawrence, Wade H.
Finsterwald, Peter
Calvert, G. W.
Munuer, Charles
Parker, Wade
Oxley, A. B.
Cramner, Claude
Crippen, Clarence
Chappell, J. M.
Goff, Harry E.
Patterson, J. A.
White, Wm.
Hambletou, J. S.
Laird, Armstrong
Mansfield, Jervis
Vanbiber, Jessa
Edmundson, Clyde
Roach, Orr
Lepley, T. W.
Burtt, Fred

Foster, I. M.
Brooks. W. J.
Laughlin, Murn
Gardner, W. E.
Barnhill, L. A.
Carr, P. D.
McKibben, Harry
Bobo, Harry
Jordan, H. E.
Banks, Edward
Moore, E. C.
McWhorter, John
Mall, Armstrong
Gould, Wm.
Hedges, F. A.
Slaughter, Isaac
Hill, S. B,
Gossage, Warren
Beasley, C. M.
Kincade, F. M.
Smart, G. M.
Sanders, H. L.
Simmons, Wm.
Forrest, A. L.
Hunter, Hurbert
Brandenburg, Sylves
Goff, W. D.
Wilson, Joseph
Dickson, Wm.
Edgar, W. W.
Stout, J. J.
Olds, Frank E.
Reeves, Vergal A.
Hastings, R. C. M.
White, F. P.
Crippen, H. M.
Chaney, Chas. B.

Sweringer, W. E.
McAdoo, E. D.
Marquis, C. G.
Pidcock, Samuel
Woodworth, Fred
VanDyke, Jas.
Morrataty, T. B.
Cook, John N.
Penney, Albert
Griffith, T. J.
Kinney, Wilber
Eavner, G. D.
Baird, W. W.
Simmons, Aaron
Mansfield, Perl
Cooper, Wm.
Kincade, F. R.
Martin, Aaron
McNutt, E. C.
Mooney, C. E.
Winning, Peter J.
Penney, George A.
Carsey, Samuel A.
Woodyard, James H.
Hanning, Fred
Woodyard, H. B.
Albaugh, H. D.
McWhorter, George
McClanahan JamesJr
Sams, D. A.
Hoffner, Connard
Crofford, Alva
Dalton. Harry L.
Stokee, Charles
Perry, Jasper N
Gabriel, A. E.
Gandee, John S.
Burch, Ray
Hawkins, P. W.
Johnson, A. L.
Kinney, Melvin
Wolf, Mervin

Robinett, Alford
Penrod, A. J.
Berhs, Charles F.
Watkins, Frank
Baird, Robert F.
Moore, Willie G.
Hutchens, James
Beckler, William
Tucker, Charles F.
Jones, Thomas B.
Pennell, Wm. J.
Reeves, James P.
Brickles, Ross C.
Williams, Lewis B.
Slaughter, Ray E.
Woodyard, T. J.
Winning, Thomas
Hutchens, William
Meredith, Bert
Martin, Aaron E.
Sutton, F. F.
Swarm, Clarence
Mansfield, Elza B.
Bobo, G. H.
Simmons F. M.
Shall, George
Reeves, C. W.
Simmons, Arthur J
Beasley, C. A.
Stephenson, F. S.
Mansfield, Elmer
Woodruff, David M.
Dewey, G. W.
Thomas, Thomas
McCoy, James O.
Mace, Eli
Penney, Jerry
Sherman, Ralph
Byer, P. E.
Woodgerd, Charles
Bowers, Wm.

Almoud, Michael
Thompson, Wm.
Mace, Leander
Williams, William
Lane, Orvid D.
Mills, William
Cabeen, J. H.
Woodworth, E. C.
Kinney, C. A
Burnfield, James A.
Hofner, John
Burnley, Isaac
Cramblet, James
Burnley, F. B.
Hooper, Ralph
Martin, Wm J.
Sanders, B. R.
Parfitt, John
Wilson, Robert
Mirner, Edgar
Parfitt, James
Dowler, H. P.
Kelley, J. L. C.
Reeves, Emmett
Stanley, P. J.
Arnold, Ralph
Jones, C. L.
Carmichel, Robert
Dowler, James
Perry, Charles H.
Barnhill, Frank D.
Thomas, Ivor
Pickering, A. S.
Carpenter, James
Mansfield, Elza
Mansfield, Edward
Copeland, Thomas A
Jones, Perl A.
Hall, W. W.
Baker, Owen
Holland, George
Cooper, R.. M,

Amesville Grange, No. 798. Patrons of Husbandry.

Brawley, R. G.
McCune, S. R.
Hixson, Mrs. John
Goddard, W. R
Fleming, G. L.
Brawley, E. H.
Fleming, J. T.
Warrener, Wm J.
Marquis. Wm.
Goddard Gladys
Goddard Estella
Henry Lucy
Goddard Augusta
Henry, Jessie
Henry C. D.
Brawley, Mrs. E. H.
McCune, C. B.
Wyatt, G. E.
Glazier L. B.

Henry Mrs. C. D.
Fleming, Lucy E.
Wyatt C. P.
Anderson J. O.
Lovell O. M.
Finch, Emma
Phillips, D. G.
Marquis, Wm.
Brawley, M. G.
Phillips, Mrs. G. A.
Glazier, Mrs. L. B.
Phillips, John
Kuhns, J. W.
Phillips, W. R.
Anderson, Mrs. J. O.
Lovell, Mrs. O. M,
Finch, E. H.
Wyatt, C. H.

Henry, Mrs R. B.
Linscott, B. W.
Fleming, Daniel,
Keirns, R. R.
Hixson, Ethel
Henry, Millie
Perry, Charles
Howard, Effie
Warrener, Mary E.
Hill, Carrie
Perry, Mrs. C.
Hixson, John
Fleming, Mrs. J. T
Hixson, Carrie
Warrener, Annie A.
Howard, Ota
Hixson, Emma J.
Smith, Lewis

. . . . . Farm Residence of Mr. and Mrs. C. H. Boudinot. . . . . .

MR. C. H. BOUDINOT was born on the farm where he now lives February 13, 1863. His father, Tobias, was a native of Meigs county, while his mother, Elizabeth Southerton, was born in England, coming to the United States in 1833. His father was an Athens county Infirmary Director for two terms.

The present Boudinot farm was settled by his grandfather over fifty years ago, dying some years ago at Mt. Vernon, O., at the advanced age of more than 102 years.

His great uncle, Elias Boudinot, was a descendant of the French Huguenots, was a member of Congress in 1777, becoming president of that body in 1782, signing the treaty of peace with Great Britain the next year in his official capacity. Washington made him Superintendent of the mint in 1796. For several years he was a Trustee of Princeton College, which had conferred upon him the degree of L. L. D..

The subject of this sketch was at one time a student of Nathee College and was married to Celia Sawyer on September 1, 1898, she having been born in Morgan county on May 14, 1877. To them two very bright and interesting children have been born, Goldie, Aug. 21 1899, and Warren Parker, Sept. 13, 1901.

Belonging to their family also is Fletcher Boudinot, Mr. B's nephew. who has lived with him since he was three months old, now a young man over 21 years. He sits in the swing on the Indian mound. He is a young man of splendid life and habits. This mound is one of those built by the Mound Builders, and was found to contain skeletons, so that this beautiful country scene is directly connected with very ancient history.

Residence and Farm of Mr. and Mrs. O. B. Miller, of Lodi Township.

OLIVER B. MILLER is one of the best and most successful farmers of Lodi township, as the view of his fine home herewith shown will readily suggest. To farming he evidently was born and carefully trained. Mr. Miller first saw the light of day August 8, 1849, on the farm adjoining his own. His father, D. D. Miller, was a native of new Jersey, having been born in 1812, when Great Britain was trying for the second time to destroy the United States.

In 1838 Mr. Miller came to Lodi township and settled the farm on which the subject of this sketch was born, where he lived for fifty years. In 1840 he married Sarah Bodwell, who was born in Ames township in 1817.

October 26, 1876, Oliver Miller married Samaria Riggs, who was born in Meigs county, March 30, 1852, the same county in which her father was born May 11, 1811, dying December 4, 1873. Her mother was born in Gallia county in 1816, dying July 1, 1884.

Mr. Miller's father died in July, 1890 his mother following August 27, 1897.

Mr. Miller has confined his efforts to farming and stock raising, making a specialty of Delana sheep, of which he now has a fine flock of one hundred and fifty head, dividing his attention with short horn cattle. His farm of two hundred and fifteen acres is delightfully adapted to this purpose, being well watered and of excellent soil. Five years ago Mr. and Mrs. Miller took a six month's trip south and southwest, spending a few months at Hot Springs, Arkansas. To see a beautiful farm, scientifically and successfully handled, one has but to visit this beautiful place, the pride of Lodi township.

Residence of Mr. and Mrs. Charles Lœffler, of Rome Township.

CHARLES LŒFFLER, the subject of this sketch, was born in Athens County, January 1, 184i, and is the son of Earnest and Elizabeth Lœffler. For a number of years Charles attended the public schools of Nelsonville, but finally moved with his parents to the home farm on Sugar Creek, where he was employed till 1899. Tiring of agricultural persuits he went to Wheeling, West Virginia, where he was employed as a cook for four years, receiving therefore a good salary. His duties here being of such an exacting character, caused his health to fail, and he was therefore compelled to resign. He returned to Athens county and re-engaged in farming, under which persuit his health is greatly improving. March 9, 1904, Mr. Lœffler was married to Miss Cora E. Anthony, daughter of James and Jane Anthony. Upon their marriage Mr. and Mrs. Lœffler moved to their farm in Rome township, March 16, 1904, where they now reside. Their home is a happy and an attractive one, and gives evidence of thrift and prosperity.

Whatever measure of success Mr. Lœffler has attained or may yet attain, is due to his own determination to surmount all obstacles and persist for the prize of his ambition. He is nobly assisted by his devoted wife, one of the most estimable young women of the county.

Farm Residence of Mr. and Mrs. J. Gaston Coe, of Dover Township.

THE COE family is one of the oldest in the United States. The family came to this country from Suffolkshire, England, where they had lived for many generations. Those who have read "Fox's Book of Martyrs," have noticed that "Roger Coo" (the English style of spelling), of Millford, Suffolkshire, was burned at the stake by order of Queen Mary in September, 1555, at Yoxford in that shire.

Robert Coe, born in Suffolkshire, England, in 1596, was the first Coe emigrant to the new world, coming with his wife Anna and their three sons. They sailed on the ship Francis, from Ipswich, Suffolkshire, April 10th, 1634. They arrived at Boston, Massachusetts, in June of the same year, and settled in Watertown, near Boston. From here the family scattered, one branch settling in Connecticut. From Stratford, Connecticut, Josiah Coe (great grandfather of the subject of this sketch) came to Ohio, in 1806. He settled near Nelsonville, and purchased a site for a mill, but finding later on that his location afforded no water power, he abandoned the idea of building a mill in that place, and proceeded to build what is now known as the Robbins mill in Nelsonville. Of the several mills

which he built along the Hocking River, some of the foundations and remains of dams are yet in evidence. He bought the Cable farm, which is now a part of Athens, and there spent the latter part of his life.

His son James was a miller by trade, and he spent most of his life on Monday Creek, near Nelsonville. This son was born January 8th, 1800, in Stratford, Connecticut, and came to Athens County with his parents in 1806.

Johnson Coe, son of James, was born near Nelsonville. November, 5th, 1826. He did not devote himself entirely to one occupation but tried several, nine years of his life being spent in the coal business. This was at a time previous to the building of railroads and the coal was shipped on the canal to the various places where it was sold. Later on he turned his attention to farming. He died in Nelsonville. February 8th, 1890.

Gaston Coe, oldest son of Johnson Coe, was born at Nelsonville, September 2d, 1853. As shown above, he comes from a long and splendid line of ancestry, some of whom at least died in early martyr days for conscience sake. Mr. Coe spent his first twenty-two years under his father's roof.

April 18th, 1877. he was married to Isabella, daughter of Peter Martin. Mrs. Coe was born in Athens County May 18th, 1853. To them three children have been born. one dying at an early age.

Celia is the wife of J. T. Hope, Jr., while Lettie Maud is still at home. She is a graduate of the Athens High School, being a member of the class of 1903.

The family holds its church membership in M. E. Church at Chauncey, all being active and interested workers in all the enterprises of the church.

Mr. and Mrs. Coe have two grandchildren, Geraldine Coe Hope, aged three years, and Alton Russell Hope, aged one year. Their pictures appear in the group in the corner of the home view.

Mr. Coe is regarded as one of the best and most successful farmers of Dover Township, and his premises among the finest, as the picture herewith shows. They are an enterprising, social, Christian family. deeply interested and active in all that pertains to the welfare of society.

Upon their marriage, Mr. and Mrs. Coe at once moved on to the farm where they now live, and have resided there continuously ever since.

Residence of Mr. and Mrs. William R. Angell, in Lee Township.

THIS pretty country place is the home of Mr. and Mrs. William R. Angell, in Lee township, about three miles from Albany. He is the son of Hector and Lydia Angell, now deceased, and was born in Lodi township, September 26, 1849, and grew up on the farm, leading the life of a farmer lad and attending the common schools till he acquired a fair education.

On October 6, 1874, he was married to Miss Emma McVay, the daughter of Jacob McVay, one of the well-known citizens of the county. In 1878 they bought the farm of 105 acres, on which they have since resided, and by close attention to business and by studying the problems that confront every thoughtful agriculturalist and solving the same after careful consideration, they have succeeded well.

Mr. Angell is now giving his attention almost exclusively to the dairy business, converting the milk

from his Jersey herd of sixteen cows into wholesome butter which commands the highest market price. He has always been a breeder of good stock and has exhibited sheep at the county fairs for twenty six

years, winning first premium invariably. Mr. and Mrs. Angell have four children as follows: Halbert E , born Oct. 16, 1875; Grace, born Dec. 3, 1878; Mary Lydia, b. March 4, '80; and Lucy Pearl, b. May 10, '85.

HADLEY H. WICKHAM.

IN presenting the leading facts in the life of Hadley H. Wickham, it will be seen that it is the career of one of the representative citizens of Athens county. What success he has achieved has been accomplished in a quiet, unobtrusive way. Hadley H. Wickham is the son of Mr. and Mrs. Warren W. Wickham, and was born in Rome township, near the Bern township line, in 1842. He came from sturdy New England stock, the Wickham family originally coming from England and settling in Vermont. His great grandfather, Joseph Wickham, left a British vessel and served in the Revolutionary War, his grandfather, John Wickham, served in the War of 1812. His grandmother was a Culver, whose ancestors came over in the May Flower. The family of John Wickman came from New England in the early years of the nineteenth century and settled in Rome township. Later he moved with his family, with a team of oxen as the only means of travel to Big Darby Creek, northwest of Columbus. The country then was low and swampy, and on account of the frequent attacks of malaria, the family removed to Athens county, locating at the mouth of Marietta Run, in Bern township. The parents of Hadley H. Wickham were born in Athens county, and lived practically their entire lives in Rome and Bern townships. The death of the mother occurred April 5, 1893, and the death of Warren W. Wickham occurred on July 13, 1904, at Stewart, at the advanced age of ninety years. When twenty years of age, Hadley H. Wickham enlisted in the service of his country, joining Company A, Ninety-second O. V. I., serving until the close of the Civil War, and was mustered out at Washington, D. C., in June, 1865. He was in many severe engagements, notably at Chickamauga, Lookout Mountain, Missionary Ridge, Rocky Face, and in the en-

RESIDENCE OF H. H. WICKHAM, NORTH COLLEGE STREET, ATHENS, OHIO.

gagements with Sherman on his Atlanta campaign, and with "Sherman to the Sea." He was wounded at Chickamauga and Rocky Face, Ga. At the close of Civil War he returned to Bern township, and in 1868 went to Missouri where he spent the winter teaching school. In 1869 he was married to Keturah E. Broadwell. Mrs. Wickham was born in Cincinnati in 1847, and was the daughter of Mr. and Mrs. Henry Broadwell, whose farm is now the present site of the town of Broadwell. For an extended time after his return from Missouri, he engaged in farming and stock raising, and later engaged in the mercantile business at Mineral, where he was located seven years. Subsequently he bought a farm in Canaan township. and is now the owner of 252 acres of improved farming land in that township. Mr. Wickham was elected treasurer of Athens county in 1888 and served two terms. He began the practice of pension attorney in 1884, and has been highly successful. He is still actively engaged in that business. He is now a stockholder and director in the First National Bank of Athens, and for eight years served in a similar capacity with the First National Bank of Pomeroy. He is a member of the Masonic bodies up to Knight Templar, and is a member of Columbus Golden Post, G. A. R., of Athens.

FARM OF H. H. WICKHAM IN CANAAN TOWNSHIP.

ANDREW JACKSON, of Chauncey, Ohio, is one of the Dover township citizens with an interesting history. He was born in Athens, December 8, 1844, being a resident of the county all his life. At the breaking out of the war he responded to the call for troops and enlisted December 6, 1861, for three years, or so long as the conflict might last. He was a member of Company D, Seventy-fifth Regiment, O. V. I. He was in sixteen battles, among them being some of the bloodiest conflicts of the war, such as Gettysburg, Gainesville, second Bull Run, Cedar Mountain, and the siege of Ft. Wagner, where, on August 19, 1863, he received several terrible wounds. His lower limbs were terribly shattered, the knee cap of the left leg being destroyed and his right leg so torn that it was amputated the same day. His right shoulder was also badly injured.

He was lying in front of the rebel barricade when piles of powder exploded on the enemies side, sending pieces of shells, etc., into the Union ranks. He was in the Army of the Potomac till after the battle of Gettysburg, when he went south to Morris Island, where he received his terrible wounds. He was then taken to Beaufort, South Carolina, hospital; then removed to Ft. Schuyler, New York; afterward to David's Island, New York Harbor; thence to Central Park hospital, New York City, from which he received his discharge January 20, 1865. He was never taken prisoner, nor at any other time wounded. Returning to his home at Chauncey, arriving there August 19, 1865, just two years from the day he was wounded. January 1, 1868, he married Margaret Ann Border, daughter of Solomon Border, a native of Pennsylvania.

Mrs. Jackson was born near Chauncey, September 8, 1845. They have seven children, all living but one. Miss Addie was for a time deputy post mistress at Chauncey.

Mr. Jackson has some rare relics of the war. One is a piece of a rebel flag, captured at the third day siege of Gettysburg, when the greatest charge was made; also a piece of his regimental flag, the blue part of which was pierced by seventy bullets and pieces of shells. He has a fine gold medal, a "reward for gallant bravery." He is a member of the K. of P. Lodge, No. 709, at Chauncey, also of the G. A. R., Columbus Golden Post of Athens, No. 89.

His nice home is on Sandy Ridge, near Chauncey. Mr. Jackson is a familiar figure in Athens and elsewhere. His patriotism and sociability take him to State and National encampments of the G. A. R.

Country Home of Henry Tribe, in Alexander Township.

HENRY TRIBE, whose home appears herewith, was born in Alexander township, Athens county, Ohio, January 30, 1842, on the farm where he now resides. His parents, George and Sarah Tribe, were both born at Wisborough Green, Sussex county, England, in 1812, and came to America to the farm above mentioned in 1832. On the breaking out of the war, Henry Tribe enlisted in Company C, One Hundred and Forty-first Regiment, Ohio National Guards. His enlistment was July 14, 1863, and for one hundred days. Upon the closing of the great struggle he was honorably discharged. December 31, 1871, Mr. Tribe was married to Sarah Oxley, daughter of Sidney and Elizabeth Oxley. Mrs. Tribe was born in Athens township, in July, 1851, and died December 13, 1892.

Mr. and Mrs. Tribe had eight children, all of whom are living, five still at home. The home farm consists of two hundred and fifty acres, and at once presents a picture of thrift, enterprise and neatness.

Residence of Mrs. James T. Morrison, of Coolville, Ohio.

JAMES T. MORRISON, (deceased.)

MRS. JAMES T. MORRISON, Coolville.

JAMES T. MORRISON was born November 27, 1822, in Wayne township, Jefferson county, Ohio, and died in Coolville, Ohio, October 24, 1903.

His father, John Morrison, and his mother, Sarah Turner Morrison, were born and married in Pennsylvania, and came to Jefferson county, O., in 1817, and in 1838 came to Athens county, where they lived to an old age, dying within one year of each other, in 1875 and 1876.

Mary A. Laflin was born October 27, 1833, in Barlow township, Washington county, O. Her father, Hon. Harley Laflin, was born in Washington county and her mother, Annie Shields Laflin, was born in Wood county, Virginia, now a part of West Virginia. They lived their entire married life of sixty-one years on the farm where they died within five days of each other in 1892.

James T. Morrison and Mary A. Laflin were married May 20, 1857. Their children were Fannie, who died in infancy; Mamie, wife of the late Owen C. Hoobler; and Dora, wife of Otto Barth. Mr. and Mrs. Barth have one son, Carl Morrison Barth, born October 21, 1893.

Mr. and Mrs. Morrison have lived in the home shown in the picture above since November, 1866. This house was built in 1841 by Dr. John Pratt. Mr. Morrison was connected with the Coolville Flouring Mill from 1852 until the time of his death, except a few years after selling to John Clifford, but later he went into the Steam Mill company, which built a mill in 1875. Then into the company which tore down the steam mill and the old original water mill and erected the mill in 1882 which burned in 1886. He continued in the new company which built the present mill.

Mr. Morrison was actively engaged in the lumber business from 1858 until within a few years of his death, beginning in Meigs and Athens counties and then later in West Virginia. He also had large land interests.

Residence of Mr. and Mrs. Carlos D. Henry in Bern Township.

LOCUST VALLEY STOCK FARM.

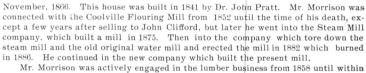

CARLOS D. HENRY, farmer and stock raiser, was born in Bern township, Athens county, Ohio, December 22, 1859, is the youngest son of the late Charles and Fanny M, (Dean) Henry and grandson of John and Margaret Henry, who came to America from Ireland in 1788 and settled on the farm where our subject now lives in 1817. His youth was spent in assisting his father in the management of the farm and attending the public schools, where he received his education. He lived with his parents until their death and then succeeded them on the old homestead, as did his father, he being the third generation. He was united in marriage, June 3, 1886, to Miss Hanna L. Bean, daughter of Archibald and Adaline Bean, of Wayne Co., Ill. She was born at Pleasanton, Athens Co., O., April 18, 1858. In 1865 she moved with her father's family to Wayne Co., Ill., where she received her education and taught in the public schools of the county for eight years.

By this union were five children, four of whom still live. Charles Guy (deceased), Harry Glen, Ralph McDougall, Clara Elenor and Wilbur Carlos. The homestead contains two hundred and ninety-eight acres of land, and is one of the finest in the county.

Mr. Henry and his wife are members of the Presbyterian church at Amesville. They are also members of the order of Patrons of Husbandry, No 798, a flourishing society at Amesville.

JAMES WILLIAMSON, whose home in Glouster, Ohio, is shown here, was born at Lanerickshire, Scotland, November 2, 1868. His father was born in Lanerickshire, Scotland, in 1841, while his mother, Janette Gillan, was born in Lanerickshire, Scotland, in 1839. His father was known in Scotland as "Shaft Sinker." Believing a larger and better field awaited them in America, young Williamson emigrated to this country with his parents in 1880, settling at Shawnee, Ohio, in 1887, finally locating at Glouster, where their shaft sinking business was continued. They put down most of the shafts in that vicinity.

December 24, 1889, Mr. Williamson was married to Miss Amelia Smith, who was born at Brynmaide, South Wales, England, October 6, 1871. Mrs. Williamson's parents were both born in England. Mr. and Mrs. Williamson are the parents of six bright and interesting children, George, John, Celia, Janet, Lizzie and James. Mr. Williamson is a member of the I. O. O. F., and is considered one of the most progressive citizens of Glouster. He has prosecuted his business in several states besides Ohio, his contracts reaching into many thousands of dollars, and nothing in his line is too large or difficult for him to undertake.

Aumiller & Edington, Clothing, Men's Furnishings and Shoes, Nelsonville, Ohio.

THE firm of Aumiller & Edington, of Nelsonville, Ohio, had its beginning in 1899, when Messrs. Aumiller and Edington went to Orbiston, Ohio, and opened a general merchandise business, known as the Orbiston Store Company. After conducting this business for less than a

year, they sold out to the Sunday Creek Coal Company. In August of the same year they came to Nelsonville and purchased the Standard Clothing Company's business, at their old stand, corner Washington street and the Public Square, and then the firm name was changed to Aumiller & Edington In August, 1904, the business was moved to their present commodious quarters in the Miners and Merchants Bank building, corner Columbus street and Public Square. Their present apartments were designed and arranged specially for their business, and their rooms being so light, convenient and handy.

Their line consists now of clothing, men's furnishings and men's and boys' shoes. By confining themselves strictly to these lines, they are able to give their patrons a larger assortment, with better prices and better goods.

Both Mr. Aumiller and Mr. Edington are experienced business men, having devoted their lives to it, and their fine business ability has won for them a large patronage. They carry the largest stock in their exclusive lines of any business house in Nelsonville, and are thus able to fit and please all classes. To see an emporium of fashion and goods, one has to but visit Aumiller & Edington's.

ATHENS COUNTY HISTORY
CONTINUED.

MOUNDS OF ATHENS COUNTY.
By CLARENCE MATHENY.

have been confined chiefly to those on Wolfs' Plains. Located on this bit of territory are seventeen conical mounds. The most prominent work done in this county was that by Prof. E. B. Andrews some thirty or thirty-one years ago for the Peabody Museum, of Cambridge, Mass. The majority of the mounds were opened. The most prominent mounds are the following: The Beard Mound; the Smith Mounds called the Geo. Connet Mounds by Prof. Andrews; the school House Mound; and the Connet

Bird's Eye View of Wolf's Plains where Mounds are Found.

Mounds. By Prof. Andrews' measurements, the Beard Mound is 30 feet high with a diameter at the base of 114 feet. The Smith Mound is 40 feet high and 175 feet in diameter at the base. These are the two most prominent mounds. A description of the work by Prof. Andrews will be given with many of the details omitted.

The Beard Mound is the second in size of the mounds on the Plains. One side has been removed to make way for the public road. This removal of the dirt leaves a bank about fifteen feet high and almost vertical. More of this bank was dug away and the excavation deepened to make it on a level with the surface of the surrounding land. It has never been adequately explored. Nothing of importance was found except a celt of

Continued on page 83.

NATHAN S. HATCH was born August 27, 1836, in Hocking county, Ohio. He was married to Lydia A. Parsons, January 10, 1855,. To them five children were born, three sons and two daughters. Mrs. Hatch died July 20, 1879. Afterward Mr. Hatch married Mrs. Louisa P. Johnston, daughter of Elam and Almira Frost. Mrs. Hatch's two sons, Harvey and Alva Johnston reside in Hall county, Nebraska, and are among the best agriculturists and stock raisers in the great and fertile Platt valley.

Mr. Hatch is a veteran of the Civil War, having enlisted in 1863 in Company I, 116 Regiment. He was severely wounded in the left shoulder at the battle of Piedmont, West Virginia, lying thirty-six hours on the battlefield. On the evening of the second day he was assisted to the field hospital where his wound was dressed. General Hunter withdrawing with his marching force, the wounded soldiers fell into the hands of the enemy, and Mr. Hatch, in company with others, was taken a prisoner to Andersonville, Georgia. Here he was detained for five and a half months, suffering all the deprivations and hardships for which that awful place is known. He was one of the famishing when the miracle of the gushing spring relieved the burning thirst of thousands of the boys in blue. Mr. Hatch's discharge is dated December 17, 1865. His present residence is one and a quarter miles northwest of Frost, Athens county. For many years he has been a member of the Troy Baptist church, and he lives close to her teachings of charity and hospitality, for these are prominent features with Mr. Hatch.

JAMES O. IMES, son of Richard and Jane Holmes Imes, was born June 10th, 1837, in Waterloo Township. He spent his early days on the farm, working in summer and attending school in the winters. From 1857 to 1861, his time was spent in academic work and teaching school. Answering the "call to arms," he enlisted as private in Company D, 75th O. V. I., October 29th, 1861, for three years. He participated in all the great battles in which his regiment was engaged, such as second Bull Run, Chancellorsville, and Gettysburg. He was promoted to Sergent Major March 1st, 1863, and commissioned Second Lieutenant August 19th, 1864. He was captured at the battle of Gainesville, August 17th, 1864. He served as a prisoner in Andersonville, Savannah, and Milan, Georgia. He was finally paroled, and mustered out of the service at Columbus. Ohio, January 13, 1865. Three years later he went to Missouri, where he engaged in school teaching and contract work. In 1875 he married Frances M. Laney, of Waterloo, New York. He then returned to his old home, and until recently resided with his aged parents. September 30, 1904, Mr. Imes was appointed postmaster at Marshfield. He is the father of three sons, Dr. L. L. Imes, of Indianapolis, Ind., Rupert, a rural mail carrier, and Richard P., a stationary engineer.

Richard Imes is one of the oldest citizens of the county. His grandfather, Captain Isaac Barker, an old sea captain, emigrated to Ohio from Massachusetts about 1797, and settled near the present site of Athens. In 1836 he married Jane S. Holmes and settled on the farm now owned by his son, J. O. Imes. His life was linked with nearly all the early life and incidents of both the county and the city of Athens. There are those now living in Athens belonging to the seventh generation of the Imes family. To read his life is to read the history of the county.

JAMES. O. IMES.

RICHARD IMES.

RESIDENCE OF CHARLES WILLIAMS, NEAR ATHENS.

THE subject of this sketch is the son of James Harvey and Sarah Hull Williams, and was born in Lodi township January 13, 1858. His experiences reach back into days of hardship and deprivation. He remembers his first suit of clothes to have been made by his mother, who bought the wool at one dollar a pound, and did the whole process of manufacturing it into wearing apparal. At the time of Morgan's raid he, together with the other members of his family, accompanied neighbors nearly two miles to a sort of block house, where they all took refuge. His father being in the war, and his mother left with four children, the eldest of whom was only seven yeare old, Charles contributed his share toward the support of the family, and continued this till he was sixteen years old. At the age of twenty-five he married Mary E, daughter of Charles Brown, descendent of one of the earliest settlers of the county. His great grandfather, William, was a native of Wales, but came to this country, settling in the fertile Shenandoah Valley, Virginia, where he became a slave holder. Upon the breaking out of the Revolutionary War he liberated his slaves. Charles' father was born in Zanesville, Ohio, and came to Athens county as one of its first settlers. His mother's father was a soldier in the war of 1812, and was in Hull's surrender on Lake Erie. When his mother was a girl of ten years, she, together with her parents, floated down the Ohio river to Pomeroy, from which they subsequently emigrated to Athens county, settling in Athens township. For eleven years after his marriage, the subject of this sketch worked for H. D. Mirick but he afterward purchased a farm in Lodi township, where he lived for ten years, devoting himself to stock and fruit raising. Only recently he purchased the farm of one hundred and eighty acres where he now lives.

Residence of Mr. and Mrs. Leroy S. Woodworth, Dover Township.

THOUGH fifty-nine years old, Leroy S. Woodworth may properly be called one of the pioneers of Dover township, as he has been a resident of that township for nearly forty years. Fifty-nine years ago he was born in Trimble township, where he grew to young manhood. He then moved to his present home, one mile north of Millfield, where he owns a well-improved farm of eighty acres. He was married in 1868 to Sarah B. Riddell. They are the parents of six living children, as follows: C. A. Woodworth, of New York; E. C. and J. E. Woodworth, of Athens; Mrs. Mabel Sanders and Mrs. Olive Sanders, of Millfield, and Miss Estella Woodworth, of Columbus.

The subject of this sketch served his country during the Civil War for two years, serving in Company G, Eighteenth O. V. I., and was in the command of General Thomas during the Nashville campaign. Has held many offices of honor and trust, serving as justice of the peace, trustee of Dover township, and for three years was a member of the board of infirmary directors. He is an active worker in the Republican party and takes the keenest interest in all national, state and county campaigns.

The Woodworth home, shown in the illustration, is as comfortable as it looks, and the latch string is always out with a welcome by the occupants for old and young alike.

Residence of Mr. and Mrs. L. R. Andrews, of Glouster, Ohio.

L. R. ANDREWS, of Glouster, Ohio, son of Mr. and Mrs. Mason Andrews, was born in York township, this county, October 3, 1863, and was reared on a farm and taught to do all kinds of farm work. He received an education in the country schools with but two terms in the Ohio University at Athens. He began teaching in 1883, and for seven years taught each winter. He was married to Lizzie B. Wolf, eldest daughter of Mr. and Mrs. Joseph Wolf, May 28, 1885. To this union three daughters were born, Adda May, Florence E. and Nellie Belle. Adda and Florence have both gone through the Glouster schools, and Adda is now a teacher in the school. Mr. Andrews farmed, taught school and had some experience in mining in the Floodwood mines, this county, until December, 1891. At this time he was employed by the Trimble Mill Company, at Glouster, Ohio, and entered their business as hardware clerk. In the spring of 1892 The Sunday Creek Hardware Company was incorporated, and Mr. Andrews becoming a stockholder was made manager of the Glouster branch of the business. This position he held for nearly twelve years, and under his management the business grew to be the largest in the Sunday Creek Valley. The work included the handling of hardware, furniture, vehicles and building material, having erected as many as twenty buildings in one season. He and Mr. S. S. Danford, of Trimble, carried also undertaking as a side line since 1898. While intrusted with the Sunday Creek Hardware Company, Mr. Andrews worked untiringly, seldom giving less than sixteen hours for a day's labor. He necessarily had several men in his employ, who speak highly of his kindness and ability as a manager. In October, 1903, the business of the Sunday Creek Hardware Company was divided, Mr. Andrews taking the vehicle and undertaking part of the business.

Mr. Andrews is now located on Front street, handles a nice line of vehicles, and does undertaking work. He is a licensed embalmer and well equipped to do work of this kind. He and his family are active members of the Methodist church, and there is no place he enjoys so much as the Sunday school room, and has served several terms as Sunday school superintendent. He has held positions of trust, the duties of which he has discharged creditably, proving him to be a man of honor.

FARM RESIDENCE OF F. L. CLARK, LEE TOWNSHIP

F. L. CLARK is one of Lee township's progressive and well-to-do farmers and stock raisers. This is the township of his birth, May 17, 1850. He was the son of William and Lydia Clark. His father was a pioneer from Harrison county, Ohio. The subject of this sketch, whose home is shown herewith, was raised on a farm and received such education as the country schools of his day afforded. August 27, 1871, he married Laura C. Ashley, of West Virginia, her native state, where she was born December 25, 1846. To them two children have been born. O. W., June 13, 1872, and May E., September 9, 1882. In 1872 Mr. Clark bought a farm of 110 acres of wood land, clearing and living there till 1878, when he moved to Zaleski, Vinton county.

Here he went into the hotel business, remaining there eighteen months, when he sold and returned to his farm, remaining there till 1888. He operated a saw mill with James Sickel. He bought 500 acres of timber land of Joseph Dana, of Athens, from which he sawed the timber and then sold the land, moving back to his original farm, where he remained till 1893. He then went to West Virginia, and with A. G. Ross and J. F. Robins, bought 160 acres of timber land. His stay here was but three months, when he returned home, where he has been ever since. His home farm now consists of 240 acres, nearly all of which is in a high state of cultivation. In addition to this, Mr. Clark has 7,000 acres of coal land near Albany and Mineral, with a vein of coal nine feet thick, destined some day to be very valuable.

MR. ROBERT WHITE.

THE residence here shown is the home of Mr. and Mrs. Fred P. White, located on North Lancaster street, overlooking the beautiful Hocking river in its winding through a broad fertile valley.

Mr. White is one of Athens young men, who started in life with no other capital than his hands and learned the tinners trade under Frank Witman, by whom he was engaged for six years. Seventeen years ago he started into business for himself and has been more than ordinarily successful. He employs a number of men and is busy the year round.

On April 19, 1888, he was married to Miss Mary E. Edmundson. They have six children, whose births are recorded as follows: Della M., born June 8, 1889; Homer E., born January 8, 1892; Carlos R., born June 12, 1891; Mary L., born June 23, 1897; Doris J., born September 8, 1899; Frederick L., born December 8, 1901. A peculiar coincidence is noted in the births of these children, four of whom were born on the eighth of the month.

Mr. Robert White, the father of the subject of this sketch, was born July 17, 1823, in Witheringwick, Yorkshire, England, and makes his home with his son.

Mr. White, Sr., was married to Mary Etherington, December 25, 1847, and they came to this country in 1851. Mrs. White died on March 17, 1901. Mr. White has been a resident of Athens over half a century, and is well known, having been a coal dealer here for many years. He was the first man to use a horse team for hauling and drayage in Athens, competing with Jasper Carsey, who used oxen exclusively for many years.

Farm Residence of Mr. and Mrs. William Pierce, in Lodi Township

WILLIAM PIERCE was born in Mercer county, Pennsylvania, in 1846. He was the seventh child in a family of eleven children, eight sons and three daughters. His father, David Pierce, was born in Westmoreland county, Pennsylvania, the son of John and Margaret (Scott) Pierce. William's mother, Mary (Robb) Pierce, was born in Mercer county, Pennsylvania. the daughter of Robert and Mary (Smith) Robb.

David Pierce's family moved to Athens county, Ohio, in 1851, and settled on a farm. Here William spent his boyhood, working on the farm in summer and attending district school for a few months each winter. After the close of the Civil War he was a pupil at Miller's Seminary for a few terms; also a student at Atwood Institute.

In 1867 William commenced teaching school, an occupation which he followed for thirty-two years, except a period of six years while in the west. In 1869 William went to Montana, and for six years was a miner, prospector, teamster, Indian trader and hunter. He traveled over that country from the mouth of Milk river to the Idaho line, and from the Yellow Stone National Park to the "Whoop-Up Country" in the British possessions.

He became acquainted with some of the most noted characters of that day. Among others was General George A. Custer, Colonel Tom Custer, Charley Hard, H. Beadler, Dick Berry, Dan Blevin and Liver-Eating Johnson. Among Indians he was acquainted with are the following chiefs: Sioux, Standing Buffalo, Sitting Bull, Long Dog, Tunica and Red Stone. Gros Ventres, White Eagle and Bear Child. Crows, Horse Guard and Two Bellies. In 1879 William Pierce was united in marriage to Emma M. Barnhill, daughter of Samuel and Eliza J. (Kebaugh) Barnhill. They have four children, two daughters and two sons. The view accompanying this sketch shows Mr. Pierce's fine home in Lodi township.

MR. AND MRS. JOHN ARTHUR TULLIS, OF NELSONVILLE, OHIO.

JOHN ARTHUR TULLIS was born in Clark county, Ohio, November 11, 1836, and came to Nelsonville, Ohio, in 1879, and established the Nelsonville News, making it the first successful newspaper published in the town. In 1884 he disposed of his publishing business on account of ill health. After two years of retirement he again entered the journalistic world, and in 1886 began the publication of The Valley Register. In the beginning it was made an independent paper, but after the lapse of two years was changed and became the organ of the Republican party, and was published by Mr. Tullis in that interest till the time of his death, which occurred June 20, 1899. Since that time The Valley Register is being edited and published by Mrs. S. E. Tullis and their two daughters, Anna and Mabel Tullis.

Mr. Tullis was united in marriage with Miss Susan E. Deaton, of Champaign county, Ohio, March 31, 1859. They were the parents of three daughters. They were both members of the Methodist Episcopal church, as are also their daughters. The eldest, Addie Amelia, was born February 5, 1860, and married Emerson M. Smith, April 18, 1884, then of Columbus, Ohio, now of Spokane, Washington. The second daughter, Anna Viola, born April 23. 1875, married Theron C. Hulburt, of Seville, Ohio, May 29, 1905. The youngest. Mabel Clare, born April 5, 1878, is still at home. Mrs. S. E. Tullis commenced the millinery business in St. Paris, Champaign county, Ohio, in 1867, and is now conducting a millinery business in Nelsonville, where they removed in 1879.

PICTURESQUE ATHENS.

1. Soldiers' Monument and College Campus.
2. College Street, Looking South from Washington St
3. University Terrace, Looking North.
4. Sunnyside" Looking North from Brick Plant.
5. Mulberry Street Looking East from Court Street.
6. "Autumn Leaves," View in College Campus, Looking East.
7. Washington Street Looking West from College Street.
8. "Flat Iron Square," "Currier Building" in Center.
9. Court Street Looking South from State Street.
10. State Street Looking West.
11. Union Street Looking West from Court Street.

J. V. Oxley's Blacksmith Shop, Athens, Ohio.

J. V. OXLEY, son of Eli Oxley, was born near Dresden, Iowa, May 19, 1868 and came with his parents to Alexander township, Athens county, Ohio, in 1874. He lived on a farm till he was eighteen years old. December 24, 1892 he was married to Martina Cowan, who was born in Lodi township, July 1, 1871.

Mr. and Mrs. Oxley have four children, two boys and two girls.

Four years ago Mr. Oxley came to Athens and opened a blacksmith shop, he having learned the trade ten years ago, and has worked at it continuously ever since. He is a successful and scientific workman in all the branches of his profession, which is proven by his large and increasing patronage.

Residence of Mr. and Mrs. D. T. Johnson, in Dover Township.

D. T. JOHNSON was born in Dover township, on what is known as Sand Ridge, November 10, 1858. He is the son of Eli and Lydia A. Johnson. His father was born in Perry county, Ohio, April 11, 1816, while his mother was born in Bedford county, Pennsylvania, July 10, 1823, coming to Ohio with her parents in 1831.

Mr. Johnson's parents were married April 20, 1841, and settled on and cleared the farm where the subject of this sketch was born. Here his parents both died 'midst the scenes of their life-careers, the mother dying December 19, 1893, and the

father October 27, 1894. His father was one of the early hunters, with a local record, among other feats, killing five deer in one day and forty-seven during the season.

October 24, 1883, Mr. Johnson married Alice, daughter of Calvin and Rosanna Mingus, of Dover township, Mrs. Johnson having been born in Morgan county March 10, 1862.

Mrs. Johnson's father was a veteran of both the Mexican and Civil wars, while her great grandfather was a veteran of the Revolutionary war.

To Mr. and Mrs. Johnson have been born five children all living but one, Ray Elmer, who died at the age of fourteen years

The Johnson home is one of the nicest country homes in Dover township, being situated opposite the Infirmary. Mr. Johnson has always been a farmer, and therefore has his farm of 160 acres under a high state of cultivation, upon which he has a fine large house, a picture of which is shown in connection with this sketch.

Residence of Dr. and Mrs. A. E. Lawrence, Coolville, Ohio.

DR. ARTHUR E. LAWRENCE, son of Moses Lawrence, was born near Guysville, Ohio, December 7, 1867. He attended Medical College at Columbus, Ohio, from which he graduated in March, 1890. On December 24, 1890, he was married to Florence V. LeGoullon, at Guysville. To Dr. and Mrs. Lawrence two children have been born. Majel, aged 13 years and Arthur E. Jr., aged 10 years. Shortly after his graduation. Dr. Lawrence located in Coolville, 1891, for the practice of his profession, where he still resides. The home shows prosperity as well as a keen sense of the things beautiful.

Residence of Mr. and Mrs. Solomon Huntington Johnson, Trimble Township.

SOLOMON HUNTINGTON JOHNSON was born in Trimble Township, January 23, 1837, on the farm where Hollister is now located. He was the fifth son of John B. and Adeline S. Johnson. The common schools and his father's fireside furnished his education. With the exception of his army life he has devoted himself to farming and stock raising, confining his stock breeding to the finest draft horses.

On President Lincoln's first call for troops, he enlisted in Company H. Twenty-second Ohio Volunteer Infantry, where he served four months Being discharged he reenlisted in Company A., Sixty-third Regiment O. V. I. where he served as first lieutenant from August 19, 1861 to October 30. 1862 when he was discharged. He was with his regiment at New Madron, Island No. 10, Inka, Tiptonville and Corrinth, where his regiment lost 48 per cent. of its total force, while at Farmington Mr. Johnson was wounded by a shell. On his return home he engaged again in farming and stock raising.

Mr. Johnson has always been one of the leading men of his community, both in business and politics, and has ever been noted for his splendid memory of political events. He has always been a staunch Republican, and has preached Republicanism from the stump in many a campaign. He was township trustee two terms, 1876 and 1877, Justice of the Peace two terms, and Trimble's first mayor, occupying that office two terms. Different times he has been prominently spoken of for State representative, but his willingness to see others served first has kept him out of the race.

In 1865 he was married to Miss Elizabeth Jones, with whom he lived most happily till 1889, when she died, since which time his home has been made with those occupying his house. Mr. Johnson is a Master Mason, a member of the Church of Christ, and through his genial and social disposition he has won for himself a host of friends far and near.

Farm Residence of Mr. and Mrs. Henry A. Matheny, Alexander Township.

whom he feels especially indebted are Judge J. M. and Perry Wood, and the ever genial Dick McKinstry. He is passionately fond of music, the study of which he began at an early age, and he has been a member and teacher of numerous musical organizations.

He believes that no home can be poor where the members of the family understand and enjoy music. He was married to Fannie M. Henry, daughter of Parker and Elizabeth Henry, September 4, 1884. They have two children. Letha Mayme, who is a student in the musical and elocution department of the Ohio University, and Raymond Henry, who is also in the preparatory studies for college work.

They own and live upon the farm known as the Alanson Hibbard farm on east Margarett's creek. He is a member of the Albany Lodge, No. 156, F. &. A. M. and the Modern Woodman of America. He belongs to the Students Agricultural Union, and has been for many years special correspondent for the American Agriculturist.

HENRY A. MATHENY, son of Charles and Fanny Dorr Matheny, was born on the banks of Sugar Creek, in Athens township, September 29, 1861. In the spring of 1865 his parents bought the William Stanley farm in Alexander township, which still remains the old family homestead He received his education in the common schools and at the Atwood Institute, at Albany. Among his teachers to

B. C. Wise's Dining Room, Nelsonville, Ohio.

THE interior picture here shown is the dining room of Hotel Nelson, in Nelsonville, Ohio. Mr. B. C. Wise, the present genial host, has made a reputation for himself as a caterer and hotel proprietor. In connection with the hotel he operates a short order restaurant, serving hot and cold lunch day and night. The dining room is also used for serving ice cream.

Mr. Wise finding Hotel Primrose more suitable to his business, has leased that property and will conduct the hotel business after April 1, 1906.

THE MATHENY FAMILY ORCHESTRA.

FIRST : PRESBYTERIAN : CHURCH : ATHENS, : OHIO.

THE First Presbyterian Church Society was organized in Athens in the year 1809 by Rev. Jacob Lindley. The first ruling elders were ordained in 1813. The church organization was incorporated at the State capitol in Columbus in 1827. Rev. Jacob Lindley served as its first pastor from 1809 until 1827. The first building was erected in 1828 and remodeled and enlarged in 1865. For many years this building served both for a school house and a church. Many of the old citizens of Athens recall the days when they went to school in the basement of the First Presbyterian Church. All the education that some of the old people got they received in that memorable old building. It remained on the lot until the year 1902 when it was removed to give room for the new commodious edifice that now graces the corner, a handsome picture of which is herewith shown. This church property is valued at over $40,000 and is one of the most modern and expensive church properties in southern Ohio.

The membership now numbers 426, and is composed of many of the leading families of this city.

The following ministers have served the congregation: Jacob Lindley, John Spaulding, Robert G. Wilson, and also President of the Ohio University, Samuel Davis Hogue, William Barba, Timothy Sterns, N. B. Purington, W. H. McGuffey, and he was also President of Ohio University, Wells Andrews, Aaron Williams, M. A. Hogue, Addison Ballard, Alfred Ryors. S. Dieffendorf, John H. Pratt, James F. Holcomb, E. W. Schwefel, James M. Nourse, Isaac Monfort, W. A. Powell and G. Walton King, who after a very successful pastorate of six years is now away on a years leave of absence, studying in the Union Theological Seminary and Columbia University, New York City.

: : : Residence of Mr. and Mrs. L. B. Glazier, Near Amesville, Ohio. : : :

LOUIS BARNARD GLAZIER, farmer and stock raiser of Ames township, Athens county, Ohio, was born January 26, 1860. He is the son of John Henry and Sarah Ann (Henry) Glazier, and grandson of Loring Brown and Jane (Henry) Glazier, and of Mathew and Mary (Park) Henry, and great-great-grandson of Captain Benjamin Brown, who was prominently identified for many years among the early settlers of Athens county and who was a captain in the Revolutionary War, coming to Ohio from Massachusetts in 1776.

Our subject was born and reared in the house in which he now resides and on the farm formerly belonging to his father and grandfather. He was educated in the common school and Amesville Academy. He was married October 16, 1890, to Metta Adela Selby, of Bern township, Athens county, Ohio, daughter of Warren and Emily (Garretson) Selby, and grand daughter of Dyar and Tabitha (Calhoun) Selby, early settlers of Bern township and of Isaac and Beulah (Kirk) Garretson, of Jefferson county, Ohio.

They are the parents of two children, Myron Selby, born September 22, 1891 and Clifford Russell, born June 20, 1901. Mr. Glazier is a director and vice president of the First National Bank of Amesville, a trustee in the Presbyterian church, and president the Ames township board of education. He has a good stock farm of about 400 acres, and, being a man of unassuming character, his greatest pleasure is found in the careful attention to the best interests of the home and farm, being not unmindful, however, to the public welfare and that of the community in which he lives.

Mrs. Glazier was born February 15, 1866. She is a descendent of Captain Calhoun, a revolutionary hero from the State of New York. Her early life was spent on a farm and her education received in the common school and at Bartlett Academy. For a period of eight years she was a teacher in the public schools of Washington and Athens counties, Ohio. She is a member of the Presbyterian church and of the Woman's Christian Union of Amesville.

ATHENS COUNTY HISTORY
CONTINUED

MOUNDS OF ATHENS COUNTY.
By CLARENCE MATHENY.

greenstone. This was found a few feet below the surface and had been accidentally dropped and buried. This "mound" gives

good opportunity to study the method used by the Mound-Builders in the construction of these mounds. It shows them to have been built by dumping quantities of dirt on the growing heap. Perhaps a peck at a time was dumped on. These individual quantities are still plainly visible, there having been of course different kinds and colors of dirt used in the process of building. Each one now presents an oval appearance resembling a small heap. Many years were evidently used in constructing this mound. At various levels, there are evidences of a heavy growth of vegetation having covered the surface of the unfinished

mound. Whether they were slow in building simply because of insufficient means, or whether they added so much each successive year, can not be conclusively ascertained. It should be more carefully explored.

The mounds spoken of by Andrews as the Geo. Connett mounds are located on the farms of David Smith and Frank Smith on the northern part of the Plains. One of the mounds about 6 feet high and 40 feet in diameter was opened by digging a trench 5 feet wide through the center. An abundance of

Continued on page 85.

Residence of Mr. and Mrs. E. A. Dutton, at Hockingport, Ohio.

EDWIN A. DUTTON, whose fine home near Hockingport is herewith shown, traces his ancestry back to February 5, 1759, when Kingman Dutton, was born in Delaware county, Pennsylvania. His mother, Mary Craig, was born November 21, 1763. His parents were married in 1784. They moved from Philadelphia, Pennsylvania, about 1787, to Hampshire county, Virginia, and from there to Wood county, Virginia, in 1802, and settled on Little Kanawah about two miles from Parkersburg. They remained here until December 11, 1806, when they removed to Hockingport, Ohio, settling on the farm now owned by Edwin A. Dutton. To them the following named children were born: James, Jane, John, Kingman, Samuel, Craig, Mary and Ruth. Mrs. Dutton died at Hockingport in 1834 and her husband followed her in 1837.

Samuel was born in Hampshire county, Virginia, February 8, 1794, and died in Hockingport, Ohio, February 7, 1883. Nancy Brookhart was born November 15, 1800, and died at Hockingport February 10, 1861. Samuel Dutton and Nancy Brookhart were married January 18, 1821. Their children were James B. and Lydia E. Dutton. Samuel inherited the old homestead where he lived to a good old age, and died respected by a large circle of friends.

James B. Dutton was born November 21, 1821, and died May 10, 1873. Hannah Humphrey was born June 30, 1827, and died March 28, 1886. These two were married October 12, 1853, and had three children—Clara E., Edwin A. and Lucy I. Edwin was born February 26, 1859. Letha R. Curtis was born November 12, 1858, they being married November 12, 1884. Their children are Herbert P., Walter R. and Clarence E. Edwin A. owns the farm his ancestors settled nearly a century ago, and is one of the first and best farms in the county. Scientific farming and good management have had much to do in making this place so attractive and valuable.

Both Mr. and Mrs. Dutton are both active members of the Methodist Episcopal church, and are also members of Troy Grange, No. 905. They have represented Athens county at several sessions of the State Grange.

A GROUP OF OLD PIONEERS OF ATHENS, OHIO.

Top Row	1. Eliakim H. Moore	2. Jacob Lash	3. G. M. McDougal	4. Rev. H. Gortner	5. John Cornwell
	6. Rev. M. V. B. Ewins	7. Joseph M. Dana	8. N. H. Van Vorhes	9. Abner Frost	
Center Row	10. William Nelson	11. A. J. Wilmarth	12. Mathew Patrick	13. Ephriam Brown	14. John Welch
	15. Dr. E. G. Carpenter	16. T. H. Norton	17. D. B. Stewart	18. David Goodspeed	19. Samuel Pickering
Lower Row	20. Francis Beardsley	21. John A. McCune	22. Hull Foster	23. Jacob Swett	24. A. G. Brown
	25. William Golden	26. John B. Brown	27. A. B. Walker	28. Richard M. Drake	29. Mrs. Frost

F. BURR MODIE, ARCHITECT.

F. BURR MODIE, whose picture is here presented, came to Athens about two years ago and established an office as architect. He had the distinction of being the first architect to open an office in Athens, consequently had a great deal of pioneer work to do in his line.

The Athens County Atlas Association, the publishers

of this book, employed him to make the maps of all the townships and the county that are shown herewith, and the character of his work speaks more than words of his ability as a draughtsman.

Mr. Modie is happily married to a devoted wife, and their home has been blessed with a sweet little girl now less than a year old. In June of 1905, Mr. Modie moved his family to Lancaster where he might enjoy a broader field in his profession. He maintains an office in that thriving city.

JULIAN GIFT, whose nice home in Alexander township herewith appears, is one of a family of four boys and one girl. Mr. Gift's father, J. B. Gift, was born in Perry county, March 10, 1838, while his mother, Jane Evans Gift, was born in Athens county. September 3, 1838, she being the daughter of Aaron and Rachael Evans. His father came to Athens county in 1858, locating in Trimble township. Subsequently he removed to Alexander township, where he died April 3, 1895. He was the first man to make shipments of coal and household goods by rail in the Sunday Creek Valley, when he removed from Trimble township to Alexander township. He brought with him four cars of coal which he helped to mine at Mine No. 4, unloading the same near Albany, which was then the terminus of the railroad. His mother is still living and makes her home with Julian.

June 16, 1897, the subject of this sketch was married to Edna C., daughter of Mr. and Mrs. R. M. Patterson, Mrs. Gift having been born in Alexander township, August 29, 1876. To Mr. and Mrs. Gift two children have been born, the eldest Vena, dying at about the age of two years. Adena, their surviving child, whose picture is presented in this work, was born February 11, 1904, and is a child of rare merits.

For several years Mr. Gift has been closely identified with the agricultural and political interests of his home township, which has honored him by electing him to places of honor and trust. For about three years he made a business of butter and cheese manufacture, but at present is principally engaged in stock raising, utilizing his farm of over one hundred and eighty acres to this end. Both Mr. and Mrs. Gift exercise themselves in all lines and departments of advancement and improvement.

MR. AND MRS. JULIAN GIFT AND BABIES.

In the picture above showing the farm residence, may be seen Mr and Mrs. Gift, their little daughter and Mr. Gift's mother, and another devoted member of the household, Rex, the faithful dog. On the left are good likenesses of Mr. and Mrs. Gift and their two babies Vena (deceased) and Adena. On the right is shown Rex and Adena. The artistic eye of the official photographer caught this pose as he was leaving after finishing his work. As soon as the engravers saw this picture they at once asked permission to use it for artistic calendars, etc. Permission was granted, and this plate, the most artistic piece of picture making in life, in this book, will have wide publication.

ADENA AND REX.

ATHENS COUNTY HISTORY
CONTINUED.

MOUNDS OF ATHENS COUNTY.
By CLARENCE MATHENY.

charcoal was found underneath which was a skeleton with the head to the east. It had been enclosed in a wooden structure rather roughly made. Part of this had only been charred by the action of the fire. Much of the middle part of the body had been burned to a cinder. It is thought that this burning was accidental, that a layer of dirt had been placed over the box and then the fire made. By some misfortune the fire got into the wooden structure and consumed part of it with a part of its contents. On the bottom or floor of the box in which the body had been laid were found about five hundred copper beads, forming a line almost around the body. These beads were formed from strips of copper hammered out and rolled up in the shape of a tube. Owing to the difficulty in obtaining copper and the crudeness of the tools with which they worked, these beads must have been very valuable. They probably constituted the property of the man. About fifty shell beads were also found.

The most valuable relic found in this research was an instrument of copper found in the ashes with the bones. It was about 5½ inches long and chisel-shaped. At the wide end it is over 2 inches broad. The part corresponding to the handle of a chisel is a little less than an inch in diameter. The copper had been carefully and neatly hammered out into a perfectly smooth sheet, then so folded as to make a chisel-shaped instrument. It was hollow. What it was used for it is unsafe to conjecture.

A small mound on the old Connett farm was opened. Ashes, charcoal, and bones were found. The conditions were similar to those just described except that the bones were scattered over a considerable space. Some of the bones in this mound and in the one previously named were in an excellent state of preservation.

A pottery "whistle" was also found. It was formed from yellow clay and had not been burned. It was merely a tube about 7 inches long and a little less than an inch in diameter. Several mounds called by Prof. Andrews the Zenner Mounds were explored. These are located on the farm now known as the "Michaels" farm. Nothing more than some ashes and burnt human bones were found.

The School House Mound is so called because it was plowed down to make a suitable location for a district school house. This was done in 1875. Owing, possibly, to the fact that the

lower part of the mound was never removed, no bones were plowed up. In this mound was unearthed a very peculiar article, consisting of several layers of buckskin between which were two rows of copper beads. Many who saw it thought it was a buckskin pouch in which the beads had been placed. Prof. Andrews, however, thought it to have been a piece of ornamented dress. This latter is perhaps the most reasonable supposition. It was about 8 inches square with the buckskin very well preserved.

Two mounds on the old Jewett farm were explored at this time. This is the farm recently purchased from the late Peter F. Martin by the Johnson Coal Mining Co. This exploration furnished nothing of interest except a few fragments of bones, some charcoal and ashes. Burnt earth was quite abundant.

A badly decayed skeleton was obtained from a mound on the farm then owned by Mr. Alanson Courtney, but now under the management of Mr. A. V. M. Courtney. This mound showed no charcoal, and very few ashes.

The large Connett Mound was subsequently opened and explored with very successful results. It is about 18 feet high with a diameter of 85 feet. A tunnel was dug to the center of the mound. Its foundation was similar to that of the Beard Mound except for the absence of black dirt, or "kitchen refuse."

(Continued on page 93.)

THIS page is devoted to one of the best known men in Nelsonville, Dr. I. P. Primrose, of the firm of Primrose & Hyde. He has been practicing medicine in Nelsonville since before the Civil War, and by his acts of philanthropy, generosity and kind heartedness in his large and widely extended practice of medicine. has enshrined himself in the hearts of thousands who have appealed to him and got relief in the time of great physical distress. In his palmy days, the night was never too dark nor the distance too great for him to respond promptly to a call no matter whether he would ever get a cent for it or not. He has prescribed and furnished hogsheads of medicine to the indigent sick and attended their wants with the same care as he did the oppulent. He has prospered by liberality and has closely devoted a long life to his profession.

Dr. Primrose was born in Uniontown, Muskingum county, Ohio, October 18, 1831, the son of Reuben and Hester A. Primrose. He began the study of medicine in New Straitsville, in 1858, and studied four years.

He enlisted as army surgeon on August 7, 1861, in Company A, Thirty-first Regiment, O. V. I., as second lieutenant, and after serving eighteen months he was promoted to first lieutenant. He resigned from the service in November, 1862, and located in Nelsonville, February 27, 1863, and began the practice of his profession. In 1864 he organized an independent company, known as the Thirty-sixth O. N. G., and was commissioned as colonel, and served six months. He attended Starling medical college in Columbus the year of 1864 and 1865, and received a doctor's degree, at once returning to Nelsonville and resuming his practice.

He was married to Miss Jane Harbaugh in 1852. To them six children have been born, five of whom are living: Hester A. Coleman, Sarah A. Alderman, Binnie L. Curtis, Loving L. Primrose, Miss Blanch Primrose. Adda C. died in July of 1880.

Dr. Primrose, although always a busy man in his profession, has found time to serve the public in an official capacity. He has served as member of the board of education, member of the city council, board of health, and in 1863 represented Athens county in the General Assembly. He was president of the Athens County Medical Society for six consecutive years.

He has dealt largely in real estate in Nelsonville for the past forty years, and has built on an average of one house a year during that time, some of which are among the finest in the city. The first property he ever bought is on Fort street, between Washington and Madison.

His present handsome and comfortable residence, which is shown in the illustration, is located on North Fort street and is one of the finest homes in the city. It was built in 1892. Hotel Primrose also shown on this page. is the best located hotel property in Nelsonville. Dr. Primrose bought and remodeled this property in April, 1902.

Thus is given a sketch of a long and useful life, which seems inadequate, and at best, gives but little conception of the man himself. The history of the life of Dr. Primrose as the people among whom he has toiled for a half century, see and know it, listening with a sympathetic heart to the aches and pains to which the race is heir. would take volumes to describe and the work would be imperfectly done. Broad minded, sympathetic and generous to a fault, he has gone in and out of thousands of homes carrying sunshine and hope to the afflicted.

HOTEL PRIMROSE.

DR. I. P. PRIMROSE.

THE NELSONVILLE FOUNDRY AND MACHINE COMPANY.

Mr. and Mrs. John W. Jackson.

JOHN W. JACKSON was born in Morgan county, Ohio, April 30, 1829, and died in Nelsonville, Athens county, January 27, 1901, aged seventy-one years. He came with his parents to Athens county and settled in what is now known as Happy Hollow, in the year 1838, where he resided until 1879, when he moved to Nelsonville, where he resided until his death.

Mr. Jackson began business life as a farmer, and followed his vocation until his death. When a young man he purchased a tract of land which is now a part of the Maple Hill coal works, going in debt for the most of it, but was able to meet all his financial obligations. He was president of the Nelsonville Foundry and Machine Company, a member of the board of county commissioners, having been elected to that position in the fall of 1899, a member of the Odd Fellows of Nelsonville, having been elected several times to the office of Noble Grand.

Mrs. Kate White Jackson, a daughter of Hiram and Melissa Foster White, was born in Athens county in 1834, a niece of the late Uncle Hull Foster, of Athens, so well known to everybody in the county, and a grand daughter of Major John White of revolutionary fame, was united in marriage to John W. Jackson, April 14, 1864.

THE Nelsonville Foundry & Machine Company was incorporated under the laws of the State of Ohio on April 4, 1881, by Thomas E. Knauss, Charles A. Cable, Webb W. Poston, A. H. Carnes and C. E. Poston. The company was organized for the purpose of doing a general foundry and machine business, repairing machinery and constructing mine cars. The business was started in the brick foundry building and the two-story building as shown by cut, the foundry department, of course, doing all of their work in one foundry building.

The machine and blacksmith departments were located on the ground floor, and the pattern making and car building departments on the second floor of the two-story building. The increase of the business, however, led to the construction of an addition to the foundry building, the construction of an iron-clad pattern storage room, the construction of a separate building for the blacksmith and car building departments and two additions to the machine shop. All of the different departments are equipped with machinery adapted to the building of machinery used in the equipment of coal mines.

The line of the work engaged in was extended from that above mentioned to include the manufacture of a full line of coal mine equipment and machinery, consisting of haulage engines for slope and drift mines, hoisting engines, both geared and direct connecting for shaft mines, chain hauls and retarders for handling loaded and empty cars on inclines, mine cars of all sizes and styles, mine car wheels, axles and irons, wire rope sheave wheels and rollers for haulage and hoisting purposes, mine ventilating fans, stationary engines, bar screens, revolving screens, shaker screens, steel weigh baskets and chutes, elevators and conveyors, steam actuated, crossover dumps, Mitchell gravity crossover dumps and a general line of castings, all of which they are well prepared to make. They have furnished work of various kinds for use in almost all of the coal producing states in the union, and have the reputation of turning out machinery that is first-class in every respect.

R. H. Jackson is the son of the late John W. Jackson, and is the present secretary and treasurer of the company, and is one of Nelsonville's most euterprising and energetic young men. The management of the company is largely in his hands and he has made a marked success of the business.

Dr. Charles L. Wilson.

DR. CHARLES L. WILSON, whose picture is here presented, is a familiar face to the people of Athens and adjoining counties, among whom he was the trusted general practitioner of medicine for many years succeeding the Civil War. By his skill as a physician, his devotion to his patients and his kindly

character, he endeared himself to thousands who cherish his friendship next to that of a father.

By his labors in surgical practice, at the head of the Indianapolis Surgical Institute, he won wide recognition in his profession.

Dr. Wilson is a native of Athens county, the son of the late Josiah Wilson, Esq., and received the degree of M. D. from Western Reserve College in 1854 and began the practice of his profession in Graysville, Monroe county; afterward returning to Athens county where he practiced at Albany and later in Athens. His college fraternity was Beta Theta Pi; he is a Companion M. O. Loyal Legion of the U. S., a member of the G. A. R.; U. S. pension agent 1866–72, and a prominent and distinguished Mason, being a member of Athens Commandery No. 15, Knight Templars. He is enjoying a well-earned rest from an active life, and is living with his children in Indianapolis, Indiana.

Farm Residence of Dr. George B. Parker, in Canaan Township.

THE beautiful farm residence herewith shown is the property of Dr. George B. Parker and was purchased from John Finsterwald in 1902. The farm embraces 328 acres, a large part of which is on the Hocking bottom and is considered one of the best farms in the valley. Dr Parker, who makes his home in Athens, has a tenant on this place, but gives general oversight in the management. He also owns the Warren farm which adjoins this place, making him a combined acreage 395 acres. He also has a farm of 170 acres near New England not far from his Hocking tract.

He owns quite a good deal of residence property in Athens, and has an elegant ten room brick residence in course of construction on east Union street, the finest building site in Athens, which he will occupy as a home when completed.

Dr. Parker was born in Alexander township, Athens County, in September, 1857, where he grew up, as most boys, in the country, going to school, farming and teaching school till he was 24 years old. He entered the Physio-

medical College in Indianapolis and graduated therefrom in 1881. He began the practice of medicine at Guysville, and after four years, moved to Chillicothe where he practiced with marked success for fourteen years. He came to Athens in July, 1901, and has been farming and practicing his profession since.

He was married to Miss Sarah Tedrow, daughter of Mr. and Mrs. Noah Tedrow, of New England, in 1879. They have two children, Sidney aged 16 years and May aged 11 years.

FARM RESIDENCE OF W. B. RICE, NEAR STEWART.

THIS neat, well-kept and attractive country place is the home of Mr. W. B. Rice in Rome township, near Stewart. Seated in the front yard is Mr. and Mrs. Rice and their happy family of six girls. The environment here as elsewhere, is a true index of the character of the people. Industry and thrift is apparent on every hand. Mr. Rice is a native of Rome township, and is the son of James Rice, who was born December 28, 1824, yet living, and Mrs. Rexavilla Beebe Rice, who was born November 12, 1826 and died August 22, 1892.

Mr. Rice, who is now in his forty-sixth year, was married to Miss Maggie McGraw, September 24, 1891, who was at that time twenty-four years old. Mrs. Rice was the daughter of Mr. and Mrs. Anthony McGraw. They have six children, all girls. The eldest, Lenora was born October 30, 1892; Louise, born June 14, 1894, and passed the Boxwell examination April 15, 1905. She is said to be the youngest Boxwell graduate in the county. Meldred, born September 7, 1895; Rexavilla, born April 14, 1897; Marguerite, born December 23, 1899, and Gertrude, born August 5, 1904. Mr. Rice has a fine farm of two hundred and eighty-seven acres.

ALEXANDER WARD NELSON was born in Nelsonville, September 4, 1825. His father came from Shrewsburg, Massachusetts, and bought a large tract of land, upon a part of which is now the city of Nelsonville. In August, 1814, Mr. Nelson, with his family, reached the site of the town which bears his name, and proceeded to erect a double log cabin on the southwest corner of the public square. June 16, 1818 he laid out the village, to which he deeded the school grounds, public square, cemetery and canal grounds. May 20, 1835, Mr. Nelson died, his son Ward being but ten years old. Ward worked on a canal boat, and finally rose to be captain. He enlisted in Company G, Eighteenth O. I., for services in the war. He afterwards was with J. F. Camp in the real

WARD NELSON.   DOUGLAS NELSON.

estate business. He was an ardent Republican and always worked for that party's success. He married Alpha Steenrod, and to them nine children were born, Douglas being the eldest. Mr. Nelson was a member of Phil Kearney Post, No. 38, G. A. R., at the time of his death.

Douglas W. Nelson was born February 4, 1859, and married Katharine Sanderson in 1881. He was a member of Sons of St. George, Red Men and Eagles. He was one of the best business men of Nelsonville, owning one of the largest business blocks in town. He was quite a politician, and always interested in the Republican party. He had sympathy and charity for all. He died September 13, 1904.

⚜ ⚜ ⚜ ⚜ ⚜ ⚜ ⚜ ⚜ ⚜

RESIDENCE OF DR. AND MRS. J. M. HIGGINS, ATHENS, OHIO.

THE handsome residence here shown is the home of Dr. John M. Higgins, one of Athens' successful medical practitioners. He is the son of the late Joseph S. Higgins, who served the county as one of its commissioners.

The Higgins family is one of the oldest families of the county. Andrew Higgins moved to what has since been known as the Higgins' homestead, about three miles south of Athens, in 1798. Michael Higgins, his son, owned and lived on the farm until his death in 1870 at the age of 75. His second son, Joseph S., the father of the subject of this sketch, bought the old home place and lived on it until his death in 1901. After his death the place was sold by the heirs to Cyrus M. Higgins, the brother of Dr. Higgins. The farm has thus been owned wholly or in part by the Higgins family for 107 years.

Joseph S. Higgins was married to Hannah W. Hibbard, the daughter Rev. John M. Hibbard, in 1851. To them were born ten children, five boys, Joseph W., Cyrus M., Daniel N., John M., of Athens. and Charles H., of Zanesville; and five girls, Mrs. Lottie Wood, Mrs. Mary Francis, and Miss Annetta M., of Smithfield. O.; Miss Elizabeth, of Martin's Ferry, O. Emma died at the age of eighteen.

Dr. Higgins has two children, Louise and Monroe, both growing into young womanhood and manhood.

Residence of Mr. and Mrs. Henry Gilkey, Alexander Township.

HENRY GILKEY, whose home is shown herewith, is a native of Alexander township, having been born here December 28, 1840, and having lived here continuously ever since, with the exception of ten years he spent in Meigs county. His parents were among the first settlers of Alexander township, his father having come here with his parents when a mere boy.

Mr. Gilkey's father, William Gilkey, was born in Alleghaney county, Penna., in 1818, while his mother, Frances Hill Gilkey, was born in Fredericksburg, Va., April 21, 1815. His father began life for himself a poor boy, but by industry and frugality was a well-to-do farmer at his death in 1896.

Henry Gilkey married Cyntha A. Reeves, May 26, 1862, and to them three children were born: J W., Nellie May and Frances A. Mrs. Gilkey dying. Mr. Gilkey married Mrs. Mary A. Dudley Nov. 6, 1897.

The Gilkey family occupies a prominent place in the life and affairs of Alexander township. They give close attention to all those principles of life helpful to individuals as well as to the community at large.

The early Gilkeys had to contend with rude conditions, but having inherited those sturdy and sterling qualities necessary to success, they applied themselves so dilligently and conscientiously to every task that success in life was assured.

The younger Gilkey generation, of which Henry is a splendid example, have not allowed these virtues and dispositions to die out; hence their home is a hospitable one, a beautiful one, and withal, one of which the community may well feel proud.

Superintendent Aaron Grady.

AARON GRADY was born near Morgantown, Pike county, Ohio, on August 31, 1848. He is the son of George and Mary Ann Grady. He attended school in Pike, Ross and Highland counties, and began teaching in Pike county near the place of his birth Nov. 4, 1867. About this time his parents moved to South Webster, Scioto county where he followed at the close of his school.

He later took the scientific course and graduated from the Lebanon Normal College. He had charge of the Sciotoville schools two years, where he married Miss Hattie Allard. To this union there was born two sons and one daughter. The oldest son, G. Otto, is now Superintendent of the Ceredo W. Va., schools the younger son, W. Earl, is in business in Bluefield, W. Va., and Clare, the daughter is at home.

Mr. Grady went to Wheelersburg from Sciotoville and remained there eleven years as superintendent of schools. While in Scioto county he served nine years as County School Examiner.

After leaving Wheelersburg, he served one year as Principal of the Ironton High school. He next served three years in a similar capacity at Troy, Ohio, under Chas. L. Van Cleve, and was elected for the fourth year but resigned to accept the Superintendency of the Ludlow, Ky. schools, where he served for six and one-half years, when he resigned to accept the superintendency at Nelsonville, O., Jan. 4, 1900, which position he still fills.

The schools at Nelsonville are on the accredited list of the Ohio State University, and placed in the first grade by the State School Commissioner.

Mr. Grady has served as School Examiner of Athens county since September, 1902. He has been a hard worker all his life and has always had employment whenever he wished it.

PROF. L. C. CRIPPEN, the versatile man of letters and business, prominent in the history of Athens and adjacent counties, as educator and successful business man. A man of fine physique, tall, broad-shouldered, commanding stately bearing. He was born March 15, 1842, at Frost, Rome township, eldest son of James Riley and Paulina Crippen. His childhood was spent at what is called the "Old Crippen Place," opposite Cook's Crossing, on the Hocking river; his boyhood at his father's homestead, where now is the site of the village of Frost.

He enlisted in the Civil War the winter of 1863, in Company A, Ninety-second Regiment, Ohio Infantry. His army record is short, as he was taken ill with measles, that dread disease of the war, shortly after enlisting, and was not in active service. He lay in the hospital at Nashville, Tennessee, many months, becoming so prostrated, so emaciated his recovery was dispaired of.

Soon after the close of his army career he entered the Ohio University. His journal of this period tells of difficulties as he looked longingly forward to a life of usefulness, but at this time handicapped by ill health as the result of his army life. He tells the story in his own words. "Struggling against ill health, ignorance, poverty and obscurity, the dull routine of an unpretending student can be of no interest to any but the writer, who, should he be so fortunate as to be ever surrounded by more favorable circumstances may wish to look back with a "retrospective eye" upon the obscure path he traveled in youth," tells the story in his own words, of the obstacles and the ambitions of his boyhood.

He was united in marriage to Lucy M. Waterman, youngest daughter of Asher and Bathsheba Waterman, at their home near Coolville, August 18, 1867. Her parents were godly people of the old pilgrim stock, training their children in the fear and admonition of the Lord. Mrs. Crippen answered well to this early training, serving her God in the beauty of holiness. Her Christian life and faith was an inspiration to her husband, an example of true piety to the hundreds of talented young men and women who subsequently came under his care. His loyal love and appreciation of the wife of his youth and manhood is expressed in these verses addressed

MAPLE HILL.

TO MY WIFE. WRITTEN JANUARY, 1878, AT MALTA, OHIO.

Let me sing you a song of devotion,
A song of my love, dear, for you,
I bring not a pearl from the ocean,
A gem from the mine to your view,
But my offering's my heart's warm emotion
A love that forever is true.
Yes, the love I have long felt for you,
A love that forever grows new,—
I bring not a gem from the ocean,
But a love that forever is true.

I know that your love is as loyal
As ever true woman could show:
I know that its gift is as royal
As ever a queen could bestow.
Then why should heart not employ all
Its love 'til it channels o'er flow?
Yes, with love does my heart ever glow
With love does my heart overflow,
Aye, with love to my wife ever loyal
My heart does forever o'er flow.
MALTA, OHIO, January 13, 1878.

He entered the National Normal University, of Lebanon, September 1873. Graduated with honors from the scientific and classic courses. After teaching successful schools elsewhere, in the year 1881, he took the professorship of the old Historic Bartlet Academy. The thoroughness of his methods may be illustrated by the popular verdict of his admiring pupils, "WE HAD TO LEARN," and the high aspirations he held before his students may be told in the words of a former student: "We carry a pleasant memory of his work and will always be the better men and woman for the ideals he held before us and the way he developed the manhood and womanhood of his pupils."

The latter years were spent in the life insurance work for the most part. He was a staunch. Prohibitionist, watching with a jealous eye, the advancement of the temperance cause, giving liberally to all benevolences. One son, five daughters. The only son, well loved, talented, died December 12th at Lancaster, Ohio, while engaged with his father in their work as teacher and exponent of rapid shorthand writing. Soon after the death of his

son he removed with his family to their home, Maple Hill, near Frost, where died his beautiful seventeen year old daughter, Eunice, January 28, 1891.

His death came after a year's illness, December 23, 1904. His friends will rejoice that we have the assurance of his acceptance into the heavenly kingdom. Buried on Christmas morning in the family lot at Bethany. The last thought of him as he lay in his blue army robe, in the casket, lined with white tufted satin, whilst the sweetly swelling notes of the faith inspiring hymns was wafted to troubled hearts, is of one

" sustained and soothed
By an unfaltering trust, approached his grave
Like one who wraps the drapery of his couch
About him, and lies down to pleasant dreams."

His face peaceful and calm, his form commanding stately in death even as in life.

Contributed by his daughter,
CLARA.

Interior View of The Thacker Dry Goods Company Store, Nelsonville.

THE interior view here presented is that of The Thacker Dry Goods Company, which is located in the Cable-Hickman block, opposite the post office in Nelsonville. This store has the reputation of being the best of its kind in the city. They carry a complete line of dry goods and their goods are all bought at the fashion centers and are up to the minute in color and design.

The business is owned by a stock company known as The Thacker Dry Goods Company, and was incorporated under the laws of Ohio, in March, 1903. The store was opened April 9, 1903. The incorporators are Mr. and Mrs. Orin Thacker, Miss Alice Thacker, of Columbus; James Sheppard and Frederick W. Thacker, of Nelsonville. The store is under the successful management of Frederick W. Thacker, who thoroughly knows the business, and the store is enjoying a largely increasing trade each year.

IGNATS SCHENTZ OLD HOME AND OLD STORE.

THEODORE SCHENTZ RESIDENCE.

THE A. K. SCHENTZ COMPANY, BUCHTEL.

THERE was never a better illustration of the motto "In Union there is Strength" than is here presented by I. Schentz, wife and four sons, in business at Buchtel, Ohio. The A. K. Schentz Company doing a general merchandising business, was organized in 1903 and is exclusively composed of Mr. and Mrs. Schentz and their four sons, whose store and several residences are shown on this page. By industry and united effort they have become well-to-do, and they constitute a progressive and enterprising firm.

Ignatz Schentz, the father, is the son of Joseph and Grace Schentz and was born in Steinbach, Baden Germany, January 31, 1847. He came to this country in 1864 and married Miss A. K. Siegel, of Clermont county, Ohio, July 25, 1870.

They have had five children, the only daughter Anna, now deceased, and four sons, Edward, Theodore, Henry and John, the residences of all of whom are herewith shown. Mr. Schentz came to Athens county from Clermont county in 1883, engaged in mining and started a little store in the old homestead shown above. In 1898 he moved to the present location, a picture of which is shown herewith. The company was incorporated in the name of the good wife and mother, Mrs. A. K. Schentz, who has always taken an active part in the business and partly to her business sagacity the present prosperous business has been established. Scrupulous honesty, strict integrity and close attention to business, all working harmoniously with but one aim in view, is the secret of the frugality and prosperity of this family.

EDWARD SCHENTZ RESIDENCE.

HENRY SCHENTZ RESIDENCE.

The Buckeye Block, Nelsonville, Ohio, built by T. Erven Wells, the second story of which is occupied as the "Home" of the Buckeye News.

T. ERVEN WELLS, editor Buckeye News, Nelsonville, was born near Wirt Court House, West Virginia, and began the printing business at an early age as "devil" in a country office. He came to Nelsonville in April, 1882, and soon purchased the Nelsonville News, which he has owned and operated for twenty years. When he acquired possession of the plant it was in a delapidated condition and scantily supplied with material. From this meagre beginning has grown the magnificent plant now known as the Buckeye News, which is second to none in Southeastern Ohio.

T. ERVEN WELLS, Editor Buckeye News.

Residence of T. Erven Wells, Editor of the Buckeye News, West Washington Street, Nelsonville.

Dr. and Mrs. Milo Wilson.

DR. MILO WILSON and his wife, Mrs. Josephine B Wilson, Superintendent and Matron, respectively, of the State Hospital at Athens, are fitting examples of right persons in right places. From every standpoint they are fitted for the important positions they so ably occupy.

Dr. Wilson was born near Findlay, October 16, 1870, attended Findlay college, and later graduated from the Ohio Medical University and then took a post-graduate course in the Philadelphia Polyclinic and college for graduates in medicine. For some years he practiced his profession in Putnam county, but became associated with the State hospital November 15, 1898, as first assistant to the superintendent. Mrs. Wilson having been born in Clark county, Illinois, but living in Athens county since she was six years old, has been

identified with the institution since June, 1891, filling different positions of responsibility. Their training, practice and natural endowments readily suggested them as proper and efficient successors to the vacancies caused by the resignation of Dr. and Mrs. Rorick, and to these positions the board of trustees called Dr. and Mrs. Wilson in May, 1905.

Coming to the institution nearly seven years ago, Dr. Wilson found the demand for a wider knowledge of the pathology of nervous diseases, and that he might be able to diagnose and treat these cases with the best possible results, he very studiously applied himself to a deeper research of all medical authorities on the subject. To this he added much personal investigation, so that today Dr. Wilson is an acknowledged authority on nervous diseases as well as one of the best specialists in the country in that particular field.

ATHENS COUNTY HISTORY
CONTINUED.

MOUNDS OF ATHENS COUNTY.

By CLARENCE MATHENY

Near the center was a pile of bones and ashes. Over this was a pocket of bark filled with pieces of bones. They had evidently been picked up and placed in the pocket while the mound was in process of formation. Two plates of copper and a stone tube were also found. The first copper plate was a very thin one with its edges notched. Near each end a hole had been drilled possibly for the reception of a string or thong. The other was a thin plate of copper, curled till the edges were almost brought together. It is hardly large enough to have been a wristlet. The stone tube was about seven inches long and over an inch in diameter. The material resembles oolitic limestone and is highly polished. For various reasons this is an interesting and valuable relic.

This is about all that has been done in the way of scientific exploration of the mounds of this county. The articles obtained by these researches are now in the Peabody Museum. Through the kindness of the curator of this museum, Dr. F. W. Putnam, much of the preceding information was secured. Some few bones and fragments of pottery are in the museum of the Ohio

Continued on page 98.

Residence of Mr. and Mrs. George Van Meter, Luhrig, Ohio

he first went to working the Hocking mines. He earned twenty-seven dollars with which he brought his family to Glen Ebon. He was married to Miss Ida Carr on August 4, 1884. They have four children, all of whom are shown in the picture along with their father and mother: Alma, Vina, William and Clifford.

THE accompanying picture of the home of George Van Meter at Luhrig, proves the question that a man can mine coal, save his money and gain a competency. Mr. Van Meter not only owns this comfortable home but has a farm of one hundred and five acres and operates a general store in Luhrig.

He was born in Mason county, West Virginia, in 1863 and moved to Middleport ten years later, coming to Athens county in about 1886, and has been a coal miner nearly all of his life. His father was Gwin Van Meter, a soldier in the Union army from West Virginia, and after the war operated a flat boat assisted by his son.

The subject of this sketch walked from Middleport when

Residence of Mr. and Mrs. D. W. Cornell, Guysville, Ohio.

THE picture shows the comfortable home of D. W. Cornell, of Guysville, one of Athens county's most prosperous and highly respected citizens. He has been engaged in general merchandising in Guysville thirty-nine years, and has demonstrated that the large town or city is not the only place to make money. Mr. Cornell was born in Chester, Meigs county, January 20, 1842, and is consequently sixty-three years young. He graduated from the Ohio University in 1863. Broad minded, liberal in his beliefs and opinions, he has won a host of friends. He is prominently identified with the Masonic order, being a member of Savannah Lodge No. 466, A. F. & A. M; also Athens Commandery No. 15, Knight Templars, being a past officer in each body.

Mr. Cornell's parents, Dr. John and Christine Cornell, came from New York to Ohio in 1832, and settled in Meigs county, where he practiced medicine until his death in September, 1873.

Mr. Cornell, the subject of this sketch, was one of a family of ten children. He was married to Miss Amy Calvert, a native of Rome township, October 10, 1869, with whom he has lived happily ever since. They have no children, but an adopted daughter, Mrs. Mary Harper, who has a bright little girl, makes their home with Mr. and Mrs. Cornell, and the child is the life of the household, making glad the hearts of its grand parents.

Many times have the people of his township shown confidence in the integrity of Mr. Cornell by making him township treasurer and township clerk. A man of large land interests along with his merchandising, he exerts a powerful influence in his community. Many a man reduced to poverty has been extended credit by Mr. Cornell, through purely philanthropic motives and helped to his feet. Should he at any time decide to remove from Guysville and dispose of his property, he and his family would be sadly missed.

THE farm scene and residence here shown is the home of Christopher Basom, in Carthage township, one of the best farms and prettiest home sites in the township. Mr. Basom, who was born in Coshocton county, December 10, 1834, settled on this farm in 1859. He cleared away the dense woods which at that time covered almost the entire farm and has lived there ever since. He has an abundance of all kinds of fruits, which he cultivates with quite a profit. He also gives a good deal of attention to stock raising and breeds good cattle. He has good grazing land and keeps it well stocked. Mr. Basom was married to Elizabeth Jane Algo, March 15, 1860. There were four children born to them: Joseph S., April 17, 1861; James M., October 1, 1862; Hester Anna, April 18, 1864, and Sarah Emily, June 3, 1866. Mrs. Basom died May 28, 1869.

Residence of John Niggemeyer, Carthage Township.

THE picture here presented is that of one of Athens county's industrious and enterprising young men, Mr. George E. Beasley, who was born and reared about Hebbardsville, attending the public schools in winter and making himself useful on the farm and about the store and hotel owned by his father, David Beasley.

George Beasley, our subject, has always been an ardent Republican and interested himself in township and county politics. He was appointed deputy sheriff under C. H. Porter, and held that office for nearly four years, making one of the

THE picture herewith shows not only the residence and farm of one of the best and most prosperous farmers in Carthage township, but is also a picture of practically all of John Niggemeyer's family. Mr. Niggemeyer, the subject of this sketch, is one of those thriving German-Americans who started with nothing but good health and a strong determination to succeed, and is now enjoying the product of a life time of hard work and strict economy, and is consequently in comfortable circumstances. One of the reasons for Mr. Niggemeyer's success, lies in the fact that he has always put brains into his efforts. He knows his farm like a book and has studied the nature of the soil so that he gets the best results from his toil and effort. In about thirty-five years he has accumulated a farm of nearly four hundred acres, which is one of the best improved farms in the township. He makes his land pay good returns on the investment.

John Niggemeyer is of foreign birth and lineage, having been born in Paterburn, Germany, June 24, 1843. He came to America in 1860, locating in Carthage township, Athens county, Ohio, in 1867. Here, October 26, of this same year, he married Margaret Staab, who was born in Noble county, March 16, 1845. Mrs. Niggemeyer's parents, also, were born in Germany. Mr. and Mrs. Niggemeyer are the parents of nine children. Lena, Mary, John B., Adam, Katharine, Anthony and Elizabeth (twins), Isabella and Lawrence. All of these children are living. Mrs. Niggemeyer died Sept. 22, 1904.

best deputies the county ever had. Fearless and energetic, he performed his duties in a highly commendable manner, in fact, he served so faithfully and well, that his name was prominently mentioned for sheriff, but in consideration for friends who had as good a claim as he, he did not permit his name to go before the Republican primary, preferring to wait till a more convenient time. Mr. Beasley is now thirty-eight years old and is in the prime of young manhood. He was happily married to Miss Ella Headly, of Middleport, November 11, 1900.

THE accompanying excellent pictures show the familiar face of Willis Gaylord Hickman and the interior of his modern drug store in Nelsonville. Mr. Hickman was born in Mt. Vernon, Ohio, October 16, 1839. His mother died at Somerset, Ohio, when he was three years old. He lived with his father until he was seventeen, taking in the

WILLIS GAYLORD HICKMAN.

meantime a common school education. He worked at the printers trade and afterwards blacksmithing, until March, 1862, when he enlisted in Company E of the First Battalion of the Eighteenth United States Infantry and served three years, being discharged at Lookout Mountain, Tennessee, March 27, 1865. He participated in the battles of Corinth, Perryville, Stone River, Hoover's Gap, Tullahoma, Chickamauga, Mission Ridge, Dalton, Resaca, Burnt Hickory, Kennesaw Mountain, Smyrna Church, Peach Tree Creek, Chattahoochee, the siege and capture of Atlanta and Jonesboro.

After returning home he became a student in the Normal at Lebanon. He returned to New Lexington and

was deputy clerk for one year in the office of his father, who was the probate judge of Perry county. In 1868 he came to Nelsonville and went into the drug business with his brother, W. C. Hickman, under the firm name of Hickman Bros. In 1873 Joseph Smith became his brothers successor, and in 1876 Mr. Smith retired from from the firm and he has since carried on the business alone. Mr. Hickman has many times been honored by his fellow citizens by electing him to responsible offices. He has served as township trustee, member of the school board of Nelsonville, in 1880 elected one of the commissioners of Athens county and held the office for six years, being one of the best commissioners the county ever had,

and in 1900 he was elected county treasurer and served four years.

He was married to Miss Lorana L. Wolf on November 2, 1871, who died May 31, 1878, leaving two children—Robert D. and Perley W. He married Miss Dora Wolf, of Nelsonville. They have had two children, Emma now deceased and Mildred.

Mr. Hickman stands high in the councils of Masonry, being a Knight Templar and 32nd degree member of the Scottish Rite, consistory. He is a member of the I. O. O. F. lodge, Past Grand of the subordinate lodge and Past Worthy Patriarch of the encampment. He is also a member of Phil Kearney Post, G. A. R.

Hanson & Faires Livery and Garage, at Nelsonville.

Mr. Hanson who is shown in the automobile in the picture, is general agent for all automobiles and does general repairing. He is a young man of about twenty-eight years, and in the common vernacular, is a hustler and has been very successful.

The firm has been in business in Nelsonville but a comparatively short time and has built up a good business. Everything in their barn is new and first-class, so that their numerous patrons are always well taken care of and are furnished good horses and comfortable rigs.

THROUGH the enterprise of H. M. Hanson, of the firm of Hanson & Faires, who operate a livery and sale stable, Nelsonville enjoys the distinction of having the first automobile garage in Athens county. They take care of automobiles or rent them, and do a good business in connection with their horse livery.

Residence of Dr. S. E. G. Pedigo, Marshfield, Ohio.

HON. ELIAKIM H. MOORE.

JUDGE JOHN RUDOLPH DE STEIGUER.

COLONEL WILLIAM S. WILSON.

HON. CHARLES TOWNSEND.

PROMINENT : ATHENIANS : NOW : DECEASED.

DR. HUGH M. LASH.

CHARLES W. HARRIS.

THOMAS A. BEATON was born in Athens, Ohio, February 13, 1837. His parents, George A. and Jeanette Beaton, emigrated to Athens from Inverness, Scotland, in 1822.

The death of his father, at an early age, made it necessary for him to leave school and seek employment for his own support, also to assist in the support of his mother and sister.

Although deprived of the benefits of a school education, though a naturally observant mind, by association with people of prominence and absorbing information, he came to be recognized by those who knew him as a man of exceptional general information.

At the breaking out of the Civil War he was prevented from enlisting as a volunteer because of a slight lameness. He, however, entered the service as Wagon Master of the 13th O. V. I., serving in West Virginia, and was at the battle of Carnifax Ferry.

When the 5th Tennesee Cavalry was organized he was appointed quartermaster of that regiment by its colonel, W. B. Stokes, with the rank of captain. He was afterwards appointed by the United States Government Inspector of Horses with the rank of captain, and stationed at St Louis. He held this position until the close of the war. He was appointed Superintendent of Mails at the capitol. Washington, D. C., by President Andrew Johnson, and was also in charge of the mails at the White House, also appointed by President Johnson to that important position.

After the war he returned to Athens and engaged in the grocery business with Albert H. Crippen. Later, he formed a partnership with General C. H. Grosvenor, under the firm name of T. A. Beaton & Company, operating stage lines, mail contracts and a general carrying and stable business.

From early manhood he took an active interest in politics. The latter years of his life were spent in Columbus, Ohio, in the growth of which city he was actively interested, being identified with its Board of Trade in securing for Columbus new industrial and commercial enterprises

He was a man of strong will, quick discernment and an exceptionally good judge of human nature. He was always zealously interested in affairs relating to the public good. As a friend he was loyal and steadfast.

He died in Columbus, Ohio, November 7, 1895.

The subject of this sketch was the father of George A. Beaton, whose love for Athens, her environment and his boyhood friends suggested the "Athens Home Coming."

LEOPOLD FRIDAY, ESQ.

LEOPOLD FRIDAY, ESQ.

JUDGE ERASTUS A. GUTHRIE.

ALONZO L. ROACH.

MILBURY M. GREENE.

LIEUT. H. T. BROWN.

GEORGE PUTNAM.

Residences and Drilling Machine of L. D. Shields and Sons, Chauncey.

L. D. SHIELDS.

CHARLES C. SHIELDS.

HOMER SHIELDS.

WE herewith present the beautiful homes and fine Cyclone drilling apparatus of L. D. Shields and Sons. These gentlemen, while living in Chauncey, are known in several different states, having done prospecting in Ohio, Pennsylvania, West Virginia, Michigan, etc., for the leading coal companies. They began their business in 1885, and therefore, with their twenty years experience makes them valuable and reliable workmen. Their specialty is water, well, pump and electric wire holes for coal miners. They make a careful study of their business, and employ the best methods and machinery, having operated the spring pole drill, shot and diamond drills, and later the cyclone or hollow rod drill, the one now in general use in the Ohio coal field. Their Ohio field is for the most part in Hocking, Perry, Athens and Guernsey counties, and they are proud to refer to coal companies operating in this field for information about them or their work.

Residence of Mr. and Mrs. George Crawford, Canaan Township.

GEORGE CRAWFORD was born in Carthage township, Athens county, Ohio, March 6, 1858. He is the son of Daniel and Julia A. Crawford, who came to Athens county in 1857. His father was a native of Harrison county, while his mother was born in Guernsey county. In 1893 the subject of this sketch came to Canaan township, where he has resided ever since. November 13, 1888 he was married to Caroline, daughter of Martin D. and Abigal Mansfield.

The home farm of the Crawford family consists of one hundred acres, and the house is one of the cozy, comfortable, neat ones of Canaan township, as the picture herewith shows.

Mr. and Mrs. Crawford are among the the reliable and sturdy citizens, always interested and active in everything that pertains to the welfare of the community.

The careful student of human nature would know this from looking at the picture. Actions speak louder than words

CYCLONE DRILLING MACHINE.

Norman J. Theiss.

NORMAN J. THEISS is the son of Julius and Katie Theiss, and was born in Ironton, Ohio February 15, 1883. He came with his parents to Nelsonville when just of school age and graduated from the high school, May 27, 1902. On November 19, 1901, he was appointed under direct contract an agent for a number of fire insurance companies, being the youngest fire insurance agent under direct contract in Ohio. He represents fire, tornado, life, health, accident and plate glass insurance. He enjoys a lucrative and growing business.

To Mr. and Mrs. Crawford have been born three children, the first one dying in infancy. The other two, both appearing in the home picture, is John, aged twelve years, and Theodore, aged ten years. The little girl in the picture is Bernice Dorr.

and environment of any home speaks more than volumes that might be written about it, and the people who occupy it. Neatness due to care is the forerunner of thrift and prosperity, These virtues the Crawfords possess, and their home is an open house to their friends the country round.

Dr. W. B. Dailey's Dental Parlors, North Court Street, Athens.

DR. DAILEY'S OPERATING ROOM.

DR. W. B. DAILEY, the subject of this sketch, and the interior of whose palatial Dental Parlors in Athens are herewith shown, was born near Albany, in Meigs county, July 5, 1872, and is the son of J. F. and Amelia Dailey. His grandfather was the late W. M. Dailey, near Albany.

In 1897 Dr. Dailey graduated from Ohio University with the degree of Ph. B. Two years after finishing his literary work in Ohio University, he graduated from the dental department of the University of Maryland, at Baltimore, with the professional degree of D. D. S. He spent one year with Dr. Basom, after which he opened an office in Albany where he remained for four years. In October, 1904, he came back to Athens and began the

DR. DAILEY'S RECEPTION ROOM.

practice of his profession in a finely furnished suite of rooms in the Fulton block, north Court street, where he still remains.

May 2, 1894, he was married to Miss Bertha Foster, daughter of W. B. Foster, of Athens. To the family of Dr. Dailey have been added two children, Lloyd, aged nine years, and Margaret, aged five years.

Residence of Mr. and Mrs. Freeman Marshall, in Lodi Township.

THE picture herewith shows the home of Freeman Marshall, in Lodi township. Mr. Marshall was a native of Carroll county, Ohio, where he was born, in Center township, October 2, 1824, being the son of William and Susannah Marshall. Mr. Marshall's father was a native of Virginia, while his mother was born in New Jersey. Mr. Marshall has always been of a strong religious character, a close student of the Bible, and an ardent believer in the cardinal principles of immersion, repentance, and the doing of good works for happiness in this life and in the life to come.

Mr. Marshall having married Mary A. Readinghouse, they removed from Jefferson county to Athens county in 1851, settling near Jerseyville. Here they raised a family of ten children, all of whom but two sons are living. On the 2nd of January, 1902, Mrs. Marshall died in the triumphs of Christian hope and faith.

Mr. Marshall has always been engaged in farming and stock raising, and is regarded as one of the best and most successful farmers and stock breeders of Lodi township.

July 3, 1901, his house, together with all its contents, the accumulation of over fifty years, was destroyed by lightning. Not discouraged, he rebuilt the same year. At one time he was a large land owner, having about five hundred acres, but at present has but about one hundred acres, the rest having been deeded to his children.

Upon the breaking out of the war, Mr. Marshall was one of the first to respond to the call for troops, serving till he received an honorable discharge for disability. As yet, the government has failed to recognize his services with a pension. His aged mother-in-law, Mrs. Readinghouse, whose picture is shown elsewhere, makes her home with him, together with some of his children and grandchildren.

ATHENS COUNTY HISTORY
CONTINUED.

MOUNDS OF ATHENS COUNTY.

By CLARENCE MATHENY

University. Other mounds have been opened with less interesting results. It seems strange that the Smith Mound and the Beard Mound, the two largest on the Plains, have never been fully explored. They certainly deserve a more careful examination.

A small mound located on the very top of the hill bordering the eastern part of Wolf's Plains and a little northwest of the house now occupied by Mr. J. Taylor, superintendent of the Johnson Coal Mining company's mine here, was opened by two or three of the citizens in the spring of 1905. They were in search of copper and stone articles and more especially inscriptions. At the bottom of the mound and lying on a huge flat stone was a skeleton apparently of a woman. The lower limbs were crossed. The bones had been much decayed by the action of water. The explorers stated that the bones were remarkably large. The jaw bone would fit over that of the average man of to-day and leave plenty of place besides. The forearm bones were 5 inches larger than those of the average man. Charcoal was found in three different layers.

Many years ago Mr. Woodruff Connett plowed into two skeletons in a small mound on his farm. Subsequent explorations were made by a party from Athens with no significant results. It was probably not very closely examined.

Continued on page 101.

Residence of Mr. and Mrs. John L. Evans, in Lodi Township.

JOHN L., son of Lorenzo D. and Ann Evans, was born in Lodi township, April 13, 1842. His early life was spent on the farm and devoted himself to such work as belongs to agricultural life. He was married to Lucretia Barnes June 6, 1861. To them ten children have been born; the first two, Arminta and Clinton, dying in infancy. Hattie, Frank, Carrie, Hollas, Blanche, Annie, Fred and Edna still living, the last two at home. Hattie, Frank, Carrie, Hollas and Blanche have been married; Hattie, Frank and Blanche having since died.

Mr. Evans still resides in the township of his birth, his home herewith being shown. His farm consists of 130 acres of good grazing, farming and rich coal land. He has served as Justice of the Peace and member of the Board of Education for several years, and in 1904, was elected under the new school code for a term of four years.

In 1902, as a member of the Board of Education, he was largely instrumental in establishing a Township High School at Judson, and actively engaged himself in securing pupils for the same, as well as for select schools. He is the only member of the present board who cast his vote to continue the Judson High School. He is at present, as he has been for the last twelve years, claim collector and practicing lawyer in Justices courts.

In 1899 he was, through recommendation of Judge DeSteiguer commissioned Notary Public by Gov. Asa S. Bushnell, and in 1902, through recommendation of Judge J. M. Wood, received a like commission from Gov. Geo. K. Nash. His commission expiring, Judge Wood again recommended him for Notarial services, and in 1905 he received his commission from Gov. Myron T. Herrick. Mr. Evans is interested in all that pertains to peace and prosperity, and is one of the reliable citizens of Lodi township.

FRED EVANS, son of John L. and Lucretia Evans, was born in Lodi township, April 17, 1880. His early life was spent on the farm and in the common schools. Later he attended select schools at Judson, where he assisted in securing teachers and scholars. Here he completed the High School course, including latin, algebra, rhetoric, physics, psychology, etc., under Professors C. R. Cline and G. W. Christman.

In the summer of 1904, he matriculated in Ohio University, where he expects to finish his course. In 1900 he began teaching at Federal, in Ames township, and has taught consecutively ever since. Mr. Evans is deeply interested in all things pertaining to education and religion. He is a consistent christian, having united with the Christian church at Graham's Chapel in 1903. He is one of the aggressive, model young men of the county.

Residence of Jacob Katzenbach, in York Township.

THE residence here shown is the home of Mr. and Mrs. Jacob Katzenbach, a portrait of each appearing in the opposite corners of the picture. These good people are of the highest type of the thrift of German-American citizens. By industry and economy, they have accumulated considerable property, saving from day to day, always making their income exceed their expenses, thus following the true principle of thrift and economy.

Jacob Kitzenbach was born August 27, 1829, in Balborn, Rhinpfalz, Bavaria, Germany. He emigrated to this country in 1859 and first located in Philadelphia, Pennsylvania, and resided there until 1865. He was married in 1853 to Miss Catherine Wixler, also a native born German, who was born in Markgrouingen, Wurttemburg, on September 2, 1832.

Mr. Katzenbach entered the government service as stationary blacksmith at Fort Monroe in 1862 and served until the close of the Civil War. He came to Ohio in 1865 and settled in Athens county where he has resided continuously ever since.

Mr. and Mrs. Katzenbach are the parents of fourteen children eleven of whom are living, three having died in infancy. Six sons and five daughters, all of whom are married except the youngest. Mr. Katzenbach is a genial and pleasant fellow, always looking on the bright side and takes things as they come, always making the best of it. He has given his children a good home and all the education they would take.

ELM ROCK IN YORK TOWNSHIP.

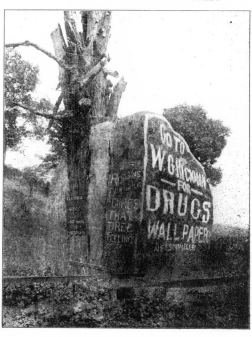

THIS peculiar freak of nature—an elm tree, growing out of a massive rock is located south of Nelsonville not far from the residence of Jacob Katzenbach shown also on this page. It is known as Elm Rock, because the tree that found such an unusual and unwelcome place to grow was a sturdy elm.

Residences of Joseph Wolf and Frank E. Bennett, Nelsonville, Ohio.

JOSEPH WOLF'S RESIDENCE.   FRANK E, BENNETT'S RESIDENCE.

THE two houses shown in the illustration are the homes of Joseph Wolf and his son-in-law, Frank E. Bennett, in East End in the city of Nelsonville.

Joseph Wolf, the subject of this sketch, was born in Porter county, Indiana, January 1, 1836. His father, William D. Wolf, was a native of Athens county, the son of Christopher Wolf. who was the original owner of a large tract of land in the western part of Athens township, now known as Wolf's Plains, named after the owner.

When the Indians relinquished their reservation here, William D. Wolf, the father of our subject, moved to Indiana where Joseph was born in the wilds surrounded by friendly Indians, who came to the cabin frequently to fondle the "pale face" baby. When Joseph was two years of age his parents returned to Ohio, and after six years residence in Athens county removed to Hocking county near where Haydenville now is. There Joseph was reared and given such education as could be obtained from the common schools of that day. On reaching his

majority he bought a farm of eighty acres south of Nelsonville, where he made his home until moving to Nelsonville about two years ago. He was one of the most successful farmers in York township, and as the years went by, he increased his eighth section to within a few acres of a full section. In connection with his farming, he mined coal, dealt largely in timber and lumber, and was superintendent of the B. B. Sheffield mine at Floodwood for five years.

Mr. Wolf is now serving his second term as county commissioner and has made a conscientious and faithful official. Honest, open and frank in all his dealings, he has inspired a lasting confidence among the people he serves.

Mr. Wolf was married to Miss Sarah N. Rogers, a native of Hocking county, November 19, 1857. To them have been born twelve children, eleven of whom grew to young manhood and womanhood, and nine are yet living. The children in order of their years are Frank L., Eugene O.,

Charles J., Sylvester E., Lizzie B. (now Mrs. Riley Andrews), James W., Dora M. (now Mrs. Will Philipps), Cora E., a twin of Mrs. Philipps died in infancy, Homer V., Minnie F. (now Mrs. Ed Humphrey), Nellie B. (now Mrs. Frank Bennett, Myrta A. (now Mrs. Charles Bennett).

FRANK E. BENNETT was born in York township, Athens county, Ohio, July 11, 1874, a son of John W. and Mary L. (Thornton) Bennett. He was reared on a farm and educated in the common school, living with his father until he grew to manhood.

He was married December 6, 1902, to Nellie B. Wolf, daughter of Joseph and Sarah N. (Rogers) Wolf. To this union two children were born, William V., and one died in infancy.

Mr. Bennett is employed at the Sunday Creek company mine, No. 205. Since his marriage he has resided in Nelsonville.

: : : Residence and Store of R. R. Marquis, at Mineral. : : :

THE accompanying picture shows the general store and residence of R. R. Marquis, in Mineral, a thriving little village in the western part of Athens county. Mr. Marquis, the proprietor, was born in Sharon, Noble county, Ohio, February 6, 1850, and came with his parents to Athens county in the fall of 1861. He received a common school and academic education and taught his first term of school when but sixteen years of age, near Big Run in this county. He continued teaching for fifteen years and was very successful, his services commanding the highest wages paid at all times. After having been principal of the Amesville Academy, he quit teaching and engaged in business, and at present deals in general merchandise at Mineral.

Mr. Marquis was married in November of 1878 to Miss Emma Ellis, who is still living. They have two children, now grown to womanhood, Glenn, aged twenty years and Carrie, aged seventeen years. As the picture herewith shows, Mr. Marquis and family are nicely and comfortably situated, and look on the bright side of life at all times.

ATHENS MASONIC BUILDING.

THIS fine three story building is the home of the Masonic lodges of Athens, and is a fine monument to the fidelity and loyalty of the Masonic brethren in this masonic division and proves their devotion to the ancient and honorable institution of masonry, the oldest secret order in the world. The first two floors of the building are devoted to commercial purposes, while the third floor is used by the several Masonic bodies exclusively.

Paramuthia Lodge, No. 25, commonly known as the "Blue Lodge," was instituted in Athens, October 2, 1814 thus making it the first fraternal organization in Athens county. Its number indicates that it is among the earlier lodges of the State, American Union No. 1, at Marietta, being the first Masonic lodge in Ohio.

The other masonic bodies meeting in this building are Athens Chapter, No. 39, instituted in 1849, Athens Council, No. 15, instituted in 1850, Athens Commandery, No. 15, instituted in 1857, and Order of Eastern Star instituted October 26, 1904. All these bodies have a large membership and are in a prosperous condition. There are 147 members in the Blue Lodge, 123 members in the Chapter, 100 members in the Council, 151 Sir Knights in good standing in the Commandery, and 91 members of the Order of Eastern Star, notwithstanding this lodge is less than a year old. It began with 31 charter members.

Early in the history of Athens, Paramuthia Lodge, No. 25, F. & A. M., held its meetings in a building located near where the city stand pipe now stands, in the school house lot. This was known for many years as "Mason Hill." Sometime in its early history this building was destroyed by fire and all of the early records were lost. The date of the destruction is lost to history so far as the writer can ascertain. The lodge next met in the second story of a building located on or near where Grones & Links store now is. This building along with several others burned in about 1853. The lodge then moved to the third floor of the First National Bank building and remained there until the building shown in the illustration was ready for occupancy.

ATHENS COUNTY HISTORY
CONTINUED.

MOUNDS OF ATHENS COUNTY.
By CLARENCE MATHENY.

Mrs. Pennelia Courtney at one time owned a small pottery kettle and a full set of teeth obtained from a mound in this locality. The kettle was of about one pint capacity.

A survey of these mounds was made at a very early date by Mr. Hildreth. The original notes and drawings of Mr. Hildreth are in the possession of the Ohio State Historical and Archaeological Society. These notes and drawings were made in 1840. It will be seen from what has been said that these mounds were simply places of burial. No other supposition seems acceptable since there are remains found in nearly every mound. Some do not give evidence of burial, but they are rare and have probably offered unfavorable conditions for the preservation of human remains. Those who believe them to have been for purposes of defense should study more carefully their location. As to their having been used for religious rites nothing can be said except that, under such conditions, it is difficult to account for the presence of the bones so often found. There is little doubt that they were merely sepulchres.

Dr. F. W. Putnam of Cambridge, Mass., thought from the remains found that southern Ohio was originally the meeting-place of two distinct races of people. He based his supposition on the fact that there is an apparent dissimilarity between the skeletons disclosed in the different mounds.

It must not be inferred from the preceding paragraphs that those mound mentioned include all the mounds found in Athens county. Mounds and embankments are numerous all over the county. All evidence points to the theory that this was a prominent locality in that prehistoric age in which these great earthworks were constructed.

After all, the information obtained by no means established the theory that the Mound Builders were a highly cultured race. They had evidently reached an advanced state of civilization compared to the American Indian in his former condition. They were more industrious as well as more accustomed to labor for food. To provide sustenance for so many as there must have been of them and then to find time to erect the vast number of earthworks must have required some better means of providing the necessaries of life than simply hunting and fishing. But, however, much we may wish to think of the Mound-Builder as a very refined man, we must at the same time concede that nothing so far known lends any valuable evidence in support of that view.

Now naturally arises the question of the fate or destiny of those who constructed these ancient earthworks. Some think they were overcome by the Aztecs and the Pueblos of Mexico and southwestern United States. Conjectures, however, are easily made. No man knows what became of them. Whether they were overcome by other tribes of people or by some fatal

Continued on page 106.

The corner stone of the Masonic Hall was laid with appropriate ceremonies on October 10, 1877, and was formally dedicated June 24, 1878. The report of the building committee shows that the building cost $13,206. The first Master of Paramuthia Lodge was John Lewis; the first High Priest of the Chapter was Leonidas Jewett, and the first Thrice Illustrious Master of the Council and first Eminent Commander of Commandery was S. B. Pruden in each body. The building is under the general charge of a board of trustees, one from each of the four bodies. The board at present is composed of Peter Kern, B. A. Headley, Fred W. Bush and W. K. Scott.

Residence of Mr. and Mrs. William Gilkey, Alexander Township.

WILLIAM GILKEY, Jr., the son of William and Frances Gilkey, was born in Alexander township, Athens county, September 24, 1844. His father was born in Pennsylvania, December 15, 1816, dying in Alexander township, in Athens county, Ohio September 6, 1896. Mr. Gilkey's mother was born in Virginia, April 22, 1812, dying at the old home in Alexander township, Athens county, March 16, 1891. January 30, 1873, Mr. Gilkey married Martha J., daughter of Jesse F. and Elizabeth Carrell. Mrs. Gilkey having been born at Rokeby, Morgan county, Ohio, December 18, 1850. Mrs. Gilkey's father was a native of West Virginia, having been born in Harrison county, March 25, 1824, while her mother was born in Croyden, New Hampshire, December 31, 1833 dying in Athens township, September 4, 1880.

To Mr. and Mrs. Gilkey have been born four children, all of whom are living, three still at home. They have two grand children.

Mr. and Mrs. Gilkey are active and interested members of the Methodist Episcopal church, where they make their Christian characters count for good. They have one of the finest homes in Alexander township.

E. P. TOTMAN'S STORE AND RESIDENCE, SHARPSBURG.

THIS page is devoted to the illustration of the residences and business places of two of Athens county's most energetic and successful young business men—Elisha Parker Totman, of Sharpsburg, and Marion Perley Totman, of Broadwell, both of whom are engaged in general merchandising as a main line, while each indulge in side lines. As an illustration, E. P. owns and operates a flouring mill at Sharpsburg, which is shown on this page along with his residence and interior of store.

Both of the Totman brothers were born on a farm one-half mile southeast of Big Run, Athens county, Ohio, E. P. having first seen the light of day, June 21, 1856, while Marion P. was born October 7, 1861. They still jointly own the old home farm.

E. P. TOTMAN'S FLOUR MILL, SHARPSBURG

Our subjects were of a family of eight children—four boys, Elisha Parker, Charles Presley, Marion Perley and Sherman Elsworth, and four girls, Louisa, Ada, Myra and Inez, all of whom are living except Charles Presley, who died in a hospital in Columbus from an operation for appendicitis, and is now sleeping in the cemetery at Broadwell, Ohio. The father died December 12, 1886, leaving the old home so lonely that the mother abandoned housekeeping and has since been making her home with her children.

E. P. Totman was united in marriage with Lucy Ogg, daughter of Aaron and Theodocia Ogg, at Broadwell, Ohio, November 13, 1881 and commenced keeping house at Big Run, Ohio. He followed the carpenter trade for several years; then he and his brother, M. P. Totman formed a partnership after the style of Totman Bros. and purchased the store property and goods of the Federal Coal Company of Broadwell, Ohio, and did a successful business together for four years, and then E. P. sold his interest in the store and property to M. P. and moved to Sharpsburg and entered into the merchandising business where he is still engaged. He has been very successful and has gathered together a sufficiency of this world's goods.

To Mr. and Mrs. Totman have been born five children, one of them having died when fourteen months old. The family now consists of his wife and four children, two boys, Ferdie, twenty-one years of age; Roy, nineteen, and two girls, Sylvia. fourteen and Goldie ten years of age. They all make life a pleasure and look to the future for more lasting happiness.

M. P. Totman was united in marriage with Edith E. Wickham, daughter of W. W. and Harriet A. Wickham. of Broadwell, Ohio, February 3. 1884, and commenced keeping house in Marion. Ohio; living there only one year and then moving back to Broadwell and went to farming. After farming three years he bought the store and property of Holdcroft & McCune, and did a successful business for several years. He

INTERIOR E. P. TOTMAN'S STORE. SHARPSBURG.

then entered into business with his brother, E. P., as above stated; then purchased the interest of E. P., and has been at Broadwell until this date, having been very successful in business.

His family consists of his wife and two children. One daughter, Bessie May, now twenty years of age and married to Clarence E. Gorham. Their home is here represented. One boy, Walter W., nineteen years of age still at home. The home is a pleasant and happy one through the uplifting of Christian influence and a deep veneration for and the observance of the principles of the Christian religion and the practice of Christian virtues.

How the Totman brothers won success and achieved a competence is an open secret among the people with whom they have lived and transacted business. The spirit of honesty and fair dealing was instilled into them by precept and example of their parents. They were reared right and were started right. The lessons of industry and frugality were held up as cardinal virtues in the Totman household and these coupled with uprightness and straight forward dealing in every transaction brought confidence of the people and every thing else that makes for a successful career followed.

These gentlemen have not alone profited by their success, but the communities have been benefitted by their having lived in them. They take an active interest in everything of a public nature and have always stood for the best in citizenship,—all that was for the uplifting of the community, morally or intellectually.

The accumulation of property, when done by fair means is good, but the building of a noble character is better and there is none to say that the Totman boys have not built broadly and well. They have thus the confidence and high regard of all the people in their respective communities, and have proven themselves worthy of the same.

RESIDENCE OF MR. AND MRS. CLARENCE GORHAM, BROADWELL

M. P. TOTMAN'S STORE AND RESIDENCE, BROADWELL.

PHILIP AND REBECCA MEEK NICE.

THE accompanying pictures show the home and family of Fred H. Nice, in Waterloo township. We also present the pictures of Mr. Nice's father and mother. Early in the forties his parents, Philip and Rebecca Meek Nice emigrated to Rome township, Athens county, from near Moundville, Virginia, and on a small farm brought up a family of eighteen children, of whom Frederick, born June 14, 1859, was the sixteenth. Here the subject of this sketch spent his early life. June 30, 1879 he married Rominia A. Adams, of Marshfield, and the following year settled on the farm where he now lives, having lived there continuously ever since. He found the farm an unbroken forest, but by dint of perseverance he cleared it and placed it under a high state of cultivation and made it the prettiest country home in the township and one of the nicest in the county. To do so, however, many hardships had to be gone through. Mr. Nice gradually gave his attention to the lumber business, and to-day he is a fine judge of timber, in which he is a large dealer. On his farm have been located some of the best gas and oil wells in the county, all of which Mr. Nice is sole owner. This affords him a splendid revenue, as the oil is of the finest quality and the gas of heavy pressure. Nine children have been born to Mr. and Mrs. Nice, named in order of their births as follows: Millard Wayne, Leonard Blaine, Frederick Riley, Madge Neoma, Clara Eldora, Grace Irene, Ethel Belle, Ray Ernest and Iny Stanley, deceased, who appears on the mother's lap in the group picture. Mr. Nice received only such education as the common schools furnished, though his children have fared much better. Leonard Blaine is a successful teacher, and is a student in the Medical College in Columbus.

FRED H. NICE AND FAMILY.

Residence of Mr. and Mrs. S. D. Webb, Albany, Ohio

SAMUEL D. WEBB was born in Columbia township, Meigs county, Ohio, April 26, 1865. He is the second son of David L. and Elizabeth (Gregory nee Shirkey) Webb.

On April 10, 1886 he was married to Miss Lizzie V. Castor who was born in the same township, April 10, 1868, and whose parents are William G. and Emeline (Vale) Castor. The record of the children of this marriage is as follows: Earl C., born July 31, 1888; Carol C., born March 31. 1895.

S. D. Webb was reared on a farm and in the winter attended the district school in the old school house, on his father's farm, on the bank of Brush Run, the house having been destroyed by the memorable cyclone of May 12, 1886.

March 5, 1881 he was granted a teacher's certificate at McArthur, Ohio, and on July 11, following, he began teaching in Vinton township, Vinton county, Ohio. This profession he followed continuously till April 23, 1897, the last six years being engaged in high school work; always being recognized as one of the leaders in the profession, holding "Professional Certificates" in different counties.

In the spring of 1893 he was elected principal of the Albany public schools, which position he held for four successive years.

During the summer of 1894 he removed his family from his farm on "Flower Hill," Columbia township, to Albany. where they have since resided, owning one of the most beautiful homes in Athens county; located on an eighteen-acre tract of land. The home is equipped with all the modern conveniences. This residence, a picture of which appears herewith, was erected by the present owner in 1904.

At present (1905) Mr. Webb is a traveling salesman for The Jarecki Chemical Co., of Sandusky Ohio, having been employed in that capacity since November, 1897. He receives a handsome salary and is one of the thrifty business men of the town.

Mr. Webb is a member of the I. O. O. F., having become a Past Grand some years since, and has served his district as D. D. G. M. He is a prominent member of the order of the United Commercial Travelers, belonging to Council No. 262 at Athens, Ohio. In 1881 he became a member of Laurel Grange No. 1030, P. of H., and his wife and son are are both active members of this organization.

Mr. Webb is also one of the members of the Board of Deputy State Supervisors of Elections of Athens county, Ohio, having been appointed by the Secretary of State in 1901.

Residence of Mr. and Mrs. Henry Newton Hewitt, in Waterloo Township.

HENRY NEWTON HEWITT, whose residence in Waterloo township is here shown, was born in 1828 on the farm where he now resides. He was the son of Pardon Hewitt, who was born in an old log house now used as a stable on the same farm, in 1804. Pardon Hewitt was the son of Moses Hewitt, who was born in Worcester, Massachusetts, in 1767 and came to Ohio in 1790 and settled in a block house on what is now known as Blennerhassett Island. Here he married, and after two children were born he joined a command of Indian fighters. Moses, while a man of slight stature, was noted for his physical prowess and could perform feats that seemed almost impossible for man to do. While Indian fighting on the Kanawha he was captured by Indians and marched by them across Ohio to Sandusky, a place of Indian headquarters. The story of his escape, published in Howe's History of Ohio, is quite thrilling. He slipped the thongs with which he was bound, one night, and after nine days he arrived at a camp on the Muskingum near the mouth of Wolf creek, nude as Adam and almost famished.

The grandson, H. N. Hewitt, our subject, was married to Mary Young, the daughter of Alexander Young on Hamley Run in 1850, she being twenty-three years old. Her father was born in Virginia in 1795, the son of a rich slave owner. He came to Ohio when about seventeen years old.

Alexander married Hannah Cramby, the aunt of Bishop Earl Cranston of the M. E. church, in 1825. Hannah was the daughter of an Englishman and was one of a family of ten children, nine of them are yet living.

To Mr. and Mrs. Hewitt, whose pictures are shown in the corner of the illustration, were born ten children, five sons and five daughters, three sons are living, one of whom is J. C. Hewitt, an energetic young business man of Athens, engaged in the lumber business, and four of the daughters are yet living.

Mr. and Mrs. Hewitt have twenty-one grand children and two great grand children.

| Buckeye Cliff, Between Mineral and Carbondale. | Residence of Mr. and Mrs. James Henry Finsterwald, Near Guysville. |

THE above bit of natural scenery is known as Buckeye Cliffs and is located on the wagon road between Mineral and Carbondale, jointly on the Hewitt and Beckler farms. The rocks are 75 to 100 feet high and make a pretty picture almost any time of the year. Tradition has it that a white man chased by Indians ran or fell over this cliff, but the story has but little foundation. It derives its name from a large buckeye tree that grew from the cleft in the rock.

THIS comfortable and prosperous looking country place is the home of Mr. and Mrs. James Henry Finsterwald, and is located on the Hocking, about two miles from Guysville.

Our subject, J. H. Finsterwald. was the son of Fritz Finsterwald, now deceased, who was one of Athens county's most prominent and highly respected citizens. In the Republican county of Athens Mr. Finsterwald, Sr., a Democrat, was elected one of the county commissioners in 1876, and served two terms. It was during his administration that the present court house was constructed. Henry, the son, was born in Ames township, December 2, 1848, and moved with his parents when about eight years old to his his present home. He grew up on the farm, attended the common schools and a short time at the Ohio University and then fitted himself for business by taking a commercial course in Cincinnati. He was married to Miss Addie Stout, the daughter of Charles Stout, of Carthage township. They have three children, a daughter who married Superintendent C. H. Copeland, of Hamden; Fred, aged nineteen years, who is a student in the Ohio University, and Fern, aged twelve.

Mr. and Mrs. Finsterwald have about 750 acres of good land, the home farm containing about 450 acres. They are well to do citizens, and are highly respected by their neighbors and acquaintances. Mr. Finsterwald also runs a livery business in connection with his brother Lewis, at Guysville.

WESLEY A. WEBB was born in Columbia township, Meigs county, Ohio, December 5, 1862. He is the eldest son of David L. and Elizabeth (Gregory *nee* Shirkey) Webb. The subject of this sketch was reared on a farm and received a good common school education; commenced teaching school when eighteen years old and taught fourteen years.

He went to Nebraska in July, 1884, but returned home in October. He was married April 10, 1886, to Elizabeth Caster, who was born in the same township, September 8, 1867, and whose parents are Lewis and Lovina (Greene) Caster.

Mr. and Mrs. Webb commenced house keeping near Dyesville, Ohio. They are the parents of one child, Alma Edith, born July 3 1888. Mr. Webb was elected township clerk of Columbia township, three consecutive terms, and was a notary public for six years. He is a member of Albany Lodge, No. 156, F. & A. M. Mr. and Mrs. Webb have been members of Laural Grange, No. 1030, about twenty-five years. He was elected assistant steward of the Ohio State Grange in December, 1892, and served one term, declining reelection because he had changed his occupation and could not attend to Grange work. His daughter is a member of Albany Grange, No. 1611.

Mr. Webb was appointed a railway postal clerk in March, 1894, with headquarters at Columbus, Ohio, and moved from his farm to that city the following month. He lived in that city about three years and worked on several different routes as a substitute postal clerk, and received a permanent appointment July 16, 1895, on the B. & O. S-W. railway, between Cincinnati, Ohio and Grafton. West Virginia, but afterwards transferred to the Norfolk & Western between Columbus, Ohio and Kenova, West Virginia.

June 24, 1897 he was transferred to the Ohio Central and Kanawha & Michigan railroad between Columbus, Ohio and Gauley Bridge, West Virginia, and is now (1905) on that run. He is a member of the Railway Mail Association, and was elected a delegate to the National Convention, held at San Antonio, Texas, June 7, 1900. After attending the convention he made a pleasure trip to Monterey, Mexico,

In 1895 he purchased the farm on which he now lives, and moved his family from Columbus to Albany, Ohio, July 1, 1897, where they have since resided. His present home which is shown in this illustration was completed May 1, 1905, and is a very fine farm residence.

Farm Scene of Hough L. Harner, of Alexander Township.

HOUGH L. HARNER, the subject of this sketch, and whose fine farm home and dairy herd we herewith present, was born May 1, 1882, in Monongahela county, near Morgantown, West Virginia, in which State he resided till in his twentieth year. In 1892 he came to Alexander township, locating on the P. C. Henry farm of three hundred and sixty-eight acres, this being the center of the township. With pride Mr. Harner can look to a long line of splendid ancestry. His father, P. F. Harner, was for some time president of the county court of Monongahela county, and was also one of the county's commissioners for six years. P. F. Harner was the son of Philip Waugh and Sarah Fear Harner, and was born March 15, 1848 in Fairchance, Fayette county, Pennsylvania. In 1849 he came to Morgantown, Virginia, now West Virginia, coming with his parents, both of whom were Germans, but emigrated to the United States in 1791.

Mr. Harner's parents were married in December, 1868, his mother being Margaret O. Robinson, daughter of John D. and Elizabeth Robinson, to them being born three boys and two girls, Hough L being the youngest of the family.

January 14, 1904, Hough Harner and Miss Grace Dowler, daughter of D. D. Dowler, were married. Mr. Dowler is known as the veteran school teacher of Ath-

ens county, he having taught eighty-eight terms, extending over a period of forty years. He was also justice of the peace for Canaan township for eighteen years, and always took an active interest in all matters of an educational nature, as well as whatever would tend to dignify law and its observance.

In 1865 Mr. Dowler was married to Electa Poston, and Mrs. Harner is one of their family of five children.

Mr. Harner is a practical and scientific dairyman, and takes interest and pride in his business, which he conducts so as to make it a profitable enterprise.

THROUGH the courtesy of Mr. George A. Beaton, of New York, we are enabled to herewith present four beautiful and artistic views of the Athens State Hospital, located across the Hocking, southwest of the city of Athens and in full view of many of her citizens.

This institution, now one of the largest in the State, was provided for by legislative enactment of April 13, 1867. Dr. W. P. Johnson was then the representative of Athens county. There was much competition for the location of the Hospital, but finally Athens secured it by her citizens buying and donating to the State one hundred and fifty acres of land known as the Coates farm. The corner stone was laid November 5, 1868, the ceremonies being conducted by the officers of the Grand Masonic lodge of Ohio, and not less than one thousand members of the order from various parts of the State were present. In the corner stone were placed: Holy Bible; constitution of Ohio and all States of the Union; names of members Fifty-eighth General Assembly; names of State officers; proceedings of the Grand Lodge of Ohio; laws of Ohio 1867: program of days proceedings, roll of members of Paramuthia Lodge No. 25; copy Cincinnati Commercial; Cincinnati Gazette; Cincinnati Chronicle; Weekly Enquirer; Athens Messenger; specimen of coins of the United States and list of grand officers of Ohio Masons.

The building was completed and furnished for reception of patients, January, 1874. The

original building was 853 feet in length and was 4072 feet around, but many additions have been added since then. Four new and commodious cottages have been added within the past two years, and at this time 1294 patients are being taken care of in the building. The park or grounds about the building as the picture indicates, contains some of the most beautiful natural scenery in the State. Nearly all the walks and drives are paved, and all the patients except the helpless and decrepit are given an airing every day of the year that the weather will permit. A beautiful location, excellent water. picturesque surroundings makes this indeed an ideal spot for taking care of the State's mentally unfortunate.

MOUNDS OF ATHENS COUNTY.

By CLARENCE MATHENY

epidemic, or whether they perished through internal wars, no one can definitely ascertain. That they have lived their day and perished without leaving to future races the slightest information as to their condition except what is contained in their mounds and other earthworks is, to express it mildly, a sad fact. However, it may be, at least two separate and distinct races of people have previously thronged the land that we now claim as ours. Why these races failed to grow and to become powers of note, it is beyond the power of human understanding to explain. They were a people of some degree of civilization, not of culture; they were great in number; they were industrious and actively inclined; they were adepts at the art of pottery making and of stone and copper implement-making; they were particularly numerous in Ohio, especially in southern Ohio; and they were a warlike people. Such facts as these are quite evident, but more than these is simply some man's theory. These are important fields for investigation; and it is altogether possible that a few more years will bring to light much valuable and interesting information along these very lines. Let us at least hope that it may be so.

Continued on page 111.

Elmer M. Enlow.

ELMER M. ENLOW, whose picture is here presented, is the leading photographer in Athens. In June of 1897, he bought a part interest in the gallery owned and operated for several years by J. C. Brannan, and after six months bought out the entire plant and has successfully conducted the business since.

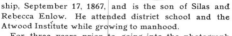

Mr. Enlow was born in Lee township, September 17, 1867, and is the son of Silas and Rebecca Enlow. He attended district school and the Atwood Institute while growing to manhood.

For three years prior to going into the photograph business, he was an attendant in the Athens State Hospital.

June 3, 1896 he was married to Miss Charlotte Dick, of New Lexington. They have one son, Garrett, who was born March 28, 1897. They own their comfortable new home on Elmwood Place in east Athens.

Lorin Charles Nye.

LORIN CHARLES NYE was born near Chauncey, Ohio, June 21, 1869. He is the youngest son of Jane Harvey Nye, and was reared on the farm adjoining the Nye cemetery. In May of 1891, he started into

the tinning and roofing trade with C. A. Cable in Nelsonville, and the following July, on the 27th day he was married to Miss Mary Brawley, the daughter of John Brawley of near Chauncey. They have three children: Charles E., aged 13 years; Earl L., 7 years and Dorris F., 5 years.

In November of 1891, Mr. Nye located in Trimble and carried on a general roofing business until May, 1895, when he moved his family and business to Bremen, Ohio. In 1900 he moved to Athens and has been very successful, having added to his plant the equipment for manufacturing gas heating stoves. Owing to the excellence of his product, he has established quite a large trade and his stoves are shipped broadcast wherever natural gas is used.

Mr. Nye is a member of Sereno Lodge No. 479, I. O. O. F. and also Athens Encampment No. 175. He has served as Chief Patriarch Athens Encampment, and in May, 1905 became a member of Athenian Lodge No. 104, K. of P.

Residence of E. M. Blower, Trimble, Ohio.

Farm and Residence of Mr. and Mrs. William H. Linscott.

WILLIAM H. LINSCOTT was born December 18, 1847, in Ames township, Athens county, Ohio. He is the son of George and Sarah Linscott, mention of whom is made on another page of this work. A member of a family of twelve children, early thrown upon his own resources, Mr. Linscott through careful management and strict application to his farming interests, has become one of Athens county's leading farmers. The above illustration represents his farm on Stroud's Run, and from a standpoint of scenery can scarcely be rivaled in Athens county.

Nor is this a picture farm alone. The general appearance of thrift is some indication of its value as an agricultural and grazing proposition. It is in a high state of cultivation and brings good returns at all times. Mr. Linscott and his estimable wife put brains into their management and make every effort count. The character of the soil, the proper rotation of the crops, etc., have all been thoroughly studied out in an effective way.

Upon this farm is the famous "Linscott" spring as shown herewith coming from a rock in the hillside. This spring has a capacity of two hundred thousand gallons of water daily, and is the largest fresh water spring in this section of Ohio. The water is as pure as Nature itself, and is cool and refreshing all the summer through. The picture here shown is one of the most artis-

and happy life in the country that would be difficult to duplicate.

Mr. Linscott was married to Nancy Coulson, October 7, 1891, and they have lived upon the Stroud's Run farm since.

Nancy Coulson was born September 3, 1859. She was the daughter of James Coulson, son of John Coulson, born in London, England, August 5, 1784, he being the son of Charity Death Coulson, daughter of James Death, Sr., of London, England. John Coulson came to the United States about 1800, and settled in Washington county, Pennsylvania. A blacksmith by trade, he came to Ohio in 1837 and purchased four hundred acres of land in Dover township, two hundred acres in Sunday Creek valley, and two hundred acres in Sugar Creek valley. Upon this land is now located the Continental Coal Company's mine, No. 209, known as "the Coulson mine."

John Coulson married Sarah Mustard in 1811. James Coulson born February 15, 1814, gradutaed from Washington, Pennsylvania, 1837, and was a surveyor by profession, serving some years as county surveyor of Athens. He married Sarah A. Mounts, daughter of Joseph and Nancy McGlothlin Mounts, who came to Ohio, April 15, 1844, and settled on Coulson farm on Sugar Creek.

Thus briefly is described the lives and short genealogy of two of Athens county's most estimable citizens, but it would require more than our space would permit to give a fair estimate of the high character of these people, whose deeds of charity and pure beneficence has made for them an enviable place among the people with which they come in contact every day.

Their home is a most hospitable one and the latch string is always out to their numerous friends the country round. While no children have been born to them, their hearts have been kept young and their fancies free through personal association and keeping in touch with the world at large. They are both of a public spirited nature and are always found on the right side of ever public question in their community, whether of social, educational or moral nature.

It will be noticed in the personal sketch of Mrs. Linscott that her ancestry came from Eng-

MRS. WILLIAM H. LINSCOTT.

MR. WILLIAM H. LINSCOTT.

tic in this work and has won the admiration of all who have seen it. The man sitting by the spring is easily recognized as Mr. Linscott, while the lady is his excellent wife as they appear day by day attending to the multiplicity of their duties about the home and farm. The faithful dog, the ducklings swimming in the water, the old spring house—all make a picture of peaceful

THE FAMOUS LINSCOTT SPRING.

land. She has in her possession a piece of crockery ware that was brought to this country over one hundred years ago and has been handed down from generation to generation. She prizes this heirloom of another century very highly. The crock may be seen setting in the window of the spring house, and is guarded with scrupulous care by its owner.

M. I. EWERS, son of Johnathan and Rosana Ewers was born in Belmont county, April 21, 1846, and moved to Coolville, Athens county, in 1850. He lived on a farm near there until 1864, when he enlisted in Company E, One Hundred and Seventy-fourth Regiment, O. V. I., and served one year. After the close of the war he went west and remained there until November 22, 1873,

M. I. EWERS.

when he married Amanda M. Melchi at Joy, Morgan county, Ohio, and settled in Stewart, Athens county, Ohio, November 10, 1875, and went into the manufacturing of stogies and has followed that business almost continuously ever since. He has been very successful. The Red Star stogie of his manufacture is known far and near.

Mr. and Mrs. Ewers were the parents of four children as follows: Grace, born March 27, 1876 and died June 26th of the same year; Maggie, born July 11, 1877; Frank B., born September 6, 1879 and was married to F. E. Kimes, May 28, 1902; Murry M., born September 19, 1881. Mrs. Ewers, the wife and mother, died January 2, 1905.

In politics Mr. Ewers is a Democrat, both by birth and adoption. He has many times been honored by his party by nomination and election. He was justice of the peace of Rome township six years, and has been a notary public for twelve years. He was the postmaster of Stewart under Cleveland's administration. He is at present the nominee of the Democrat party for sheriff of Athens county, and has served as central committeeman of his party in Rome township almost continuously for the past twenty years. He is president of the school board of Stewart, special school district, and has always taken an active interest in local affairs of a public nature. He has been a member of the I. O. O. F. Lodge, No. 753 since 1881, and is a member of United Commercial Travelers of America.

Residence of Mr. and Mrs. John Morris, Ames Township.

THIS comfortable cottage in Ames township is the home of Mr. and Mrs. John Morris, thrifty and enterprising agriculturalists, owning a farm of one hundred and seventy-five acres, which judging from the home and environment, is made to yield a good income on the investment.

Mr. Morris, our subject, is the son of Joseph Morris, deceased since August 22, 1854, and Caroline Morris, who died September 12, 1894. He was an excellent citizen, progressive farmer and generous neighbor. He has served as trustee of Ames township for a number of years, and has proven himself a careful guardian of public funds, using the same care in the township's business as if it were his own. He is also a member of the Township Board of Education. His parents came to this county from Pennsylvania in about 1850.

Mr. Morris was married to Miss Sarah Lewis, January 1, 1882. They have three children; Joseph, who was born February 16, 1884 and married Miss Maud Howard, July 29, 1905; Charles, born August 2, 1886 and Pearl born July 19, 1889.

Mrs. Morris is the daughter of John and Elizabeth Lewis, and was born October 26, 1851. Her father died April 8, 1895, and her mother is still living.

W. R. Goddard.

HERE is the picture of one of Bern township's most highly respected citizens and most progressive farmer and stock raiser, Mr. W. R. Goddard, who was born March 28, 1849. His grand parents came from the New England states and his parents were Abram Wood Goddard and Maria J. Cutler Goddard, of Washington county.

Mr. Goddard was married in 1878 to Miss Anna Blake, and two children were born to them. In 1881 he was again married to Miss Fannie E. Henry, and seven children have been born to them, all of whom are living.

Mr. Goddard formerly lived in Washington county, where he served as county treasurer from 1878 to 1880. He has a fine stock farm and is a large fruit grower, which he conducts in a scientific manner and makes good returns on the investment. He is interested in all public affairs and lends his time and influence to all propositions tending to advance the public good.

Residence of Mr. and Mrs. George Myers, York Township.

JOHN G. MYERS.

THE thrift of the German-American is proverbial, and no exception is found in Mr. and Mrs. George Myers, whose comfortable home and commodious barn in York township are herewith shown. These are sturdy citizens, and by industry and frugality have accumulated a sufficiency of this world's goods.

Mr. Myers, our subject, was born June 9, 1842, in Hocking county and was the son of John G. and Elizabeth Myers. He was married to Elizabeth Whetstone, the daughter of Jacob and Mary Whetstone on April 2, 1868. They have three children, all living: Mary, who married F. P. Brady, and is living near Buchtel; Isadore, who is still at home, and John W., who was married to Miss Ella Welden and lives in York township.

The Myers farm embraces three hundred acres, the large part of which lies in the Hocking bottoms. To those who are familiar with the adaptability and fertility of Hocking bottom farms, nothing further need be said of the value of Mr. Myers' holdings.

Along with the residence and barn are shown the pictures of Mr. and Mrs. Myers and the late John G. Myers, the father of the subject, who was one of the prominent men of York township in his day and generation. Whatever success the son has achieved is due largely to the training and direction given by the father, who held principle higher than pence, and cultivated the disposition to regard honesty, frugality and charity as the crowning virtues.

GEORGE MYERS AND WIFE.

Farm Residence of Charles A. Howard, on Stroud's Run.

LEWIS LEE HOWARD.

MR. AND MRS. LEWIS V. HOWARD.

THE accompanying picturesque illustration shows the residence and part of the farm of Charles A. Howard on Stroud's Run. In 1896 our subject entered the Ohio University, and after spending two years in that institution his father left this farm for Charles to take care of, and in the seven years succeeding, he has demonstrated that he can make a success of agricultural pursuits.

The Howard family came from Virginia, where Charles' grandfather, Lewis Lee Howard was born on March 2, 1804. He married Elizabeth Miller on December 13, 1827, and came to Athens county in August of 1835. He raised a family of fifteen children, seven boys and eight girls. At the time of his death, September 27, 1896, there were sixty-eight grand children, fifty-nine of which are still living.

Lewis V. Howard, the father of our subject, was born June 28, 1851, and was married June 18, 1871. He moved to the farm shown in the picture in 1873, built the residence in 1880, and remained here until the fall of 1898, when he moved to what is known as the Johnson farm near Amesville. He was a successful farmer and raised a family of eight children, five girls and three boys.

The Howards are all industrions and enterprising citizens and are highly respected by their neighbors.

MR. O. W. BEAN is a product of Athens county, and has lived here practically all his life. He was born near Nelsonville, July 13, 1836, and is the son of William Thomas and Sarah Ester

O. W. BEAN.

(Mansfield) Bean. Mr. Bean's present home is about two miles south of Nelsonville, and is one of the finest and most picturesque places in that vicinity.

The farm lies on the banks of the Hockhocking river, and partakes most liberally of the beautiful scenery for

which this stream is noted. His farm is one of the very productive ones, as Mr. Bean is an agriculturalist who puts brains into his work and is therefore a practical and progressive farmer.

Together with farming Mr. Bean devotes much time to the raising of fine stock, and he has some splendid specimens of his breeding ability. He has also dealt largely in mineral lands and real estate in general. Mr. Bean is one of those quiet, unassuming gentlemen, and is always on the side of right. His influence for good is felt throughout the community, and he is the centre of a large circle of friends.

. . . Residence of John William Bennett, in York Township. . . .

JOHN WILLIAM BENNETT, whose home is here represented, is one of the substantial farmers of the Hocking valley. He was born in Baltimore, Maryland, August 17, 1849, the son of James and Pricilla Bennett. On April 21, 1871, he was married to Miss Mary L. Thornton. To them have been born nine children: Loving L., Frank E., Charles W., John M., James V., Clarence E., Walter H., Evert L. and Mary E., the last two died in infancy.

Mr. Bennett owns three hundred and seventy-three acres of land, two hundred acres in Henry county, Ohio, splendid black soil, and is withal a very successful man. In politics he is a Democrat, and has had the honor of the nomination for county offices many times. At one time he ran against Hon. D. L. Sleeper for representative and ran ahead of his ticket eight hundred. He ran

THE OLD HOMESTEAD.

equally well at another time for county commissioner against Abner Juniper. He has never been defeated for a township office and has been trustee of York township for the past six years. Mr. Bennett is a faithful member of the Methodist church and an enthusiastic worker in the Sunday school of which he has been superintendent for the past eighteen years, many of these years he has not been absent for a single Sunday. His fidelity to his church and Sunday school is illustrative of his persistency to duty in everything that engages his attention. John W. Bennett does nothing by the halves or in a half-hearted manner. He throws his whole soul into whatever he undertakes, and therein lies the secret of his success in business, in farming, in digging coal or anything to which he directs his energies. He is an excellent citizen, a kind husband and father, and withal a good man.

Residence of Mr. and Mrs. A. P. Hatch, Lodi Township.

A. P. HATCH, the subject of this sketch, and the son of William Hatch, was born in Nelsonville, Ohio, October, 15, 1876. Here he lived till he was about twenty years old, when he moved to Dover township. Shortly after this he married Edna I., daughter of George and Elizabeth Everett, of Ames township, May 4, 1897. Mrs. Hatch

was born in Ames township, February 11, 1876. Her mother dying when Edna was less than a year old, she was taken by her grandmother, Mrs. Rose Everett, with whom she made her home till her marriage. Mr. Hatch's grandfather was A. Poston, one of the early and successful coal operators of the county.

For a time the subject of this sketch was in the employ of the government as rural mail carrier out of Athens. He is a member of Eagle Aerie at Athens, No. 529, and also of the Modern Woodman of America camp at Jerseyville.

To Mr. and Mrs Hatch have been born three chil-

dren, Floyd. October 23, 1899; Maggie September 15, 1901; Garnett, February 8, 1903.

Mr. Hatch now lives in Lodi township. where he is regarded as one of the pushing. energetic farmers of the community. We herewith show his home and family in the accompanying pictures.

Residence of John C. Harner, Alexander Township.

JOHN C HARNER, son of P. F. and Margaret O. Harner, was born in Morgantown, West Virginia, May 26, 1878. His father was born at Oliphant Pennsylvania, March 15, 1848, while his mother. Margaret O. Robinson Harner, was born at Morgantown, West Virginia, September. 1847. Mr. Harner's parents still reside at the old homestead in Morgan. town.

The subject of this sketch was married to Mary E., daughter of Mr. and Mrs. J. I. Shriver, of Morgantown, March 10, 1898, who was born near Morgantown, West Virginia, August 22, 1876, dying near Athens, Ohio, October 28, 1904. To Mr. and Mrs. Harner were born three children, Mary O., now aged six years; Fairchild, now four years old, and Ruth, the youngest, now but two years old.

Mr. Harner has been engaged in the dairy business all his life, his father having trained him to it. When he came to Athens county from West Virginia in October, 1902, he brought his dairy herd with him and located where he now lives, in Alexander township, where he owns a fine dairy farm of two hundred and fifty acres, on which he has a choice herd of thirty-five graded cows.

Mr. Harner is a member of the K. P. Lodge at Morgantown, and sym. pathizes with any and every fraternal and business enterprise that is calculated to help and build up, being a young man of enterprise and and good business ability.

ATHENS COUNTY HISTORY
CONTINUED.

THE HOCKING CANAL.

Athens county has had her share of the 700 miles of canals in this state, Athens being the terminus of the 60 mile Hocking Canal which joined the Ohio canal at Carroll in Fairfield county. The different canals with their seven reservoirs were built at a cost of $16,000,000, several of these to-day are entirely abandoned others nearly so.

There was great rejoicing when the canal reached Nelsonville in 1840. It was then opened for business and the first load of Hocking Valley coal started to market. Stone coal was a new thing to most people and this boat with its load attracted many to the canals bank as it made its way north. Late in 1841, the canal was completed to Athens and the entire canal opened up. It had thirty-one locks and eight dams, with a width of 80 feet.

The expense of this division known as the Hocking canal, because it followed closely the valley of the Hock-hocking river, was built at an expense to the state of about $950,000. This canal was the first state improvement to open up the immense resources of the Hocking Valley. In 1856 railroads began to crowd in and with their switches right to the coal banks they carried away much of the canal trade.

Such terrible floods and freshets as are seldom known to-day devasted the valley in 1847 and again in 1858 damaging the banks of the canal to a great extent and required large expenditure of money to repair them. After the flood of 1873, when the magnitude of the damage was discovered for the canal was almost entirely destroyed from Logan to Athens, it was decided to abandon it between Nelsonville and Athens. In many places the old banks can still be recognized and they stand a monument to a by-gone day but point to one stage of development which was a most necessary step in our progress. We can scarcely realize now with what joy the canal was welcomed for the "incalculable blessings it would bring and the wonderfully increased prosperity that would follow close upon the opening of travel and traffic on that great waterway."

EDUCATION IN ATHENS COUNTY.
By SUPT. F. S. COULTRAP.

Space will not permit a careful review of the schools from their inception in the county to the present time. Nothing therefore will be attempted further than to note a few things which have been epoch-making periods in the growth and development of the common school sytsem.

History records that in the early settlements of Ohio only the weak or crippled or naturally slow were employed to teach, the strong and vigorous being needed to clear the forests and till the soil. But this depended upon the class of, people that came into a community and the inspiring souls who were the leaders in educational thought and sentiment. Athens county seems to have been peculiarly fortunate in this regard; her pioneers being of a type of citizenship who were especially concerned about the education of their children; for history notes the fact that along with the development of great physical strength due to the struggle for mere existence was a constant longing and planning and striving of these back-

Continued on page 116.

O. B. SLOANE.

O. B. SLOANE'S GRANDCHILD.

O. B. SLOANE, whose picture and some of the results of his efforts are shown on this page, was born in Washington county, Pennsylvania, March 14, 1848. When ten years of age he came with his parents to Ohio. After living on the farm for a few years, his parents moved to the village of South Salem in Ross county, Ohio, where he attended the public schools and later had the advantage of an academic course, which he pursued through the junior year. This comprised all of his educational advantages so far as school was concerned. On leaving school he was engaged in the mercantile business for a few years with his father. Having ambition to engage in business for himself, his father bought a stock of dry goods in Athens, and on June 21, 1871, our subject, arrived here, a total stranger and took charge of the store. After two years, he with a partner bought the stock and continued the business successfully. The partner desiring to go south, Mr. Sloane bought his interest and continued the business

until 1903, having built up a large department store occupying thirteen rooms, and did a volume of business second to none in Athens. Desiring to retire from active store business, he sold his stock. To say that he has prosecuted business to a successful issue is evinced by his acquirements of property, now owning and operating four large farms in Athens county, besides land interests in the west, a number of dwellings in Athens, the large block herewith shown on the corner of Court and State streets in Athens, and two large double business blocks in the city of Duluth, Minnesota.

On January 9, 1872, Mr. Sloane was married to Miss Sarah Alice Leffingwell, of Ross county. There was born to them one daughter, Jessie Pauline, now the wife of Dr. R. W. Bowden and residing in the city of Duluth, Minnesota. They have one child, Richard Sloane Bowden, whose picture is also shown herewith along with his grandfather.

Mr. Sloane has never entertained political aspirations, but has attended strictly to business. On account of his peculiar fitness, he was selected by his fellow citizens as a member of the Board of Public Affairs of the city of Athens.

Thus is noted the main incidents in the life of one of Athens most prosperous and successful business men. These cold facts are indeed inadequate in giving an estimate of the character of the man. Mr. Sloane has led a busy life, and his strict attention to every detail of his business brought him the success he merited, but life has been more to him than business routine. His interest in the welfare of the city of his adoption has always been next to that of his own. Were he not a modest man, instances of philanthrophy and charity by the score might be cited, which reflect honor and credit to his magnanimity

INSTITUTED September 4, 1895, with the following officers: C. L. Kennedy, P. C.; O. G. Hawk, C. C.; A. O. Hunter, V. C.; S. E. G. Pedigo, Prelate; G. L. Pake, K. R. & S. and M. of F.; S. F. Beverage, M. of Ex.; F. H. McVay, M. of W.; G W. Duffee, M. at A ; E L Wilson, I. G.; C. E. Baughman, O. G. Meetings continued for some months in a rented hall, but with great inconvenience. On the 12th day of the following July, O. G. Hawk and G. L. Pake were in the home of A. H. Dixon. By mutual consent the following plan was put into effect at the meeting of the 17th: Pake proposed "that we build a new hall." Dixon made a motion to that effect, which was seconded by Hawk. In keeping with this the following committees were appointed: On plans and specifications, F. P. Phillips, O. G. Hawk and W. D. Ziggafoos; finance, Z. Z. Bridge, E. L. Wil-

son and S. B. Phillips; location, Charles Burt, G W. Duffee and O. G. Hawk. Plan for building 32x60 was accepted, and each member of the lodge loyally and voluntarily subscribed $5.00. The new building was occupied on the evening of November 27th. Success has attended the lodge numerically and financially from its very beginning; the two story building being properly equipped on the second floor for lodge purposes, while the lower floor is fitted for public entertainment. A $500 government bond is placed in reserve with ample funds remaining in the treasury.

OUR HONORED DEAD—H. F. McCoy, Sept. 6, 1897; C. L. Kennedy, Feb. 25, 1902; H. S. King, April 16, 1902; Leonard Martin, April 8, 1903; C. H. Dumaree, June 27, 1905. CHARTER MEMBERS—G. L. Pake, G. W. Duffee, Charles Burt, S. F. Beverage, J. J. Lyons, S. E. Robinett, J. E. Hamilton, J. Ryan, E. L. Wilson, S. E. G. Pedigo, A. H. Dixon, M. Young, F. P. Phillips, O. Weethe, S. B. Phillips, E. B. Ward, J. E. Braley, Sam Baughman, Silas Scott, F. M. Schwarzel, George Beckle, O. G. Hawk and A. O. Hunter.

MEMBERS K. P. No. 692.

George P. Doll,
J. F. Beckler,
L. D. DeVore,
H B. Stright,
William Flemming,
Charles McCoy,
G. A. Hunter,
F. W. Stanton,
Jerome Mace,
W. L. Bridge,
Ira Barnes,
M. E Andrews,
Curtis Todd,
J. P. Snyder,
Marion Lewellen,
H. C. Beverage,
W. E. Sturgill,
A. J. Stevenson,
William DeVore,
Martin Pinny,
W H. Partlow,
Joseph McBride,
J E Nanna,
Jacob Pollock,
John Dalton,
C. C. Pierce, Jr.,
Martin Pidcock,
George Smith,
Conrad Hoffner,
R. M. Gillilan,
C. C. Woods,
T. W. Ashton,
Bert Martin,
William Madison,
F. C. Betts,
Will Williams,
J. W. Nanna,
B. A. Irwin,
H. D. Albaugh,
Mason Nichols,
T. B. Jones,
G. B. Stanley,
John S. Martin,
Charles Bell,
William Todd,
F M. Martin,
George Moriarty,
Fred Burt,
W. T. Glanville,
J. W. Cottrill,

Robert Jackson,
James Rankin,
William Beckle,
Geo. McCollins,
B. F. Beckler,
E. E. Doolittle,
H. W. Severs,
W. U. Finney,
Marion Graham,
Garrison Cox,
T. F. Hamilton,
J. P. Emish,
S L. Withers,
V W. Clendenin,
Bert Russell,
Alfred Bailes,
J. W McDaniel,
Carl Coots,
Lon Hutchins,
Milford Russell,
Edward Cox,
J. W. Johnson,
B. F. Kizor,
Patrick McBride,
Chris Betts,
Albert Todd,
Elsworth Cox,
Samuel Gilham,
Bert Carter,
H. D. Nanna,
George Gabriel,
C. O. Rizer.
R. P. Imes,
James McHarg,
Frank Sturgill,
J. O. Russell,
Alvan H James,
Alvin Sturgill,
G. W. Weatherby,
W. A. Thomas,
M. H. Stanley,
Aaron Martin,
John Loper,
Howard Robbins,
William Pierce,
H. Stinemyer,
John Cooper,
L. E. Vincent,
J. R. Lostro,
Harvey Carter,

L. B. Nice.

A. H. DIXON.   G. W. DUFFEE   E L. WILSON.
G. L. PAKE.   O. G. HAWK.

. . . . Residence of Joseph W. Jones, Glouster, Ohio. . . . .

THIS is the residence of Joseph W. Jones at Glouster, Ohio, at present United States pension agent of Ohio and located at Columbus. He was born on a farm in Athens county, March 8, 1836, a son of David and Sarah (Dixon) Jones. His parents were natives of Pennsylvania. His father was an early settler in Athens county, and here Mr. Jones was reared to manhood and educated in district and select schools. He remained on the home farm until his twentieth year, and by the time the Civil War began he had made an encouraging start in life. In 1861 he enlisted in Company A, Sixty-third Regiment, Ohio Volunteer Infantry, commanded by Colonel John Sprague. The regiment was sent to the front and the first engagement in which Mr. Jones participated was the memorable fight at New Madrid. After that he took part in the fighting at Island No. 10, Fort Pillow, Farmington, Corinth and Iuka Springs, and in a number of less important engagements. In November, 1864, he was promoted to be second sergeant of his company, and he served in that rank until honorably discharged in 1865. He made a three-year record as a soldier.

Returning to his home Mr. Jones engaged actively in farming and dealing in live stock. After a few years he gradually drifted into the real estate business, buying and selling farms on his own account, and in time became one of the prosperous farmers in his township. He was several times elected to the office of justice of the peace by the citizens of Glouster, Ohio. In 1898 he was appointed United States pension agent at Columbus for a term of four years by President McKinley. He took up his residence in Columbus in August of the same year, and has since devoted himself conscientiously and unreservedly to the performance of the duties of his office, with such success that any pension agent in the United States might be proud of his record. As a Republican Mr. Jones has always been active and influential, and his counsel has been sought by other party leaders in local, county and State politics. He keeps alive the associations of the Civil War by membership in W. P. Johnson Post, No. 340, Grand Army of the Republic, and he is a member of Bishop Lodge, No. 470, A. F. & A. M., of Bishopville, Morgan county, Ohio.

Mr. Jones was married December 8, 1864, to Miss Martha E. Anderson, daughter of George S. Anderson, of Hocking county, Ohio, who died January 10, 1881, after having borne him seven children, named as follows: Sara E., Ella S., James S., Joseph E., Elmer L., Alice B. and Silas H., who died January 10, 1881. Mr. Jones' present wife was Miss Laura Wyatt, daughter of Jacob L. Wyatt, of Glouster, Ohio, who has borne him three children, as follows: Louise F., David W. and Dana.

. . . Residence of Mr. and Mrs. O. L. Strahl, in Canaan Township. . . .

GAY VALENTINE, No. 182,467.

ONE would travel a long way before finding a more thrifty and industrious married couple than Mr. and Mrs. O. L. Strahl, of Canaan township, a picture of whose home is here presented. They have solved the problem of how to make money out of a farm, having in their favor, however, one of the best farms in Canaan township.

Mr. Strahl was born in Salem, Iowa, September 13, 1850. He came to Ohio with his parents, John and Hannah Strahl in 1852, and has lived in this county ever since. He was first married to Miss Mary Sherrod, of Hamden, Ohio. To them was born one son, John M., who is now living in Dayton Ohio. Mrs. Strahl died in 1880, and Mr. Strahl was again married to Miss Nancy Watkins November 10, 1886, the daughter of the late Christopher Watkins, one of Athens county's substantial and highly respected citizens.

Mr. Strahl was for fifteen years a bridge carpenter on the Baltimore & Ohio railroad, but has for several years been devoting his attention to agricultural pursuits, breeding and raising grade stock, such as Short Horn cattle, Delaine sheep and Percheron horses. No common stock is kept on the place. He has long since learned that it pays to raise the best in everything. His herd of Short Horns is headed by Gay Valentine, No. 182,467, which is herewith shown along with two heifers. His stock is always in demand and finds a ready market at a high price. He is always an easy winner on stock displayed at the county fair.

Country Residence of George B. Lash, in Alexander Township.

GEORGE B. LASH, while living in the city of Athens, has a fine and picturesque country home in Alexander township, a picture of which is here shown. Mr. Lash was born near Athens in May, 1862, and is the son of Abraham

ABRAHAM LASH AND WIFE.

Lash, being of a family of six children. He is the grandson of William Lash, a native of Pennsylvania. He came, however, to Athens county, Ohio, and became one of its pioneers, whose life was subject to pioneer conditions.

He was also a soldier in the War of 1812, upon whom fell heavily the vicissitudes of that great conflict. Jacob Lash, the great grandfather of George, was a native of Germany and possessed those sterling qualities which have made the Germans famous for thrift and industry. Mr. Lash's mother was Isabell McKinstry, daughter of John McKinstry, a well-known and highly successful farmer, who believed in the possibilities of the soil when properly treated. His mother was of Scotch-Irish descent, than which there is no better blood known. The pictures of Mr. Lash's parents are given in connection with his home picture.

The subject of this sketch was married to Ella E. Carr in 1885. They have one child, Greta, nine years old, who sits in the buggy in the picture. Mr. and Mrs. Lash lived on the old home farm of the former, till September, 1904, when they moved to the A. W. Connett residence in Athens, which they had purchased. Mr. Lash is a member of the Modern Woodmen and I. O. O. F., and is withal an excellent citizen, always being found upon the side of justice and right in his relation to his friends and neighbors, on all questions of public concern.

Residence of C. A. Nice, Big Run, Ohio.

C. A. NICE, whose handsome residence is here shown, is one of the hustling young men of Athens county, and has met with considerable success in mechandizing farming, and stock raising at Big Run, Ohio. He was born March 2, 1866, and was the son of Alfred and Mary Nice. He took such education as the common schools afforded, and on December 8, 1889, he married Miss Sarah Katharyne Rowan, the daughter of Thomas and Hannah Rowan.

Two children have been born to them, Lulu May, born December 22, 1892, and Dale, born February 22, 1896. He owns a large farm in Washington county and breeds registered short horn cattle very successfully.

He opened and operated the first coal mine at Big Run, and successfully managed the same for about eight years.

Mr. Nice is an excellent citizen and a successful business man. He has a happy family and is contented.

Residence of Eli Oxley, Alexander Tp.

ELI OXLEY, the subject of this sketch, was born in Coloraine township, Belmont county, Ohio, November 6, 1833. He came to Athens county with his parents October 7, 1845, since which time he has been a resident of the county. Of his parents family, three brothers and two sisters are dead.

July 11, 1858, Mr. Oxley married Miss Mary E. Starkey, who died in January, 1900. On April 19, 1903, he married Mrs. Amanda J. Foster. Mr. Oxley is the father of four children, Winfield. R. J., Mary E. and J. V. September 12, 1862, Mr. Oxley responded to the call for troops, and enlisted in Seventh Regiment, Ohio Volunteer Cavalry. He was a gallant soldier, serving three years. He was in some of the hardest battles of the war, among them being Atlanta, Nashville, Knoxville, Columbus, Georgia, etc. The picture accompanying this is of Mr. Oxley's home near Pleasant Hill. In the corner of the picture is shown the likeness of of his father, Eli, taken from an oil painting, executed in 1820. His father was born March 17, 1797, and died February 9, 1865.

PETER HIXSON.

THE HIXSON family is one of the best known families in Athens county, and is noted for its sturdy worth and good citizenship. Peter Hixson, the father of the Hixson family under consideration, was a prominent farmer and business man, and reaped largely of his honest efforts and keen business sagacity. He was born in Bedford county, Pennsylvania, August 29, 1822, and died at his home in Ames township, November 21, 1902. He came to this county with his father, Amos Hixson when a mere lad and early started out in life without a dollar. By hard work and persistent effort he acquired seven hundred acres of good farm and mineral land and considerable personal property besides. He was a man of deep conviction and was largely identified with all matters of public concern.

Peter Hixson was married twice. His first wife was Margaret Carter, and to them were born seven children, named as follows: John, Amos, George, Daniel J., Sarah A., Hannah and Margaret. George, Sarah, Hannah and Margaret have passed to the beyond, the remainder all prosperous and are living in Athens county. They are industrious and enterprising citizens and are highly respected by their neighbors.

The accompanying illustrations show the residence and business property of Daniel J. Hixson in Amesville, the third son, who was born December 3, 1849. Growing up on the farm he was married to Miss Lucy A. Hill, daughter of Amasy Hill, April 6, 1873, with whom he lived happily until her death, May 4, 1905. Mr. and Mrs. Hixson began life together on the Sayre farm which had been given him by his father. After four years they moved to the old homestead, the Sheldon farm of two hundred acres and lived there until 1899, when they moved to Amesville. In 1903 Mr. Hixson sold his farm interests. He was in the livery business two years, and during his life, he, associated with his father, bought wool extensively. At present he is a director of the First National Bank of Amesville, and has many other business interests.

THE JOHN R. PATTERSON STORE PROPERTY.

M. A. NOYES was born in Grafton county, New Hampshire, March 2, 1834, and came with his parents, Jonathan G. and Fanny D. Noyes to Athens county, Ohio, in the fall of 1837. He was married to Caroline Byron, daughter of William and Mary Byron, at Stewart, Ohio, January 10, 1858. To this union three children were born, two daughters and one son: Mrs. Luster Clark, Mrs. Eaton Chase and William B. Noyes, who married Miss Emma Carleton, daughter of Dr. E. L. Carleton, of Coolville, Ohio.

Mr. and Mrs. Noyes are very pleasantly situated, with all their children living on farms of their own within a mile of their own home. All are connected by telephone. Mr. Noyes has never taken a single dose of medicine prescribed by a physician, and a twenty dollar bill would pay all doctor bills he ever paid out in raising his family. His general health is now good. On the 11th day of April, 1864, he with six others, James I. Caldwell, Oliver Tedrow, John Yeaer, B. Beabout, H. K. Norris and John Parsons, started from New England on the old M. & C. railroad for the gold mines in Montana. Went from Omaha, Nebraska with ox teams, arriving at Virginia City, Montana, August 9th, after being on the road about four months. He says he believes he has been at one standpoint where he could see a thousand buffaloes, near the foot hills of the Rocky Mountains. After returning to this county in 1868, he purchased the old homestead, his father having died while he was away. He was elected township clerk in 1875, and served four years. He is now, as to service, the oldest Notary Public in Athens county, having served for twenty-four years at the expiration of his present commission.

ATHENS COUNTY HISTORY
CONTINUED.

EDUCATION IN ATHENS COUNTY.
By SUPT. F. S. COULTRAP.

woodsmen after a vigorous intellectual and moral manhood that would match their physical strength. Such was the character in large measure of the people who settled Athens county.

Ames township was singularly fortunate in the prominence of its earliest inhabitants. The first family was that of George Ewing, father of Thomas Ewing, the first graduate of the Ohio university; then came Judge Ephriam Cutler followed by Sylvanus Ames, father of Bishop. R. Ames of the M. E. church and many others of like spirit and worth. Such were the men who, in 1804, established the first public circulating library west of the Alleghanys. It consisted of fifty-one volumes and formed the nucleus of the now famous "Coonskin Library." It had its name from the medium of exchange with which the first supply of books was purchased. About seventy-five volumes of this library in after years found their way into the library of the Ohio university where they still remain.

First, of course, came the private schools with teachers of little knowledge, but more or less inspired by the parents who had made their way to Athens county with much difficulty, urged on by the thought that when there their children would be entitled to all the privileges of the schools the same as the children of the rich. Rude school houses were soon constructed with large fire-places, slab benches, and oiled paper windows; the supposed incentives to study, being the head marks in spelling, the dunce block, and the famous bundle of sticks which hung on the wall near the master's desk. But there must have been other and much stronger incentives to study found in the homes in the strong men of the communities and in the real character and influence of the teachers themselves in many instances or else how can we account for so many strong men from the west in those earliest times finding their way to the councils of the nation.

The law of 1821 provided for the laying off of townships into districts and the election of three of said householders as a school committee of each of said districts.

In early times debating clubs were prominent and the school houses were the usual places of meeting. Between 1821 and 1825 school legislation was much debated in these numerous debating clubs and the chief topic of discussion was whether the state should or should not tax one man to educate the children of another, and much good is said to have come from these discussion.

In 1824-5, an act was passed by the general assembly establishing free schools in Ohio. It provided for an election of three directors in each school district, and authorized a levy

Continued on page 119.

Residence of Mrs. Winnie Gift Moore, Athens Township.

THIS beautiful country residence and farm scene is the home of Mrs. Winnie Gift Moore, about three miles south of Athens. This farm has a remarkable history, in that it was purchased from the government by Cornelius Moore when Indians were plentiful in these parts. He lived to a ripe old age, and the farm went to his son, Matthew, who died at the age of eighty-two years, and left the farm to his son, Luzern D. Moore, the husband of our subject, who died October 15, 1896, at the age of forty-one years. Thus the farm is still and always has been in the Moore family.

Mrs Moore is the daughter of J. B. and Jane Gift, and was born in Trimble, Athens county, Ohio, February 6, 1864, and when eighteen years of age she removed with her parents to near Hebbardsvile. On June 20, 1883, she was married to Luzern D. Moore.

There were six children born to them as follows: Zoah G., born September 19, 1884; Aletha E., born July 31, 1886; Clarence Lash, born April 23, 1888; Orley D., born June 30, 1890, and Elmer G. and Ralph L., twins, born in 1895 and died the same year. Clarence Lash, at the age of ten years and six months was stricken with typhoid fever and died. The death of the father in 1896 left the widowed mother with the care of the farm and four small children, a cruel fate, but she assumed the responsibility thrust upon her and successfully surmounted her difficulties, proving herself a most capable woman in every particular.

Mrs. Moore, as the picture shows, is comfortably situated, and her mother, Mrs. Gift, spends a large part of her time here.

Residence of James P. Southerton, Dover Township.

THE residence here shown is the home of James P. Southerton, one of the earliest settlers in Dover township. He was born in the Parish of Sussex, England, December 17, 1811, and came with his father's family, James Southerton, Sr., to this county in 1821, and who settled on the land near where our subject now resides. He was educated in the subscription schools of pioneer days. Mr. Southerton has helped clear two farms, and when he settled on his present farm it was in woods. He was married in June, 1836, to Elizabeth H., daughter of James Musgrave, a native of Virginia. She was born in Tyler county, Virginia, and came to Muskingum county, Ohio, with her parents in 1833, and to this county in 1835. There have been born to Mr. and Mrs. Southerton thirteen children, six of whom are yet living as follows: Sarah A., William B., Clark N., L. Horton, Hiram and Maria.

Mr. Southerton worked at the cooper trade for about forty years during the winter season and attended to his farm of two hundred and twenty-three acres of valuable land during the remainder of the year. Mrs. Southerton died at an advanced age in 1903. Mr. Southerton, who is now ninety-four years old, has become quiet feeble. The picture shown herewith was taken several years ago.

SUPERINTENDENT ALVIN DILLE.

ALVIN DILLE was born on a farm near Plantsville, Ohio, October 31, 1873, the son of Lewis C. and Louisa Dille. His father's people came from England to New England, thence to Ohio at an early period and settled on the Ohio river at a place known as "Dille's Bottoms." His mother's family came from Germany to Pennsylvania and then to Ohio in about 1802. Mr. Dille was educated in the country schools, Bartlett Academy and Ohio Northern University, graduating from the latter institution in 1895. He began teaching in 1892, and has followed that profession ever since. He has been identified with the schools of Athens county the greater part of his professional career. Was elected superintendent of Albany schools in 1903. He was married in 1902 to Miss Bertha Wickersham, of Michigan City, Indiana.

AUGUSTUS J. FRAME.

THIS Atlas would not be complete without the accompanying picture of Ex-County Auditor Augustus J. Frame, one of the best known and kindliest men in Athens county. His handsome residence on East State street is shown on page twenty of this book, where a biography of Mr. Frame will also be found.

Mr. Frame is the secretary and treasurer of the publishers of this work, and to his suggestion and valued assistance, the general excellence of the township and county maps is due. He is a loyal friend, a faithful and competent official, and a devoted husband and father.

R S. DENT was born in Belmont county, Ohio, in 1836, and is a descendant of John Dent, of Georgetown, Maryland, who was sent to Ohio as government surveyor in 1802–03, and Verlinda Beall, his wife, the daughter of Samuel Beall and Elinor Brooke, daughter of Major Thomas Brooke, of Prince George's, afterwards Frederick county, Maryland. Samuel Beall was a near relative of Colonel Ninian Beall, the great indian fighter, commander of the Provincial forces, and member of the house of Burgesses of Maryland, who emigrated from Scotland about 1655.

Mr. Dent's parents moved to Bealsville, Ohio, in 1837, where his father died nine years later, after which he lived with his uncle, G. W. Marshall, until sixteen years old, when he learned the carpenter trade, which he followed for twenty years. He married January 1, 1861, Malvina Evans, daughter of Aaron Evans, of Amesville, Ohio, and great granddaughter of Evan Evans, of Berks county, Pennsylvania, who was a Revolutionary soldier. They began housekeeping in Dover township, within one mile of Millfield, the place where they now live. They moved to Alexander township in 1864, where they lived for about twenty-three years. He was always much interested in politics and served in various minor offices being justice of the peace for nine years and assessor for several terms. He has always been a leader in church organizations wherever he has lived, and has been Sunday school superintendent for thirty years. He was superintendent of the county Infirmary for nine years, during which time the institution was greatly improved under his careful and judicious management.

In 1899 he moved to Millfield where he was engaged in the mercantile business for two years, being succeeded by his son, Evans S. Dent, and son-in-law, Louis W. Russell. He is now postmaster at that place, and also a member of the board of Infirmary directors.

He had seven children, all of whom are living, except Octa A., wife of Cyrus M. Higgins, who died in January, 1899. Sarah J, wife of Benjamin Vorhes, lives at Williams, Iowa. The third daughter, Royal D. Sprague, lives at Chauncey Ohio, and the youngest, Besse M. Russell, at Millfield, Ohio. The eldest son, Elmer A., is a graduate of the Ohio University, and also of Yale College. He received the degree of Doctor of Divinity from the Ohio University in 1902. He is now pastor of the Jefferson Street M. E. church, Hartford, Connecticut. Alva E, is a carpenter and lives on his farm near Hebbardsville, Ohio. Evans S. is the senior partner in the Dent–Russell company at Millfield, Ohio.

John Gleason's Monumental Works, Athens, Ohio.

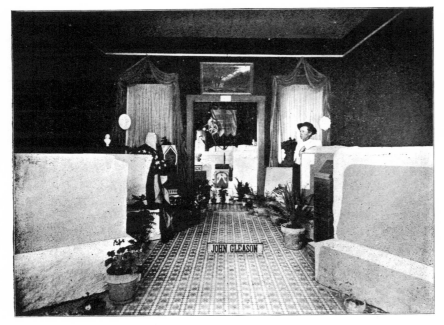

THE beautiful picture is a view of John Gleason's salesroom and a peep into his work shop on Dean Avenue in Athens, Ohio. No higher classed monuments are produced in Southern Ohio than that turned out by John Gleason, the leader in sculptural art work in this section. He is a practical man and an artist combined. He has been established in Athens over seventeen years and is continually adding to his plant and keeps abreast of the times. He is well equipped in every way to turn out elegant work, having recently installed a ten horse power engine and can supply the demands of the most exacting. No better proof can be offered for this statement than a glance at the accompanying picture, which shows a handsome line of samples of the product of his factory. His work is always the best, always the lowest, and always reliable.

Fletcher Stanton Coultrap.

FLETCHER STANTON COULTRAP, at present the efficient superintendent of Athens Public Schools, was graduated from the Ohio University in 1875 After teaching for two years at Wheelersburg, he was elected superintendent of the Nelsonville, Ohio schools and remained there until 1898, and through his efficient management, these schools were brought to a high standard. He came to Athens Public Schools in the fall of 1898, and is regarded as one of the strongest school men ever employed here. He was recently reelected as superintendent till 1907.

Mr. Coultrap is a live and energetic school man. He has done a great deal of institute work in several counties, and is now serving his eleventh appointment as county school examiner.

In 1888 he was chairman of Athens county's educational display at the Columbian Exposition. He is a member of the board of control of the Ohio Teachers Reading Circle, a board of but eight members in the State. He was a delegate to the general conference of the M E. church at Omaha in 1892, and in 1893 was appointed by Governor McKinley to take charge of the miners relief fund in the Hocking and Sunday Creek valleys, and distributed about $3600.

Residence of Mr. and Mrs. Charles S. Moore, Athens Township.

THIS neat and attractive country residence is the home of Mr. and Mrs. Charles S. Moore and family, and is located about three and one-half miles south of Athens in Athens towhship. The farm embraces ninety acres of good tillable and pasture land, and the picture indicates that Mr. Moore knows how to make the farm a success.

Our subject, is the only son of Spencer P. and Malissa Martin Moore, and was born July 31, 1872. His father died when Charles was a small child, leaving his mother with three young children to support and educate, and in this she proved her efficiency under discouraging circumstances.

Mr. Moore received a fair education by attending the country school and early in life the farm he now owns, fell to his management, so his education has been a practical one. He was married to Miss Minta Parker, the daughter of Andrew Parker, a neighbor, February 22, 1892, and to them have been born four children, two sons and two daughters, named as follows: Raymond, Herbert, Edna and Bertha, all of whom are living and are shown in the picture along with their parents.

Mr. Moore's mother makes her home with her son, but she happened to be absent at the time the picture was taken.

... Residence of Mr. and Mrs. George L. Bryson, Ames Township. ...

ARCHIBALD BRYSON, the subject of this sketch, was born in Bedford county, Pennsylvania, August 27, 1813, and came with his parents to Ames township, Athens county, Ohio, in the autumn of 1816. His father, David Bryson, a pious and industrious man procured a tract of land near the center of the township where he reared his family of six children, two sons and four daughters. Archibald, the eldest son, bore his full share of the toil and hardships necessary to clear the land and support the family. When five years old he was lost for several hours in the woods, during which time he wandered a distance of several miles. He obtained a fair education for those early times and was during his entire life a great reader, being particularly fond of historical works. He possessed an excellent memory and while always giving due respect to the opinions of others, he was unswerving in his own convictions. He was strictly honest and straightforward in all his dealings, never seeking public honor nor personal favor. In habits he was strictly temperate, abhorring the use of liquor or tobacco in any form. Physically he was strong and athletic.

When twenty-one years of age he became the owner of a good farm from his father's tract, which was a life long home for him and his faithful companion, whom he chose a year later in the person of Miss Henrietta Davis, who was born near Lake George, New York, February 15, 1814 and came with her mother and only brother to Ames township in early childhood. Her early life was fraught with hardships of the severest kind, but amidst them all she developed a character of true worth and Christian piety. She possessed a mind of rare ability and a nature of tenderest sympathy. She was an excellent reader and amidst all her domestic duties found time to acquire a good knowledge from the best of books, which together with her excellent judgment made her life of inestimable worth to both children and grandchildren.

She was married to Archibald Bryson on October 11, 1835, and they moved at once to their farm home, where for a period of nearly sixty years they lived and shared together the joys and sorrows of domestic life. They were blessed with twelve children, seven sons and five daughters. The eldest son, a teacher of bright prospects, died at the age twenty with fever. One son was accidentally killed by a falling tree; a son and a daughter died almost simultaneously with flux, and one daughter died in infancy. Of those who grew to manhood and womanhood three have since died, namely: David, John and Ida. Those still living are Maurice, George, Fanny and Jane. The latter remained at home with her parents as long as they lived, and now resides in Amesville.

Mrs. Bryson died August 1, 1895, aged eighty-one years, five months, and sixteen days. Archibald Bryson died March 27, 1902, aged eighty-eight years and seven months. The old home has since been occupied by their grandson, George L. Bryson, a model farmer, and the same spirit of generous hospitality is manifest as in days of yore.

ATHENS COUNTY HISTORY
CONTINUED.

EDUCATION IN ATHENS COUNTY.
By SUPT. F. S. COULTRAP.

of one-half mill upon the dollar to be appropriated for the use of the common schools. But no common schools entirely free can be said to have been established till after the passage of the school law of 1838.

The early custom of the teachers boarding around was not without its advantages. It did not afford favorable opportunity for study, it is true, but it gave the teacher a valuable opportunity of knowing the children and of making the acquaintance of the parents and of getting their hearty support in the accomplishment of his work.

In 1853, an act was passed authorizing a tax of one-tenth of one mill on the grand list for the purchase and sustaining of school libraries and apparatus under the direction of the commissioner of common schools. Each family was entitled to receive one book, whether or not it was represented by a child in any of the schools. The establishment of libraries in each school district soon cultivated a taste for reading which ultimately changed entirely the intellectual character of the several communities. Three years after its passage and before the wholesome effect of the school library tax law could be realized, the law was repealed, but the libraries remained in the several districts for many years and resulted in great good. An act of 1838 created the office of superintendent of common schools. It was repealed in 1840, and the secretary of state was made state superintendent. In 1853 an act was passed creating the office of state commissioner of common schools.

The famous Akron law which provided for free graded schools in Akron only was afterward amended to extend the law to any incorporated town or city contingent upon the petition of two-thirds of the qualified voters. Under this law Athens established her high school and had her first graduating class in 1858; and Nelsonville high school graduated her first class in 1878. At the present time Athens and Nelsonville have high schools of the first class; Glouster, Marshfield and Albany, high schools of the second class and Coolville, Guysville, Trimble, Stewart, Amesville and Chauncey high schools of the third class.

On March 22, 1892, an act was passed known as the Boxwell law providing for the graduation of pupils from the ungraded schools. This law in its amended form provides for the admission of said graduates into the high schools of the county free of charge, provided there is no township high school in the township to which said graduates belong, the townships being required to pay the tuition of their respective graduates who enter said high schools. This law has proven quite a stimulus

Continued on page 122.

ASA J. LINSCOTT.
S. G. LINSCOTT.
ELZA LINSCOTT.
ALBERT LINSCOTT.

WITHIN a few rods of the highest elevation in Athens county, in the northern part of Ames township, is the beautiful home of Alexander Linscott, now deceased. Mr. Linscott was born June 4, 1843, on the old homestead now owned by G. W. Linscott. On May 2, 1864, he enlisted in the Union army, and was honorably discharged September 3, 1864. He married Lucy A. South, March 18, 1866, moving at once to the farm on which he spent the remainder of his life. A man of stalwart principles, highly intelligent and industrious, he succeeded in establishing for himself the highest respect of the community. Successful as a farmer, at his death on November 11, 1895, the community realized the loss of an honored

citizen. His family consists of seven children, namely: Lola, now Mrs. T. H. Boudinott; Flora, who married P. H. Druggan, but died April 26, 1904; Edna, now the wife of Lewis W. Kasler, living near Athens. Asa married Orpha, daughter of J. H. Jones and resides in Columbus Ohio. Elza married Ninnette Mingus, and now lives in the old home.

THE LUCY LINSCOTT FARM, SHOWING THE HIGHEST POINT IN ATHENS COUNTY. ALTITUDE 1068 FEET.

Albert married Edna, daughter of Kelly Kasler, and is one of Ames townships prosperous farmers. S. G., who for some years was a teacher of Athens county and the traveling representative of the Columbus Press-Post, is now the Democratic nominee of the Ninth-Fourteenth Senatorial District for State Senator. He is an ardent Democrat, and if elected will make a capable representative in the General Assembly of Ohio.

The knoll to the rear of the barn is the highest point above sea level in Athens county. The altitude, 1068 feet was established by the United States government engineers in making the geodetic survey of this section. Only a few places in the county have an altitude of over 1000 feet.

From the point in question one can get a view as far as the eye will carry, giving an idea of grandure not surpassed in Ohio.

THE LINSCOTT FAMILY.

THE accompanying illustration is a representation of one of the large families of Athens county. Mrs. Sarah Newlin Danes Linscott, deceased, whose husband George Linscott died in 1879, was one of the early pioneers of Ames township. The mother of twelve children, nine of whom are living. She enjoyed eighty-seven years of Athens county's progress. In the picture is her family, namely: Seth, Lorenzo, Harvey, Alexander, William, Israel, George, Mrs. Nancy South, Mrs. Mary Morris, Mrs. Eliza Donaldson and Mrs. Sarah Keirns.

MRS. T. H. BOUDINOTT.   MRS. L. W. KASLER.   MRS. P. H. DRUGGAN.

Seth Linscott's Farm and Residence in Ames Township.

MR. AND MRS. LINSCOTT AND FAMILY.

THIS picturesque and prosperous looking farm scene and residence is the home of Mr. and Mrs. Seth Linscott and family in Ames township. one of the most highly respected families in that section of the county.

Mr. Linscott, our subject, is the son of George and Sarah Linscott, prominent farmers in this section in the earlier history of the county, and was born August 2, 1836. He grew to manhood leading the usual life of a boy on the farm, taking advantage of such education as those times afforded.

On January 10, 1858, he was married to Miss Susan E. Morris, who was born October 21, 1840. The Morris family was thrifty and prosperous and the union was a happy one.

To Mr. and Mrs. Linscott have been born twelve children, eight of whom are yet living. The names of the children are: George, Pearl, Harvey, Caroline, Daniel, Oliver, Nora, Adaline, Alonzo and Emmett.

Mr. Linscott has a farm of one hundred and seventy-five acres, which he handles with such skill as to produce not only a good living for his large family, but also pays returns on the investment. He has studied the soil so thoroughly that other things being equal, farming is no guess work with him.

A portion of his farm is especially adapted to producing fruit which he raises in large quantities, selecting only that quality and kind that goes on the market at a good price.

Mr. and Mrs Linscott are proud of their large family, a group picture of which is shown herewith.

. . . Residence of Mr. and Mrs. Israel J. Linscott, Ames Township. . . .

THIS beautiful rural picture shows the home and a part of the farm of Mr. and Mrs. Israel J. Linscott, in Ames township, Athen county. This farm embraces an acreage of less than a quarter section, but is regarded as one of the best tracts of land in the township, the best agricultural township in Athens county. The beautiful home with its shade trees and broad lawn, the neat and commodious barn, the well cultivated growing crops, and the character shown in the pictures of the family itself—all is indicative of thrift and frugality of these excellent people.

Mr. Linscott, our subject, was born February 7, 1850, took a common school education and grew to manhood as a farmer's boy. He was married on September 10, 1874, to Miss Georgiana Kasler, the daughter of Frederick Pember and Jane Kasler, old residents of Ames township, who died April 6, 1883, and February 20, 1871, respectively.

To Mr. and Mrs Linscott have been born two children, Ethel, now the wife of John Howard, who lives on North Lancaster street, Athens, Ohio, and Nellie, who lives with her parents. Both of the daughters, together with Mr. and Mrs. Howard's little son, Arthur M., are also shown in the illustration.

Along with a general agricultural business, Mr. Linscott has given quite a little attention to horticulture and stock raising, both of which branches he has made quite remunerative.

THE STEWART MILL SITE.

THE OLD STEWART MILL, EAST OF ATHENS.

We here present in miniature a picture of the will-known Stewart Mills, east of Athens, now owned and operated by Otto Barth. This was for many years early in the last century, the business centre of Athens. Here it was that the first postoffice was established. We give it space more as a pretty picture than for historical illustration, as the building, compared with the mill site is modern.

Another familiar land mark is herewith shown. It is the "Old South Bridge," one mile farther up the river from the mill. On account of the dam at the mill, there is a good stage of water for boating, and Naptha launches have

THE OLD SOUTH BRIDGE, NEAR ATHENS.

been run successfully on this reach. The bridge is of the old type of wooden structures and served its purpose in days gone by, but a modern steel structure will take its place before many years, and this excellent half-tone picture of the bridge will be regarded with more than passing interest.

In 1881 a colored man was hung from the north end of this bridge by a mob of citizens of the county, supposed to be from Albany where the victim committed his crime.

A. B. ALLEN, M. D., was born at Bellville, Kansas, on February 22, 1874. While just a small child his parents moved to Ohio and settled at the forks of Sunday Creek, then known as Allen's Store Postoffice. Was raised on the farm till about twelve years of age, when he started as clerk in a general store owned by Collison Bros., and spent about a year with this company; then changed to the store of Joe Worden, where he spent several months; then returned to school, and when sixteen years of age finished his course in the Glouster High School, being a member of the first graduating class from the Glouster High School. After graduating he served as assistant postmaster for one year, at which time he began to study medicine under Dr. A. J. Crawford. Attended lectures at the College of Physicians and Surgeons, Baltimore, Maryland, for three winters, graduating in the spring of 1895. He then returned to Glouster, Ohio, and entered into partnership with his former preceptor, Dr. Crawford, remaining with him till August 1, 1904. They then dissolved partnership, Dr. Allen starting in by himself, but remained only till October, 1905, when it became necessary for him to have help. Dr. James G. Blower then joined him, forming a partnership of Drs. Allen & Blower.

On the first day of April, 1896, he was united in marriage to Miss Gweune Thea Williams, of Glouster, Ohio. To them have been born two children: Dorotha A., eight years old and Harold Russell, six years old.

Dr. Allen is well equipped, both physically and educationally to achieve the success in the general practice of medicine that has been his. Whole souled and cordial, he at once wins the kindly feelings of his patients and establishes a confidence in his ability, that is necessary and highly desirable. Dr. Allen recently organized a stock company for the establishment of a hospital for Glouster, an institution that is very much needed for Glouster and and neighboring towns and villages, and at this writing the hospital proposition give evidence of success.

Residence of Mr. and Mrs. Jas. A. Palmer, Athens, Ohio.

THIS elegant residence is the home of Mr. and Mrs. James A. Palmer, on North College street, Athens, Ohio. Mr. Palmer was the son of John and Lydia Dutton Palmer, and was born in June, 1850, in Palmer township, Washington county, Ohio.

On October 12, 1887, he was united in marriage to Miss Emma R. Roach, the daughter of Alonzo L. and Maria Childs Roach, one of Athens most popular young women. They have three children, all growing into young manhood and womanhood. Miss Edith, the eldest, graduated from the Athens high school in the spring of 1905, and is now a student in the Ohio University; J. Alonzo and Horace D. are active boys attending the public schools and assisting their father who conducts small dairy business. Mr. and Mrs. Palmer are faithful members of the Methodist Episcopal church and a Christian atmosphere pervades their home. Mr. Palmer is an enthusiastic Mason and is identified with all the several bodies of York rite Masonry, from the "Blue Lodge" to Knights Templar. He is also a member of Coolville Lodge, No. 527, I. O. O. F.

ATHENS COUNTY HISTORY
CONTINUED.

EDUCATION IN ATHENS COUNTY.

By SUPT. F. S. COULTRAP.

to the work in the ungraded schools as shown by the fact that during the thirteen years the law has been in operation about seven hundred pupils have been graduated and advanced to the high schools of the county. The law enacted establishing township boards of education in place of the local directors for the employment of teachers and the act passed April 25, 1904, limiting said boards to five members would seem to be wise, but grave apprehensions are felt in many places that it may not bring the best results the tendency so far seeming

to be to pay all teachers the same salary regardless of the wide difference often in culture training experience and efficiency of said teachers.

Steps looking toward partial centralization in some parts of the county under the act passed April 25, 1904, give promise of much good. Complete centralization of the ungraded schools at the present time is not practical because of the bad roads in many parts of the county, but partial centralization by suspension of some of the sub-district schools is practical where the enumeration is small, the cost of conveying the pupils to an adjoining district being but a small fraction of the expense necessary to maintain a separate school.

The teaching force of the county has improved much in methods and efficiency during the past four years, due in large measure to the numerous reading circles formed in the county. The object of these circles was to secure systematic reading and study of the O. T. R. C. books recommended by the state board of control. The average enrollment in these circles for

the past four years is 520, thus making Athens county the banner county of the state in the O. T. R. C. work.

By far the most important event in the progress of the schools of the county was the passage of the Sease bill establishing two normal schools in the state, one of which was located in Athens. The Athens county teachers were quick to avail themselves of the many advantages of this normal school of the Ohio university and the schools of the county are reaping the benefits due to the "broader scholarship," higher culture and better training of her teachers.

The hope is entertained that ere long the normal college will so transform public sentiment that none but thoroughly trained teachers will be entrusted with the education of the youth of the county, and thus we look to the near future for the comprehensive system of schools which will be adequate to the needs of the schools of the county and worthy of the age in which we live.

ATHEN'S : COUNTY'S : THREE : CENTENARIANS.

MARGARET TWADDLE READINGHOUSE, whose picture accompanies this sketch, was born in Jefferson county, Ohio, Mar. 10, 1805, where she lived till womanhood. April 2, 1828, she was married to David Readinghouse, and in 1857 they came to Athens county, locating in the village of Jerseyville. To Mr. and Mrs. Readinghouse one child was born, Mary A., who became the wife of

MARGARET TWADDLE READINGHOUSE.

Freeman Marshall. Mr. Readinghouse died in 1886, his aged wife continuing to live in Jerseyville till 1896, when she made her home with her daughter, Mrs. Marshall, where she still resides. Her one hundreth anniversary was appropriately celebrated by a large gathering of relatives and friends. The picture shown herewith was taken June 6, 1905. Mrs. Readinghouse has never had a week's sickness in her life, notwithstanding she is the oldest person in the county, and one of the oldest in the State.

MARY MARGARET McLAIN, was born near Pt. Pleasant, West Virginia, on Old Town Creek, June 10, 1805, and is therefore over one hundred years old. In her seventeenth year she was married to Henry Board, of Pennsylvania. Two children were born to them, but after six years of married life Mr. Board died and his widow returned to her home near Ripley, West Virginia.

In 1832 she was married to I. N. De-Wees, and to them

MARY MARGARET McLAIN.

were born seven children, five sons and two daughters, three of these sons were veterans of the Civil War.

Mrs. DeWees is active, both mentally and physically, and drove to Athens a short time ago with her son, M. M. DeWees. She has a pipe that is said to have belonged to old Black Hawk. It is made of red rock and has five large silver bands around it. It is over one hundred years old.

JANE MEANS (nee Cubbinson), was born in Washington Co., Pennsylvania, July 15, 1805, making her one hundred years old July 15, 1905. She was married to Andrew Means at an early age, and came to this State, locating in Muskingum county when she was about 54 years of age. She remained in Muskingum about eighteen years, when she came to this coun-

JANE MEANS.

ty and located in the neighborhood where she now lives. She was the mother of five children, two of whom are living, Mrs. Louise Phillips, with whom she lives, and James Means, a resident of Ross county. Five generations are represented in the various families of this remarkable old lady, who walks about with apparent ease, goes up stairs and down unattended, in short, is as active in every way as many people are an ordinary life time younger. She is still in good health.

Prof. Dafydd Joshua Evans.

PROF. DAFYDD JOSHUA EVANS was born in 1846, on a farm near Oak Hill, Jackson county, Ohio, of Welsh parentage. Until his eighteenth year Prof. Evans worked on the farm and attended the district school. In his eighteenth year he began teaching, and after teaching two winters, six months each, he entered the Ohio University, matriculating March 26, 1866 and graduated in the classical course in 1871.

His boyhood home had good substantial Welsh books, some of which were excellent translations (translated and published by his uncle) of standard Biblical and Theological English works, which Dafydd read more than once. From his graduation in 1871 to 1873, Prof. Evans was in public school work as superintendent; since 1873 he has been in college work, having occupied the chair of Latin in Ohio University since 1882.

In 1872 he married Lydia Margaret Lash, daughter of Jacob and Susan Morrison Lash. To them four children were born, the eldest son, William M. died in his twentieth year. The second, Jacob Claire, is a chemist in Denver, Colorado; the third, Rhys Dafydd, is a student in the Ohio University. Their only daughter, Margaret Lucile, is the wife of Arther Howe Carpenter, mettallurgist in Denver, Colorado, to whom two children were born, Franklin Dafydd and Margaret Annette.

PICTURESQUE CLIFFS ON NORTH HILL, ATHENS, OHIO.

Residence of Adam Niggemeyer.

Residence of William H. Katzenbach in York Township.

THIS comfortable residence is the home of Wm. H. and Sadie Katzenbach, near the famous Elm Rock, shown elsewhere in this work, and is located opposite Green Lawn cemetery, the burial ground of the city of Nelsonville.

Mr. Katzenbach is the son of Jacob Katzenbach, and is an enterprising and industrious citizen.

THE accompanying cut represents the mining property of Jacob F. Schuler, Sharpsburg, Ohio, the best equipped mine in that section of the county. Mr. Schuler began to operate this property on a small scale several years ago. He has an eight or nine foot vein of excellent coal, and at first supplied only the local trade, but he increased his equipment and went into the wholesale and retail trade and established a coal office and yard in Marietta, which is to-day handling all the coal it can get, the business being handicapped at times by a lack of cars on the railroad.

The mine is equipped with electrical machines of the latest and most improved patterns, and every facility is provided for mining coal in large quantities in the most economical manner. Mr. Schuler also maintains a general store, a picture of the interior of which is also shown herewith. He is ably assisted in the management of

INTERIOR OF JACOB SCHULER'S STORE.

both his store and mine by his children now grown to manhood and womanhood.

Mr. Schuler has been remarkably successful since he went to Sharpsburg. When he moved there about ten years ago he had but nineteen dollars and a large family to support. By industry and close attention to business, and by careful management, he has built up a large business, and to-day possibly could show assets of a thousand dollars for every cent he had when he began business. His success came by no royal road. The opportunity and the man met, and he had sufficient forsight to grasp the situation. A disposition to do hard work brought the reward he has so thoroughly merited. Not alone has he toiled, for every member of his family has assumed their part of the work and responsibility. They are a help at all times, and the united work of all has merited the success they have achieved.

He has been a coal miner and farmer, but took up photography about twenty-one years ago and has had splendid success. He maintains an art gallery in Stewart where he has a flourishing trade. He has gone about the country doing view work and has in his collection, some rare bits of artistic scenery.

Residence of M. M. DeWeese, Carthage Township

Residence of B. F. Swope, Glouster, Ohio.

THE cozy residence shown in the illustration is the home of M. M. DeWeese, in Carthage township. It is a picture of home and contentment. The old lady shown in the picture is Mrs. Mary Margaret McLain, who celebrated her one hundredth anniversary on June 10, 1905, and whose cabinet half-tone and biography will be found on page 123 of this book along with two other Athens county centenarians. Mr. DeWeese, our subject was born at Ripley Jc., W. Va., in 1853. He left home to seek his fortune at the early age of fourteen.

JOHNSON M. WELCH.

JOHNSON M. WELCH, a lawyer and a Major in the war of the rebellion, is a native of Athens county. His father was the late John Welch who was for thirteen years, on the Supreme bench of Ohio. He was born April 20, 1832, and at an early age matriculated at the Ohio University. Leaving the institution at the age of nineteen, he began the study of the law under the tuition of his father, when he was appointed to a clerical position in the Interior Department at Washington. Ill health compelled his retirement from that position and he spent several months in travel, recruiting his health.

In 1856-7 he was ingaged in mercantile pursuits in Athens, but, resuming the study of the law he completed his course and was admitted to practice in 1858. He was thus engaged until the breaking out of the war.

In July, 1861, he recruited Company C, 18th Ohio Infantry. His regiment was attached to the Army of the Cumberland. He served as Captain, with credit, until his promotion to a Majority, June 1863.

During Major Welch's time of service he was largely employed on staff duty. He participated in most of the battles of his department, including Stone River and Chickamauga At Stone River he received a severe shell wound in his left leg. During the winter and spring of 1864, he commanded his regiment. He

filled the arduous position of Provost Marshal of Chattanooga, and discharged the muitifarious duties of that office with signal ability.

On his return from the army he resumed the practice of law, and on the retirement of his father from the Supreme bench, formed a law partnership with him, the firm of Welch & Welch being well and favorably known.

Of late years he has become largely interested in the mineral lands of southeastern Ohio, and he has conducted, with success, operations of great magnitude.

While holding pronounced views upon all the political questions of the day, Major Welch has never en-

tered actively, into politics, being content to preserve in the community simply the relations of a skillful lawyer and an enterprising business man.

In civil and military life he is distinguished for his great tact and administrative ability, which have enabled him to conceive great projects and carry them through to a successful conclusion.

For many years he was Vice President of the First National Bank of Athens, and President of the Athens Gas Light Company.

Major Welch was married, in 1853, to Adaline Carpenter. She died in 1866 and in 1870 he married Ella Cadwallader, of Marietta.

. . . . . . Mr. Cyrus Rose and Father, Matthew Rose . . . . . .

MATTHEW ROSE

WE here present the pictures of Matthew Rose and his son, the late Cyrus Rose, whose lives were identified with Athens for many years. Matthew was born in Canada, October 7, 1807, and died at Boscobel, Wisconsin, in July of 1904. In early boyhood he moved to New York and in 1835 came to Athens. For a time he lived at Coolville, then returned to Canada and back to Ohio. He served through the Mexican war, and returning from the service, located at Cleveland. After some years he moved to Wisconsin. He married Lydia Mott Dewey, of Montpelier Vermont, in Canada, in 1840. She was born February 11, 1811, and died October 30, 1901, in Marietta, Ohio. Cyrus Rose was born in Watertown, New York, February 4, 1831, and came to Athens when about four years of age. He learned the harness trade in Marietta and attended College at Delaware. He married Cornelia S. Reed, of Reedsville, Ohio, September 20, 1853, and located in Athens the following year, where he followed his trade for over half a century. To Mr. and Mrs. Rose were born eleven children, four of whom are living, as follows: Edward T., Maria Bell—now Mrs. W. B. Lawrence, Frank, Cyrus and Fannie E., now Mrs. J. E. Snow.

Mr. Rose was a licensed local preacher and member of the Methodist Episcopal church. He was a christian man in all the word implies, carrying his religion into his business and daily walk and conversation. An excellent citizen and highly respected, he went down to the grave loved and honored by all classes of people.

CYRUS ROSE

WILLIAM Elsworth Day, was born in Carthage Township, Athens County, Ohio, October 29, 1861, is a son of William and Sarah Blazer Day, of Lodi Township, Athens County, Ohio. He was married to Cora C. Southerton, of Dover Township, Athens County, Ohio, May 17, 1882. To this union were born three children; Charles W. now a successful clothing merchant of Athens; James S. one of the leading farmers of Carthage Township, and the youngest, Pearl E. still with his parents.

MR. AND MRS. WILLIAM E. DAY

Mr. Day has followed agricultural pursuits the greater part of his life and still owns an excellent farm in his home township. About nine years ago, he purchased property in Athens, a picture of which is shown on this page. Since his removal to Athens he has been engaged in various real estate transactions. By careful management and frugal living he has accumulated considerable wealth.

Cora C. Southerton Day, wife of William E. Day, was born in Dover Township, Athens County Ohio, February 7, 1864. She is the daughter of Charles W. and Lydia Deshler Southerton of Dover Township, Athens County Ohio.

RESIDENCE OF MR AND MRS. W. E. DAY

RESIDENCE OF MR. AND MRS. WILLIAM DAY.

WILLIAM Day, father of W. E. Day, war born in Lodi Township, Athens County, Ohio April 26, 1838, and was married to Sarah A. Blazer, May 13, 1858. He with his family removed to Carthage Township, where he engaged in a general farming business, devoting much of his time to the raising of sheep and cattle. August 27, 1864, he enlisted in the One-hundred and Seventy-fourth Ohio Volunteer Infantry, and served his country faithfully until discharged, June 28, 1865: He was a member of the A. F. & A. M. Fraternity, at Coolville. He died at the old farm house, November 9, 1896. Sarah Blazer Day wife of William Day, daughter of George and Susan Moore Blazer, was born in Lodi Township, Athens County Ohio, May 9, 1840.

The pictures of Mr. and Mrs. Day and their home are shown on this page.

THE DAY HOMESTEAD, IN DOVER,

CHARLES W. Southerton was born on the old homestead, in Dover Township, May 22, 1831 and was married to Lydia A. Deshler, December 9, 1857.

Mr. Southerton died in his native Township, May 1, 1894, from the effects of injuries received by his team running away on his farm.

Mrs. Southerton died at the old home Aug. 27, 1896.

The residence of Mr. and Mrs. Southerton together with their photographs are shown herewith.

The old Day homestead in Dover Township, where Mr. and Mrs. W. E. Day began life together, is also shown herewith.

RESIDENCE OF MR. AND MRS. CHARLES W. SOUTHERTON.

=RESIDENCE OF C. L. POSTON, ATHENS, OHIO.=

CLINTON L. POSTON, son of Lorenzo D. and Lucinda M. Parkinson Poston, was born at Nelsonville, November 19th, 1847. At the proper age, he began attendance at the public schools of that place and, at an early age, during the summer months, he began to take an active interest in his father's business, buying stock for the farms, helping in the store and office and about the coal mines, thus acquiring knowledge of business and habits of industry.

Beginning with 1867, he attended the Ohio University, after which he took charge of his father's store, selling goods on commission until, in the year 1873, he became one of the active purchasers of his father's entire active business, under the firm name of Poston Brothers. This business was conducted until September of 1881, at which time his brothers sold their interests to McClintick and Smith, lawyers and fine business men, of Chillicothe, Ohio. This partnership was continued, under the firm name of C. L. Poston & Co., until 1893, at which time Mr. Poston purchased from his partners their entire interests in the business. After this, new mines on lands which had been acquired by purchase and lease, were opened near Nelsonville and the business was continued by C. L. Poston until September 1st, 1902, at which time the entire mining property, excepting the coal in the lands which is retained on a royalty basis, was sold to J. P. Morgan syndicate, which sale included houses, railroad tracks, tipples, and all the electrical mining machinery

C. L. POSTON.

and appliances necessary for the operation of the mines, also a large general store, a large ice plant and cold storage, and a meat plant for both wholesale and retail business, in all aggregating a business of about half a million dollars a year.

Having greatest faith in the mineral wealth of the Hocking Valley, Mr. Poston was not slow to seize upon every opportunity to invest in coal properties and found time to purchase, sell and become the lessor of perhaps more coal lands than any other man in the Hocking Valley.

His active operations now in the production of coal are in the Pittsburg seam, known as No. 8 coal, in Jefferson County, Ohio, where, with Calvary Morris, of Cleveland, Ohio, they are the owners of 3800 acres of that unexcelled steam coal. These mines, under the active management of his son, L. D. Poston and son-in-law,

T. R. Biddle, are producing a large tonnage daily.

Mr. Poston is member of the board of directors of The Sunday Creek Company organized in 1905, which is the second largest coal company in the world. The Sunday Creek Company absorbed five large coal companies in the Hocking and Sunday Creek valleys in Ohio and in the Kanawha valley in West Virginia. This company is now oprating sixty large mining properties, thirty-three in the Hocking and Sunday Creek valleys and twenty-seven in West Virginia.

October 28th, 1869, C. L. Poston was married to Delia Kessinger, daughter of Joseph L. and Mary E. Jewett Kessinger. They have one son and one daughter, both living. Lorenzo Dow Poston and Grace M., wife of Dr. T. R. Biddle.

‖ LORENZO D. POSTON. ‖

LORENZO D. POSTON was born in Hampshire county, Virginia, March 29th, 1812, and came to Athens county, Ohio, in September, 1830. For about two years after arriving he worked out by the month, then engaged in buying and selling live stock until October, 1833, when he settled in Nelsonville in the mercantile business. The letter of credit on which he purchased his first stock of goods was given him by J. N. and J. H. Norton and Ezra and William Stewart, of Athens. Soon after the completion of the Hocking Canal, a branch of the Ohio Canal from Carroll, Ohio, to Athens, Ohio, 1842, he engaged in the coal business and was one of the pioneer operators in the development of that great industry, which, as he alway predicted, would become the greatest in the state. In this business, in which he had great agricultural and mercantile interests, he continued until 1873, at which date, by a sale of the property

LORENZO D. POSTON.

and a lease of the mines, he turned over to his sons, William W. and Clinton L. and his son-in-law, E. P. Pendleton, his coal mining and mercantile business. He was a man of great energy, strict integrity, fine business capacity and an excellent citizen; and was exceptionally successful in all his undertakings. His death occurred December 16th, 1875, and he left a large estate which was divided among six sons and one daughter.

History of Daniel Fleming and Family, Ames Township

DANIEL FLEMING was born in Athens county, near Bishopville, October 22, 1822. He is a son of John and Christina Fleming. John Fleming was born in Germany in 1777, and came to the United States and settled in New York at the age of fifteen.

In 1819 he came to Ohio, having purchased an interest in the Ohio Land Company's grant. Being possessed of considerable means, he contributed liberally in the upbuilding of the country. Knowing of the scarcity of money in the west, he brought several hundred dollars in silver, mostly of the denomination of one dollar, which were carefully divided in half or quartered, as the case demanded, in making change.

After remaining in Ohio six years, he returned to New York City, taking his family with him. John Fleming died there in 1841, and his wife, Christina (Smith) Fleming, died in Ames township in 1863.

Our subject attended the public and private schools of New York until about seventeen years of age, when he secured work on a sailing vessel plying between New York and New Orleans, making several trips between those points. Becoming acquainted with the engineers of the "New York and Harlem" Railway, then being built by George Law, one of the few millionaries of that day, he engaged as fireman on one of their crude, but at that time wonderful engines. He was afterwards sent to the "Mohawk and Hudson" Railway, which connected Schenectady and Albany. In this postion he was an engineer and ran the "John Bull," an engine which was built in England, and which was exhibited at the Columbian Exposition held at Chicago in 1893. He was also employed on the steam vessel "Oregon," which, owing to her size and the fact that she was propelled by steam, was an object of much curiosity.

In 1845, Mr. Fleming returned to Ohio and the

RESIDENCE OF MR. AND MRS. DANIEL FLEMING

scenes of his childhood, and purchased a farm of fifty acres; he was married May 16, 1846, to Lucy P. Gardner, daughter of Thomas and Margaret (Smith) Gardner.

Thirteen children were born to them, seven of which survive—Joseph, William, John, Theodore, Lincoln, Julia and Edith.

: : : : Residence of Mrs. and Mrs. Joseph C. Fleming, Stockport, Ohio : : : :

Mr. Fleming has all his life been a very active man, and has accumulated considerable of this world's goods—in fact he is possessed of more wealth than any other person in Ames township. His business, that of stock dealer and wool buyer, has given him a large circle of acquaintances.

For more than forty continuous years he has been a Trustee of Ames township, and in the administration of its affairs, uses the same careful judgment today that has brought him success in private life.

Mr. Fleming is in his eighty-third year but gives his personal attention to all his business affairs and directs them with the sound judgment of a man two score years younger.

In 1896 Mr. and Mrs. Fleming celebrated their fiftieth wedding anniversary. There were present at that time a host of relatives who came to join hands with this elderly couple and wish them many more years of happy wedded life.

Mr. and Mrs. Fleming are enjoying a comfortable old age and while the former is as active both physically and mentally, as he was a score of years ago, Mrs. Fleming is afflicted as to locomotion, but is otherwise in very good health.

The handsome residence here shown is the home of the eldest son, Joseph C. Fleming, near Stockport, Morgan county, Ohio. The home is indicative of the prosperity that he enjoys through his own efforts and frugal living. He was married to Miss Julia Carpenter, the daughter of Mr. and Mrs. Lewis Carpenter. Their home has been blessed with two children.

Residence of Mr. and Mrs. Lon Minx, Kissimmee, Florida.

AWAY in the southland, where nature blossoms and blooms the year around, and winter is comparatively unknown, is the beautiful and comfortable home of a daughter of Mr. and Mrs Daniel Fleming, Mrs. Julia Flemming Minx, who was born December 26, 1854 at the old homestead, and was married to Lon A. Minx December 18, 1879. Their home which is shown in the accompanying illustration, is located at Kissimmee, Florida, where Mr. Minx is engaged in the practice of law, and has the management of extensive orange groves, which is one of the leading industries of the peninsula state.

Mr. and Mrs. Minx have three children, and in this mild climate life is easier than in the north where nature does not work so assiduously for man, who has to supply with strenuous activity what nature fails to produce.

The house setting up on small pillars, the small single chimney, and the luxuriant growth of shrubbery, would indicate to the careful observer that this is a picture of a place where rigorous cold winds and snow covered ground are not known.

Residence of Mr. and Mrs. Theodore Fleming, near Amesville.

ABOUT one mile north of Amesville is located the commodious farm residence shown in the accompanying illustration, the home of Theodore M. Fleming a son of Mr. and Mrs. Daniel Fleming. The subject of our sketch was born at the old Fleming homestead in Ames township, April 17, 1858. He grew up as a farmer's boy, and early engaged as a practical agriculturalist. Farming and stock raising is so familiar to him as to have become a second nature. He studies the various soils he

has to deal with and knows for what it is best adapted. He breeds good stock which commands good prices in the markets and is, withal a successful man and is comfortably situated.

Mr. Fleming was married to Miss Marcella Woodyard, daughter of Mr. and Mrs. Nathan Woodyard, on June 19, 1881. Mrs. Fleming was born in Morgan county October 27, 1858. They have four children living: Nellie, William D., Theodore, Jr., and Cora, two having died in infancy.

ATHENS COUNTY HISTORY
CONTINUED.

THE SALT INTEREST ONCE OF ATHENS COUNTY, OHIO

BY F. M. CHASE, CINCINNATI

I gladly contribute my allotted portion of the work, necessary to place before the people of Athens county, a complete history of the same, going back to the formation of the state, and ending with 1905—a round one hundred years.

In writing of the salt interest of this county, I must depend somewhat on my personal experience in this line of business, as well as on such information as I have obtained from others, whose knowledge far antedates that of my own.

The first salt furnace in this county was built by Resolved Fuller, Senior, 1838-40, on the site, so long known as the Ewing-Vinton & Co. Works, a small affair, using wood as fuel and do-

F. M. CHASE

ing for the time, only a local business. In 1842, this furnace was leased by Calvary Morris and Norman Root—Morris & Root—who sold out their lease to Ewing, Vinton & Co., in 1844, and

Continued.

WE here present an excellent picture of the home and premises of one of Ames township's most successful farmers and stock raisers, Mr. John T. Fleming, another son of Samuel and Lucy Fleming. Thrift, industry and frugality can be read in every feature of this illustration. The picture tells the story of success of this stalwart citizen better than words.

Mr. Fleming was born June 17, 1856, and was married December 17, 1879 to Flora A. Linscott, the daughter of George S. and Mary Owen Linscott, one of the prominent families of Ames township. They have four children, who together with Mr. and Mrs. Fleming are shown in the picture.

Mr. Fleming does a general farming business and conducts it with such skill that he realizes largely on his investment. He has done much for the county in importing and breeding high bred draft horses. thus introducing and fostering a class of horses that make good farm animals and beside command a high price in the markets of the world. One of his best horses is shown in the corner of the picture.

Residence of Mr. and Mrs. G. Lincoln Fleming, Ames Township

THE residence here shown is the home of G. Lincoln Fleming, the youngest son of Daniel and Lucy Fleming, who lives on Ewing Run near the old homestead where he was born August 23d, 1861. He was married to Miss Ella E. James, the daughter of Mr. and Mrs. Samuel James, on October 26, 1886. Four children have been born to them: Florence, Bertie, Fanny and Effie, three of whom are living.

Mr. Fleming, like his brothers, has made a success of agricultural pursuits. He has traveled over this country quite a little, having been through the west in 1884, through the south to southern Florida in 1899, and through the north-west to Seattle in 1903. He is an enthusiastic member of the Masonic lodge at Amesville and is withal a public spirited and useful citizen.

at which time the furnace, and one thousand acres of land adjoining was bought by last named firm. This was in 1845. The firm of Ewing, Vinton & Co,. was composed of Thos. Ewing of Lancaster, the first graduate of the Ohio university as I have always understood ; Samuel F. Vinton of Gallipolis, and for thirty years congressman from the Athens, Meigs and Gallia district; Nicholas Biddle of Philadelphia, former president of the Bank of the United States, and Elihu Chauncey, a capitalist of the same city, and for whom the town of Chauncey was named. This firm made extensive improvements, in the way of building additional and larger furnaces, putting down a shaft 106 feet to a 6 foot vein of coal, building the large hotel still standing in the village ; and in many other ways did they contribute to the prosperity of that vicinity and surrounding neighborhood. In the year 1852, they leased the furnaces to Chas. R. Smith, and his brother-in-law, John Haming. Later on, possibly in 1855, Mr. Smith retired and left all in the hands of Mr. Haming who remained in the business until 1856, when the writer took possession by lease from Thos. Ewing, who, by this time, had full ownership of the property. I continued manufacturing salt in connection with other business, until April, 1863, when I sold out my remaining stock of goods to Mr. Ewing, and was succeeded by Col. F. Steele, his son-in-law. By this time salt was being made in Syracuse, New York, and in Michigan, at much less expense than at Chauncey, and Mr. Ewing decided to change the old order of manufacturing by abandoning the open kettle for that of evaporation in large vats. This change involved heavy expense, but was only a temporary success, and in about the year 1878 or '80, all was abandoned, and now a few piles of debris is all that marks the once busy place.

In 1845, Samuel B. Pruden of Harmony built two furnaces, directly across Hocking river from the place just described. This venture was a success for years, and was constantly in operation until about 1875, when it was abandoned by his son Charles Pruden, who had carried on the works several years after his father's death.

In 1845, James Fuller and A. B. Walker of Athens, built two furnaces at what is now known as Beaumont—then Tyler. This venture was a great success in the hands of Fuller & Walker, until they sold out to M. M. Greene and his half-brother, Geo. T. Gould, in about 1859. The firm of M. M. Greene & Co. was in active operation until the year 1870, when Mr. Greene, being elected president of the Hocking Valley Railroad, withdrew, leaving all in the hands of Mr. Gould.

A very disastrous flood in Hocking in 1873 caused the loss of many thousand barrels of salt, and the coal shaft was filled with water, requiring constant pumping for near six months before any business could be done in the mines, and, of course, a complete stagnation of all business for the time. In about 1882, all work here was suspended, and now, the once busy place, is as dead as night.

Continued

Residence of Mr. and Mrs. James Linscott, near Canaanville, Ohio.

THIS beautiful residence is the home of the youngest daughter of Daniel and Lucy Fleming—Marcie Fleming Linscott, the wife of James A. Linscott. and is located near Canaanville.

Mr. Linscott was born in Ames township, October 4th, 1867, and is the second son of the late G. S. and Mary Owens Linscott. His youth was spent in working on the farm and attending school. He remained with his parents until he grew to manhood. After his father's death in 1885, he came to Canaanville and purchased 315 acres of land where he and his wife now reside. There has been added to the original tract 145, making in all a farm of 560 acres, underlaid with good coal and for agricultural purposes one of the best farms along the Hocking.

Mr. and Mrs. Linscott were married October 31st, 1888. Beside the large farm spoken of, they have real estate and other interests in Athens, Ohio. They are industrious and frugal citizens and lend their influence for good in every public matter.

The have no children.

THE DANIEL FLEMING FAMILY.

MR. AND MRS. JAMES LINSCOTT.

Residence and General Store of William Fleming, Federal, Ohio.

THE picture herewith shows the residence and general store of the second son of Daniel and Lucy Fleming—Wm. Fleming, who is located on a farm at Federal and conducts a general merchandising business. He was born in Ames township, January 7th, 1849, and growing to manhood on the farm, he was married to Miss Jane Smith the daughter of Mr. and Mrs. Edmund A. Smith on September 7th, 1871. They have four children living. Along with the general store he conducts a farming interest of considerable magnitude.

Residence of George W. Linscott's in Ames Township.

THE OLD LINSCOTT HOMESTEAD

G. W. LINSCOTT, whose home is here represented, owns and resides upon the old Linscott Homestead in Ames Township. He was born June 28, 1854. On September 6, 1874, he married Nancy James. Of this union there were five children, viz.: Jesse, accidentally killed some years ago, was a young man of sterling qualities and bright prospects; Lena, now the wife of George Anderson: Carl, living at home; Lucy, who died in 1892, and an infant daughter who died at same time. Mrs. Linscott died November 30, 1892, being the third death in the family within a few days.

Mr. Linscott was again married to Nancy Koons, August 23, 1893. Of this union there is one child, viz: Homer.

Mr. Linscott is a breeder of fine Short Horn Cattle, having some of the finest specimens in Ohio. Herewith is shown two of his herd:

Little Lady—registered, volume 54, American Short Horn Registers' Association. Also Duchess of Ames, recorded in same volume.

Mr. Linscott represents everything that is progressive in farming and stock raising. Like many other successful farmers, he has learned that it pays to raise the best, whether it be cereal, stock or fruit. He combines his long time experience in all these lines with a liberal education on the subjects gained by reading agricultural, horticultural and stock journals, thus getting the benefit of the experience of others. He studies the nature of the soil he has to deal with and knows what kind of soil will produce the best kind of crops. With all this, it is needless to add that he has made a success of his business and is comfortably situated.

GRANDMOTHER LINSCOTT

✤ ✤ ✤ ✤ ✤ ✤ ✤ ✤ ✤

Shown in connection with the old homestead is the mother of one of the largest and most progressive families of Athens county. Sarah Newlin Danes-Linscott wife of George Linscott, Sr., was born June 11, 1818, on Wills Creek, Gurnsey county, Ohio. She married George Linscott October 26, 1834. George Linscott died April 19, 1879. Of this family eleven lived to maturity, all of whom became prosperous, and have also reared large families. On June 5, 1905, at the ripe age of eighty-seven years, Grandmother died. Nine children, sixty-five grand children and ninety great-grand children survive her.

✤ ✤ ✤ ✤ ✤ ✤ ✤ ✤ ✤

. . . Residence of Mr. and Mrs. Harvey Linscott, Ames Township. . . .

HARVEY LINSCOTT was born November 29, 1840. In 1866 he married Ellen, daughter of Frederick and Jane Kasler. Of this union there were five children, viz.: Edward, Olive, Etta, Arza and Fred. Mrs. Linscott died about twenty years ago. He was married again to Pearl Wolfe, of Zaleski, October 26, 1886. There were two children of this union, viz.: Harlan and Marie. Mr. Linscott lives on the Aaron Evans farm, in the northern part of Ames township, and is a successful farmer, stock raiser and fruit grower.

On July 4, 1861, at Wrightsville, Morgan county, Ohio, he enlisted in Company B, 36th O. V. I. He was mustered into service August 12, 1861, at Marietta, Ohio, a member of one of the regiments that made much of the history of the Civil war, passing through all the skirmishes and forced marches under command of Burnside, McClellan, Sheridan, Grant and Rosecrans. He was actively engaged in the following battles besides: South Mountains, Antietam, Bull Run, Winchester, Kernstown, Berryville, Fisher's Hill, Lynchburg, Hanover Gap, Chicamagua and Missionary Ridge. At the battle of Chicamagua Mr. Linscott was twice wounded. He passed successfully through the war, enlisting at the age of twenty years. He was mustered out July 27, 1865, at Wheeling, West Virginia, and was discharged at Columbus, Ohio, August 2. 1865, having been inactive service of his county over three years.

RESIDENCE OF MRS. ELLA SIX.

THE beautiful farm residence shown herewith is the home of Mrs. Ella Six, about two miles east of Nelsonville. On March 14, 1835, William Six bought this farm, one of the best tracts of land along the Hocking, of Christopher Wolfe and the title has been in the Six family ever since.

December 28, 1854, Wm. Six married Miss Cassandra Wells, of Athens and there were born to them two sons, W. W. and David, The former was born October 1, 1855, and the latter September 2, 1859. On April 19, 1860, the father died and left the widowed mother and two young sons. Mrs. Six, was a woman of more than ordinary mental and physical energy. Industrious and frugal, she brought up her two sons with well grounded ideas that accounted in a large measure for their subsequent success. She conducted the farm with unusual success until her sons were old enough to relieve her of the resposibilty.

The elder son W. W. was married to Miss Ella Roach the subject of this sketch, September 27, 1881. To them were born three children William R., Mary C. and Garnet O. On January 26, 1889, David Six was married to Miss Flora Sheffield, of Athens. To them were born two children; one son and one daughter.

The Six brothers were active and energetic business men, ran a large dairy and tilled their large farm, their mother having lived with them until her death, February 17, 1889. Soon after her death her eldest son Wm. W. died. It was on April 27, 1889, thus leaving our subject with the care of her fatherless children and a large farming interest to look after, much as had Mrs. Cassandra Six been left a generation before. She proved herself as equal to the occasions as had her mother-in-law. The estate was divided and our subject kept the old homestead which is shown in the illustration. She has conducted the farm most successfully and demonstrated her business ability to a marked degree.

Her only son Wm. R., a promising young man, died September 23, 1899.

D. C. Cornwell & Co., Athen, O.

WE here present a picture of the optical room of D. C. Cornwell & Company on Court Street Athens, Ohio, the successor of D. C. Cornwell who started in business in Athens in 1869 and has maintained ever since the leading jewelry store of the town. Mr. Cornwell is still connected with the business but in April 1904 he associated with

him his nephew C. A. Cornwell, a skilled watch maker and engraver who has charge of the watch and clock repair department, and B. M. Covert, his son-in-law who is a graduate of the Northern Illinois

Optical College and has had sufficient experience to become an expert in his profession.

The optical room shown herewith is equipped with all the modern instruments for scientifically testing the eye and correctly fitting glasses. No expense has been spared in making this department the best in the town or in the county.

This firm also carries a large stock of jewelry of every description, silverware, cut glass, hand painted china, in fact everything that is usually found in a first class jewelry store.

Residence of J. C. Harvey, Dover Township.

J. C. HARVEY is a son of John and Sarah K. Harvey who were among the early settlers of Athens county. The days of his childhood and early youth were spent upon the farm. He received a common school education, but has spent most of his life teaming and lumbering, making his home on Sugar Creek. He has owned several portable saw mills and cut up considerable timber in different parts of the county making the business very successful. His greatest ambition all his life has been for driving oxen, and nothing suits him better now than to drive a team of oxen with from five to ten yokes at a time.

E. R. WALKER, Auditor.

ISRAEL M. FOSTER, Prosecuting Atty.

A. W. LYNCH, Probate Judge.

COUNTY COMMISSIONERS

ANDREW MURPHY, Sheriff.

JOHN BIDDLE. JOSEPH WOLFE. S. B. HILL.

D. A. R. McKINSTRY, Clerk of Courts.

The Hocking Mining Co's Mine near Carbondale.

THIS excellent picture is an exterior view of The Hocking Mining Company's mine near Carbondale in Waterloo township on the Carbondale branch of the B. & O. S. W. railroad.

This company has a bed of 320 acres of coal lying in a vein of four and a half feet in thickness. It is what is known as the No. 6 vein and is a very fine quality of coal for steam and domestic purposes and commands a good price in the market wherever it is offered for sale.

The mine is equipped with the most modern electrical machinery, employs about 140 men and has an output capacity of five hundred tons a day. This company was organized in 1903 and is capitalized at $50,000, stock fully paid up. The officers and directors are Judge Rufus Carpenter, president; A. E. Moore, vice-president and general manager; C. D. Hopkins, secretary and treasurer; Harry G. Stalder and J. W. Jones all enterprising business and professional men of Athens county. The general offices of the company are in the First National Bank building in Athens.

History of the Foster Family of Athens, Ohio.

HULL FOSTER, SR.

MARY AMES RICE FOSTER.

FRANKLIN EVERMONT FOSTER

JOHN Foster, Sr. was was born in England in 1626 He came to America and settled at Salem. Mass. and in 1649 married Martha Tompkins. His son Ebenezer Foster was born at Salem Mass. 1677 and married Anna Wilkins Baxter. Ebenezer Foster, fifth son of the above was born at Salem, Mass. in 1710. Was married to Lydia Felton in 1731. In 1744 they removed to Rutland Mass. Lieut. Ebenezer Foster son of above was born in Salem, Mass. in 1733. In 1744 he removed with his father to Rutland. In 1757 he married Hannah Parlin of Concord. In the French and Indian war he served as a soldier under Col. John

much loved for his purity of life and willingness to assist the deserving poor of the town. He died at the home of his son Franklin in Athens. Ohio in 1890. His first wife was Orinda Carpenter, who died in 1827, leaving two sons Franklin Evermout and Warren Carpenter. His 2nd wife was Mariah Brown, by whom he had two sons William Brown and James Dickey. She died in 1866.

Franklin Evermont Foster was born at Athens, O., April 4. 1823 and spent his entire life here in the mercantile business. He was educated at the Ohio University and some of the large trees on the college campus that he and other

Murray. He purchased a large tract of land in west Rutland, where the town of Oakham was incoporated in 1762, and he was prominent in the local history of the town, having held most of the offices within its gift. He was one of the minute men who sprang to arms at the Lexington alarm in April 1775. He also had three sons in the Revolutionary war

The old Foster home at Oakham, Mass. picture of which is here shown built by Lieut. Ebenezer Foster and occupied by him is still standing. The village being without a schoolhouse he donated part of this house to be used for that purpose and a few families engaged Sarah Porter to teach there Thus sprung up a pretty romance in the courtship and marriage of Zadoc, eldest son of the family and Sarah Porter.

Zadoc Foster was born at Oakham, Mass. February 1, 1767, married Sarah Porter in 1789, moved to Sudbury, Rutland county, Vermont in 1797 and in 1798 came to Little Hocking, Washington county, Ohio, where he prepared a home for his family who joined him there one year later. In 1809 he came to Athens and conducted a tavern until his death in 1814. After his death his widow taught a private school in her home for over thirty years. She was one of the first charter members of the First Presbyterian church at Athens, Ohio.

Hull Foster Sr. was born at Sudbury, Rutland county, Vermont January 23, 1796, and came with his father's family to Little Hocking. Washington county, Ohio 1799. His first visit to Athens, Ohio was in 1805, when the village could boast of but ten or twelve small log houses and but one of them was on what is now the principal street. He spent almost his entire life here in the shoe business. In 1819 he united with the Presbyterian church and was always strong in the support of the church his mother had helped to organize and held so dear. For many years he was known as "Uncle Hull" and

students planted are still standing. In the early years of his business career he engaged extensively in buying and shipping country produce, conducting a general store here for many years. He received the appointment of County Recorder, also served on the school board. In 1850 he married Maria Davis who died, leaving one son Hull Foster Jr. In 1856 he married Mary Ames Rice at Chester, Meigs county, Ohio.

The following are the children of Franklin Evermont Foster; Hull, Sophronia Robinson, Amy Whipple, Charles Rice, Sarah Porter, Eli Crane, Orinda Carpenter Peoples, Israel Moore.

THE OLD FOSTER HOME AT OAKHAM, MASS.

Edmund Rice of Barkshamstead, county of Hartfordshire, in England, born in 1594, was of Welsh origin, and with his wife and eight children came to America in 1638 and settled near Concord, Mass. which plantation was incorporated in 1639 by the name of Sudbury. In 1660 he and other neighbors moved eight miles west of Sudbury and incoporated the village of Marlborough. He was intrusted with various important duties by the General Court and was influential in promoting the wellfare of the settlements. He died in 1663,

Joseph, the sixth son of Edmund Rice was born at Marlborough and was living there when that village was destroyed by the Indians in 1676 when he moved to Watertown, where his son Jonathan was born. He later returned to Marlborough. Jonathan Rice was born in 1679, and died at Sudbury, Mass. when 92 years old, his wife died one year later, at the same age.

William Rice, third son of Jonathan Rice was born at Sudbury in 1708 and died there in 1780.

Charles, son of William Rice was born in 1749 at Sudbury, Mass., married Susanna Moore and removed to Packersfield, now Nelson, New Hampshire, then to Belpre, Ohio in 1809. He died at Chester, Meigs county, O. aged 90 years.

He was in the Revolutionary war and fought in the battle of Concord. His brother Oliver Rice, was a major in the Revolutionary war, came to Marietta among the first emigrants to that place and assisted in laying out and incorporating Marietta and Belpre.

William Rice, son of Charles Rice, was born at Nelson N. H. in 1799 and came to Belpre with his father when eight years old. He married Sibyl, daughter of Dr. Fenn Robinson of Chester, Meigs county, Ohio.

Their daughter Mary Ames Rice married Franklin Evermont Foster Sept. 18, 1856.

ATHENS COUNTY HISTORY
CONTINUED.

lard mines at Monday Creek, and this necessitated a heavy supply in store for such times as the canal was closed by ice.

In the year 1846 or '47, Judge Pruden built a furnace at his home place, Harmony, four miles east of Athens, on the south bank of Hocking river. So long as this stream was free from mill dams, and before Pomeroy came to the front in the way of salt manufacturing, Judge Pruden had a ready market along the river. But many years before his death his sales were only local, and not sufficient to make his investments pay, and all was abandoned by his son, some years after his death about 1885.

During the salt "boom" in Athens county, Rodolph De-Steiguer Sr. built two small furnaces, one on what is now known as the Mansfield farm, five miles east of Athens, and one "factory" four mile west of Athens. These furnaces were failures, so far as salt making went, for I can find no account of a barrel of salt ever being made at either place.

Salt making in Athens county was once a great factor, and at one time the source of more revenue than any other pursuit. Cheap fuel and stronger salt water about Syracuse and in Michigan, made it impossible for Athens county to compete. Many canal boat loads of salt have I sent out from Chauncey to Lancaster, Circleville, Chillicothe, Columbus, Newark, Akron,

and Cleveland. But what a change now, as I pass along the streets of the above named cities, I see salt from places, once supplied from Athens county. That salt manufacturing could yet be made a successs in Athens county, I have no doubt, if furnaces were located so as to secure fuel at less expense than in olden times.

And now in this hurried and imperfect way I have written what seems to me a correct history of the Salt Interest once of Athens county. If any errors, they are of the dates only, immaterial so long as facts are stated.

I cannot conclude this article without offering my sincere thanks to those having the matter in charge for asking me to help as best I could in so laudable a work as placing on record so complete a history of Athens county as I understand the work in hand to be. It will be of service and source of pleasure to all who follow those who engaged in putting out this official map of their native or adopted county. That it be a complete success and satisfactory to all concerned is my sincere wish.

F. M. CHASE. Cincinnati, Ohio.

October 16, 1905.

HISTORY OF ATHENS COUNTY'S COAL INDUSTRY
BY L. A. SHANTON.

The coal business of today is more to Athens county than was the salt industry of three quarters of a century ago. It is the chief industry of the county, and is destined to remain such

for many decades to come. The supply of coal in this territory is almost inexhaustible with a rapidly increasing trade. This commodity forms the sure foundation for great wealth, and is a standing invitation to manufacturing industries to get close to our surpassed fuel supply. Athens county coal is the best of its kind to be found, and our facilities for mining and shipping are increasing and improving, and consequently the demand for our unsurpassed fuel article is broadening and multiplying, so that a prophecy today of marvelous things in the coal business will be recorded history tomorrow, vouchsafed from all parts of the county.

FORMATION.

As is wellknown the formation of coal is due to a rank and luxuriant vegetable growth, covering a period of many centuries and having periodic growths of many decades each. These rank growths being of the early flora, and belonging to the carboniferous age, must eventually yield to the stronger actions of nature and become submerged by oceanic floods or tides, which would so completely overcome and envelope these fallen forests as to render it impervious to the air. Here, lying low and encased in water which, because of the geological period, was comparatively warm, the abundant vegetation was compelled to undergo a chemical change, a sort of combustion. The great heat thus generated by pressure of the overlying mountains of Glacial drift and oceanic waters, heat native to the great bulk of vegetable matter and generated by chemical action, volcanic heat, &c., reduce the mass to a state in which fixed carbon and
Continued.

CAPT. NEHEMIAH WARREN.

CAPTAIN NEHEMIAH WARREN, the father of Warren Brothers, of Athens and Mrs. A. P. Linscott of Cannanville, was born in Clover, Columbia county, N. Y., April 13, 1823, and died at Canaanville July 23, 1881. He was a resident of Athens and Athens county for fifty-four years, a man of good judgment, successful in business

and instilled such principles into his sons that accounts in a large measure for their success.

He entered the army as First Lieutenant on September 2, 1862, and was promoted to Captain May 25, 1863, and resigned May 15, 1864. He held the office of Sheriff of Athens county one year and a half by appointment and one term by election in 1874-5.

THIS beautiful and comfortable home is the residence of Mr. and Mrs. Augustus P. Linscott, near Canaanville, on the Athens-Guysville pike. The general thrift in evidence in the picture tells the story of the fertility of Hocking bottoms. There are 315 acres in the farm which has been known for years as the N. O. Warren farm and is one of the best farms in the valley.

Mr. Linscott the present owner is the son of George S. and Mary Owen Linscott, who spent most of their lives in Ames township, near Amesville. He was born in Athens township on Sugar Creek, January 29, 1859, and grew to manhood in Ames township leading the ordinary life of a boy on the farm.

He was married to Miss Lydia Warren, the daughter of the late Capt. Nehemiah Warren, an ex-Sheriff of Athens county, April 13, 1880. They began life together on the old Linscott homestead in Ames township, and in 1887 bought the farm where they now live. In 1898 they came to Athens to give their children better school advantages, and in 1903 they returned to the farm.

Nehemiah W., the son, is employed by the Standard Oil company as its agent in Athens, and Flossie E., has not yet finished her scholastic studies, and is now in King's School of Oratory in Pittsburg.

The Linscott home is a most hospitable one and is always open with a cordial welcome to their friends whom they number by the score.

THE LINSCOTT FAMILY.

Residence of Preston D. Patton, Near Frost, Ohio.

THIS comfortable country residence is located on a farm of 226 acres on the Hocking river near Frost and is the home of Preston D. Patton, one of Athens county's prominent and well to do citizens.   Mr. Patton was born in Rome township November 25, 1840, the son of Joseph and Pamelia Butts Patton.

His father came to Athens county with his parents in 1830, and lived in Rome township the remainder of his life, dying in January, 1903. He bought the farm where his son, P. D., now lives, in 1864. This farm was known as the Josephus Butts farm and was purchased of the heirs by our subject in 1903.

Mr. Patton received only a common school education and has spent the greater part of his life in farming and stock raising.   For several years he has been making a specialty of breeding standard bred Short Horn cattle and disposing of them mostly for breeding purposes. He has bred and raised some of the best individuals in the county.

On May 2, 1864 he enlisted in Co. A., 141st Regiment, O. V. I., and served four months, being mustered out in the following September.

Mr. Patton was married to Olive Patton, the daughter of Elijah Patton, a native of Troy township, in November of 1888. In the picture is shown Mr. Patton as he appears about his work from day to day, and his uncle, Warren Patton, and his brother Oscar Patton, both making their homes here, are also shown.

RESIDENCE OF PRESTON D. PATTON.

History of Warren Brothers, Athens, Ohio.

ATHENS long noted for her progressiveness has nothing of which it may be more justly proud than its livery service. The credit being mainly due to Samuel and Jesse Warren, proprietors of Warren Brothers Livery, feed and sale stables, who with the able assistance of Mrs. Jesse Warren, conduct the finest and most up-to-date livery barn in southern Ohio. They are natives of Athens county, coming to Athens in 1885, possessed of little excepting an honest purpose and an ambition to succeed. They thus began at the bottom and by anticipating the needs of patrons commanded a continually increasing patronage that enabled them to improve and enlarge their service and in 1881 erected and have since occupied the large commodious barn shown in the accompanying cut. Equipped with modern improvements and stocked with only high-class rigs of nearly every style and variety in the catalogue and deserving of particular mention and of which they are especially proud is their good service for Funerals, Weddings, etc. They having a line of Hacks that for numbers and quality would be creditable to a large city. They are both practical horsemen and have thereby been able to secure and keep in good serviceable condition driving horses in keeping with their other appointments and suitable and pleasing to their high class patronage. They have a number of draft teams, wagons and other necessary equipment for the delivery of sand and all

WARREN BROTHERS LIVERY BARN

kinds of heavy hauling and delivering and for the accommodation of this department of their business, they have a large barn on North Court street entirely separate from their Livery.

Their residence, located a few doors west of their livery barn on Washington street, is on the second floor of the Warren block, built by them in 1900, is shown in the accompanying cut.

They have taken part in the recent growth and development of Athens and have purchased and erected a number of substantial dwelling houses, equipped with modern improvements that they rent. They also have a large acreage of farm lands near Athens, on which among other things, they have the finest bred and perhaps the largest herd of Shetland ponies in this section of Ohio.

They are patriotic and public spirited and among Athens most substantial citizens financially, having fairly demonstrated that industry, forethought and honest methods when properly applied is the sure road to success. Though justly proud of their self-achieved success, they have not been unmindful of others and they with Mrs. Jesse Warren have without ostentation, above and over all been generous and charitable.

WARREN FAMILY

Wm. A. Hibbard Funeral Director and Undertaker

THE handsome Warren building herewith shown is occupied on the ground floor by Wm. A. Hibbard, funeral director and undertaker, The building is located on Washington street directly opposite the post office and is without exception the finest equipped undertaking establishment in southern Ohio. The second floor is occupied by Warren Bros. for a residence.

Mr. Hibbard engaged in the undertaking business in 1896 and was associated with L. R. Glazier the firm doing also a general furniture business, After a few years Mr. Glazier withdrew and H. H. Wickham became a partner under the firm name of Hibbard & Wickham. This firm disposed of their furniture business in 1902 when Mr. Hibbard began undertaking alone in his present location and has enjoyed a good business ever since. He spares no pains or expense in adopting modern equipment in all branches of the business. He has elegant funeral cars, fine large team, competent assistant, casket lowering device, morgue table, engraving machine, in fact his establishment is equipped in every way to take care of his large patronage. He carries a large assortment of caskets, in fact, the largest stock in the county and has a lady assistant when the patrons so desire.

In 1901 Mr. Hibbard organized a branch of the Harrison Mutual Burial Association and has since been president. The association now has over two thousand members and has proven to be the most successfully conducted organization in the state.

WARREN BUILDING

Prof Edson M. Mills.

EDSON M. MILLS, professor of Mathematics of the State Normal college, of Ohio University, was born on January 14, 1855, and is therefore in the prime of life, vigorous and alert in body, quick and active in mind.

Without even favorable opportunity and without financial help, he secured an education by dint of his own toil, energy and courage, and has become a potent educational force in Ohio.

Successful as a rural school teacher, he was called to the graded schools, high schools, principal, superintendent of common schools, respectively; then to Findlay College, Defiance College and finally to his present position which he fills with great success—a teacher of

teachers. A prominent educator has said of him: "As an instructor in his line of work, whether in the county institute or the class room, Prof. Mills has no peer in the state. He has the happy faculty of so correlating theory and practice, knowledge and pedagogy, that the principles of teaching are acquired by and through the academic mastery of the subjects. His original and marvelous work would make a valuable contribution to the literature on the teaching of mathematics."

The Athens National Bank

WE here present a picture of The Athens National Bank building, erected in 1905, the largest and highest structure in Athens and withal a modern and complete office building - an ornament to the city of Athens and a compliment to her rapidly growing industries.

The building is owned and was erected by The Athens National Bank, organized under the laws of the United States, on may 10, 1905, and chartered by the general government May 16 of the same year. It was capitalized at $100,000 and the stock was subscribed by about thirty-five of the most progressive business men of the town and county.

The board of directors and officers are: Dr. W. N. Alderman, president; H. D. Henry vice president; L. G. Worstell, J. Halliday Cline, Henry Zenner, J. Gaston Coe, Don C. Cable, S. L. McCune and Geo. B. Lash. J. D. Foster, Jr. is the cashier and Fred L. Alderman is the teller.

The building occupies a ground space of 51x90 feet and is five stories high above the basement. The south side of the first floor is occupied by The Athens National Bank, while the north room is used for business. The three floors above are divided into elegant suites for offices, while the fifth floor is the home of the Elk lodge. The building is equipped with an elevator, steam heat, gas and electric light. It is modern in all of its appointments, nothing having been spared to make it a model in its class.

The walls are built of vitrified brick with stone trimmings, as the illustration shows, making it a handsome piece of architecture and a substantial building, a lasting monument to the enterprise of those who are responsible for it.

.... The Glouster Bank ...

THE Glouster Bank was organized in 1891 with E. A. Lewis, President, S. W. Smith, Vice President, David Edwards, Cashier.

In 1892 the business had so increased it was necessary to have more room and the present bank building was erected. Later, C. E. Duncan was elected bookkeeper. The business increased and he was promoted Assistant Cashier, and Miss Etta Duncan bookkeeper.

Shortly after the death of D. Edwards, in 1903, R. L. Lewis was made Vice President, C. E. Duncan Cashier.

The bank is conducted on conservative and unquestionably legitimate banking principles. Any business intrusted to it will be cared for to its customers entire satisfaction.

The stockholders are individually responsible for $250,000, consisting of real estate and personal effects outside the bank.

The officers at the present time are: E. A. Lewis, President; R. L. Lewis, Vice President, and C. E. Duncan, Cashier.

THIS well kept and prosperous looking farm residence is the country home of Mr. and Mrs. William R. Phillips, about one mile west of Amesville. Here the Phillips' with their two bright and interesting children, spend the summer months, looking after the interest of their large farm which is well stocked with high bred horses and Short Horn cattle, while they spend the winter months in the comfortable home on South Court street in Athens, Ohio, known as the Judge John Welch residence, as it was occupied by him until his death, when it was purchased by Chas. H. Welch, a grandson, who sold it to Mr. Phillips. This is one of the most beautiful home sites in Athens, situated as it is high above the street and facing the beautiful natural forest in the campus of Ohio University. An elegant picture of the home is also shown on this page.

Mr. Phillips, our subject, is one of the most enterprising young business men in Ames township, and besides conducting a stock farm of several hundred acres, he has large real estate investments in Athens. Since the death of his father in 1896, he has successfully managed the estate, assuming a responsibility at seventeen that would try the courage of mature years. He has not only kept the property together, but has so conducted affairs that he has made good returns on the investment.

Mr. Phillips is the son of Ezra and Ellen Ring Phillips, both now deceased and was born October 22, 1879. His father was a prominent

farmer and stock dealer before him, and was born April 3, 1835, dying September 5, 1896. Our subject's grandfather, Capt. Ezra Phillips, was one of the early pioneers of Ames township, having been born in 1801. His grandmother was Mary Ann McDougall Phillips, of one of the best families of the county.

The farm here illustrated is known as the old John Brown farm, and passed to the Phillips family by the purchase of Ezra Phillips in 1881. At his death September 5, 1896, the property passed to his wife, who died March 1, 1898, and it then became the property of the son, W. R. Phillips, who has successfully managed it ever since, and has demonstrated that he is a practical agriculturalist and stock raiser. One of the elements of his success lies in the fact that he early became convinced that the most profitable stock to handle is the very best stock he can get. In consequence, he has a fine herd of registered cattle and devotes the greater part of his time to this industry.

Mr. Phillips was happily married on October 23, 1901, to Miss Adda Alderman, the accomplished daughter of Dr. and Mrs. W. N. Alderman, of Athens, whose history will be found on another page. They have two children, both girls, Eleanor and Alice, who are the life of the household and the joy of their devoted parents.

On the opposite page Eleanor is shown with her grandfather, Dr. Alderman, who is sitting on the steps of his residence on College street.

Mr. Phillips is a member of the Masonic fraternity, and is on the roster of the Amesville lodge. He and Mrs. Phillips stand for the best in citizenship, are public spirited and contribute freely to everything of a public nature that tends toward advancement and the uplifting of the community, both morally and educationally.

Few families are surrounded with brighter prospects and none are more deserving of all that makes life tolerable and desirable.

RESIDENCE OF WILLIAM R. PHILLIPS SOUTH COURT STREET ATHENS, OHIO.

Old Fashioned Fire Place.

HERE is a picture of comfort and contentment and takes one back an hundred years when stoves for cooking and heating were unknown and when all heat for domestic purposes was obtained from the huge open fire place. The picture here shown is the interior of one room in Mrs. Mary Patton's home in Rome township.

She has retained the primitive utensils of former days as well as the old fire place and all was arranged especially for this picture.

THE accompaning pictures show the home of Dr. Wm. Nelson Alderman on College street Athens, Ohio, his office building on Washington street and the Doctor himself who is one of the most prominent physicians of Athens and one of her most successful business men. He was born near Trimble, Morgan county, Ohio, Nov. 27, 1853, a son of

DR. WILLIAM NELSON ALDERMAN

Nelson J. and Susannah Wiemer Alderman. He grew to young manhood on the farm and began to battle with the world in the mercantile business with his brother S. J. Alderman at Bishopville, Ohio. After three years, he retired from the firm and began the study of medicine with Dr. George E. Carpenter in Athens. After one year he studied with Dr. H. D. Danford of Trimble, remaining with him until his graduation from the Medical College of Ohio at Cincinnati, February 28, 1877. He practiced with his perceptor until the following September when he went to New York and took a course of lectures at the Bellevue Medical College, graduating Feburary 28, 1878. In July 1878, he located in Nelsonville and in the spring of the following year formed a partnership with Dr. I. P. Primrose under the firm name of Drs. Primrose & Alderman. He soon secured a large clientage and when he moved to Athens in May of 1890 the firm then including Dr. Hyde, had the largest practice in Nelsonville.

Coming to Athens and succeeding Dr. H. M. Lash, Dr. Alderman soon established a lucrative practice and is today considered a leader in his profession but for the past few years, his business interests have become so numerous that he has gradually relinquished general outside practice and devotes his time professionally to consulation and office practice. Dr. T. R. Biddle was taken into partnership in 1892 and was succeeded by Dr. D. H. Biddle in 1902 so the firm name has been Drs. Alderman & Biddle for the past thirteen years.

Dr. Alderman has always been a very busy man and while he has always taken care of a large medical practice, he has found time to devote to public local affairs, being public spirited and enterprising in everything he has had to do.

He was one of the organizers of The Nelsonville Sewer Pipe Company and is now its vice-president and a director. He was one of the leading spirits in the organization of The Athens Brick Company in 1891, one the best manufacturing plants in Athens and has been president of the company since its organization. He is president and a large stockholder in The Athens Foundry & Machine Company, a thriving institu-

RESIDENCE OF DR. WILLIAM NELSON ALDERMAN.

tion and is a director of The Nelsonville Brick Company which was organized in 1904. He was the chief promoter in the organization of The Athens National Bank, capitalized at $100,000 in 1905, and was elected president of the company which has now under construction a magnificent five story office building, a

ALDERMAN BLOCK

picture of which is shown on another page. He was treasurer of the Athens School board for ten years, at present the president of the Board of Trustees of Public of Affairs of Athens, president of the Athens Board of Trade, member of the Medical board of U. S. Pension examiners since 1889, member of the Athens county and State Medical societies, a Knight Templar and an Elk.

The handsome office building shown herewith, located on Washington street, he built in 1899 and occupies the entire second floor for his professional and business offices.

Dr. Alderman was married to Miss Sarah A Primrose the daughter of his former partner Dr. I. P. Primrose, in Nelsonville, February 25, 1880. To them have been born two children Addie P. now Mrs. W. R. Phillips and Fred L. book-keeper in The Athens National Bank.

ATHENS COUNTY HISTORY
CONTINUED.

In the year 1842 or '43, Samuel B. Denman, a brother-in-law of Thomas Ewing, built a furnace in connection with a grist mill, just north of the old Morris homestead, one mile north of Chauncey. This was a complete failure and resulted in the financial ruin of the projector.

Possibly, in 1844, Jas. Pugsley, in connection with his brother, and some others built a furnace on Bailey's Run, just east of the Morris homestead. This was also a failure as the hauling in wagons to the canal added so much to the cost of the salt, that successful competition with works directly on the canal, was impossible.

In the year 1846, a Mr. Eggleston built a small furnace on Green's Run in the northern part of Dover Township. This was only for local sales; no market, or shipping point, nearer than Chauncey, and was a failure after a few years effort to make it a success. This was abandoned in 1857. The above named furnaces were all built in Dover township.

In 1852, John Ballard and his son James and Charles P. built a furnace on the banks of Hocking river at what is now known as Armitage. This was a great success for many years. In 1860 they leased all to Joseph Herrold, and the place for years was known as Herrold's Salt Works. In about 1870, the land was sold; the furnaces remained idle for years, and finally abandoned in about 1885. One thing that mitigated against success at this place was the fact all coal used had to come from the Bal-

Continued

The Athens Messenger

Athens County Gazette.

THE ATHEN MESSENGER is the pioneer newspaper of Athens county and while it has borne that name about sixty-two years practically the same paper began its existence in 1825, under the name of Athen Mirror owned and edited by Hon. A. G. Brown. Isaac Maxson succeeded Mr. Brown in 1830 and was it called the Western Spectator until 1836 when it was purchased by Abram Voorhes who christened it The Hocking Valley Gazette and Athens Messenger. Succeeding owners and editors: Nelson H. Van Voorhes, A. J. Van Voorhes, George Walsh in 1844, then N. H. Voorhes who published it until 1861; T. F. Wildes until 1862; Jesse Van Law till Nov. 1865; J. W. Stinchcomb till November 1866; J.R.S. Bond till March 1868; Charles E. M. Jennings until his death June 8, 1896, since that time Fred W. Bush has been its editor and manager. The paper was incorporated in July of 1895 with a capital stock of $11,000. In November of 1905 the capital stock was increased to $15,000 and The Athens Daily Messenger, the first daily paper in Athens county was established in connection with the weekly, and gives promise of a successful career.

The board of directors and officers are J. B. Allen, president; Harry G. Stalder, secretary; Rachel Jennings, treasurer; John Finister-

wald, L. G. Worstell and F. W. Bush.

The Athens Journal, a Democratic weekly, was established by Col. R. W. Jones in 1875. After his death it was published by his daughter Miss Jennie Jones, now Mrs. A. J. Frame, until 1885 when C. I. Barker became the publisher. Thomas H. Craig purchased an interest with Mr. Barker in 1887. In the following year Calvin S. Welch purchased Mr. Barker's interest. Under this ownership W. S. Jones became editor in March 4, 1889. In October 1890 A. Price Russel succeeded Mr. Jones as editor and was succeeded by Wm. M. Entler who remained as editor, until 1894 when A. E. McGrath became editor, Mr. Craig having purchased Mr. Welch's interest in 1895. On December 1, 1895, Curtis V. Harris purchased an interest and has since been the editor and manager.

The Athens County Gazette, a Republican weekly was established in Glouster, Ohio in 1888 by Hon. J. M. Allen and was moved to Athens in 1895. In 1897 it absorbed The Albany Echo. David R. Richards purchased an interest with Mr. Allen in 1895. In 1899 Mr. Allen sold his interest since which time the plant has been owned by Mr. Richards and C. H. Bryson equally. Mr. Bryson is its editor and Mr. David Richards is the business manager.

THE ATHENS JOURNAL.

Residence of Mr. and Mrs. Edwin Chase in Carthage Township.

THIS beautiful country place is the home of Mr. and Mrs. Edwin Chase in Carthage township. Mr. Chase was the son of William S. Chase who was born in New Hampshire, August 27, 1822, his father having come there from England. When eleven years old he came with his parents to Ohio, then almost an unbroken wilderness, and in 1852 bought the farm shown in the picture. He was married to Tobitha Tribbet in 1853, who came to Ohio with her parents when she was quite young. She was of Swedish decent and was born in New Jersey, February 6, 1830. To them were born four children; Eaton, Hannah, Lydia and Edwin, the subject of this sketch, now lives on and maintains the old homestead, one of the best farms in the township.

Edwin Chase was born September 28, 1868 on the farm where he now lives and was married to Miss Lucy Jeffers on January 6, 1899. They have four children who together with Mr. and Mrs. Chase are shown in the accompanying picture. The children are Gladys age six years; Bessie age four; William aged two and Mildred age six months.

❀   ❀   ❀   ❀   ❀   ❀   ❀

ATHENS COUNTY HISTORY
CONTINUE.

volatile combustible matter form the chief elements. This change was not to petrifaction or decay, but liberating the oxygen and hydrogen, and leaving the pure carbon. The value and kind of coal depend primarily upon their relative proportion of oxygen and hydrogen driven off, and the purity of combustible carbon remaining. Geologists say that it takes about 3,000 years of carboniferous growth to produce 30 feet of coal or 10,000 years of this exotic life to produce 113 feet of coal. From these figures we can form some notion of the time consumed in the construction or formation of our great coal veins.

GEOLOGY.

The coal of Athens county belongs, Geologically, to the
Continued.

Residence of J. B. Clayton, Athens, Ohio.

JEFFERSON BAIRD CLAYTON was born in Athens, Ohio, August 6, 1839. His father, David Moore Clayton came to Athens about 1837 and was married to Susannah Baird, daughter of Moses Baird, formerly of Guernsey county, Ohio. D. M. Clayton was a merchant in Athens for many years, and later was postmaster and agent of Adams & Harnden Express Companies during the Civil War. Lenna Belle Clayton, a daughter, lived to be 11 years old and died same year as her father in 1868. J. B. Clayton received his education in the public schools and graduated from the Ohio University in 1862, having taken a full classical course. He has always made Athens his home although for a number of years in the employ of the Standard Oil Company in the cities of Louisville. Charleston, S. C., Baltimore and Philadelphia. He was married to Florence C. Sloane, daughter of John M. Sloane, of south Salem, Ohio in 1875. They have three children. David Roy, Earle Sloane and Mary Florence who have received their education at the public schools and Ohio University. For a number of years J. B. Clayton has been the sole owner and manufacturer of the Standard remedy known as "Dr. Seth Hart's Cough Syrup." He held the position of member of the Board of Education of Athens and for five years past, and at the present time holds the position of Township Clerk and Clerk of the Township Board of Education. The testimony of both boards attest his efficiency and correctness in the discharge of his duties.

❧   ❧   ❧   ❧   ❧   ❧

RESIDENCE OF DR JOHN L. HENRY.

Residence of Dr. J. L. Henry, Athens.

JOHN L. HENRY, M. D., eldest son of Charles and Kate (Lindley) Henry was born in Canaan Township, Athens county, Ohio, October 25, 1866. His childhood was spent on a farm near Canaanville.

When about six years of age his parents moved to Athens township, buying a farm about two miles east of Athens. Here the subject of this sketch attended district school until 1884 when he entered the Ohio University, which he attended for a little over three years with the exception of two intervals which were spent in teaching district schools.

In 1887 he began the study of medicine under Dr. R. M. Steele, of Athens, Ohio, later attending the Columbus Medical College from which he graduated in 1891.

Soon after graduating he began the practice of medicine in Athens, Ohio, on South Court street, having an office in the Norton Building where he remained for over 10 years.

In 1901 he formed a partnership with Dr. K. Tinker and then moved his office to 18 West Washington street, where he is now located.

Sept. 19, 1897, Dr. Henry was married to Ora M. Cotton, daughter of H. M. and Nancy (Withers) Cotton. They have two children, Ruth Marie, born October 13, 1900 and John Cotton, born March 13, 1901.

Dr. Henry is a member of the Athenian Lodge No. 104 Knights of Pythias, of Athens Company No. 54 Uniform Rank, Knights of Pythias; of Sereno Lodge No. 479 Independent Order of Odd Fellows and of Mohawk Tribe No. 174 Improved Order of Redmen.

Residence of John C. and G. P. Ackley,
OF LODI TOWNSHIP.

THE farm residence here shown is the home of John C. and G. P. Ackley in Lodi Township near Pratt's Fork, two industrious and highly respected citizens. They are the sons of the late George W. and Elizabeth Ackley. natives of Greene county, Pennsylvania. and moved with their parents to Ohio when eleven and thirteen years old respectively and settled near this farm when it was all in woods. Fourteen children were born to them, nine boys and five girls. All lived to maturity except one boy who died when one month old.

Mr. and Mrs. Ackley were good and faithful members of the Christian church and led exemplary lives. The farm in question was where they settled when they were married. Mr. Ackley is a Democrat in politics and is a successful farmer and stock raiser.

G. P. Ackley who with his brother John C. owns the farm was married to Miss Mary Jeffers, the daughter of George and Elizabeth Jeffers in 1896. They have four children: Wayne E., age 9 years; Willard H., age 8 years; George R., age 4 years and Floyd A., his twin died March 11, 1900, age 11 months and 9 days.

Both sons like the father are Democrats. They operate their farm of 189 acres so as to make good returns on the investment and are well to do and respected citizens.

RESIDENCE OF JOHN C. AND G. P. ACKLEY.

Athens County Veterans of the Civil War.

TOP ROW:-- Richard Monroe, Thos. Maxwell, Rufus Bean,   E. A. Weekly, Thomas Morris, Capt. John P. Dana, Major Elmer Golden, John Kale, Capt. Josiah B. Allen, Henry Dixon.   SECOND ROW:
Isaac Nice, Eli Oxley, H. H. Wickham, Ezra Walker, W. H. Brown, J, M, Goodspeed, S. N. Hobson. Marion Tippie, Michael Love, Charles Harrison, Peter Finsterwald, John Brooks,   THIRD ROW:-- Zespheniah
Fulton, James Diltz, Eli Roush, Will E. Dean, Andrew Jackson, C. D. Gist, Esaias Daily,   John Tippie,   FOURTH ROW:--Charles Brown, D. C. Beverage. Capt. David Putnam, A. W. Lynch.

Residence of Mr. and Mrs. Elmer K. Stout, in Carthage Township.

THIS beautiful rural picture is the home of Mr. and Mrs. Elmer K. Stout, in Carthage township. Mr. Stout is one of the most successful farmers in this section of the county and has made quite a success in breeding and raising registered Aberdeen Angus cattle, some fine specimens of his stock was shown in the foreground of the accompanying illustration. He has the only herd of Aberdeen cattle in the county and is justly proud of his efforts along this line, believing the Angus to be the best breed of cattle to raise and has been in the business about twelve years.

Mr. Stout is the son of Seldon C. and Mary J. Stout. He grew up on the farm attending the public schools in the winter and in the meantime making himself useful on the farm. He was married to Miss Lydia Russel, November 10, 1897. They have one child, a bright boy born August 2, 1899, named Seldon Dwight. Mr. Stout has lived on the old homestead about twenty-two years and is prosperous. He and his excellent wife are highly respected citizens and liberally endorse every effort towards the uplifting and bettering of humanity.

LADY OF SHADE VALLEY.

The accompanying photograph shows a fine four year old Angus cow registered number 48851 and name Lady of Shade Valley. She is one of the Meggie family, sired by Barnet's Boy, number 20643. The dam was Alice of Woodland, number 14569.

143

WE here present one of the most picturesque and artistic farm scenes found in this work of beautiful pictures. The picture was taken when nature was in bloom and while there is that in the picture which holds the attention and admiration of the artistically inclined, the man who enjoys a picture of prosperity and a comfortable farm home is pleased with the illustration.

Both the accompanying pictures represent the home and environment of W. W. Blackwood, one of the best citizens in Carthage Township and one of its most intelligent and prosperous farmers. He has two hundred acres of excellent land and does a general farming business turning his hand to that which promises best returns.

Mr. Blackwood was the son of Isaac Blackwood who enlisted as a soldier in the Civil War and was in many engagements until he was captured by the enemy and confined in the prison-hell at Andersonville and died from neglect and starvation.

Our subject was married to Miss Isabel Griffin, a native of Troy township, Athens county, Ohio, a member of one of the highly respected families of that township, in 1886. They went to housekeeping on the farm where they now live. The neat, comfortable residence and commodious barns and stables indicate the value of the

RESIDENE OF W. W. BLACKWOOD

soil of this farm which is one of the best for general farming and stock raising in the township.

Mr. and Mrs. Blackwood are the parents of five children, all living, four girls and one boy, who are securing and have secured a liberal education and have laid the foundation for useful citizenship: Aletha, age 18; Linnie, age 16; Velma, age 13, Frank, age 12 and Fay, age 10.

Intelligent and aggressive, this happy family have learned the lessons of frugality and industry, are excellent citizens, generous neighbors and their home is noted for its hospitality.

ATHENS COUNTY HISTORY
CONTINUED.

Continued

Waverly period or group, making it a comparatively young coal formation. It is a part of the great Appalachian coal belt which extends from Pennsylvania to Georgia. Athens county lies wholly within this valuable coal belt, and is the second richest county in coal in the state and has the largest output.

The Nelsonville seam, known as the Middle Kittaning seam, is the thickest of any in the state, reaching a thickness some places of 13 feet. While this seam lies high, and is composed mostly of drift coal, yet it is among the richest in the country. The seam almost approaches the surface near Nelsonville, the river bed and banks often revealing it. Many bluffs also throughout the county show the coal cropping out. The seams, therefore, are rather uneven, both as to depth and thickness. Following the river from Nelsonville there is a gradual dip of the seam till about five miles south of the city where it is lost beneath the bed of the Hock-hocking river on Section 8 of York township.

The slope to the southeast is at the rate of about 25 feet to the mile, while near the farm of A. H. Montgomery, in Rome township, the course is a little more to the east, and the slope

Continued

Residence of Culbert M. Pierce.

IN the accompanying picture is seen the residence of Mr. Culbert M. Pierce, near the picturesque little village of Pleasanton. Mr. Pierce was born in Mercer county, Pennsylvania, June 11, 1848, being one of a family of eight boys and three girls, of whom one girl and three boys are dead, all others but one living in Athens county. Culbert came to Athens county, Ohio, with his parents, David and Mary Pierce, in the spring of 1815.

His father was born in Westmoreland county, Pennsylvania, August 3, 1805, and died in Athens county, January 18, 1868.

Mary Pierce, his mother, was born in Mercer county, October 11, 1815, and died at her home in this, Athens county, two miles east of Pleasanton, January 8, 1894.

Mr. Pierce volunteered the 31st day of August 1864, in Company D, of the 174th O. V. I., and remained with his regiment until the close of the war, being discharged June 28, 1865. Returning to his home he then made a trip through the western states and on his return took up farming and stock-raising in which he is still actively and successfully engaged.

On March 15th, 1881, he was united in marriage to Miss Columbia Woodruff, daughter of Merril and Lucinda Woodruff and to this union was born six children, three boys and three girls, Jesse, Maude, Emery, Fahye, Estella and Cora Pierce.

The baby in the picture, the only grandchild, Durward, is the son of Jesse, the oldest child, who was married to Miss Bertha Parker, Dec. 31, 1903.

BISHOP CHARLES C. McCABE, D. D.

Charles Cardwell Mc-Cabe was born in Athens, Ohio, October 11th, 1836. He was the son of Robert and Sarah McCabe, well and favorably known in Athens, O. He received a college education; entered the ministry in the Ohio Annual Conference of the Methodist Episcopal church in 1860.

He enlisted as chaplain of the 126th Ohio Infantry, and on the battle field of Winchester, Va., was captured and sent to Libby Prison. On his release he rejoined his regiment, but was pressed into the service of the Christian Commission where he accomplished splendid results for his unfortunate comrades. He gave sixteen years of efficient work to the Church Extension Society of the M. E. church. At the session of the General Conference, in Cleveland, O., 1896 Chaplain McCabe was elected and ordained bishop in the Methodist Episcopal Church. There is no American Methodist more popular than he, and as a bishop he is greatly beloved and his services are most highly valued.

BISHOP EARL CRANSTON, D. D.

Earl Cranston, D. D., son of Earl Cranston and Mrs. Jane Montgomery Cranston, was born in Athens, O., June 27, 1840. He is an alumnus of the Ohio University, received the degree of Doctor of Divinity from both Allegheny and Cornell colleges in 1883. He enlisted at the first call for troops in the Civil War. He afterward recruited a company and was assigned to the 60th Ohio; Captain Cranston shared in General Grant's campaign with the army of the Potomac to the investment of Petersburg.

He was licensed to preach and entered the ministry in the Methodist Episcopal Church at the age of twenty-seven. He soon filled important charges in Ohio, Illinois and Colorado. He served the church as presiding elder several years and also gave much supervision and liberal donations to the Denver University which have borne splendid fruits. He was elected Publishing agent of the Western Book Concern in 1884 and filled this most responsible position with great efficiency for a period of twelve years.

At the General Conference in 1897 Dr. Cranston was elected and ordained a bishop in the Methodist Episcopal Church. His official work meets the highest expectations of his church and Bishop Cranston is estimated and everywhere welcomed as one of the greatest bishops in the church of his choice.

DAVID H. MOORE, D. D.

David Hastings Moore, another Athenian, was born September 4th, 1838. He was the son of Hon. Eliakim

CENTER

BISHOP E. R. AMES, D. D.

UPPER

BISHOP EARL CRANSTON.

LOWER

BISHOP DAVID H. MOORE.

BISHOP C. C. McCABE.

H. and Mrs. Amy Barker Moore. Early in life he entered the ministry in the Methodist Episcopal Church, but not until after he had graduated honorably from the Ohio University. In 1860 he became a member of the Ohio Annual Conference. In 1862 he volunteered as a private but was elected captain of Company A, 87th Regiment Ohio Volunteer Infantry. Afterward he was promoted a major, then lieutenant-colonel of the 125 O. V. I. He had charge of a regiment during almost the entire Atlanta campaign, his colonel having been placed in charge of a brigade. Dr. Moore served a number of the leading charges in Ohio as pastor. He was president of Cincinnati Wesleyan Female College for five years. He was chancellor of the Colorado Seminary and University of Denver for ten years and soon after was elected to the editorship of the Western Christian Advocate; this position he held until the General Conference of 1900 elected him a bishop in the Methodist Episcopal Church. After his ordination as bishop he was officially assigned to China, Japan and Korea where he remained for four years and was then assigned to work in the United States.

It is seldom one fills so many official positions, yet it is well said that every position was well filled. His versatility as a writer, his eloquence as speaker and his wise administrative ability combine to make him the great man that he is.

ATHENS COUNTY HISTORY
CONTINUED

is only 12 feet to the mile. The Nelsonville field is claimed to be the original or normal middle Kittanning seam, and is the best in volume and quality. Its fixed carbon and volatile combustible matter are of a high per cent. Dover and Trimble townships contain among the most valuable basins of the Upper Freeport coal seam in the western field. In Dover township the seam ranges from 6 to 8 feet thick at a depth of from 75 to 125 feet.

POWER AND VALUE.

The power exerted by an ordinary man during day of labor is reckoned as equivalent to the power exerted by one pound of coal, when that power is liberated by combustion. This man will labor three hundred days in a year, and his year's strength, therefore, is equal to three hundred pounds of coal.

Now the coal area of Athens county is estimated at 140,000 acres, and engineers and expert miners assign a uniform or average thickness of coal vein or veins as being 6 feet, with 7,500 tons of coal to the acre. This gives one billion, fifty million tons or two trillion, one hundred billion pounds of coal to the county. On the basis that a man's strength or energy for a day is equal to one pound of coal, we have the combined strength of two trillion, 100 billion men for one day, or the strength of the same number of men seven billion of years of 300 working days each.

Suppose that this man's daily strength or energy is worth one dollar and a half an average wage. By this methods, then, the value of the coal of the county reaches the enormous sum of three trillion, one hundred fifty billion dollars in potential force or energy. But to calculate by another method. The actual cost of mining coal, at this writing, is 90 cents a ton. By this process of reasoning it is found that the value of the county's coal in money, is 945 million dollars.

At the present time there are about 6,500 miners operating the coal interests of the county, the largest number of any county in the state. These miners produce 3¾ million tons a year. There being one billion, fifty million tons of coal in the Athens county field, it will take the present mining force and equipment 200 years to mine the total estimated product of the county.

HISTORY.

The history of the discovery of coal in Athens county began with a hunter, and but a trifling incident in his career. It was away back nearly a century ago, when a hunter, by the name Roberts, was on a chase. Tiring, and being thirsty, he stooped at a murmuring brook to slake his thirst, when, upon rising he saw something queer before his eyes, in the rugged banks. Upon examining it he found it to be coal. Just what he did relative to his discovery, neither tradition nor history repeats to us. Suffice it to say, however, that some local speculation and enthusiasm were the outcome.

Sometime following this incident, specimens of coal were carefully sent to the legislature for examination, hoping thereby to interest the law making body to do something to provide an outlet for what was believed to be a great product.

J. F. Somers, a gentleman hailing from the east, was one of the earliest to take hold of the coal interests of the county, and to put forth efforts to development.

As early as April, 1830, Athens county coal was mined for commercial purposes. At this time James Knight loaded a wagon with 58 bushels and hauled it to Columbus with six horses and sold it at 4 cents a bushel, Gill and Greer being the purchasers. Up to this time about the only demand in a commercial way was by the local blacksmith, and this demand was almost entirely supplied from a mine at the north side of Johnson's hill about a half mile northwest of Nelsonville, the farm now owned by the Nelsonville Coal & Land Co., better known as the W. B. Brooks property.

But nearly each and every land owner mined coal for his own uses, and also such as he might market to his neighbors. The Hocking Valley canal being completed in 1840, capitalists were anxious for investment in the rich and promising coal fields of the county, such being readily recognized as a fine business venture. The demand for the product was increasing while the rude means of obtaining the product were decreasing at a proportional ratio.

Among the early operators was Thos. Ewing, at one time United States senator from Ohio, and later a member of Pres. Lincoln's cabinet, associated with Mr. Ewing was Samuel F. Vinton, also a United States senator. The Thos. Ewing mine was at Chauncey. Afterwards these gentlemen were joined by Nicholas Biddle and Elihu Chauncey of Philadelphia, the town of Chauncey receiving its name from the Philadelphian. This combination of enterprise and capital further proceeded to tap the Nelsonville seam at Dorr Run, now comprising the west end of the city of Nelsonville. Their eminent success attracted oth-

Continued

er prospectors and capitalists, among whom were James Fuller and A. B. Walker, both of Athens. This was about 1845. Mr. Walker had an extensive and successful business experience, among other things being that of operating a salt furnace near Chauncey. This partnership was dissolved in 1855. These brothers-in-law opened mines a little to the north of those being operated at Dorr Run, and extended their operations to both sides of the river. Their product readily found the large places of commerce and consumption through the canal, the coal being hauled in wagons and loaded on to the canal boats by wheelbarrows.

Launcelot Scott, who was born in England, Nov. 2, 1804 emigrating to the United States in 1834, was one of the earliest miners of the Hocking Valley. His father before him was mine boss in Willington Colliery, England, where young Scott received his knowledge of the coal business. In 1838 he came from Gallia county with the Hon. Samuel F. Vinton, locating at Chauncey, where they opened a mine in the Bailey Run coal vein, about two miles above Chauncey, on what is now known as the Aaron Lewis farm. This was one of the first coal mines opened and worked in the Hocking Valley.

The coal was hauled to Chauncey and used in the salt furnaces at that place. Mr. Scott afterward supervised the sinking of the coal shaft at Chauncey to the No. 6, or Nelsonville coal

A. Poston and John Meyers formed a partnership about 1860, and operated at Doanville. This partnership lasted for only a couple of years when Mr. Poston entered the firm of The Co-operative Coal company, who continued operating the same plants. Finally Mr. Poston freed himself of the mining business by selling all his interets to Lama & Doan in 1885.

The mines in Trimble and Dover townships were opened in 1880 upon the completion of the Ohio Central railroad through this field. This railroad corporation bought 12000 acres of coal land, and set to developing it with a large force of men and equipping the plant with modern machinery and facilities.

Upon the death of Mr. Scott, the business, came under the management of his son-in-law, Mr. L. D. Poston, who, however, because of his splendid business ability, gave the business an added impetus. He proceeded to enlarge and re-equip the operating departmnets. Hence, he soon became recognized as one of the best coal operators in the Hocking Valley.

During the days of the canal the winter operations of the mines consisted in digging and piling the coal up on the bank of the canal ready for shipment so soon as the ice was sufficiently out to permit shipment, the coal being hauled from the mines to the canal by horses and oxen. Tramways were constructed in the 50's. These were little wooden railroads, leading from

worked out, C. L. Poston purchased all the interests of his partners, since which time Mr. Poston has been sole owner.

Mr. Poston continued in active operations till Sept. 1, 1902, when he sold all of his interests except the coal itself to the Morgan Syndicate, locally known as The Continental Coal company. By lease and ownership he had about 1800 acres, some of which had been worked to a large extent. He reserved several hundred acres, however, which is now being worked on royalty. He yet owns the old mine of his father's opening in 1873, but its output is limited to only about 3,000 tons per month. Mr. Poston is yet the heaviest coal operator in the county, as owner and lessee, as well as one of the oldest and most prominent in the Hocking Valley. The new and promising Sugar Creek mines he leased to the Continental Coal company. The Poston family has been more closely identified with the coal interests of Hocking Valley than any other one family and they have done more, probably, to develop that great natural industry. In all their operations they have been eminently successful. In addition to all his Athens county interests, Mr. C. L. Poston has some valuable and extensive coal holdings in Jefferson and Belmont counties.

But thus far there has been no specific reference to the city of Athens. About 1867 a shaft was sunk near where the B. & O. depot now is, but the depth being about 250 feet, and the

HERROLD'S MILL, WEST OF ATHENS.

seam. In 1840 he moved to Nelsonville and opened the first shipping and coal mine at that place in company with Mr. Steenrod, but dissolving their partnership soon after Mr. Steenrod continuing at the mine just opened, while Mr. Scott opened new mines at Robbins Hill, adjoining Nelsonville on the west.

In 1859, W. B. Brooks, a banker and merchant of Columbus came to Nelsonville and associated himself with Mathew Vanwormer of Nelsonville, who together purchased 300 acres of coal land across the river from Nelsonville for many years known as Mine No. 29, where they conducted an extensive and profitable business, but the partnership was dissolved one year later, Mr. Brooks continuing the business. He enlarged his holdings by purchasing 600 acres on Sec. 19, immediately adjoining Nelsonville and enlarged the plant in proportion. For a long term of years, Mr. F. L. Preston of Athens had the management of this splendid business. Screens, compressed air power, automatic pumps and an ice breaking machine, enabling the plant to operate all the year round, were some of the new facilities introduced. By these appliances, Mr. Brooks was able to mine, load and ship as much as 105 cars a day when he was afforded railroad facilities. During the year 1857, two million bushels were mined in the vicinity of Nelsonville alone. In the summer of 1867 Thaddeus Longstreth came from Warren county and entered the coal firm of W. G. Power & Co., and in less than two years bought the entire interests of his partners, including the site of the plant.

the canal to the mines. Finally shutes were added, being a great addition to the tram facilites. Up until about the breaking out of the war Mr. Poston had operated only leased fields, shipping as above described, but war conditions making new and increased demands, he seized upon these advantages and opportunities by purchasing a large tract of coal land and putting it under operation. All of these operations were mostly confined to the immediate vicinity of Nelsonville because of her shipping facilities, but upon the completion of the C. & H. V. railroad in 1870, the industry again received a new awakening. The canal being a branch off of the Ohio canal from Carroll to Athens, offering good shipping facilities so far as it could, was soon outdistanced though, by the facilities of the railroad. To keep pace with demands and openings, Mr. Poston adds to his holdings by the purchase of 250 acres of coal land. Refitting the plants &c. he leases to his sons, C. L. and Wm. together with his son-in-law, E. P. Pendleton, for a term of 20 years, retiring from active participation in 1873, dying in December, 1875.

Mr. C. L. Poston was the managing partner of the firm of Poston & Pendleton. In 1880 W. W. Poston and Mr. Pendleton sold their interests to Messrs. McClintock & Smith of Chillicothe. Shortly after this combination the new firm added 400 acres in the Monday Creek Valley to their coal lands, the company now known as C. L. Poston & Co. They increased the force of men till their output was about 150,000 tons per year. This firm continued till 1893, at which time the mine being well

coal so faulty &c., the project was abandoned. But it is safe to say that very soon this vein will turn out great qauntities of marketable coal.

The Continental Coal company has under lease about 10,000 acres of coal land two miles northeast of the city of Athens and already has three shafts in operation. In its lease this company binds itself to mine a large tonnage per year, paying the lessee the usual royalty.

Johnson Brothers Coal company, an independent concern, owns in fee simple about 5,000 acres of valuable coal land, only one mile north of the city. This company already has a large shaft in operation, while two more are sinking.

The New Pittsburg Coal company, located only about one mile northwest of Athens, has about 4,000 acres under control, with one shaft in operation and two more under construction. The Luhrig Coal company has two shafts only three miles west of Athens on its 2,000 acre field in lease and ownership. This is the newest coal company in the field, all the rest being old, with new openings. The coal production of the United States is a little less than one million tons a day (about the same as that of Great Britain for an entire year a third of a century ago, leading all nation of the world; and with a demand above its supply, it is no dream to suppose that its annual product will be 500 million tons. It is a matter of pride and concern that Athens county is a vital factor and consideration in this vast yield, producing one one-hundredth of all the coal of the United States.